MANAGING BANK ASSETS AND LIABILITIES

Strategies for risk control and profit

MANAGING BANK ASSETS AND LIABILITIES

Strategies
for
risk control
and
profit

Marcia L. Stigum

Rene O. Branch, Jr.

DOW JONES-IRWIN
Homewood, Illinois 60430

Chapters 2–6 of this volume are largely drawn from material
in *The Money Market: Myth, Reality, and Practice*, by
Marcia L. Stigum, published by Dow Jones-Irwin in 1978.

This publication is designed to provide accurate and
authoritative information in regard to the subject matter
covered. It is sold with the understanding that the
publisher is not engaged in rendering legal, accounting, or
other professional service. If legal advice or other expert
assistance is required, the services of a competent
professional person should be sought.
*From a Declaration of Principles jointly adopted by a Committee
of the American Bar Association and a Committee of Publishers.*

ISBN 0-87094-297-2

Library of Congress Catalog Card No. 82–71069

Printed in the United States of America

1 2 3 4 5 6 7 8 9 0 K 0 9 8 7 6 5 4 3

To Claudia Branch
and
Peter Hanson

Preface

In recent years, banking has been changing at an exponential rate due, in part, to the changing economic environment (particularly high inflation and high interest rates), the regulatory responses stirred partly by these changes, and the increasingly international character of banking—especially the tendency for domestic banking at the wholesale level to merge with the international Eurodollar market. As a result, the time is ripe for a book that carefully examines tactics and strategies for managing bank assets and liabilities for risk control and for profit. No existing book on banking addresses these questions on a sophisticated level in the context of the current regulatory and market environment.

This book is an in-depth guide on how to manage a bank's assets and liabilities so as to maximize profits while maintaining liquidity and holding interest rate exposure to an acceptable level. It should be of interest to bankers at institutions of *all* sizes, since care is taken to point out (1) the differences in the options open to money market, regional, and small banks, and (2) the implications of these differences with respect to the choice of optimal tactics and strategies for institutions of widely differing sizes. The book should also be useful to managers of savings and loan associations and other thrift institutions, because the choices and options facing them strongly resemble those facing bank managers. In addition, the special problems facing these institutions are alluded to throughout this book.

Corporate financial officers who preborrow long term or run a financing subsidiary also find themselves managing a "book" of fixed-rate assets and liabilities of various maturities and consequently face some of the same liquidity and interest rate exposure questions that banks do. As a result, the information in these pages should also be helpful to them.

An additional audience will be found among dealers (know thy customer), bank stock analysts, bank examiners, and people who are simply interested in finance and banking.

Finally, this book should be of use as a text in university courses on bank management either at the undergraduate or MBA level, and should also provide useful supplementary material in theoretical courses on finance and banking. Current texts used in such courses rarely provide any institutional background on the money and bond markets, the intricacies of domestic banking, and the Eurodollar operations of domestic and foreign banks. The last omission is particularly glaring because (1) the Eurodollar and other Eurocurrency markets are the international capital market of today's world, and (2) half or more of the assets and liabilities on the balance sheets of top U.S. banks arise from Euro transactions.

We anticipate that some readers, including students and bank trainees, will be relatively new to the money market and to banking. Part I provides all of the background needed for such readers to understand the rest of the book. In it, the instruments traded in the money market, how yields on them are calculated, and how banks under the control of the Federal Reserve System create our money supply are briefly discussed. Part II continues the introductory material by describing in considerable detail the domestic and offshore operations of U.S. banks and the operations of foreign banks in the U.S. The real meat of the book, the management of bank assets and liabilities, is dealt with in Parts III and IV.

Readers interested in knowing more about the operation of individual sectors of the money market should read *The Money Market: Myth, Reality, and Practice* by Marcia Stigum (Dow Jones-Irwin, 1978). This best-selling book is currently widely used throughout the money market as a reference and training guide; it is also used as a text in finance courses at colleges and universities across the country.

A number of examples of simple money market calculations are included in it. Readers who need descriptions of all key money market formulas and examples of how they can be used should refer to *Money Market Calculations: Yields, Break-Evens, and Arbitrage* by Marcia Stigum (Dow Jones-Irwin, 1981).

Final words of warning before we begin. In every area of life people develop special terms or give common terms special meanings to describe and to communicate with each other about their particular interests and activities—*jargon.* The money market is no exception, and this book uses money market jargon extensively. To aid the reader, each jargon term used is carefully defined the first time it appears in the text, and there is a Glossary at the end of the book in which a wide range of money market and bond market terms are defined. In addition, the pronoun *he* is used frequently throughout this book. It is our opinion that *he* has for years been used to mean *person,* and that any attempt to avoid this use of the term leads to nothing but bad and awkward English.

We would like to express our deep thanks to Mrs. Nancy Rosa who labored with patience and good spirit on the typing of this manuscript.

Finally, acknowledgement and thanks are due to the Morgan Guaranty Trust Company of New York for the use of several concepts and formats which were developed by that institution. Needless to say, responsibility for errors, omissions, and opinions belongs solely to the authors.

One final note: as this book went to press, an unprecedented spate of difficulties at, and sometimes failures of, major financial institutions, domestic and foreign, was rocking both the domestic U.S. and the Euromarkets. Brief descriptions of these and of their implications for sound bank management are given in Chapter 14: A Postscript. Institutions covered include Drysdale Securities, The Penn Square Bank, the Chase Manhattan Bank, the Continental Illinois Bank, and the Banco Ambrosiano together with its subsidiaries.

Marcia L. Stigum
Rene O. Branch, Jr.

Contents

PART II

THE BUSINESS OF BANKING

PART III

LIQUIDITY AND INTEREST RATE EXPOSURE

PART IV

TACTICS AND STRATEGIES

Abbreviations and acronyms

This book frequently uses street abbreviations of the names of various institutions and acronyms. The most common are:

Abbreviations

B of A	Bank of America
Chase	Chase Manhattan Bank
Manny Hanny	Manufacturers Hanover Trust Co.
Morgan	Morgan Guaranty Trust Co.

Acronyms

ARBL....................	assets repriced before liabilities (measure of interest rate exposure)
C & I loans	commercial and industrial loans
IBA	International Banking Act (1978)
IBF......................	International Banking Facility
FCM	futures commission merchant
LIBOR	London interbank offered rate (on Euros)
MMC	money market certificate
ROA	return on assets
ROE.....................	return on equity

1

Introduction

Banks carry out a wide range of important functions: (1) creating money, (2) making loans, (3) allocating credit, (4) influencing interest rates, and (5) engaging in international finance. All this is widely known.

What is less widely appreciated is that banks, like other enterprises producing services or goods, are private firms that operate in a largely capitalistic economy, and *that their major goal and responsibility to stockholders is to maximize profits*. Sears, GM, and dairy farmers are all working to make profits; so too, are banks.

As Adam Smith noted, what makes a market economy function efficiently is that firms are drawn *by the profit motive* to do whatever task—distribution, manufacturing, or financial intermediation—society needs done. To this it should be added that, in a *growing* economy, it is crucial for firms to earn profits and to retain some portion of them to augment capital. Only by adding to their capital can firms operating under uncertainty expand to meet the growing needs of their customers without unduly leveraging their balance sheets. This fact of life is the fundamental reason that making profits is not only a major objective, but also an *imperative* for banks and other financial institutions. Without a growing capital base, banks cannot continue to service the expanding needs of their customers.

Since their money and credit creation functions are of great importance to the functioning of the economy, banks have been regulated longer and more heavily by state and federal authorities than most other businesses. Still, within the area of freedom left by externally imposed constraints, banks do and should seek to maximize profits.

BANKING AS A BUSINESS

The basic nature of banking is that banks act as an *intermediary* between lenders and borrowers. Specifically, they gather funds from consumers and business firms and lend these to borrowers. In intermediating between borrowers and lenders, banks do three things: (1) they gather funds; (2) they substitute their credit for that of ultimate borrowers (i.e., they make credit judgments and assume credit risks); and (3) they assume interest rate risk because intermediation generally calls for a *maturity transformation*—using short-term deposits to fund longer-term loans.

To the extent that banks perform these functions efficiently, they should expect to receive some reward; *that reward is the basic source of bank profits.*

Above-normal profits

Most banks are not content to earn just a normal return for acting as an intermediary. In addition they seek, when it is possible and prudent, to earn *above-normal* profits by structuring their asset and liability maturities so as to earn extra profits by assuming *additional interest rate risk*. The times it is appropriate to do so and the tactics and strategies that banks should use in such situations are discussed in later chapters.

Here, three crucial points should be made: (1) Banks, like all other enterprises, operate under *uncertainty*, which means they are subject to *risk;* they can plan their future costs, revenues, and profits, but they can *never* be certain that external events will permit them to achieve these goals. (2) In seeking to maximize profits under uncertainty, a bank more than any other business firm is essentially choosing a particular structure for its balance sheet with respect to the types and maturities of its assets and liabilities. *For a bank, more than for a nonfinancial institution, profit maximization calls for selecting, under uncertainty, an optimal balance sheet.* (3) Before a bank acts to alter the structure of its assets and liabilities so as to increase its potential profitability, it must ensure *two* things: (*a*) that it has and will be able to maintain adequate liquidity—the ultimate penalty for failing to do so being the inability one day to open its doors; and (*b*) that it holds interest rate risk to an acceptable level—the example of the First Pennsylvania Bank (discussed in Chapter 7) demonstrating that failure on that count leads to major problems.

As noted in later chapters, a bank cannot take steps to change its liquidity without altering its interest rate *exposure* and thus its profit prospects; the converse is also true. These aspects of a bank's balance sheet—liquidity, interest rate exposure, and profit potential—are all inextricably intertwined. A bank can examine each feature separately, but it *cannot determine* them separately; the best it can do is to seek an optimal mix of these features given its current position and current economic conditions.

HOW TO RUN A BANK

The topic of this book is *how to run a bank,* not in the sense of how to hire clerks and process paper, but rather *how to make, at the highest levels, the tactical and strategic decisions that will structure the bank's balance sheet so as to maximize its profits subject to the constraints that liquidity risk be held to an acceptable level and that interest rate exposure be assumed only on favorable risk-reward terms.* Because banking is changing at an exponential rate due to rapid changes in the economic environment and in banking regulation, and to the increasingly international character of banking, it is difficult to imagine a more timely topic for banks, thrifts, and other financial institutions.

Two recurring themes

Our terse definition of banks as a specific type of financial intermediary describes the generic aspects of banking that apply across the board to all banks. In discussing banks and thrifts, it is a constant problem, as well as a source of interest, that these institutions *differ widely* with respect to the lines of business in which they engage and the freedom they have to restructure their assets and liabilities. In effect, banking is *many* lines of business: there are small retail banks with basically a local clientele; there are large money center banks whose clientele are a varied mix of wholesale and retail customers and whose business operations are spread via offshore branches around the world; and in between there are a host of medium-sized and regional banks, each of which operates in its own fashion and within its own particular market.

Repeatedly in describing tactics and strategies for maximizing profit, we will distinguish between banks that differ with respect to size or line of business, since the tactics and strategies which they can and should utilize differ widely.

A second theme to which we will allude often is the constantly changing nature of banking, occurring partly as a competitive response to changes in regulations imposed on banks and thrifts. Consequently, this book should be thought of not so much as a recipe book for success in managing a bank's balance sheet, but rather as a set of guidelines for analyzing the implications of various strategies and tactics, a necessary first step for coping successfully with new situations and opportunities as they arise.

Optimization and other models

For several decades, mathematical economists have labored to develop optimization models for firms, and in particular for banks, that operate under uncertainty. The goal of these theorists is to produce a model such that, if certain data are put into it, the model will tell management what tactics and strategies it should pursue—given its risk preferences—to maximize profits.

The introduction of mathematical models seems to be an exciting addition to management tools, a step in the direction of more scientific decision making. Consequently, many banks have invested much money and effort in developing such models. Often the results have been disappointing for several reasons.

Constraints. One is the need for constraints. A blank model that is unconstrained will always tell management to buy long-term municipal securities, on which interest income is tax-exempt, and to finance them with day-to-day purchases of Federal funds, the interest cost on which is tax deductible. This strategy is patently impossible, so the bank starts adding a host of constraints to its model: limits on the amounts of funds it can realistically buy in different markets, limits on its ability to add assets such as loans, complicated tax constraints if it has international operations, a constraint on the degree to which it may leverage, constraints on the minimum amounts of CDs of different maturities it must write to maintain liquidity, and so on. In effect, the bank is trying to build into the model a feel for what is possible and prudent, one that a good banker develops intuitively by operating for a long time in the market.

Unfortunately, adding such constraints is not a once and for all proposition, because the constraints constantly change. How much 6-month money a bank can buy will depend on its size, its name, and on market conditions, none of which can be counted on to remain constant over time. Similarly, how many long bonds a bank can sell at prevailing prices will depend on constantly changing market conditions. Thus, a model, to be useful, must be constantly reconstrained on the basis of a large number of highly judgmental evaluations with respect to what a bank can and, at a minimum, must realistically do in a host of different markets.

Risk preferences. Since banks all operate under uncertainty, the outcome of every move a bank makes will necessarily be uncertain. Thus, running a bank, like running any other business, involves making a series of bets. For a model to tell a bank which bets to make, the model must incorporate some measure of management's *risk preferences*—its willingness to trade the risk of loss for the opportunity to earn outsized rewards.

The need to measure management's risk preferences poses major problems for model builders. First, quantifying management's propensity to trade risk against return is difficult, perhaps impossible. Second, even if a model builder succeeds in quantifying management's risk preferences, he will have accomplished little because those preferences are *subject to change*. Management's propensity to assume risk will be much greater if the bank is experiencing poor current earnings and the projection is for even worse earnings than it would be if the bank is experiencing record earnings and forecasts the same for the future. Like the other constraints that must be added to a bank model, management's risk preferences are a *moving target*.

Doing what the old brain tells you. Banks that build optimization models usually end up with some sort of linear programming model. Constructing such a model is extremely complex and time consuming. So, too, is finding a routine to solve the model since it produces a gigantic matrix.

As noted, one problem with optimization models is that they must be severely constrained. This problem is made particularly acute because a model must always incorporate some planning horizon. It is a property of linear programming models that they tend to cram a bank into an extreme strategy at the end of the command horizon. For example, if a bank's forecast is that rates will fall, the model will cram the bank into a gigantic bond portfolio at the end of the planning horizon because, on a capital-asset-value basis, the value of the portfolio will be huge. As one model builder noted,

> If you are not careful, you will be telling the model to put out CDs here and there to preserve liquidity and to do all sorts of other diddly things, and meanwhile the machine will end up telling you to absolutely bet the

bank on bonds. To avoid that, you must add still more constraints. But by the time you do that, you are getting back to the sort of thing you do every day—*what the old brain tells you to do.*

When bankers who have sought to use optimization models realize the full dimensions of the problems associated with such models, they usually discard them and not necessarily with great regret. Many agree with the notion that a bank's management will generally be doing things the right way intuitively against its interest rates expectations. If management expects interest rates to rise, they will be funding long and vice versa. If they develop a view on the secular trend in interest rates, they will position their portfolio accordingly.

Information models. While most bank managers find optimization models of little use, to varying degrees they do employ information models. For example, some banks use simulation models to determine what profits the bank would earn if it pursued each of four different strategies under four different rate scenarios.

Some bankers find such information highly useful. Others argue that it is unnecessary. In the latter view, if management *has done its basic homework*—determining the bank's short- and long-run sensitivity to changes in interest rates—any needed calculations can be done on the back of an envelope. Bankers of this persuasion argue not only that they don't need a model to tell them what to do, but that calculating down to the last nickle or dime the possible outcomes of a tactic or strategy is irrelevant to their decision. As they see it, once management develops a view of what lies ahead and a measure of the certainty it assigns to that view, it knows what action to take; putting numbers on possible outcomes of that action will not change the probability that management will or will not take the action.

The benefits of model building

The negative view some bankers have with respect to models is probably overdone, but has its basis in a real-world situation. Bankers who decide that their bank needs a model usually begin with the *unrealistic* expectation that models can be constructed which will devise strategies and tactics for their bank. Inevitably, they find that *no* model—no matter how much effort is put into it—will do that for them.

Bankers who doubt the usefulness of models always add some qualifying phrase such as "to bankers who have not done their basic homework." In practice, it is true that a lot of bankers need to do more homework. For such bankers, the exercise of constructing a model is a good way of forcing themselves to quantify the many constraints their bank faces and to measure with greater precision the interest rate sensitivity of their bank's asset and liability structure. Another advantage of constructing a model is that it can give management useful information on the cost of self-imposed constraints. In a linear programming model, every constraint yields a shadow price. Using these, the model builder can say to management, "This is the amount of money you would save if you relaxed constraint X by $1. Are you, for example, willing to pay that amount of money—that price—to achieve the degree of liquidity you say you want?"

To the above, one caveat should be added. For a bank to build a model that serves the useful functions of forcing it to quantify its constraints, to determine the cost of those constraints, and to measure the interest rate sensitivity of its balance sheet, a tough communications problem must be solved. Typically, bankers do not understand models, and model builders do not understand the subtleties of commercial banking. Also, since each discipline has its own jargon, the two groups speak different languages.

For a bank to build a useful model, at least some of the personnel involved must be dual experts—experts on model building and on banking. Such people are hard to find, and a bank may be able to develop such personnel only by hiring trained econometricians and then giving them sufficiently broad exposure to the bank to develop a good understanding of the business of commercial banking. Doing so may be time consuming and expensive, but the alternative is to risk producing a white elephant put together by a bunch of bright bankers and bright econometricians who failed to communicate with each other. Also, bank management will never fully appreciate the information produced by its model unless that information is presented by someone who understands not only computers and models, but banking, as well.

In this book we focus on how bank management should do its basic homework and on how it should use the information thus gleaned to make tactical and strategic decisions. Any bank that wants to try its hand at model building should first master these fundamentals.

THE OUTLINE

While the audience of this book will primarily be composed of people associated with banking and thrift institutions, we want the book to be accessible to a wide audience. For this reason, we begin with fundamentals in Part I: the nature of bank intermediation, the money creation process, the instruments of the money market, and the nature of discount and interest-bearing instruments. In Part II we survey briefly the current state of domestic banking, Eurobanking, and the U.S. dollar operations of foreign banks.

In Part III, which deals with measuring and structuring a bank's liquidity and interest rate exposure, the real meat of the book begins. The reader, depending on his background, should read as much or as little of Parts I and II as he feels necessary.

BANKING REGULATIONS

U.S. banks and foreign banks operating branches in the United States are highly regulated with respect to what they may do. As background, we present in an appendix to this chapter a short description of major U.S. banking acts.

APPENDIX

THE ACTS THAT MATTER*

Edge Act: 1919. Named after Senator Walter Edge of New Jersey, who played a prominent role in its passage, this act provided for federal chartering of corporations formed to engage solely in international or foreign banking. The hope was that these Edge Act corporations would play a key role in financing American exports.

McFadden Act: 1927. This prohibits interstate banking.

Glass-Steagall Act: 1933. This severed commercial from investment banking and forced banks to divest themselves of any security-trading affiliates. The 1933 Banking Act also created the Federal Deposit Insurance Corporation and brought bank holding companies—except, as was discovered later, the one-bank holding companies—under the supervision of the Federal Reserve Board.

Douglas Amendment to the Bank Holding Company Act: 1956. This prohibits a bank holding company which is headquartered in one state from acquiring a bank in another state unless the second state specifically permits the acquisition.

Bank Merger Act: 1960. After a decade of debate over whether to apply existing antitrust laws explicitly to banking or to incorporate similar competitive standards into existing banking laws, this legislation plumped for the second course. It required the bank regulatory agencies (for the first time) to weigh the possible competitive effects of proposed mergers and acquisitions when considering applications.

---

* From "A Survey of International Banking," *The Economist*, March 14, 1981, p. 19.

Amendment to the Bank Holding Company Act: 1970. This brought one-bank holding companies under the same regulations as multibank holding companies.

International Banking Act: 1978. To bring foreign banks within the federal regulatory framework, the IBA introduced six major statutory changes:

It limited interstate domestic deposit taking by foreign banks. Previously, foreign banks had been free to open full-service branches wherever state law permitted. The new law required each foreign bank to elect a "home state" and restricted domestic deposit taking by offices outside that state.

Existing multistate branch networks of foreign banks were "grandfathered" (allowed to carry on as they were), a major concession since 40 of the 50 largest foreign banks were able to shelter under its wing.

It provided the option of federal licensing for foreign bank agencies and branches. Previously all foreign bank offices had state licences and some states applied reciprocity rules which effectively barred banks from certain countries.

The federal licensing authority (the Comptroller of the Currency) has permitted foreign banks to establish offices without regard to whether the foreign bank's home country grants equivalent access to American banks.

It authorized the Federal Reserve Board to impose reserve requirements on agencies and branches of foreign banks with worldwide assets of more than $1 billion, and to limit the maximum rates of interest such offices could pay on time deposits to the same as member banks.

It required federal deposit insurance (not previously available to foreign banks) for those branches engaged in retail deposit taking.

It amended the Edge Act to permit Edge corporations (which could conduct international banking out of state) to compete over a broader range of business, and permitted foreign banks to set up such corporations.

It subjected foreign banks to the same prohibitions on nonbanking business as domestic bank holding companies. Once again, existing nonbanking activities (including securities underwriting from which domestic banks are excluded) were "grandfathered."

Depository Institutions Deregulation and Monetary Control Act: 1980. This "omnibus act" had four main aims:

To phase out (over a six-year period) interest rate ceilings on deposits and to eliminate the .25 percent favourable differential traditionally enjoyed by the thrifts. A Depository Institutions Deregulation Committee, with representatives from the main regulatory agencies, was set up to oversee the process. All the evidence points to the committee accomplishing its task in far less than six years.

To extend nationwide the authority (previously exclusive to the New England states) to offer NOW (negotiable order of withdrawal) accounts. The maximum rate to be offered on NOW accounts has been set initially at 5.25 percent for all institutions. This ends the prohibition on the payment of interest on demand deposits.

To grant new powers to the federally chartered thrifts. A number of states have passed parallel legislation for state-chartered institutions to discourage desertion from state to federal charter. Most importantly, these powers permit S&Ls to invest up to 20 percent of their assets in consumer loans, commercial paper, and company securities; to offer credit cards; and to exercise fiduciary powers.

To override state-imposed usury ceilings on mortgages. (Some states have already taken action to raise their ceilings.)

PART I

Some fundamentals

2

Funds flows, banks, and money creation

As preface to a discussion of banking, a few words should be said about the U.S. capital market, how banks create money, and the Fed's role in controlling money creation.

Roughly defined, the U.S. capital market is composed of three major parts: *the stock market, the bond market,* and *the money market.* The money market, as opposed to the bond market, is a wholesale market for high-quality, *short-term debt instruments,* or IOUs.

FUNDS FLOWS IN THE U.S.
CAPITAL MARKET

Every spending unit in the economy—business firm, household, or government body—is constantly receiving and using funds. In particular, a business firm receives funds from the sale of output and uses funds to cover its costs of production (excluding depreciation) and its current investment in plant, equipment, and inventory. For most firms, *gross saving* from current operations (i.e., *retained earnings plus de-*

13

preciation allowances) falls far short of covering current capital expenditures; that is, net funds obtained from current operations are inadequate to pay capital expenditures. As a result, each year most nonfinancial business firms and the nonfinancial business sector as a whole run a large *funds deficit*.

The actual figures rung up by nonfinancial business firms in 1980 are given in column (2) of Table 2–1. They show that during this year business firms retained earnings of $32.7 billion and their capital consumption allowances totaled $224.9 billion, giving them a grand total of $257.6 billion of gross saving with which to finance capital expenditures. The latter, however, totaled $285.4 billion, so the business sector as a whole incurred a $27.8 billion funds deficit.

Running a large funds deficit is a chronic condition for the business sector. It is, moreover, to be expected, since every year the business sector receives a relatively small portion (9 to 13 percent) of total national income but has to finance a major share of national capital expenditures. Moreover, because of the depressed condition of the stock market in recent years, business firms have been able to obtain little financing there. Thus, the bulk of the funds they have obtained to cover their deficits has come through the sale of bonds and money market instruments.

In contrast to the business sector, the consumer sector presents a quite different picture. As Table 2–1 shows, households in 1980 had gross savings of $402.9 billion and made capital expenditures of only $313.1 billion, leaving the sector with a *funds surplus* of $89.8 billion. This funds surplus is, moreover, a persistent phenomenon. Every year consumers as a group save more than they invest in housing and other capital goods.

Most of the consumer sector's annual funds surplus is absorbed by making loans to and equity investments in business firms that must seek outside funds to cover their funds deficits. This flow of funds from the consumer to the business sector is no cause for surprise. In any developed economy in which the bulk of investing is carried on outside the government sector, a substantial amount of funds flow, year in and year out, from consumers, who are the major income recipients, to business firms, which are the major investors.

Consumers and nonfinancial business firms do not make up the whole economy. Two other sectors of major importance are the U.S. government and state and local governments. In neither of these sectors are capital expenditures separated from current expenditures. Thus, for each sector, the recorded funds deficit or funds surplus incurred over the year equals total revenue minus total expenditures, or *net saving*. Both sectors have run funds deficits in most recent years, with the result that they compete with the business sector for the

Table 2–1
Funds flows in the U.S. capital market by sector, 1980 annualized rate ($ billions)

	Sectors					
	(1)	(2)	(3)	(4)	(5)	(6)
Transaction categories	House-holds	Non-financial business	State and local* governments	U.S.* government	Financial† business	Rest of the world
1. Savings (net)	172.0	32.7	2.6	-63.5	21.6	-4.7
2. Depreciation	230.8	224.9	0	0	9.6	0
3. Gross savings (1) + (2)	402.9	257.6	2.6	-63.5	31.2	-4.7
4. Capital expenditures	313.1	285.4	0	0	15.2	0
5. Funds surplus or deficit (3) – (4) ..	89.8	-27.8	2.6	-63.5	16.0	-4.7
6. Net financial assets acquired	279.5	80.8	19.9	26.0	433.3	18.8
7. Net financial liabilities incurred ..	110.1	153.0	27.1	88.8	417.4	52.0
8. Net financial investment (6) – (7) ..	169.4	-72.2	-7.2	-62.8	15.9	-33.2
9. Sector discrepancy (5) + (8)	-79.6	44.5	9.8	-.8	0.1	28.5

* Capital expenditures are included with current expenditures in U.S. and state and local government spending accounts.
† The large size of the entries in lines 6 and 7 for this sector reflects the intersectoral and intrasectoral funds flows that are funneled through financial institutions.
Source: Board of Governors, Federal Reserve System.

surplus funds generated in the consumer sector. This is what possible "crowding out" of business borrowers by government borrowing is all about.

For completeness, still another domestic sector has to be added to the picture, *financial* business firms—banks, savings and loan associations, life insurance companies, and others. Most of the funds that these firms lend out to funds-deficit units are not funds of which they are the *ultimate* source. Instead, they are funds that these institutions have "borrowed" from funds-surplus units. If financial institutions only funneled funds from surplus to deficit units, we could omit them from our summary table. However, such activity is profitable, and every year financial firms accumulate gross savings, which exceed their modest capital expenditures, so net, the sector tends to be a *small* supplier of funds.

The final sector in Table 2–1 is the rest of the world. Domestic firms cover some portion of the funds deficits they incur by borrowing abroad, and domestic funds-surplus units occasionally invest abroad. Thus, to get a complete picture of who supplies and demands funds, we must include the rest of the world in our summary table. Also, when the exchange value of the dollar is weak, the central banks of Germany, Japan, and other countries become big buyers of dollars; they typically invest these dollars in U.S. government securities, thereby becoming financers of the U.S. government debt. When the dollar is strong, the converse occurs.

Every funds deficit has to be covered by the receipt of debt or equity capital from outside sources, and every funds surplus must be absorbed by supplying such capital. Thus, if the funds surpluses and deficits incurred by all sectors are totaled, their sum should be zero. Actually, the figures on line 5 of Table 2–1 don't sum horizontally to zero because of inevitable statistical errors. In 1980 recorded sector surpluses exceeded recorded sector deficits by $12.4 billion, indicating that some sectors' deficits had been overestimated and other sectors' surpluses underestimated. The net discrepancy was, however, small relative to the surplus and deficit figures calculated for the major sectors, so the table gives a good overall picture of the direction and magnitude of intersector funds flows within the economy.

Net financial investment by sector

Funds flows between sectors leave a residue of *newly* created financial assets and liabilities. In particular, spending units that borrow incur claims against themselves which appear on their balance sheets as liabilities, while spending units that supply capital acquire financial assets in the form of stocks, bonds, and other securities.

This suggests that, since the consumer sector ran an $89.8 billion funds surplus in 1980, the sector's holdings of financial assets should have increased by a like amount over that year. Things, however, are not so simple. While the consumer sector as a whole ran a funds surplus, many spending units within the sector ran funds deficits. Thus, the appropriate figure to look at is the sector's *net financial investment,* i.e., financial assets acquired minus liabilities incurred. For the household sector, this figure (line 8, Table 2–1) was $169.1 billion in 1980, a number of the right sign but much larger than the sector's funds surplus; the difference between the two figures is due to the statistical errors that inevitably creep into such estimates.

The big funds deficit that the nonfinancial business sector ran up during 1980 indicates that the net rise in its financial liabilities outstanding over the year must have been substantial. The estimated figure ($72.2 billion) confirms this, but again a substantial discrepancy has crept into the picture.

Similar but smaller discrepancies exist between the funds surpluses or deficits run up by the other sectors in Table 2–1 and their net financial investments.

FINANCIAL INTERMEDIARIES

As noted, every year large numbers of business firms and other spending units in the economy incur funds deficits which they cover by obtaining funds from spending units running funds surpluses. Some of this *external financing* involves what is called *direct finance.* In the case of direct finance, the *ultimate funds-deficit unit* (business firm, government body, or other spending unit) either borrows directly from *ultimate funds-surplus units* or sells equity claims against itself directly to such spending units. An example of direct finance would be a corporation covering a funds deficit by issuing new bonds, some of which are sold directly to consumers or nonfinancial business firms that are running funds surpluses.

While examples of direct finance are easy to find, external financing more typically involves *indirect finance.* In that case, the funds flow from the surplus to the deficit unit via a *financial intermediary.* Banks, savings and loan associations, life insurance companies, pension funds, and mutual funds are all examples of financial intermediaries. As this list makes clear, financial intermediaries differ widely in character. Nevertheless, they all perform basically the same function. Every financial intermediary solicits and obtains funds from funds-surplus units by offering in exchange for funds "deposited" with it, claims against itself. The latter, which take many forms, including demand deposits, time deposits, money market and other mutual fund shares, and the cash value of life insurance policies, are known as *indirect securities*. The funds that financial intermediaries receive in exchange for the indirect securities they issue are used by them to invest in stocks, bonds, and other securities issued by ultimate funds-deficit units, that is, in *primary securities*.

All this sounds a touch bloodless, so let's look at a simple example of financial intermediation. Jones, a consumer, runs a $20,000 funds surplus, which he receives in the form of cash. He promptly deposits that cash in a demand deposit at a bank. Simultaneously, some other spending unit, say, the Alpha Company, runs a temporary funds deficit. Jones's bank trades the funds Jones has deposited with it for a loan note (IOU) issued by the Alpha Company. In doing this—accepting Jones's deposit and acquiring the note—the bank is funneling funds from Jones, an ultimate funds-surplus unit, to the Alpha Company, an ultimate funds-deficit unit; in other words, it is acting as a financial intermediary between Jones and this company.

Federal Reserve statistics on the assets and liabilities of different sectors in the economy show the importance of financial intermediation. In particular, at the beginning of 1981 consumers, who are the major suppliers of external financing, held $4,493.6 billion of financial assets. Of this total, $2,241.3 billion represented consumers' deposits at commercial banks, other thrift institutions, and money market funds; $222.5 billion the cash value of their life insurance policies; and $727.1 billion the reserves backing pensions eventually due them. The other $1,820.1 billion represented consumers' holdings of primary securities: corporate stock, U.S. government bonds, state and local bonds, corporate and foreign bonds, and assorted other IOUs. Thus, in 1980 about 60 percent of the funds that had flowed out of households running funds surpluses were channeled to other spending units through financial intermediation.

Financial intermediaries are a varied group. To give some idea of the relative importance of different intermediaries, Table 2–2 lists the assets of all the major intermediaries at the end of 1980. As one might expect, commercial banks are by far the most important intermediaries. Following them at a considerable distance are savings and loan associations (S&Ls), life insurance companies, and the fast-growing private pension funds.

The reasons for intermediation

The main reason for all of the intermediation that occurs in our economy is that the mix of primary securities offered by funds-deficit units is unattractive to many funds-surplus units. With the exception of corporate stocks, the minimum denominations on many primary secu-

Table 2-2
Total assets of major financial institutions, beginning of
1981 ($ billions)

Institutions	Assets
Commercial banks	$1386.3
Savings and loan associations	629.8
Life insurance companies	469.8
Private pension funds	286.8
Finance companies	198.6
State and local government retirement funds	198.1
Federally sponsored credit agencies	192.5
Other insurance companies	180.1
Federal Reserve banks	173.8
Mutual savings banks	171.5
Money market funds*	74.4
Credit unions	69.2
Open-end investment companies	63.7
Securities brokers and dealers	33.5
Real estate investment trusts	6.3

* By December 1981, the assets of money market funds, which experienced tremendous growth in recent high-interest-rate years, totaled $186 billion.
Source: Board of Governors, Federal Reserve System.

rities are high relative to the size of the funds surpluses that most spending units are likely to run during any short-term period. Also, the amount of debt securities that deficit units want to borrow long term far exceeds the amount that surplus units—consumers and corporations that often desire high liquidity—choose to lend long term. Finally, some risk is attached to many primary securities, more than most surplus units would like to bear.

The indirect securities offered to savers by financial intermediaries are quite attractive in contrast to primary securities. Many such instruments, e.g., time deposits, have low to zero minimum denominations, are highly liquid, and expose the investor to negligible risk. Financial intermediaries are able to offer such attractive securities for several reasons. First, they pool the funds of many investors in a highly diversified portfolio, thereby reducing risk and overcoming the minimum denominations problem. Second, to the extent that one saver's withdrawal is likely to be met by another's deposit, intermediaries such as banks and S&Ls can with reasonable safety borrow short term from depositors and lend long term to borrowers. A final reason for intermediation is the tax advantages that some forms of intermediation, e.g., participation in a pension plan, offer individuals.

BANKS, A SPECIAL INTERMEDIARY

Banks in our economy are an intermediary of special importance for several reasons. First, they are by far the largest intermediary; they receive huge quantities of *demand deposits* (i.e., checking account money) and time deposits which they use to make loans to consumers, corporations, and others. Second, in the course of their lending activity, *banks create money.* The reason is that demand deposits, which are a bank liability, count as part of the money supply—no matter how one defines that supply. And today, thanks to the growing attention paid to the monetarists who argue that the money supply is immensely important in determining economic activity, all eyes tend to focus on growth of the money supply.

Just how banks create money takes a little explaining. We have to introduce a simple device known as a *T-account,* which shows, as the account below illustrates, the changes that occur in the assets and liabilities of a spending unit—consumer, firm, or financial institution—as the result of a specific economic transaction.

**T-Account for a
Spending Unit**

Changes in assets	Changes in liabilities

Consider again Jones, who takes $20,000 in cash and deposits that money in the First National Bank. This transaction will result in the following changes in the balance sheets of Jones and his bank:

Jones		First National Bank	
Cash −20,000 Demand deposits +20,000		Reserves (cash) +20,000	Demand deposits Jones +20,000

Clearly, Jones's deposit results in $20,000 of cash being *withdrawn from circulation* and put into bank (cash) reserves, but simultaneously $20,000 of new demand deposits are created. Since every definition of the money supply includes both demand deposits and currency *in circulation,* this deposit has no net effect on the size of the money supply; instead, it simply alters the composition of the money supply.

Now enter the Alpha Company, a funds-deficit unit, which borrows $15,000 from the First National Bank. If the bank makes the loan by crediting $15,000 to Alpha's account, changes will again occur in its balance sheet and in that of the borrower, too.

Alpha Co.		First National Bank	
Bank loan +15,000	Demand deposits +15,000	Loan to Alpha Co. +15,000	Demand deposits to Alpha Co. +15,000

As the T-accounts show, the immediate effect of the loan is to *increase* total demand deposits by $15,000, but no offsetting decrease has occurred in the amount of currency in circulation. Thus, by making the loan, the First National Bank has *created* $15,000 of new money (Table 2–3).

Table 2–3
Money supply

Step 1: Jones holds $20,000 in cash.
Money supply equals:
$20,000 in cash.

Step 2: Jones deposits his $20,000 of cash at the First National Bank.
Money supply equals:
$20,000 of demand deposits held by Jones.

Step 3: The First National Bank lends $15,000 to the Alpha Co.
Money supply equals:
$20,000 of demand deposits held by Jones.
+$15,000 of demand deposits held by Alpha Co.
$35,000 total money supply.

The Alpha Company presumably borrows money to make a payment. That in no way alters the money creation aspect of the bank loan. To illustrate, suppose Alpha makes a payment for $15,000 to the Beta Company by drawing a check against its new balance and depositing it in another bank, the Second National Bank. Then the following changes will occur in the balance sheets of these two banks.

The Second National Bank		The First National Bank	
Reserves (cash) +15,000	Demand deposits to Beta Co. +15,000	Reserves (cash) −15,000	Demand deposits to the Alpha Co. −15,000

The assumed payment merely switches $15,000 of demand deposits and reserves from one bank to another bank. The payment therefore does not alter the size of the money supply.

Bearing this in mind, let's now examine how the Fed regulates the volume of bank intermediation and what effect its actions have on the money supply and interest rates.

THE FEDERAL RESERVE'S ROLE

The Fed's life has been one of continuing evolution, first in determining what its goals should be and second in learning how to use the tools available to it to promote these goals. When Congress set up the Fed in 1913, it was intended to perform several functions of varying importance. First, the Fed was charged with creating an elastic supply of currency, that is, one that could be expanded and contracted in step with changes in the quantity of currency (as opposed to bank deposits) that the public desired to hold. Creating an elastic currency supply was viewed as important because, under the then existing banking system, when a prominent bank failed and nervous depositors at other banks began demanding currency for deposits, the banks were frequently unable to meet these demands. Consequently, on a number of occasions, the panic of 1907 being a case in point, currency runs on solvent banks forced these banks to temporarily suspend the conversion of deposits into cash. Such suspensions, during which currency traded at a premium relative to bank deposits, inconvenienced depositors and disrupted the economy.

The Fed was to solve this problem by standing ready during panics to extend to the banks at the discount window loans whose proceeds could be paid out in Federal Reserve notes. To the extent that the Fed fulfilled this function, it was acting as a lender of last resort, satiating the public's appetite for cash by monetizing bank assets. Today, acting as a lender of last resort remains an important Fed responsibility, but the Fed fulfills it in a different way.

Congress also intended that the Fed carry out a second and more important function, namely, regulating the overall supply of money and bank credit so that changes in them would promote rather than disrupt economic activity. This function, too, was to be accomplished at the discount window. According to the prevailing doctrine, changes in the money supply and bank credit would be beneficial if they matched the direction and magnitude of changes in the economy's level of productive activity. Such beneficial changes in money and bank credit would, it was envisioned, occur semiautomatically with the Fed in operation. When business activity expanded, so too, would the demand for bank loans. As growth of the latter put pressure on bank reserves, banks would obtain additional reserves by rediscounting at the Fed (i.e., borrowing against) *eligible paper*—notes, drafts, and bills of exchange arising out of actual commercial transactions. Conversely, when economic activity slackened, bank borrowing at the discount window, bank loans, and the money supply would contract in step.

Events never quite followed this smooth pattern, which in retrospect is not to be regretted. As theorists now realize, expanding money and bank credit without limit during an upswing and permitting them to contract without limit during a downswing, far from encouraging stable growth, tend to amplify fluctuations in income and output. In particular, unlimited money creation during a boom inevitably fuels any inflationary fires and other excesses that develop.

Today, the Fed sees its major policy job as pursuing a *countercyclical monetary policy*. Specifically it attempts to promote full employment and price stability by limiting the growth of bank intermediation when the economy expands too vigorously and by encouraging it when the economy slips into recession.

Controlling the level of bank intermediation

The Fed controls the level of bank intermediation—the amount of bank lending and money creating—through several tools. One is *reserve requirements*. Since the 1930s, the Fed has been responsible for setting the limits on the percentage of reserves that member banks are required to hold against deposits made with them. Each member bank must place all of its reserves, except vault cash, on deposit in a non–interest-bearing account at one of the 12 regional Federal Reserve banks. (All nationally chartered banks must join the Federal Reserve System.) The same requirement does not hold for state-chartered banks, many of which have opted to not join the system because of the high cost of tying up some of the money deposited with them in a non–interest-bearing reserve account at the Fed.[1] Thus, each district Federal Reserve Bank acts in effect as a banker to commercial banks in its district, holding what amounts to checking accounts for them.

The existence at Federal Reserve Banks of member bank reserve accounts explains, by the way, how the Fed can clear checks drawn against one bank and deposited with another so easily. It does so simply by debiting the reserve account of the bank against which the check is drawn and crediting by an equal amount the reserve account of the bank at which the check is deposited.

---

[1] As noted below, the 1980 Banking Act calls for the Fed to extend reserve requirements to nonmember banks and nonbank depository institutions, as well, over an 8-year phase-in period.

The member banks' checking accounts also make it easy for the Fed to circulate currency in the form of Federal Reserve notes (a non–interest-bearing *indirect security* issued by the Fed). Currency runs on banks are a thing of the past, but the Fed must still constantly increase the amount of currency in circulation because, as the economy expands, more currency is needed by the public for ordinary transactions. Whenever people demand more currency, they demand it from their commercial banks, which in turn get it from the Fed by trading reserve deposits for currency. Since the Fed, as noted below, creates bank reserves by buying government securities, the currency component of our money supply is in effect created by the Fed through *monetization* of a portion of the federal debt. All of this correctly suggests that the Fed, despite its lofty position at the pinnacle of the financial system, is none other than one more type of financial intermediary.

The second key tool of the Fed is *open-market operations,* that is, purchases and sales of government securities, through which it creates and destroys member bank reserves. Whenever the Fed, operating through the trading desk of the New York district bank, buys government securities, its purchases inevitably increase bank reserves by an amount equal to the cost of the securities purchased. When the source of the securities purchased is a member bank, this result is obvious. Specifically, a purchase of $10 million of government securities would lead to the following changes in the balance sheets of the Fed and of a member bank.

The Fed		A Member Bank	
Government securities +10 million	Member bank reserves +10 million	Reserves +10 million Government securities −10 million	

Even if the source of the government securities purchased by the Fed is a nonbank spending unit, the result will be essentially the same, since the money received by the seller, say, a nonbank dealer, will inevitably be deposited in a commercial bank, leading to the following balance sheet changes.

The Fed		A Member Bank	
Government securities +10 million	Member bank reserves +10 million	Reserves +10 million	Deposits to nonbank seller +10 million

A Nonbank Seller	
Government securities − 10 million Demand deposits + 10 million	

In the case of sales of government securities by the Fed, the process described above operates exactly in reverse and member bank reserves are destroyed.

With the exception of loans extended by the Fed at the discount window (discussed below), the *only* way bank reserves can be created is through Fed purchases of government securities, and the only way they can be destroyed is through sales by the Fed of such securities.[2] Thus, the Fed is in a position to control directly and precisely the quantity of reserves available to the banking system.

The lid on bank intermediation

Taken together, reserve requirements and the Fed's ability to control the level of bank reserves permit the Fed to set a tight limit on the level of intermediation in which banks may engage. Let's use a simple illustration. Suppose the Fed were to require banks to hold reserves equal to 10 percent of total deposits. If the Fed were then to create, say, $90 billion of bank reserves, the maximum deposits banks could create through intermediation would be $900 billion (10 percent of $900 billion being $90 billion).

Naturally, if the Fed were to increase bank reserves through open-market purchases of government securities, that would increase the quantity of deposits banks could create, whereas open-market sales by the Fed would do the reverse. For example, with a 10 percent reserve ratio, every $1 billion of government security purchases by the Fed would permit a $10 billion increase in bank assets and liabilities, whereas $1 billion of sales would do the opposite.

Our example, which points up the potency of *open-market operations* (purchases and sales by the Fed of government securities) as a tool for controlling the level of bank intermediation, is oversimplified. For one thing, the percentage of reserves that must be held by a bank

---

[2] There are some minor exceptions: In particular, movements of Treasury deposit balances between commercial banks and Fed banks affect member bank reserves, but the Fed tracks these movements daily and offsets them through purchases and sales of government securities. Seasonal and long-term changes in the public's demand for currency also affect bank reserves, but these changes too can be and are offset by the Fed through appropriate open-market operations. Finally, under the current system of "dirty" currency floats, U.S. and foreign central-bank operations in the foreign exchange market may have some effect on domestic bank deposits and reserves.

against its deposits varies depending on the type of deposit and the size of the bank accepting the deposit. Currently, required reserve ratios are being phased down to a high of 12 percent against demand deposits at large banks to a low of 0 percent against time deposits maturing in 3½ years or more. Thus, the actual amount of deposits (demand plus time) that a given quantity of reserves will support depends partly on the mix of deposits demanded by the public and partly on the size of the banks receiving those deposits.

This, together with the fact that banks may choose not to fully utilize the reserves available to them, means that some slack exists in the Fed's control over deposit creation. Nevertheless open-market operations are a powerful tool for controlling the level of bank activity, and they are used daily by the Fed to do so.

The discount window

As noted earlier, the founders of the Fed viewed discounting as its *key* tool. In practice, things have worked out differently. The main reason is that over time the Fed switched from controlling bank reserves through discounting to controlling them through open-market operations. This switch makes sense for several reasons. First, it puts the Fed in the position of being able to take the initiative. Second, the size and liquidity of the market for government securities are such that the Fed can make substantial purchases and sales there without disrupting the market or causing more than negligible price changes. The latter is important since the Fed, to fine tune bank reserves, must constantly be in the market buying and selling such securities. Part of this activity results from what is called the Fed's *defensive* operations, open-market purchases and sales designed to counter the effect on bank reserves of outside forces, such as changes in the amount of currency in circulation and movements of Treasury balances between member banks and the Fed. In addition, the Fed undertakes open-market operations to effect whatever overall changes in bank reserves are called for by current monetary policy.

The discount window still exists and banks borrow there. This activity creates some slack in the Fed's control over bank reserves, so the Fed has to limit borrowing at the window. One way it could do this would be charge a high penalty rate on discounts, one that would discourage banks from borrowing except in cases of real and temporary need. The Fed, however, has not followed this course.[3] Instead, it typically sets the discount rate at a level in step with other money market rates, with the result that banks can at times profit by borrow-

---

[3] Except for a brief experiment with a modest surcharge in 1980–81.

ing at the discount window and relending elsewhere. To limit such arbitrage and maintain control over bank reserves, the Fed has made it a policy that borrowing at the discount window is a privilege that a bank may use only sparingly and on a temporary basis.

Today, borrowing at the discount window represents a small but highly variable element in the total reserves available to member banks. In recent years, monthly figures on such borrowings have ranged from $.5 to $1.5 billion. The high numbers all occurred in times of tight money, but even in such periods member bank borrowing represented no more than 2 to 4 percent of total bank reserves.

EXTENDING THE FED'S REACH

Holding non–interest-bearing reserve deposits at the Fed imposes an opportunity cost on a member institution, namely, the interest income forgone by the institution because it cannot use these deposits productively. As interest rates rose secularly over time, so too did the opportunity cost to banks of meeting reserve requirements. As a result, the trend during the 1960s and 70s was for banks to leave the Federal Reserve System.

The Fed viewed this trend with alarm. It was prepared to live with a situation in which many small state banks were not members. However, the Fed feared that the exit from the system of increasingly more and increasingly larger banks would decrease the effectiveness of its policies and, in particular, limit its ability to control the money supply. As a result, the Fed from 1964 onward urged Congress to amend the Federal Reserve Act to make nonmember banks subject to the same reserve requirements as member banks. A second smaller but growing problem faced by the Fed was that thrift institutions outside its control began to issue *NOW (negotiable order of withdrawal) accounts*. Deposits in such accounts amount, in effect, to interest-bearing demand deposits, and as such are *money* by any reasonable definition.

In 1980, Congress passed the landmark *Depository Institutions Deregulation and Monetary Control Act*. One objective of this wide-ranging act was to increase the Fed's control over money creation. To this end, the act, dubbed the *Banking Act of 1980*, calls for the Fed to impose, over an eight-year phase-in period, reserve requirements on nonmember banks and on thrift institutions offering checking accounts, as well. At the same time, reserve requirements on savings and time deposits held by individuals at all depository institutions will be eliminated.

As a quid pro quo for the new reserve requirements, the 1980 act empowers banks and all other depository institutions to issue NOW accounts. It also empowers thrift institutions to make a wider range of investments and grants them access to the discount window. Full implementation of the 1980 act will further blur the once clear line of demarcation between commercial banks and thrifts.

Money supply and Fed control over it

As will be explained in Chapter 3, banks borrow and lend excess reserves to each other in the *Federal funds market*. The rate at which such lending and borrowing occurs is called the *Fed fund rate*. When the Fed cuts back on the growth of bank reserves, this tightens the supply of reserves available to the banking system relative to its demand for them; that, in turn, drives up the Fed funds rate, which, in turn, drives up other short-term interest rates. Thus, any easing or tightening by the Fed necessarily alters not only money supply growth, but also interest rates.

Because of this, the Fed cannot have two independent policies, one to control money supply growth, a second to influence interest rates. If the Fed focuses on pegging interest rates, money supply becomes a residual variable; it is what it is and falls outside the control of the Fed. Conversely, a Fed decision to strictly control money supply growth implies a loss by the Fed of its ability to independently influence the level of interest rates.

In implementing monetary policy, the Fed in the early 1970s focused primarily on interest rates and more particularly on the Fed funds rate. The Fed viewed money as tight if interest rates were high or rising, as easy if interest rates were low or falling. This policy stance was predicated on the view that high and rising interest rates would discourage spending and the expansion of economic activity, while low or falling rates would do the reverse.

The monetarists, with Milton Friedman at the fore, argued that this analysis was incorrect. According to their theory, giving people more money causes them to increase their spending on goods and services. Therefore, the key to achieving steady economic growth and to controlling inflation is a monetary policy that holds the rate of growth of the money supply strictly in line with the rate of growth of real output achievable by the economy. The clear implication of the monetarist position is that the Fed should seek to peg not the Fed funds rate, but the rate of growth of money.

Gradually, grudgingly, and with a prod from Congress in the form of the Humphrey-Hawkins bill passed in 1978, the Fed accepted the monetarist doctrine and shifted the focus of its policy from controlling interest rates to controlling money supply growth, the policy shift being completed under Chairman Volker.

Pitfalls of monetarism.   For monetarists, particularly those resid-
ing in the ivory towers of academe, it appeared that the mandate to
strictly control the growth of the money supply is one that the Fed
could carry out with reasonable ease and a high degree of precision. In
practice, however, the policy of controlling money supply growth—
whether wise or foolish—has posed serious problems for the Fed.

The first, and hardly trivial, problem facing the Fed has been to
determine just what money is. Clearly, the old definition of money,
demand deposits plus currency in circulation, is too restrictive since
the long-term upward trend in interest rates has spawned not only new
types of deposit accounts—NOW accounts and ATS (automatic transfer from savings to demand deposit) accounts—that can be used for
transactions purposes, but also a host of other highly liquid investment
options, including placements in money market funds. Since
liquidity—unlike virginity—is measured in degrees, drawing a line
between money and near monies necessarily involves *arbitrary*
choices. This being the case, the Fed has for some time found itself
struggling simply to define what it is supposed to control.

The Fed's difficulties in defining money are reflected in its decision
to publish four different measures of money supply (Table 2–4). Obvi-

Table 2–4
The Fed's measures of money stock

M-1:	Currency in circulation and private demand deposits, plus other transactions accounts (NOW accounts, ATS accounts, and demand deposits at savings banks).
M-2:	M-1 plus savings and small (less than $100,000) time deposits, overnight repurchase agreements (RPs) at banks, overnight Euros held in the Caribbean by U.S. residents, and money market fund shares.
M-3:	M-2 plus large time deposits and terms RPs at banks and S&Ls.
L:	M-3 plus other liquid assets including various money market instruments held by U.S. residents.

ously, the Fed cannot independently control the growth of each of
these aggregates. It currently focuses its attention primarily on M-1
and M-2.

Defining money, while a tough nut to crack, is only the beginning of
the Fed's problems in controlling money supply. A second, equally
intractable and, from a policy point of view, more serious problem is
that a large erratic element appears to be intrinsic in money supply
behavior with the result that week-to-week money supply figures fluctuate sharply (Figure 2–1); the Fed also has difficulty in seasonally

Figure 2–1

Weekly figures for M-1 (dubbed by the Fed until January 1980, M-1B) change in a highly erratic way from week to week and are rarely on target

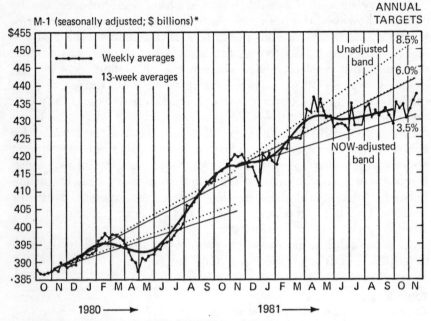

* Data not adjusted for effects of NOW accounts.
Source: The Morgan Bank.

adjusting these figures. The upshot is that underlying trends in money supply growth are hard to perceive both for the Fed and for outside observers reacting to actual and potential Fed moves.

In accepting and seeking to implement a strictly monetarist policy, the Fed—as had to be the case—has lost control over interest rates (see Figure 2–2). This permitted rates, beginning in 1980, to take off on a roller coaster ride. It also created a situation in which strong reactions by money and bond market traders to weekly money supply figures made interest rates highly volatile and unpredictable even on a week-to-week basis.

The price of a monetarist policy in a highly inflationary economy appears to be an extremely high degree of uncertainty with respect to rates in the capital market. This untoward consequence of monetarism can hardly be viewed as contributing to economic stability. The Fed knows this and would like to feed to credit market participants money supply numbers that delineate longer-term trends in money growth. Unfortunately, it can find no way to do so. Consequently, interest rates are likely to remain highly volatile until inflation is cured or the Fed

Figure 2–2
By becoming monetarist, the Fed has lost control over the Fed funds rate:
Federal funds rate (weekly averages as of Wednesday; data thru December
30, 1981)

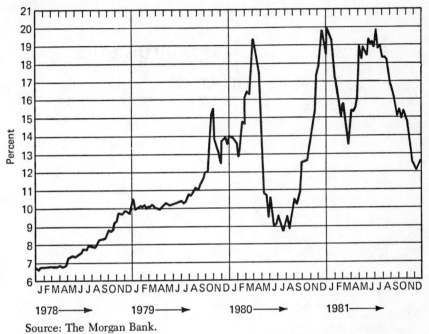

Source: The Morgan Bank.

gives up on monetarism and reverts to attempts at influencing economic activity and the rate of inflation by adjusting interest rates.

The primary purpose of this brief description of Fed policy is to
provide necessary background for Chapters 5 and 6 which cover fundamentals of domestic and Eurobanking. In Chapter 7, we will return
to the Fed and examine in greater detail current Fed policy and the
constraints it places on banks.

3

The instruments
in brief

Here's a quick rundown of the major money market instruments. Don't look for subtleties; just enough is said to lay the groundwork for later chapters.

DEALERS AND BROKERS

The markets for all money market instruments are made in part by brokers and dealers. *Brokers* bring buyers and sellers together for a commission. By definition, brokers never position securities. Their function is to provide a communications network that links market participants who are often numerous and geographically dispersed. Most brokering in the money market occurs between banks that are buying funds from or selling funds to each other and between dealers in money market instruments.

Dealers make markets in money market instruments by quoting bid and asked prices to each other, to issuers, and to investors. Dealers buy and sell for their own accounts, so assuming positions—long and short—is an essential part of a dealer's operation.

U.S. TREASURY SECURITIES

To finance the U.S. national debt, the Treasury issues several types of securities. Some are nonnegotiable, for example, savings bonds sold to consumers and special issues sold to government trust funds. The bulk of the securities sold by the U.S. Treasury are, however, negotiable.

What form these securities take depends on their maturity. Those with a maturity at issue of a year or less are known as *Treasury bills,* or *T bills* for short or just plain *bills.* T bills bear no interest. An investor in bills earns a return because bills are issued at a discount from face value and redeemed by the Treasury at maturity for face value. The amount of the discount at which investors buy bills and the length of time bills have to be held before they mature together imply some specific yield that the bill will return if held to maturity.

T bills are currently issued in 3-month, 6-month, and 1-year maturities.[1] In issuing bills, the Treasury does not set the amount of the discount. Instead, the Federal Reserve auctions off each new bill issue to investors and dealers, with the bills going to those bidders offering the highest price, i.e., the lowest interest cost to the Treasury. By auctioning new bill issues, the Treasury lets currently prevailing market conditions establish the yield at which each new issue is sold.

The Treasury also issues interest-bearing *notes.* These securities are issued at or very near face value and redeemed at face value. Notes have an *original maturity* (maturity at issue) of 1 to 10 years.[2] Currently, the Treasury issues 2- and 4-year notes on a regular cycle. Notes of other maturities are issued periodically depending on the Treasury's needs. Interest on Treasury notes is paid semiannually. Notes, like bills, are typically sold through auctions held by the Federal Reserve. In these auctions participants bid yields, and the securities are sold to those dealers and investors who bid the lowest yields, that is, the lowest interest cost to the Treasury. Thus, the coupon rate on new Treasury notes, like the yield on bills, is normally determined by the market. The only exceptions are occasional subscription and price auction issues on which the Treasury sets the coupon.

In addition to notes, the Treasury issues interest-bearing negotiable *bonds* that have a maturity at issue of 10 years or more. The only

---

[1] For tactical debt management purposes, the Treasury occasionally meets cash flow gaps by issuing very short-term "cash management bills."

[2] A 5-year note has an *original maturity* at issue of 5 years. One year after issue it has a *current maturity* of four years.

difference between Treasury notes and bonds is that bonds are issued in longer maturities. In recent years the volume of bonds the Treasury may issue has been limited, because Congress has imposed a 4.25 percent ceiling on the rate the Treasury may pay on bonds. Since this rate has for years been far below prevailing market rates, the Treasury is able to sell bonds only to the extent that Congress authorizes it to issue bonds exempt from the ceiling, the current exemption, which has been successively raised, is $70 billion. Treasury bonds, like notes, are normally sold at yield auctions.

Banks, other financial institutions, insurance companies, pension funds, and corporations are all important investors in U.S. Treasury securities. So, too, are some foreign central banks and other foreign institutions. The market for government securities is largely a wholesale market and, especially at the short end, multimillion-dollar transactions are common. However, when interest rates get extremely high, as they did in 1974 and again in 1978–82, individuals with small amounts to invest are drawn into the market.

Because of the high volume of Treasury debt outstanding, the market for bills and short-term government securities is the most active and most carefully watched sector of the money market. At the heart of this market stands a varied collection of dealers who make the market for *governments* (market jargon for government securities) by standing ready to buy and sell huge volumes of these securities. These dealers trade actively not only with investors, but also with each other. Most trades of the latter sort are carried out through brokers.

Governments offer investors several advantages. First, because they are constantly traded in the *secondary market* in large volume and at narrow spreads between the bid and asked prices, they are highly *liquid*. A second advantage is that governments are considered to be free from credit risk because it is inconceivable that the government would default on these securities in any situation short of destruction of the country. Third, interest income on governments is exempt from state taxation. Because of these advantages, governments normally trade at yields below those of other money market instruments. Municipal securities are an exception because they offer a still more attractive tax advantage.

Generally yields on governments are higher the longer their *current maturity*, that is, time left to maturity. The reason, explained in Chapter 4, is that the longer the current maturity of a debt security, the more its price will fluctuate in response to changes in interest rates and therefore the greater the *price risk* to which it exposes the investor. There are times, however, when the yield curve *inverts*, that is, yields on short-term securities rise above those on long-term securities. This, for example, was the case during much of the period 1979–82. The reason for an inverted yield curve is that market participants anticipate, correctly or incorrectly, that interest rates will fall. As a result, borrowers choose to borrow short-term while investors seek out long-term securities; the result is that supply and demand force short-term rates above long-term rates.

FUTURES MARKETS

In discussing the market for governments, we focused on the *cash market,* that is, the market in which existing securities are traded for same- or next-day delivery. In addition, there are markets in which Treasury bills, Treasury notes, Treasury bonds, bank CDs, and other money market instruments are traded for *future* delivery. The futures contracts in Treasuries that are most actively traded are for 3-month bills with a face value of $1 million at maturity and for long bonds with a par value of $100,000.

Interest rate futures markets offer institutions that know they are going to borrow or lend in the future a way to *hedge* that future position, that is, to lock in a reasonably fixed borrowing or lending rate. They also provide speculators with a way to bet money on interest rate movements that is easier and cheaper than going short or long in cash securities.

Since being introduced in 1976, futures markets for financial instruments have grown at an unforeseen and astonishing rate. In fact, futures contracts for Treasury bills and bonds have been among the most successful contracts ever launched on commodities exchanges.

The newness and rapid growth of markets for financial futures, not surprisingly, has created situations in which the relationship between the rates on different futures contracts or between the rates on a futures contract and the corresponding cash instrument get, as the street would say, "out of sync," that is, out of synchronization or line. Thus, yet another major class of traders in financial futures has been arbitrageurs who seek to establish positions from which they will profit when a reasonable relationship between the out-of-line rates is inevitably reestablished.

FEDERAL AGENCY SECURITIES

From time to time Congress becomes concerned about the volume of credit that is available to various sectors of the economy and the terms at which that credit is available. Its usual response is to set up a federal agency to provide credit to that sector. Thus, for example, there is the Federal Home Loan Bank System, which lends to the nation's savings and loan associations as well as regulates them; the Government National Mortgage Association, which funnels money into the mortgage market; the Banks for Cooperatives, which make seasonal and term loans to farm cooperatives; the Federal Land Banks, which give mortgages on farm properties; the Federal Intermediate Credit Banks, which provide short-term financing for producers of crops and livestock; and a host of other agencies.

Initially, all the federal agencies financed their activities by selling their own securities in the open market. Today, all except the largest borrow from the Treasury through an institution called the Federal Financing Bank. Those agencies still borrowing in the open market do so primarily by issuing notes and bonds. These securities (known in the market as *agencies*) bear interest, and they are issued and redeemed at face value. Instead of using the auction technique for issuing their securities, federal agencies look to the market to determine the best yield at which they can sell a new issue, put that yield on the issue, and then sell it through a syndicate of dealers. Some agencies also sell short-term discount paper that resembles commercial paper (see below).

Normally, agencies yield slightly more than Treasury securities of the same maturity for several reasons. Agency issues are smaller than Treasury issues and are therefore less liquid. Also, while all agency issues have de facto backing from the federal government (it's inconceivable that the government would let one of them default on its obligations), the securities of only a few agencies are explicitly backed by the full faith and credit of the U.S. government. Finally, interest income on some federal agency issues is not exempt from state taxation.

The agency market, while smaller than that for governments, has, in recent years, become an active and important sector of the money market. Agencies are traded by the same dealers that trade governments and in much the same way.

FEDERAL FUNDS

All banks that are members of the Federal Reserve System are required to keep reserves on deposit at their district Federal Reserve Bank. A commercial bank's reserve account is much like a consumer's checking account; the bank makes deposits into it and can transfer funds out of it. The main difference is that while a consumer can run the balance in his checking account down to zero, each member bank is required to maintain some minimum average balance in its reserve account over the week. How large that minimum balance is depends on the size and composition of the bank's deposits over the third prior week.

Funds on deposit in a bank's reserve account are referred to as *Federal funds,* or *Fed funds.* Any deposits a bank receives add to its supply of Fed funds, while loans made and securities purchased reduce that supply. Thus, the basic amount of money any bank can lend out and otherwise invest equals the amount of funds it has received from depositors minus the reserves it is required to maintain.

For some banks, this supply of available funds roughly equals the amount they choose to invest in securities plus that demanded from them by borrowers. But for most banks it does not. Specifically, because the nation's largest corporations tend to concentrate their borrowing in big money market banks in New York and other financial centers, the loans and investments these banks have to fund exceed the deposits they receive. Many smaller banks, in contrast, receive more money from local depositors than they can lend locally or choose to invest otherwise. Because large banks have to meet their reserve requirements regardless of what loan demand they face and because excess reserves yield no return to smaller banks, it was natural for large banks to begin borrowing the excess funds held by smaller banks.

This borrowing is done in the *Federal funds market.* Most Fed funds loans are overnight transactions. One reason is that the amount of excess funds a given lending bank holds varies daily and unpredictably. Some transactions in Fed funds are made directly, others through New York brokers. Despite the fact that transactions of this sort are all loans, the lending of Fed funds is referred to as a *sale* and the borrowing of Fed funds as a *purchase.* While overnight transactions dominate the Fed funds market, some lending and borrowing for longer periods also occur there. Fed funds traded for periods other than overnight are referred to as *term* Fed funds.

The rate of interest paid on overnight loans of Federal funds, which is called the *Fed funds rate,* is *the* main interest rate in the money market, and all other short-term rates are keyed to it. The Fed funds rate used to be closely pegged by the Fed. Starting in October 1979, however, the Fed, which still controls the general level of this rate, allowed it to fluctuate over a wide band.

EURODOLLARS

Many foreign banks will accept deposits of dollars and grant the depositor an account *denominated in dollars.* So, too, will the foreign branches of U.S. banks. The practice of accepting dollar-denominated deposits outside of the United States began in Europe, so such deposits came to be known as *Eurodollars.* The practice of accepting dollar-denominated deposits later spread to Hong Kong, Singapore, the Middle East, and other centers around the globe. Consequently today a *Eurodollar deposit is simply a deposit denominated in dollars in a bank or bank branch outside the United States,* and the term Eurodollar has become a misnomer. To make things even more confusing, in December 1981, domestic and foreign banks were permitted to open *international banking facilities (IBFs)* in the United States.[3] Dollars deposited in IBFs are also Eurodollars.

Most Eurodollar deposits are for large sums. They are made by corporations—foreign, multinational, and domestic; foreign central banks and other official institutions; U.S. domestic banks; and wealthy individuals. With the exception of *call money,*[4] all Eurodeposits have a fixed term, which can range from overnight to five years. The bulk of Euro transactions are in the range of six months and under. Banks receiving Eurodollar deposits use them to make loans denominated in dollars to foreign and domestic corporations, foreign governments and government agencies, domestic U.S. banks, and other large borrowers.

Banks that participate in the Eurodollar market actively borrow and lend Euros among themselves, just as domestic banks borrow and lend in the market for Fed funds. The major difference between the two markets is that in the market for Fed funds, most transactions are on an overnight basis whereas in the Euromarket, interbank placements (deposits) of funds for longer periods are common.

For a domestic U.S. bank with a reserve deficiency, borrowing Eurodollars is an alternative to purchasing Fed funds. Also, for a domestic bank with excess funds, a Euro *placement* (i.e., a deposit of dollars in the Euromarket) is an alternative to the sale of Fed funds. Consequently, the rate on overnight Euros tends to closely track the Fed funds rate. It is also true that, as one goes out on the maturity scale, Euro rates continue to track U.S. rates, though not so closely as in the overnight market.

CERTIFICATES OF DEPOSIT

The maximum rate banks may pay on savings deposits and time deposits (a time deposit is a deposit with a fixed maturity) is set by the Fed through *Regulation Q.* Essentially what Reg Q does is to make it impossible for banks to compete with each other or with other savings institutions for small deposits by offering depositors higher interest rates.[5] On large deposits, $100,000 or more, banks may currently pay

---

[3] See Chapter 11.

[4] Call money is money deposited in an interest-bearing account that can be called (withdrawn) by the depositor on a day's notice.

[5] The rates banks and thrifts may pay depositors are gradually being deregulated. See Chapter 11.

any rate they choose so long as the deposit has a minimum maturity of 14 days.

There are many corporations and other large investors that have hundreds of thousands, even millions, of dollars they could invest in bank time deposits. Few do so, however, because they lose liquidity by making a deposit with a fixed maturity. The illiquidity of time deposits and their consequent lack of appeal to investors led banks to invent the *negotiable certificate of deposit,* or *CD* for short.

CDs are normally sold in $1 million units. They are issued at face value and typically pay interest at maturity. CDs can have any maturity longer than 14 days, and some 5- and even 7-year CDs have been sold (these pay interest semiannually). Most CDs, however, have an *original maturity* of one to six months.

The quantity of CDs that banks have outstanding depends largely on the strength of loan demand. When demand rises, banks issue more CDs to fund the additional loans they are making. The rates banks offer on CDs depend on their maturity, how badly the banks want to write new CDs, and the general level of short-term interest rates.

Most of bank CDs are sold directly by banks to investors. Some, however, are issued through dealers for a small commission. The same dealers make an active secondary market in CDs.

Yields on CDs exceed those on bills of similar maturities by varying spreads. One reason for the bigger yield is that buying a bank CD exposes the investor to some credit risk—would he be paid off if the issuing bank failed? A second reason CDs yield more than bills is that they are less liquid.

Variable-rate CDs

Recently banks have introduced, on a small scale, a new type of negotiable CD, *variable-rate CDs.* The two most prevalent types are 6-month CDs with a 30-day *roll* (on each roll date, accrued interest is paid and a new coupon is set) and 1-year paper with a 3-month roll.

The coupon established on a variable-rate CD at issue and on subsequent roll dates is set at some amount (12.5 to 30 basis points depending on the name of the issuer and the maturity) above the average rate (as indicated by the *composite* rate published by the Fed) that banks are paying on new CDs with an original maturity equal to the length of the roll period.

Variable-rate CDs give the issuing bank the opportunity to make a rate play. They offer some rate protection to customers, but they also have the offsetting disadvantage of illiquidity because they trade at a concession to the market on other than roll dates. During their last *leg* (roll period) variable-rate CDs trade like regular CDs of similar bank name and maturity.

The major buyers of variable-rate CDs are money market funds. In calculating the average maturity of their portfolios, these funds treat variable-rate CDs as if they matured on their next roll date, a justifiable practice since such paper must trade at or above par on roll dates. Buying variable-rate CDs enables money funds to get a rate slightly above the prevailing rate for the relevant roll period while holding down the average maturity of their portfolios.

Discount CDs

CDs trade at a price equal to principal *plus* accrued interest. Dealers who make markets in CDs finance their CD inventory in the repo market (described below). Repos on CDs always cover principal but not accrued interest. A dealer that holds a CD inventory must therefore use his scarce capital to finance accrued interest on these securities.

To circumvent this problem and to facilitate comparisons by investors of yields on CDs with yields on discount paper—bills, bankers' acceptances (BAs), and commercial paper—some dealers proposed that banks issue discount rather than interest-bearing CDs. A few banks did this, but it did not become general practice. One reason was the Fed ruling that a bank issuing a discount CD must treat it as a deposit whose size rises over the life of the CD by the amount of the discount at issue. The Fed also required that the issuing bank calculate its reservable deposits on the basis of the constantly rising value of the deposit associated with a discount CD. This created for banks issuing discount CDs an accounting headache, which they chose to avoid by ceasing to issue such paper.

Eurodollar CDs

A Eurodollar time deposit, like a domestic time deposit, is an illiquid asset. Since some investors in Eurodollars wanted liquidity, banks in London that accepted such deposits began to issue *Eurodollar CDs*. These resemble domestic CDs except that instead of being the liability of a domestic bank, they are the liability of the London branch of a U.S. bank, of a British bank, or of some other foreign bank with a branch in London.

Many of the Eurodollar CDs issued in London are purchased by other banks operating in the Euromarket. A large proportion of the remainder are sold to U.S. corporations and other U.S. institutional investors. Many Euro CDs are issued through dealers and brokers who also make a secondary market in these securities.

The Euro CD market is younger and smaller than the market for domestic CDs, but it has grown rapidly since its inception. For the investor, a key advantage of buying Euro CDs is that they offer a higher return than do domestic CDs. The offsetting disadvantages are that they are less liquid and expose the investor to some extra risk because they are issued outside of the United States.

The most recent development in the "Eurodollar" CD market is that some large banks have begun offering such CDs through their Caribbean branches. Note that a CD issued, for example in Nassau, is technically a Euro CD because the deposit is held in a bank branch outside the United States.

Yankee CDs

Foreign banks issue dollar-denominated CDs not only in the Euromarket but also in the domestic market through branches established there. CDs of the latter sort are frequently referred to as *Yankee CDs;* the name is taken from Yankee bonds, which are bonds issued in the domestic market by foreign borrowers.

Yankee, as opposed to domestic, CDs expose the investor to the extra (if only in perception) risk of a foreign name, and they are also less liquid than domestic CDs. Consequently, Yankees trade at yields close to those on Euro CDs. The major buyers of Yankee CDs are corporations that are yield buyers and fund to dates.

COMMERCIAL PAPER

While some cash-rich industrial firms participate in the bond and money markets only as lenders, many more must at times borrow to finance either current operations or expenditures on plant and equipment. One source of short-term funds available to a corporation is bank loans. Large firms with good credit ratings, however, have an alternative source of funds that is cheaper, namely, the sale of commercial paper.

Commercial paper is an unsecured promissory note issued for a specific amount and maturing on a specific day. All commercial paper is negotiable, but most paper sold to investors is held by them to maturity. Commercial paper is issued not only by industrial and manufacturing firms, but also by finance companies. Finance companies normally sell their paper directly to investors. Industrial firms, in contrast, typically issue their paper through dealers.

The maximum maturity for which commercial paper may be sold is 270 days, since paper with a longer maturity must be registered with the Securities and Exchange Commission (SEC), a time-consuming and costly procedure. In practice, very little 270-day paper is sold. Most paper sold is in the range of 30 days and under.

Since commercial paper has such short maturities, the issuer rarely will have sufficient funds coming in before the paper matures to pay off his borrowing. Instead, he expects to *roll* his paper, that is, sell new paper to obtain funds to pay off the maturing paper. Naturally the possibility exists that some sudden change in market conditions, such as when the Penn Central went "belly up" (bankrupt), might make it difficult or impossible for him to sell paper for some time. To guard against this risk, commercial paper issuers back all or a large proportion of their outstanding paper with lines of credit from banks.

The rate offered on commercial paper depends on its maturity, on how much the issuer wants to borrow, on the general level of money market rates, and on the credit rating of the issuer. Almost all commercial paper is rated with respect to credit risk by one or more of several rating services: Moody's, Standard & Poor's, and Fitch. While only top-grade credits can get ratings good enough to sell paper these days, there is still a slight risk that an issuer might go bankrupt. Because of this, and because of illiquidity, yields on commercial paper are higher than those on Treasury obligations of similar maturity.

BANKERS' ACCEPTANCES

Bankers' acceptances (*BAs*) are an unknown instrument outside the confines of the money market. Moreover, explaining them isn't easy because they arise in a variety of ways out of a variety of transactions. The best approach is to use an example.

Suppose a U.S. importer wants to buy shoes in Brazil and pay for them four months later, after he has had time to sell them in the United States. One approach would be for the importer to borrow from his bank; however, short-term rates may be lower in the open market. If they are, and if the importer is too small to go into the open market on his own, then he can go the bankers' acceptance route.

In that case, he has his bank write a letter of credit for the amount of the sale and sends this letter to the Brazilian exporter. Upon export of the shoes, the Brazilian firm, using this letter of credit, draws a time draft on the importer's U.S. bank and discounts this draft at its local bank, thereby obtaining immediate payment for its goods. The Brazilian bank, in turn, sends the time draft to the importer's U.S. bank, which then stamps "accepted" on the draft (that is, the bank guarantees payment on the draft and thereby creates an *acceptance*). Once this is done, the draft becomes an irrevocable primary obligation of the accepting bank. At this point, if the Brazilian bank did not want cash immediately, the U.S. bank would return the draft to that bank, which would hold it as an investment and then present it to the U.S. bank for payment at maturity. If, on the other hand, the Brazilian bank wanted cash immediately, the U.S. bank would pay it and then either hold the acceptance itself or sell it to an investor. Whoever ended up holding the acceptance, it would be the importer's responsibility to provide its U.S. bank with sufficient funds to pay off the acceptance at maturity. If the importer should fail to do so, his bank would still be responsible for making payment at maturity.

Our example illustrates how an acceptance can arise out of a U.S. import transaction. Acceptances also arise in connection with U.S. export sales, trade between third countries (e.g., Japanese imports of oil from the Middle East), the domestic shipment of goods, and domestic or foreign storage of readily marketable staples. Currently, most BAs arise out of foreign trade; they may be in manufactured goods, but more typically are in bulk commodities, such as cocoa, cotton, coffee, or crude oil, to name a few. Because of the complex nature of acceptance operations, only large banks that have well-staffed foreign departments act as accepting banks.

Bankers' acceptances closely resemble commercial paper in form. They are short-term, non–interest-bearing notes sold at a discount and redeemed by the accepting bank at maturity for full face value. The major difference is that payment on commercial paper is guaranteed only by the issuing company. In contrast, bankers' acceptances, in addition to carrying the issuer's pledge to pay, are backed by the underlying goods being financed and also carry the guarantee of the accepting bank. Consequently, bankers' acceptances are less risky than commercial paper, and thus sell at slightly lower yields.

The big banks through which bankers' acceptances are originated generally keep some portion of the acceptances they create as investments. The rest are sold to investors through dealers or directly by the bank itself. Major investors in BAs are other banks, foreign central banks, money market funds, corporations, and other domestic and foreign institutional investors. BAs have liquidity because dealers in these securities make an active secondary market in those that are eligible for purchase by the Fed.

REPOS AND REVERSES

A variety of bank and nonbank dealers act as market makers in governments, agencies, CDs, and BAs. Because dealers, by definition, buy and sell for their own accounts, active dealers will inevitably end up holding some securities. They will, moreover, buy and hold substantial positions if they believe that interest rates are likely to fall and that the value of these securities is therefore likely to rise. Speculation and risk taking are an inherent and important part of being a dealer.

While dealers have large amounts of capital, the positions they take are often several hundred times that amount. As a result, dealers have to borrow to finance their positions. Using the securities they own as collateral, they can and do borrow from banks at the dealer loan rate. For the bulk of their financing, however, they resort to a cheaper alternative, entering into *repurchase agreements* (*RPs or repos,* for short) with investors.

Much RP financing done by dealers is on an overnight basis. It works as follows: The dealer finds a corporation or other investor who has funds to invest overnight. He sells this investor, say, $10 million of securities for roughly $10 million, which is paid in Federal funds to his bank by the investor's bank against delivery of the securities sold. At the same time, the dealer agrees to repurchase these securities the next day at a slightly higher price. Thus, the buyer of the securities is in effect making the dealer a one-day loan secured by the obligations sold to him. The difference between the purchase and sale prices on the RP transaction is the interest the investor earns on his loan. Alternatively, the purchase and sale prices in an RP transaction may be identical; in that case, the dealer pays the investor some explicit rate of interest.

Often a dealer will take a speculative position that he intends to hold for some time. He might then do an RP for 30 days or longer. Such agreements are known as *term* RPs.

From the point of view of investors, overnight loans in the RP market offer several attractive features. First, by rolling overnight RPs, investors can keep surplus funds invested without losing liquidity or incurring a price risk. Second, because RP transactions are secured by top-quality paper, investors expose themselves to little or no credit risk.

The overnight RP rate generally is less than the Fed funds rate. The reason is that the many nonbank investors who have funds to invest overnight or very short term, and who do not want to incur any price risk, have nowhere to go but the RP market, because (with the exception of S&Ls) they cannot participate directly in the Fed funds market. Also, lending money through an RP transaction is safer than selling Fed funds because a sale of Fed funds is an unsecured loan.

On term, as opposed to overnight, RP transactions, investors still have the advantage of their loans being secured, but they do lose some liquidity. To compensate for that, the rate on an RP transaction is generally higher the longer the term for which funds are lent.

Banks that make dealer loans fund them by buying Fed funds, and the lending rate they charge—which is adjusted daily—is the prevailing Fed funds rate plus a one-eighth to one-quarter markup. Because the overnight RP rate is lower than the Fed funds rate, dealers can finance their positions more cheaply by doing an RP than by borrowing from the banks.

A dealer who is bullish on the market will position large amounts of securities. If he's bearish, he will *short* the market, that is, sell securities he does not own. Since the dealer has to deliver any securities he sells whether he owns them or not, a dealer who shorts has to borrow securities one way or another. The most common technique today for borrowing securities is to do what is called a *reverse RP*, or simply a *reverse*. To obtain securities through a reverse, a dealer finds an investor holding the required securities; he then buys these securities from the investor under an agreement that he will resell the same securities to the investor at a fixed price on some future date. In this transaction, the dealer, besides obtaining securities, is extending a loan to the investor for which he is paid some rate of interest.

An RP and a reverse are identical transactions. What a given transaction is called depends on who initiates it; typically if a dealer hunting money does, it's an RP; if a dealer hunting securities does, it's a reverse.

A final note: The Fed uses reverses and RPs with dealers in government securities to make adjustments in bank reserves.

MUNICIPAL NOTES

Debt securities issued by state and local governments and their agencies are referred to as *municipal securities*. Such securities can be divided into two broad categories: bonds issued to finance capital projects and short-term notes sold in anticipation of the receipt of other funds, such as taxes or proceeds from a bond issue.

Municipal notes, which are an important money market instrument, are issued with maturities ranging from a month to a year or more. They bear interest, and minimum denominations are highly variable, ranging anywhere from $5,000 to $5 million.

Most muni notes are general obligation securities; that is, payment of principal and interest is secured by the issuer's pledge of its full faith, credit, and taxing power. This sounds impressive but, as the spectacle of New York City tottering on the brink of bankruptcy brought home to all, it is possible that a municipality might default on its securities. Thus, the investor who buys muni notes assumes a credit risk. To aid investors in evaluating this risk, publicly offered muni notes are rated by Moody's. The one exception is project notes, which are issued by local housing authorities to finance federally sponsored programs, and which are backed by the full faith and credit of the federal government.

The major attraction of municipal notes to an investor is that interest income on them is exempt from federal taxation and usually also from any income taxes levied within the state where they are issued. The value of this tax exemption is greater the higher the investor's tax bracket, and the muni market thus attracts only highly taxed investors—commercial banks, cash-rich corporations, and wealthy individuals.

Large muni note issues are sold to investors by dealers who obtain the securities either through negotiation with the issuer or through competitive bidding. The same dealers also make a secondary market in muni notes.

The yield a municipality must pay to issue notes depends on its credit rating, the length of time for which it borrows, and the general level of short-term rates. Normally, a good credit can borrow at a rate well below the yield on T bills of equivalent maturity because of the value to the investor of the tax exemption on the municipal security. A corporation that has its profits taxed at a 50 percent marginal rate would, for example, receive approximately the same aftertax return from a muni note yielding 5 percent that it would from a T bill yielding 10 percent.[6] For a corporation subject to high *state* income taxes, the difference between the rate offered on a municipal note issued in the firm's state of domicile and the bill rate that would give the firm the same aftertax return would be substantially larger.

---

[6] We say "approximately" because most muni notes are sold on an *interest-bearing* basis while bills are quoted on a *discount* rate, so that the rates at which the two securities are offered are rarely directly comparable.

4

Discount and interest-bearing securities

Banks deal in essentially two types of securities, *interest-bearing securities* and *discount paper*. Yields on these two types of instruments are calculated and quoted in quite different ways. Thus, a discussion of banking should be prefaced by some simple math which shows how yields on these different instruments are calculated and how they can be made comparable. We start with discount securities.[1]

TREASURY BILLS

To illustrate how a discount security works, we assume that an investor who participates in an auction of new Treasury *year bills* picks up $1 million of them at 10 percent. What this means is that the Treasury sells the investor $1 million of bills maturing in one year at a price approximately 10 percent below their face value. The "approxi-

---

[1] For a complete description, see Marcia Stigum in collaboration with John Mann, *Money Market Calculations: Yields, Break-Evens, and Arbitrage* (Homewood, Ill.: Dow Jones-Irwin, 1981).

mately" qualifier takes a little explaining. Offhand one would expect the amount of the discount to be the face value of the securities purchased times the rate of discount times the *fraction of the year* the securities will be outstanding. In our example, the discount calculated this way would equal $1 million times 10 percent times one full year, which amounts to $100,000. That figure, however, is incorrect for two reasons. First, the year bill is outstanding not for a year, but for 52 weeks, which is 364 days. Second, the Treasury calculates the discount as if a year had only 360 days. So the fraction of the year for which the security is outstanding is 364/360, and the true discount on the security is:

$$\text{Discount on \$1 million of year bills issued at } 10\% = \$1,000,000 \times 0.10 \times \frac{364}{360} = \$101,111.11$$

Because the Treasury calculates the discount as if the year had 360 days, our investor gets his bills at a discount that exceeds $100,000 even though he invests for only 364 days. The price he pays for his bills equals *face value minus the discount*, i.e.,

$$\text{Price paid for \$1 million of year bills bought at } 10\% = \$1,000,000 - \$101,111.11 = \$898,888.89$$

Generalizing from this example, we can construct formulas for calculating both the discount from face value and the price at which T bills will sell, depending on their current maturity and the discount at which they are quoted. Let

D = discount from face value.
F = face value.
d = rate of discount.
t = days to maturity.
P = price.

Then

$$D = F\left(\frac{d \times t}{360}\right)$$

and

$$P = F - D = F\left(1 - \frac{d \times t}{360}\right)$$

EQUIVALENT BOND YIELD

If an investor lent $1 million for one 365-day year and received at the end of the year $100,000 of interest plus the $1 million of principal invested, we would—calculating yield on a *simple interest basis*—say that he had earned 10 percent.[2] Using the same approach—return earned divided by principal invested—to calculate the return earned by our investor who bought a 10-percent year bill, we find that, on a simple interest basis, he earned significantly *more than* 10 percent. Specifically,

$$\text{Return on a simple interest basis on } \$1 \text{ million } 10\% \text{ year bills held to maturity} = \frac{\$101,111.11}{\$898,888.89} \div \frac{364}{365}$$

$$= 11.28\%$$

In this calculation, because the bill matures in 364 days, it is necessary to divide by the fraction of the year for which the bill is outstanding to annualize the rate earned.

Treasury notes and bonds, which—unlike bills—are *interest bearing*, pay the holder interest equal to the face value times the interest (i.e., *coupon*) rate at which they are issued. Thus, an investor who bought $1 million of Treasury notes carrying a 10 percent coupon would receive $100,000 of interest during each year the securities were outstanding.

The way yields on notes and bonds are quoted, 10 percent notes selling at *par* (i.e., face value) would be quoted as offering a 10 percent yield. An investor who bought these notes would, however, have the opportunity to earn more than 10 percent simple interest. The reason is that interest on notes and bonds is paid in semiannual installments, which means that the investor can invest, during the second six months of each year, the first semiannual interest installment.

To illustrate the effect of this on return, consider an investor who buys at issue $1 million of 10 percent Treasury notes. Six months later, he receives $50,000 of interest, which we assume he reinvests at 10 percent. Then at the end of the year, he receives another $50,000 of interest plus interest on the interest he has invested; the latter amounts to $50,000 times 10 percent times the one-half year he earns that interest. Thus, his total dollar return over the year is:

$$\$50,000 + (0.10)(\$50,000)(0.5) + \$50,000 = \$102,500$$

and the percentage return that he earns, expressed in terms of simple interest, is

$$\frac{\$102,500}{\$1,000,000} = 10.25\%$$

---

[2] By *simple interest* we mean interest paid once a year at the end of the year. There is no compounding as, for example, on a savings account.

Note that what is at work here is *compound interest;* any quoted rate of interest yields more dollars of return, and is thus equivalent to a higher simple interest rate, the more frequently interest is paid and the more compounding that can thus occur.

Because return can mean different things depending on the way it is quoted and paid, an investor can meaningfully compare the returns offered by different securities only if these returns are stated on a comparable basis. With respect to *discount* and *coupon* securities, the way yields are made comparable in the money market is by restating yields quoted on a *discount basis*—the basis on which T bills are quoted—in terms of *equivalent bond yield*—the basis on which yields on notes and bonds are quoted.

We calculated above that an investor in a year bill would, on a simple interest basis, earn 11.28 percent. This is slightly higher than the rate he would earn measured on an equivalent bond yield basis. The reason is that equivalent bond yield understates, as noted, the true return, on a simple interest basis, that the investor in a coupon security would earn if he reinvested interest. When adjustment is made for this understatement, the equivalent bond yield offered by a 10 percent year bill turns out to be something less than 11.28 percent. Specifically, it is 10.98 percent.

The formula for converting yield on a bank discount basis to equivalent bond yield is complicated for discount securities that have a current maturity of longer than six months, but that is no problem for investors and other money market participants because bills yields are always restated on dealers' quote sheets in terms of equivalent bond yield (Table 4–1) at the *asked* rate.

Table 4–1
Selected quotes on U.S. Treasury bills, November 26, 1981

Billions outstanding	*Maturity*	*Bid*	*Asked*	*Equivalent bond yield*
	1981:			
8.5	11/27	9.80	9.32	9.46
8.5	12/24	10.13	9.87	10.08
	1982:			
13.5	1/28	10.22	10.00	10.32
13.7	2/25	10.17	10.07	10.50
9.0	3/25	10.30	10.26	10.77
8.5	4/22	10.57	10.47	11.09
8.7	5/20	10.71	10.59	11.32
4.5	8/12	10.69	10.57	11.36
5.0	11/04	10.79	10.69	11.67

On bills with a current maturity of six months or less, equivalent bond yield is the simple interest rate yielded by a bill. Let

$$d_b = \text{equivalent bond yield}$$

Then, on a security quoted at the discount rate d, equivalent bond yield is given by

$$d_b = \frac{365 \times d}{360 - (d \times t)}$$

For example, on a 3-month bill purchased at 8 percent, equivalent bond yield is

$$d_b = \frac{365 \times 0.08}{360 - (0.08 \times 91)} = 8.28\%$$

From the examples we have considered, it is clear that the yield on a discount security is *significantly less* when measured on a discount basis than when measured in terms of equivalent bond yield. The absolute divergence between these two measures of yield is, moreover, not constant. As Table 4–2 shows, the greater the yield and the longer the maturity of the security, the greater the divergence.

Table 4–2
Comparisons, at different rates and maturities, of rates of discount and equivalent bond yields

Yields on a discount basis (percent)	Equivalent bond yields (percent)		
	30-day maturity	182-day maturity	364-day maturity
6	6.114	6.274	6.375
8	8.166	8.453	8.639
10	10.227	10.679	10.979
12	12.290	12.952	13.399
14	14.362	15.256	15.904

FLUCTUATIONS IN A BILL'S PRICE

Normally, the price at which a bill sells will rise as the bill approaches maturity. For example, to yield 9 percent on a discount basis, a 6-month bill must be priced at $95.45 per $100 of face value. For the same bill three months later (three months closer to maturity) to yield 9 percent, it must have risen in price to $97.72. The moral is clear: If a bill always sold at the same yield throughout its life, its price would rise steadily toward face value as it approached maturity.

A bill's yield, however, is unlikely to be constant over time; instead, it will fluctuate for two reasons: (1) changes may occur in the general level of short-term interest rates, and (2) the bill will move along *the yield curve*. Let's look at each of these factors.

Short-term interest rates

T bills are issued through auctions in which discounted prices (yields) are bid. The rate of discount determined at auction on a new bill issue depends on the level of short-term interest rates prevailing at the moment of the auction. The reason is straightforward. Investors who want to buy bills at the time of a Treasury auction have two alternatives—to buy new bills or to buy existing bills from dealers. This being the case, investors will not bid for new bills a rate of discount lower than that available on existing bills. If they did, they would be offering to buy new bills at a price higher than that at which they could buy existing bills. Also, investors will not bid substantially higher rates of discount (lower prices) than those prevailing on existing bills. If they did, they would not obtain bills, since they would surely be underbid by others trying to get just a slightly better return than that available on existing securities. Thus, the prevailing level of short-term rates determines, within a narrow range, the discount established on new bills at issue.

However, the going level of short-term rates is not constant over time. It rises and falls in response to changes in economic activity, the demand for credit, investors' expectations, and monetary policy as set by the Federal Reserve System. Figure 4–1, which plots yields on 6-month T bills for the period 1970–81, portrays vividly the volatility of short-term interest rates. It shows both the sharp ups and downs that occurred in these rates as the Fed successively eased and tightened and the myriad of smaller fluctuations over the period in response to short-lived changes in other determinants of these rates.

If the going level of short-term rates (which establishes the yield at which a bill is initially sold) falls after a bill is issued, then this bill—as long as its price doesn't change—will yield more than new bills. Therefore, buyers will compete for this bill, and in doing so they will drive up its price and thereby force down its yield until the bill sells at a rate of discount equal to the new, lower going interest rate. Conversely, if short-term rates rise after a bill is issued, the unwillingness of buyers to purchase any bill at a discount less than that available on new issues will drive down its price and thereby force up its yield.

Figure 4-1
Average auction rates of 6-month T bills

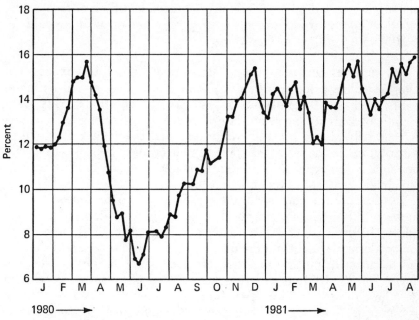

1980 ——►　　　　　　　　1981 ——►

Source: Morgan Bank.

The yield curve

Even if the going level of short-term interest rates does not change
while investors hold bills, it would be normal for the rate at which they
could sell their bills to change. The reason lies in the *yield curve.* How
this works is a function of several factors, described below.

Price risk. In choosing among alternative securities, an investor
considers three things: risk, liquidity, and return. Purchase of a money
market instrument exposes an investor to two sorts of risk: (1) *credit
risk:* will the issuer pay off at maturity? and (2) *price risk:* if the investor later sold the security, might he have to do so at a loss because
interest rates had subsequently risen? Most money market investors
are risk averse, which means that they will accept lower yields to
obtain lower risk.

The price risk to which bills and other money market instruments
expose the investor is *larger* the *longer* the current maturity. To see
why, suppose that short-term interest rates rise a full percentage point
across the board; then the prices of all bill issues will drop, *but the*

price drop will be greater, the longer an issue's current maturity. For example, a 1 percentage point rise in market rates would cause a 3-month bill to fall only $2,500 in price per $1 million of face value, whereas the corresponding price drop on a 9-month bill would be $7,600 per $1 million of face value.

The slope of the yield curve. Because a 3-month bill exposes the investor to less price risk than a 9-month bill does, it will normally yield less than a 9-month bill. In other words, the bill market yield curve, which shows the relationship between yield and current maturity, normally slopes upward, indicating that the longer the time to maturity, the higher the yield. We say "normally" because other factors, such as the expectation that interest rates are going to fall, may, as explained below, alter this relationship.

To illustrate the concept of the yield curve, we have used the bid quotes in Table 4–1 to plot a yield curve in Figure 4–2; each dot is one quote. Our results show a normal upward-sloping yield curve. Lest you try doing the same and be disappointed, we should admit that we cheated a bit in putting together our demonstration yield curve. On November 25, 1981, there were many more bill issues outstanding than those quoted in Table 4–1. Had we plotted yields on all of these in Figure 4–2, we would have found that yield did not rise quite so

Figure 4–2
Yield curve for Treasury bills, November 25, 1981

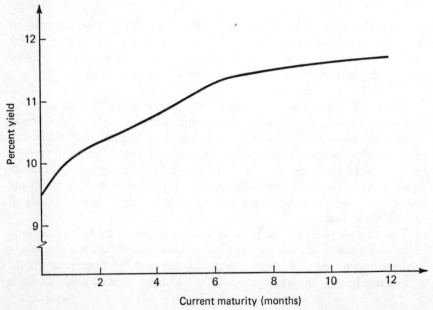

consistently with maturity; the points plotted for some bill issues would have been somewhat off a smooth yield curve. Yields may be out of line for various reasons. For example, a bill issue maturing around a tax date might be highly desired by investors who had big tax payments to make, and, for this reason, trade at a yield that was relatively low compared to yields on surrounding issues.

While the yield curve for short maturities normally slopes upward, its shape and slope vary over time. Thus, it is difficult to pinpoint a "normal" spread between, say, 1-month and 6-month bills. Yield spreads between different securities are always measured in terms of basis points. *A basis point is 1/100th of 1 percentage point.* Thus, if 5-month bills are quoted at 10.45 and 6-month bills at 10.56, the spread between the two is said to be 11 basis points. A yield spread between two securities of 100 basis points would indicate a full 1 percent difference in their yields. A basis point is also frequently referred to as an 01.

Yield realized on sales before maturity

If an investor buys 1-year bills at 10 percent and holds them to maturity, he will earn, on a discount basis, precisely 10 percent over the holding period. If, alternatively, he sells the bills before maturity, he will earn 10 percent over the holding period only if he sells at 10 percent, a relatively unlikely outcome. If he sells at a lower rate, he will get a higher price for his bills than he would have if he had sold them at 10 percent, and he will therefore earn more than 10 percent. If, on the other hand, he sells at a rate higher than 10 percent, he will earn something less than 10 percent.

The holding period yield as a simple interest rate that an investor earns on bills purchased at one rate and subsequently sold at another can be calculated using the formula

$$i = \frac{\text{Sales price} - \text{Purchase price}}{\text{Purchase price}} \div \frac{t}{365}$$

where t equals the number of days held. To illustrate, assume that an investor buys $1 million of 1-year bills at 10 percent and sells them three months later at 10.25 percent. His holding-period yield would be

$$i = \frac{\$924,166.67 - \$898,888.89}{\$898,888.89} \div \frac{91}{365} = 11.23\%$$

Bankers' acceptances and commercial paper

In talking about discount securities, we have focused on bills since they are the most important discount security traded in the money market. All we have said about yields on bills is, however, equally applicable to yields on BAs and commercial paper, both of which are sold on a discount basis with the discount being calculated on a 360-day year.

INTEREST–BEARING SECURITIES

The stock-in-trade of the money market includes, besides discount securities, a variety of *interest-bearing* instruments: Treasury and federal agency notes and bonds, municipal notes and bonds, and bank certificates of deposit. Notes, bonds, and other interest-bearing debt securities are issued with a fixed *face value;* they mature at some specified date, and carry a *coupon rate* which is the annual interest rate the issuer promises to pay the holder on the security's face value while the security is outstanding.

Some notes and bonds are issued in *registered* form; that is, the issuer keeps track of who owns its outstanding IOUs, just as a corporation keeps track of who owns its common stock. Most notes and bonds, however, are issued in *bearer* form. To prove ownership of a bearer security, the owner must produce or bear it. An issuer with $50 million of bearer bonds outstanding does not know where to send interest when a payment date comes along. Consequently, such securities carry *coupons*, one for each interest date. On the interest date, the investor or his bank clips the appropriate coupon from the security and sends it to the issuer's paying agent, who, in turn, makes the required payment.[3] Generally, interest payments are made semiannually on coupon securities. Because notes and bonds carry coupons, the return paid on face value is called the *coupon rate,* or simply the *coupon.*

Notes and bonds with a short current maturity are referred to as *short coupons,* those with an intermediate current maturity (2 to 7 years) as *intermediate coupons,* and those with a still longer current maturity as *long coupons.*

Call and refunding provisions

Once a bond issue is sold, the issuer might choose to redeem it early. For example, if interest rates fell, the borrower could reduce his interest costs by refunding his loan, that is, by paying off outstanding high-coupon bonds and issuing new lower-coupon bonds.

For the investor, early repayment on a bond is almost always disadvantageous because a bond issuer will rarely be tempted to repay early

---

[3] The procedure is different on Treasury and agency securities, which are now being issued in *book-entry* form; computerized records of ownership maintained by the Fed and banks have been substituted for actual securities.

when interest rates are rising, a time when it would be to the bond-holder's advantage to move funds out of the issuer's bonds into new, higher-yielding bonds. On the other hand, early payment looks attractive to the issuer when interest rates are falling, a time when it is to the investor's advantage to keep funds invested in the issuer's high-coupon securities.

To protect investors making long-term commitments against frequent refundings by borrowers out to minimize interest costs, most bonds contain call and refunding provisions. A bond issue is said to be *callable* when the issuer has the option to repay part or all of the issue early by paying some specified redemption price to bondholders. Most bonds offer some call protection to the investor. Some are noncallable for life, others for some number of years after issue.

Besides call protection, many bonds offer refunding protection. Typically, long-term industrial bonds are immediately callable *but* offer 10 years of protection against calls for refunding. Such a bond is referred to as *callable except for refunding purposes*. If a bond offered refunding protection through 1985, that would be indicated on a dealer's quote sheet by the symbol NR85.

Call provisions usually specify that the issuer who calls a bond must pay the bondholder a price above face value. The *call premium* frequently equals the coupon rate on early calls and then diminishes to zero as the bond approaches maturity.

Price quotes

Note and bond prices are quoted in slightly different ways depending on whether they are selling in the new issue or the secondary market. When notes and bonds other than governments are issued, the price at which they are offered to investors is normally quoted as a *percentage* of face value. To illustrate, the corporate mortgages bonds announced in Figure 4–3 were offered at a price of 99⅛ percent, which means that the investor had to pay $99.125 for each $100 of face value. This percentage price is often called the bond's *dollar price*. The security described in Figure 4–3 was offered below par, so the actual yield it offered exceeded the coupon rate of 16.25 percent.

Once a note or bond issue is distributed and trading in it moves to the secondary market, prices are also quoted on a percentage basis but always, depending on the security, in 32ds, 8ths, 4ths, or halves. Table 4–3 reproduces, by way of illustration, a few quotes on Treasury notes posted by a dealer on November 25, 1981. The first bid is 96–1, meaning that this dealer was willing to pay $96¹/₃₂, which equals $99.03125 per $100 of face value for that issue. The advantage of dollar pricing of notes and bonds is that it makes the prices of securities with different denominations directly comparable.

Figure 4–3

Pricing announcement for corporate mortgage bonds

$100,000,000

Louisiana Power & Light Company

First Mortgage Bonds, 16¼% Series Due December 1, 1991

Interest payable June 1 and December 1

Price 99⅛% and Accrued Interest

Copies of the Prospectus may be obtained in any State from only such of the
undersigned as may legally offer these Securities in compliance
with the securities laws of such State.

MORGAN STANLEY & CO.	DEAN WITTER REYNOLDS INC.
Incorporated	

THE FIRST BOSTON CORPORATION   MERRILL LYNCH WHITE WELD CAPITAL MARKETS GROUP   SALOMON BROTHERS INC
Merrill Lynch, Pierce, Fenner & Smith Incorporated

BACHE HALSEY STUART SHIELDS	BEAR, STEARNS & CO.	BLYTH EASTMAN PAINE WEBBER
Incorporated		*Incorporated*
DILLON, READ & CO. INC.	DONALDSON, LUFKIN & JENRETTE	DREXEL BURNHAM LAMBERT
	Securities Corporation	*Incorporated*
E. F. HUTTON & COMPANY INC.	KIDDER, PEABODY & CO.	LAZARD FRERES & CO.
	Incorporated	
LEHMAN BROTHERS KUHN LOEB		L. F. ROTHSCHILD, UNTERBERG, TOWBIN
Incorporated		
SHEARSON/AMERICAN EXPRESS INC.	SMITH BARNEY, HARRIS UPHAM & CO.	WARBURG PARIBAS BECKER
	Incorporated	*Incorporated*
WERTHEIM & CO., INC.		HOWARD, WEIL, LABOUISSE, FRIEDRICHS
Corporation		*Incorporated*
ATLANTIC CAPITAL	BASLE SECURITIES CORPORATION	ALEX. BROWN & SONS
Corporation		
MOSELEY, HALLGARTEN, ESTABROOK & WEEDEN INC.		OPPENHEIMER & CO., INC.
THE ROBINSON-HUMPHREY COMPANY, INC.		THOMSON McKINNON SECURITIES INC.
TUCKER, ANTHONY & R. L. DAY, INC.	ADVEST, INC.	ARNHOLD AND S. BLEICHROEDER, INC.
SANFORD C. BERNSTEIN & CO., INC.		JANNEY MONTGOMERY SCOTT INC.
LADENBURG, THALMANN & CO. INC.		NOMURA SECURITIES INTERNATIONAL, INC.

November 25, 1981

Treatment of interest in pricing

There's another wrinkle with respect to note and bond pricing. Typically, interest on notes and bonds is paid to the holder semiannually on the coupon dates. This means that the value of a coupon security rises by the amount of interest accrued as a payment date approaches

Table 4–3
Quotations for selected U.S. Treasury notes, November 25, 1981*

Publicly held ($ billions)	Coupon	Maturity	Bid	Asked	Yield to maturity	Yield value (1/32)
3.28	7¼	12/31/81	99–20	99–22	10.67	0.3646
5.81	8	2/15/83	96– 1	96– 8	11.38	0.0291
4.50	14⅜	11/15/84	104– 0	104–14	12.53	0.0126
2.25	14¼	11/15/91	107– 0	107– 4	12.95	0.0054
1.75	15¾	11/15/01	117–24	117–28	13.19	0.0039
2.00	14	11/15/11–06	108–26	108–30	12.80	0.0039

*The last issue quoted matures in 2011 but is callable in 2006. Its maturity, 11/15/11–06, indicates this.

and falls thereafter by the amount of the payment made. Since notes and bonds are issued on every business day and consequently have coupon dates all over the calendar, the effect of accrued interest on the value of coupon securities would, if incorporated into the prices quoted by dealers, make meaningful price comparisons between different issues difficult. To get around this problem, the actual prices paid in the new issue and secondary markets are always the quoted dollar price *plus* any accrued interest. For example, if an investor—three months before a coupon date—bought $100,000 of 12 percent Treasury notes quoted at 100, he would pay $100,000 plus $3,000 of accrued interest:

$$\$100,000 + 0.5\left[\frac{(0.12)(\$100,000)}{2}\right]$$

where $(0.12)(\$100,000)/2$ represents the $6,000 semiannual interest due on the notes.

Fluctuations in a coupon security's price

When a new note or bond issue comes to market, the coupon rate on it is, with certain exceptions, set so that it equals the yield prevailing in the market on securities of comparable maturity and risk. This permits the new security to be sold at a price equal or nearly equal to par.

The price at which the security later trades in the secondary market will, like that of a discount security, fluctuate in response to changes in the general level of interest rates.

Yield to maturity.   To illustrate, let's work through a simple example. Suppose a new 6-year note with an 8 percent coupon is issued at par. Six months later, the Fed tightens, and the yield on comparable securities rises to 8.5 percent. Now what is this 8 percent security worth? Since the investor who pays a price equal to par for this "seasoned issue" is going to get only an 8 percent return, while 8.5 percent is available elsewhere, it is clear that the security must now sell at *less* than par.

To determine how much less, we have to introduce a new concept—*effective yield.* When an investor buys a coupon security at a *discount* and holds it to maturity, he receives a two-part return: the promised interest payment *plus* a capital gain. The capital gain arises because the security that the investor bought at less than par is redeemed at maturity for full face value. The investor who buys a coupon issue at a *premium* and holds it to maturity also receives a two-part return: interest payments due plus a capital *loss* equal to the premium paid.

For dollars invested in a coupon issue that sells at a discount or premium, it is possible to calculate the overall, or effective rate of return received, which is the rate that the investor earns on his dollars when both interest received *and* capital gains (or losses) are taken into account. Naturally, an investor choosing between securities of similar risk and maturity will do so, not on the basis of coupon rate, but on the basis of effective yield, referred to in the financial community as *yield to maturity.*

To get back to our example, it is clear that once rates rise to 8.5 percent in the open market, the security with an 8 percent coupon has to be priced at a discount sufficiently great so that its yield to maturity equals 8.5 percent. Figuring out how many dollars of discount this requires involves complicated calculations. Dealers used to use bond tables, but all have now switched to bond calculators. A trader can thus determine in a few seconds that, with interest rates at 8.5 percent, a $1,000 note with an 8 percent coupon and a 3½-year current maturity must sell at $985.13 (a discount of $14.87) to yield 8.5 percent to maturity.

Current maturity and price volatility.   A capital gain of $14.87, which is what the investor in our discounted 8 percent note would realize if he held it to maturity, will raise effective yield more, the faster this gain is realized (the shorter the current maturity of the security). Conversely, this capital gain will raise effective yield less, the more slowly it is realized (the longer the current maturity of the security).[4]

---

[4] If you don't see this, just think—somewhat imprecisely—of the capital gain as a certain number of dollars of extra interest paid out in yearly installments to the investor as his security matures. Clearly, the shorter the security's current maturity, the higher these extra annual interest installments will be, and consequently, the higher the overall yield to the investor.

But if this is so, then a one-half percentage point rise in the yield on comparable securities will cause a larger fall in price for a security with a long current maturity than for one with a short current maturity. In other words, the discount required to raise a coupon security's yield to maturity by one-half percentage point is *greater* the *longer* the security's maturity.

By reversing the argument above, it is easy to see that if six months after the 6-year, 8 percent note in our example was issued, the yield on comparable securities *fell* to 7.5 percent, the value of this note would be driven to a *premium*, i.e., it would sell at a price above par. Note also that a one-half percentage point *fall* in the yield on comparable securities would force an outstanding high-coupon security to a *greater* premium, the *longer* its current maturity.

As these observations suggest, when prevailing interest rates change, prices of long coupons respond more dramatically than prices of short coupons. Figure 4–4 shows this sharp contrast. It pictures, for a $1,000 note carrying an 8 percent coupon, the relationship between

Figure 4–4
Premiums and discounts at which a $1,000 note with an 8 percent coupon would sell, depending on current maturity, if market yields on comparable securities were 6 percent, 8.5 percent, and 10 percent

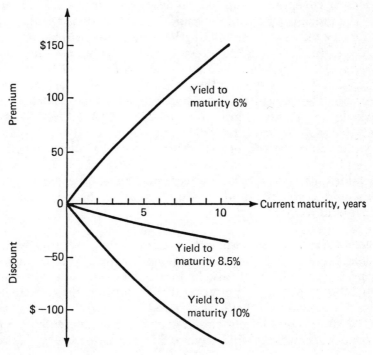

current maturity and the discount that would prevail if the yield on comparable securities rose to 8.5 percent or to 10 percent. It also plots the premium to which a $1,000 note with an 8 percent coupon would depending on its current maturity, be driven if the yield on comparable securities fell to 6 percent.

Coupon and price volatility. The volatility of a note or bond's price in the face of changing interest rates also depends on its coupon; the *lower* the coupon, the *greater* the percentage change in price that will occur when rates rise or fall. To illustrate, consider two notes with 4-year current maturities. Note A has an 8 percent coupon and note B a 6 percent coupon. Both are priced to yield 8 percent. Suppose now that interest rates on comparable securities rise to 10 percent (the big credit crunch arrives). Note A will fall in price by $6.46; since it was initially priced at $100, that works out to a 6.46 percent fall in value. Note B's dollar price drops from $93.27 to $87.07—a $6.20 fall, which equals a 6.64 percent loss of value. The reason for the greater percentage fall in the price of the low-coupon note is that capital appreciation represents a greater proportion of promised income (capital appreciation plus coupon interest) on the low coupon than on the high coupon. Therefore, for the low-coupon note's yield to maturity to rise two percentage points, its price has to fall relatively *more* than that of the high-coupon note.

Prices of government and federal agency securities are quoted in 32ds. The greater the change in yield to maturity that results from a price change of $1/32$, the less volatile the issue's price will be in the face of changing interest rates. As a result, dealers include on their quote sheets for such securities a column titled *Yield value of* $1/32$. Looking back at Table 4–3, we see that the yield value of $1/32$ on Treasury notes maturing on December 31, 1981, was .3646, which means that a fall in the asked price on this security from 99–22 to 99–21 (a $1/32$ fall) would have raised yield to maturity by 0.3646 percent, from 10.67 to 11.016. The yield value of $1/32$ drops sharply as current maturity lengthens. Thus, on bonds maturing on November 11, 2001, (the next to last line of the table), the yield value of $1/32$ was only .0039, indicating that these notes would have had to fall in value by approximately 93.5/32 for their yield to rise 0.3646 percent.

Current yield. So far we have focused on yield to maturity, which is the yield figure always quoted on coupon securities. When the investor buys a note or bond, he may also be interested in knowing what rate of return interest payments per se will give him on the principal he invests. This measure of yield is referred to as *current yield*.

To illustrate, consider our earlier example of a note with an 8 percent coupon selling at $985.13 to yield 8.5 percent to maturity. Current yield on this note would be: ($80/$985.13) × 100, or 8.12 percent. On a discount note or bond, current yield is always less than yield to maturity; on a premium bond it exceeds yield to maturity.

THE YIELD CURVE

From the examples we have worked through, it is clear that investors in notes and bonds expose themselves, like buyers of discount securities, to a *price risk*. Moreover, even though longer-term rates fluctuate less violently than do short-term rates (Figure 4–5), the price

Figure 4–5
Short-term rates are more volatile than long-term rates: Rate comparison—3-month T bill, 5-year note, and 20-year bond (monthly averages thru November 1981)

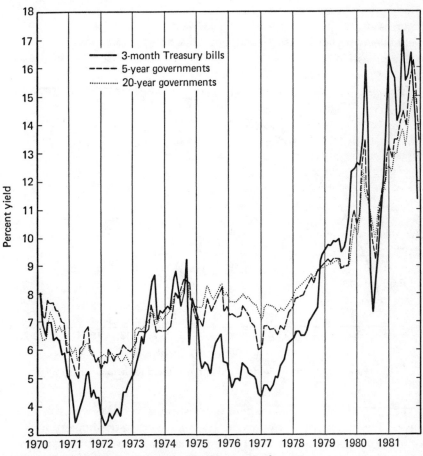

Source: Money Market Research, The Morgan Bank.

risk associated with holding debt securities tends to be greater the longer the current maturity. Thus, one would expect the yield curve to slope upward over the full maturity spectrum. And often it does.

Price risk, however, is not the only factor affecting the shape of the yield curve. Borrowers' and investors' *expectations* with respect to future interest rates are also an important—at times dominant—factor.

If the general expectation is that interest rates are going to rise, investors will seek to keep their money in short coupons to avoid getting locked into low-yield long coupons. Borrowers, on the other hand, will try to lengthen the maturity of their outstanding debt to lock in prevailing low rates for as long as possible. Both responses tend to force short-term rates down and long-term rates up, thereby accentuating the upward slope of the yield curve. The expectation that interest rates would rise was widespread in August 1975, the time of the yield curve pictured in Figure 4–6; this expectation explains in part why the yield curve sloped so steeply upward.

Figure 4–6

Yield curve for U.S. Treasury securities–bills, notes, and bonds, August 19, 1975*

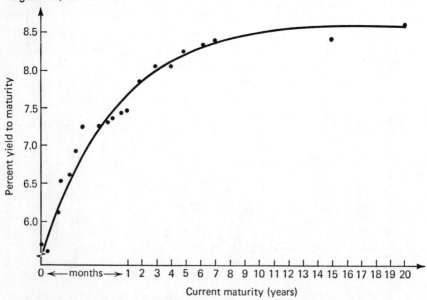

* Dots represent observed yields, yield curve is fitted to them.

People, of course, may expect interest rates to fall. When this is the case, investors respond by buying long coupons in the hope of locking in a high yield. In contrast, borrowers are willing to pay extremely high short-term rates while they wait for long rates to fall so that they can borrow long-term more cheaply. The net result of both responses is that, when interest rates are expected to fall, the yield curve (or at least some part of it) may be *inverted*, with short-term rates above long-term rates. Figure 4–7 pictures the yield curve on February 25, 1980, when

Figure 4–7
Yield curve for U.S. Treasury securities–bills, notes, and bonds, February 4, 1980

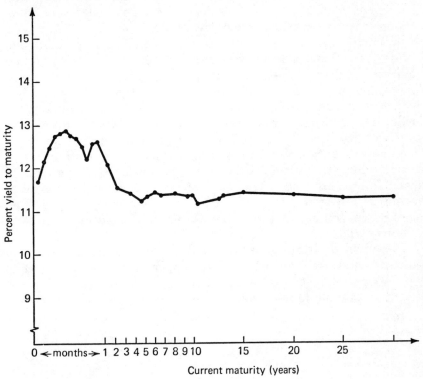

people anticipated a fall in rates. Note that after a current maturity of nine months, the slope of this curve becomes negative.

If, inspired by our yield curves, you start pouring over dealer quote sheets on governments, you are bound to discover some out-of-line yields. The reasons are varied.[5] For one thing, sale of a large new issue may cause a temporary upward bulge in the yield curve in the maturity range of the new issue. Also a security with an out-of-line yield may have some special characteristic. Some government bonds (*flower*

---

[5] One trivial reason may be a mistake in the quote sheet. These are typically compiled daily in great haste with the result that errors creep in. For this reason, such sheets often carry a footnote stating that the quotes are believed to be reliable but are not "guaranteed."

bonds to the street) are acceptable at par in payment of federal estate taxes when owned by the decedent at the time of death. These bonds, which all sell at substantial discounts, have yields to maturity much lower than those on straight government bonds.

In calculating the yield on discount securities, we found a considerable discrepancy between yield measured on a discount basis and equivalent bond yield. There are also many discrepancies—albeit smaller ones—between the ways that interest is measured and quoted on different interest-bearing securities. For example, interest on Treasury notes is calculated for actual days on the basis of a 365-day year, while interest on CDs is calculated for actual days on the basis of a 360-day year. Thus, a 1-year CD issued at 10 percent would yield a higher return than a 10 percent year note selling at par. Partially offsetting this advantage, however, is the fact that a 1-year CD would pay interest only at maturity, whereas a 1-year note would pay it semiannually. This disadvantage disappears, however, on CDs with a maturity longer than one year, since such CDs pay interest semiannually.

Another discrepancy: When government notes and bonds are sold, accrued interest is calculated between coupon dates on the basis of actual days passed since a coupon date, while on agency securities it accrues as if every month had 30 days. Thus, agency securities accrue, for example, no interest on October 31, but they do accrue interest on February 30!

These and the many other minor discrepancies among yields on interest-bearing securities have little importance for understanding the workings of the money market, but they are important to the market participant out to maximize return.

PART II

The business of banking

5

Domestic banking

In the United States, unlike most foreign countries, bank branching has always been severely restricted. Because bank charters were initially granted only by the states, banks have never been permitted to branch interstate, and in most states—California being a notable exception—even intrastate branching is restricted or prohibited. As a result, there are currently over 15,000 banks in the United States. Comparing some of these—say New York's Citibank with a bank in a small agricultural town—one might almost conclude that the most the Unites States' 15,000 banks have in common is the name *bank*. Actually that's extreme. As noted in Chapter 1, the business *all* banks are in is to receive a fee for doing basically three things: (1) gathering funds, (2) substituting their credit judgment for that of the ultimate lender of funds, and (3) assuming interest rate exposure (risk) because intermediation generally calls for a maturity transformation—using short-term deposits to fund longer-term loans. Thus, the generic aspects of banking encompass the whole spectrum of banks.

Having said that, we must hasten to add that commercial banks comprise three distinct sorts of institutions, each of which has characteristics and problems peculiar to itself. These are large money market banks, regional banks, and small banks. In one way or another, all of these institutions are subject to liquidity risk and interest rate exposure. Banks, however, depending on their size, live in different worlds, and they vary in terms of their ability to grow, to assume risk, and to control risk. Size strongly influences the options open to a bank, because a bank's size determines in large part what types of deposits it receives, whether it has access to bought money, whether it can profitably mount an offshore operation, and what sorts of loans—consumer or commercial and industrial—predominate on its balance sheet.

Size is important in determining how a bank operates, but sharp differences also exist even among banks of similar size. The precise type of business a bank does is influenced not only by its size, but by such varied factors as where it is located, whether it may branch, and the strategic decisions it has made about what sorts of business it wants to do. Among money market banks, one finds examples of these factors at work. The Bank of America (B of A), which is located in California, has always been able to operate statewide and has built up a huge branch network that siphons up consumer deposits; this network makes the B of A the only money market bank that is deposit-rich. In New York, Bankers Trust and Manufacturers Hanover have made the strategic choice to get out of the consumer business, where as Citibank has made precisely the opposite choice, namely, to court consumers and get all the business from them it can.

The variability that exist among banks dictates that we break our discussion of banking into parts. We begin by considering the nation's largest banks because they have the widest latitude in choosing how they operate—in particular, how they fund their assets; then we turn to regional and small banks.

A MONEY MARKET BANK

The nation's largest banks, true giants, are often referred to as *money market* or *money center banks*. The term money market bank is apropos, since activity in every sector of the money market is strongly influenced, and in some cases dominated, by the operations of these institutions.

The activities of a money market bank encompass several separate but related businesses. All money market banks engage in traditional banking operations: lending, managing an investment portfolio, and running a trust department. In addition, a number act as dealers in government securities and as dealers in and underwriters of municipal securities; several also have extensive operations for clearing money market trades for nonbank dealers. A final important activity in which major banks engage is offshore banking. Banks operate abroad in two ways: They participate as lenders and borrowers in the broad international capital market known as the *Euromarket;* they also operate within the confines of other national capital markets, accepting deposits and making loans in local currency.

Of the various banking activities we have described, two—trust operations and clearing operations per se, as opposed to granting dealer loans—could be described as largely off-balance-sheet profit centers. Both require capital in the form of space and equipment but do not require substantial funding from the bank. The trust department invests other people's money and the clearing operation provides a service. In contrast, the bank's three other primary domestic activities—lending, running a portfolio, and dealing in securities—have to be funded, since each involves acquiring substantial assets.

To finance its operations, a money market bank draws funds from various sources. It starts with a fairly stable base of money: bank capital and the demand, savings, and small-denomination time deposits it receives in the normal course of its commercial banking activities. The total of these is typically far below the value of the assets the bank wants to finance, so there is a funding gap that the bank fills by buying money in the Federal funds market, the CD market, the RP market, and the Euromarket.

As the above suggests, managing a money market bank involves a host of decisions concerning what assets to hold and what liabilities to incur. Before we say more about these, two comments are in order. First, one cannot separate a bank's domestic operations from its offshore operations, but we are going to try—treating domestic operations in this chapter and Euro operations in the next. Our reason is that Eurobanking is a fascinating and complex subject that deserves a full chapter. Second, money market banks are, as indicated by Table 5–1, a disparate group.

Profit and risk

However heterogeneous the nation's largest banks may be, there still are strong similarities in the way that top management in these banks views and attacks the problems of managing a large bank. First, their objective is, like that of management in any industrial, manufacturing, or other business concern, to earn *profits.* Second, banks, like nonbank firms, operate under uncertainty and thus face *risk.* Risk in banking arises from three sources. On every loan a bank makes there is a *credit risk,* that is, the risk that the borrower won't repay the money lent. On loans made at a fixed rate for some period, *fixed-rate term loans,* there is also the risk that the cost of funding might escalate during the term of the loan; this interest rate risk, which we will refer

Table 5–1
Top 10 U.S. banks, December 31, 1981 ($ millions)

	Total deposits						
	Amount	Percent foreign	Equity capital	Net income	Total loans	Securities holdings*
Bank of America	$95,976.6	42.5%	$4,048.1	$429.8	$69,642.7	$7,402.0
Citibank	72,471.1	74.1	4,871.4	673.8	65,684.8	7,404.0
Chase Manhattan Bank	58,585.7	59.5	3,209.1	441.0	49,087.0	6,134.3
Manufacturers Hanover Trust Company	42,434.9	54.2	1,925.9	285.1	35,694.4	3,502.2
Morgan Guaranty Trust Company	37,688.7	61.1	2,256.9	314.6	27,330.8	7,257.8
Chemical Bank	31,203.7	42.5	1,545.1	200.0	27,797.5	3,756.5
Continental Illinois National Bank & Trust Company of Chicago	29,881.3	49.8	1,775.8	231.3	30,773.1	2,482.1
First National Bank of Chicago	25,867.6	50.3	1,149.6	109.9	19,790.2	1,868.7
Security Pacific National Bank	23,441.6	20.1	1,331.2	208.6	19,743.9	1,722.6
Bankers Trust Company	23,276.9	58.5	1,342.3	174.9	17,248.2	3,127.5

* Securities holdings include U.S. Treasury securities, obligations of U.S. government agencies and corporations, obligations of states and political subdivisions in the United States, other bonds, notes, and debentures, federal reserve stock, corporate stock, and trading account securities.

Source: December 31, 1981 call reports. Source of Bankers Trust data, *American Banker*, February 11, 1982.

to as *interest rate exposure,* arises not only in connection with a bank's loans, but as a result of its portfolio and dealer operations. A third risk a bank faces is *liquidity risk,* which is really the risk of illiquidity. Every money market bank continually buys large quantities of short-dated (short-term) funds to finance its operations. Liquidity risk is the risk that the bank might at some point be unable to buy the monies it needs at a reasonable price or, worse still, at any price.

Because any attempt by a bank to make profits involves risks, a bank's objective inevitably becomes *to maximize profits subject to the constraint that perceived risks be held to some acceptable level.* Also, since bank analysts, investors, and bank depositors all place a lot of emphasis on current income, bankers have a strong predilection for an earnings pattern that displays steady growth over time.

Managing a money market bank

Economists' favorite term, *decision variable,* denotes something having a value that is the result of a conscious decision. *Exogenous variables,* in contrast, are things having a value more or less thrust on the decision maker by the outside world. On a bank's balance sheet, in the short run, both sorts of variables exist. Let's start with the exogenous ones.

Every bank establishes credit standards to limit credit risk. Once it has done this, a bank will normally do everything possible to meet the legitimate loan demands of any customer who fulfills these standards. Loans are a key source of bank profits, and loan customers normally provide a bank with deposits and other business, as well. The quantity of loans demanded from a bank depends largely on the state of the economy and on what funds are available to would-be borrowers from other sources. These factors are beyond the control of a bank, so loan volume is very much an exogenous variable. Bankers can wish they had more loans, but they can't decide to have them if demand for bank loans is weak.

In the short run, bank capital is also an exogenous variable, having a value that depends on past decisions. A third variable that is largely exogenous in the short run is the sum of demand deposits, savings deposits, and small-denomination time deposits received by the bank. Over time, a bank will have built up a customer base that supplies it with a fairly stable amount of such deposits. To significantly enlarge that base would take time and effort. A final important exogenous variable is the reserves against deposits that a bank must keep with the Fed.

From a bank's viewpoint, the decision variables it faces in the short run are the size and composition of its investment portfolio, the dealer position it assumes, and the quantities and maturities of the monies it buys in the Fed funds market, the RP market, the CD market, and the Euromarket.

In assigning values to these decision variables, the bank is determining in part what asset portfolio it will hold and how it will fund that portfolio. In other words, it is choosing a *balance sheet* that meets its goal of maximizing return subject to the constraint that perceived risks be held at an acceptable level.

Several facts of life are crucial for the bank in making these balance sheet choices. One is that buying money is going to be a continuing way of life for a money market bank. Capital plus what we called *exogenous deposits* minus whatever reserves have to be held against such deposits are available to a bank for funding loans. However, since money market banks as a group tend to be deposit poor, it is common for these sources of funds to be insufficient to cover loans, not to speak of funding a securities portfolio and a dealer position.

Thus, a second crucial fact of life for a money market bank is that the preservation of liquidity must be a concern of overriding importance. Here, by liquidity we mean the bank's ability to acquire money whenever it is needed in huge and highly variable sums. Since the principal source of liquidity a money market bank has is its ability to buy money, maintaining access to its markets for bought money—RP to CD—becomes the sine qua non for the continued operation of such a bank.

A third fact of life facing a bank is the yield curve. As noted in Chapter 4, money market and bond yields are normally higher the longer the maturity of an instrument except when a downturn in interest rates is anticipated. This means, as any banker knows, that one path to profits and prosperity much of the time, is acquiring assets with maturities that are longer than those of the liabilities used to fund them—*borrowing short and lending long*. A domestic banker would refer to this as running a *gap* or *gapping*. A Euro banker would call this running a *mismatched* or *short book*. Gapping or mismatching contrasts with running a *matched book*—that is, funding every asset acquired with a liability of identical maturity.

Asset and funding choices. The facts of life we have just discussed profoundly influence the asset and funding choices bankers make. Let's look first at loans. When loan demand increases, the shape of the yield curve often tempts bankers to fund those extra loans by buying the shortest-dated money they can. Yet bankers rarely do so except for short periods when they are waiting to see whether the increase in loans will be sustained. One reason is that regulators would frown on such a policy. A second and more important consideration is that funding loans with overnight money on a large scale would conflict with the bank's need for continued liquidity. As banker after banker will note:

> If we tried to finance a big increase in loans by suddenly buying a lot more overnight money, that would be immediately visible in the market and later visible in our published statements. People, particularly suppliers of funds, would begin to question why we were getting out line with "safe practices" [roughly the average of what other banks are doing] and our ability to continue to buy money might be impaired. That is something we could not allow to happen.

The upshot of all this concern is that bankers tend to fund loan increases largely through the purchase of additional CD money.

A bank's securities portfolio is a different breed of animal from its loan portfolio with respect to conditions of both acquisition and funding. On the funding side, the principal difference is that, under present Fed regulations, a bank can finance its holdings of governments and agencies in the RP market (by selling them under an agreement to repurchase on an overnight or longer basis) without incurring any reserve requirement.

Money market banks acquire portfolios of government securities for various reasons. First, there is a cosmetic motive. Traditionally *all* banks held governments for liquidity; as a result, even today a money market bank that had no governments on its balance sheet would raise eyebrows. Second, some money market banks that are dealers in government securities seem to feel that it would be awkward for them to sell governments if they did not themselves hold any such securities. Third and most important, money market banks hold governments, sometimes *very* large amounts, for profit. When economic growth slackens and interest rates are low or falling, money market banks tend to increase their holdings of governments because, at such times, governments can be financed at an attractive positive spread in the RP market.[1] The trick, of course, in a hold-bonds-for-profit strategy is not to be holding too many when interest rates start their next cyclical upswing and bond prices begin to fall as financing costs rise.[2]

Bankers feel quite comfortable financing a large proportion of their government portfolios on an overnight basis because government securities, unlike loans, are highly liquid, and banks can and sometimes do sell large amounts of such securities over short periods. Consequently, long-term funding of the portfolio, besides being expensive, is neither needed nor appropriate.

---

[1] The *financing spread* is said to be *positive* if the cost of the funds borrowed is less than the yield on the securities financed.

[2] In recent years, which have been characterized by an almost constantly inverted yield curve and by highly volatile interest rates, the case for a bank to hold any governments has become weaker and weaker. See Chapter 11.

To the extent possible, banks use the RP market rather than the Fed funds market for funding their portfolios. Generally, overnight RP money is cheaper than overnight Fed funds. Also the RP market, unlike the Fed funds market, is an anonymous market in the sense that no other banks or brokers are tracking how much a bank borrows there. Thus, a bank can make substantial use of the RP market without impairing its liquidity.

Money market banks, like other banks, also hold portfolios of municipal securities. The principal advantage of such securities is that interest income on them is tax exempt. How large a portfolio of munis a given bank holds is thus largely a function of its effective tax rate. The disadvantage of municipals is that they can't be *RPed* (financed in the RP market) but, instead, have to be financed with Fed funds or other monies.[3]

Many money market banks act as dealers in government and municipal securities. Since a dealer by definition acts as a principal in all transactions, buying and selling for its own account, a bank running a dealer operation inevitably assumes both long and short securities positions. Bank dealerships also acquire securities holdings, at times quite large ones, because they are positioning for profit. Banks finance their dealer positions in governments and munis in the same way that they finance their investment portfolios.

Mismatching the book.   Earlier we said that banks have to be concerned about interest rate exposure and liquidity risk. Matching asset and liability maturities to the extent possible would appear to be a way for a bank to limit both risks. However, it's impossible to find a banker who professes to follow this strategy. One reason is that it would be difficult, if not impossible, for a bank to do so. Few, if any, assets on a bank's balance sheet have a definite maturity. A 10-year bond or a 2-year note in the bank's portfolio might be sold tomorrow. Term loans are often prepaid, and 3-month loans are frequently rolled (renewed). Also, the latter are often made at a floating rate so that funding 3-month loans with 3-month money would not lock in a specific spread between the bank's borrowing and lending rates; instead of eliminating interest rate exposure, it would create it. On the liability side of the balance sheet, many items have specific maturities—RPs, CDs, Fed funds purchased—but a question arises as to how to view demand deposits. Technically, demand deposits can be withdrawn at any time, but in practice, demand deposits in the aggregate provide a bank with a quite stable source of funds. Besides being impractical, any attempt to match asset and liability maturities would

---

[3] For a detailed discussion of the factors, tax and other, that influence a bank's choice about what quantity of municipals it chooses to hold, see Chapter 11.

be expensive to a bank because lending long and borrowing short is a potential source of bank profits.

All bankers profess to follow the *pool* concept of funding; instead of matching specific assets against specific liabilities, they think of all the funds raised by the bank as a pool that, in the aggregate, finances the bank's assets.[4] In the next breath, of course, the same bankers will say that they RP their governments and meet increases in loans with the sale of CDs. What is really going on?

A bank typically sets up a high-level committee, which, besides making general decisions about what sorts of assets the bank should acquire, attempts to measure in some fashion, however arbitrary, the average maturity of the bank's assets and liabilities, and thereby the implicit mismatch in the bank's overall position. The committee's objective is to profit when possible from a maturity mismatch while also monitoring the size of the mismatch so that it never grows large enough to endanger the bank's liquidity or expose it to an undue rate risk. Under this approach, big increases in loans inevitably end up calling for the bank to write more CDs, whereas an increase in Treasury bill holdings can comfortably be accommodated by increased purchases of overnight money.

To this rough generalization several comments should be added. First, banks don't just react to current conditions. Management is constantly attempting to predict the future and to position itself so as to maximize future earnings. In particular, banks are constantly forecasting loan demand, deposits, and interest rates. On the basis of such forecasts, a bank might, for example, decide to issue more CDs than normal, because it expects interest rates and loan demand to rise sharply. Or it might rely more heavily than normal on Fed funds purchased, because it expects loan demand and interest rates to fall. Interest rate forecasts also strongly influence the bank's decision about the size and maturity distribution of the portfolio and dealer positions it will carry. In Parts III and IV we will examine in detail the issues raised in this and the preceding paragraphs.

The brief picture we have just presented on management of a big bank leaves much unsaid. The rest of the section fills in some of the missing subtleties.

Bank lending

Money market banks, like other banks, extend credit to consumers and make home mortgage and other real estate loans. However, the largest proportion of their domestic lending is to commercial and industrial (C&I) customers.

---

[4] Recent developments in the pricing of large loans by large banks have begun to force a change in this mode of thinking. See Chapter 11.

The environment in which banks lend has, over the last 40 years, been subject to constant, sometimes dramatic change. One result is that banks have had to continually alter their lending practices, searching for areas in which they have a real and potentially profitable role to play in supplying credit.

Before World War II, much bank commercial lending was short term. Firms in wholesale trade and commodities needed financing, often on a seasonal basis, to fill their warehouses, and their banks supplied it. The normal arrangement was that the bank would look over the customer's books once a year and decide how large a line of credit it was willing to grant this firm. The firm could then borrow, during the year, any sum up to that amount, provided no material change occurred in its circumstances after the line was granted. The customer paid for its line with compensating balances, borrowed as necessary on the basis of 90-day notes, and was expected to give the bank a *clean up* (pay off all its borrowings) at some time during the year.

When World War II came along, the situation changed. Defense contractors had to invest huge sums in new plant and equipment. They could have financed these investments through the sale of long-term bonds, the traditional approach, but that seemed inappropriate. First, they didn't expect the war to continue forever. Second, they believed they could pay for their new plant and equipment rapidly because they had a customer, Uncle Sam, who was sure to pay, and because they could depreciate their plant and equipment at an accelerated rate. So they asked the banks for term loans. The banks provided such credits with amortization built in, and while criticized at the time for doing so, they ended up successfully entering the area of medium-term commercial lending.

After the war, borrowers who had become accustomed to 5-year credits decided to try for more flexibility. On a term loan, they didn't always want to have to take down all the money right away; also, they wanted the right to prepay some or all of the loan if their cash flow improved seasonally or permanently. So bankers said, "Alright that's a revolving credit. You can have it, but at some point, you'll have to give us a clean up." The final step in this evolutionary trend came when the customer said to his bank: "I am not sure I will ever need to borrow from you, but I want to know that I can if I need to, not just now but for some number of years." In response, bankers developed a *revolving line of credit;* the customer paid balances *plus a commitment fee* and, in exchange for the latter, the bank promised to honor the line for the life of the agreement. A customer could turn such a *revolver* into a term loan simply by borrowing.

Interest rate exposure.   From the beginning of World War II until 1951, the Fed pegged yields on government bonds, and interest rates did not move much. Then, in 1951, after considerable infighting, the Treasury agreed that the Fed should be permitted to pursue an independent monetary policy. This Treasury-Fed accord spelled the end of rate pegging, and interest rates began a secular climb punctuated with periodic ups and downs. The pace of this climb was, however, slow. As a result, bankers rarely changed the prime rate that they charged their best customers, and they felt safe lending at a fixed rate not only on 90-day notes, but also on term loans; the interest rate exposure (risk) associated with both sorts of lending seemed small. Then things changed. Inflation became a problem, and to fight it, the Fed pushed up interest rates sharply and rapidly on a number of occasions starting in the mid-1960s.

The banks felt the impact of the initial credit crunch largely in terms of opportunity cost. At that point, they were not buying huge amounts of money, so tight money did not dramatically increase their cost of funding. It meant, however, that funds locked up in old low-interest term loans could not be lent out at the higher rates currently prevailing. Later, as the banks began to rely more and more on bought money, tight money did significantly increase their cost of funding; and the interest rate risk implied in fixed-rate lending became more pronounced.

To minimize this risk, banks changed their lending practices. They began adjusting the prime rate more frequently (Figure 5–1), and they started altering the rate on existing as well as on new short-term loans whenever the prime rate changed. They also made it a rule to put term loans on a floating-rate basis. The rule, of course, was not and is not always followed. As one bank officer noted: "We bankers are not as smart as we could be. When rates get near the peak and we ought to be making fixed-rate term loans, we shy away from doing so. Then, when loan demand and lending rates decline and we are out scrambling for loans, we are tempted to make fixed-rate term loans at just the time when we shouldn't." Actually, even fixed-rate term loans made during periods of high interest rates are not as advantageous to banks as one might suppose. Once rates decline, the borrower of such money is likely to say to his banker, "You're my banker and you know that the best thing for me would be to refinance this loan in the bond market or on other terms," and typically the banker lets the borrower do so without penalty, regardless of whether the loan agreement calls for one. On variable-rate term loans, the rate charged generally goes to an increasing spread above the prime rate during the later years of the loan. This maturity spread is supposed to compensate the banker for his long-term commitment, but he rarely earns it because of prepayment or renegotiation.

To some extent, bankers think of their special niche in commercial and industrial lending today as that of providers of flexible medium-term financing. Also, the money they provide is "warm" money in the

Figure 5-1

Over time, the volatility of interest rates has increased: Rate comparison—Prime rate versus Fed funds rate (monthly averages; data thru November 1981)

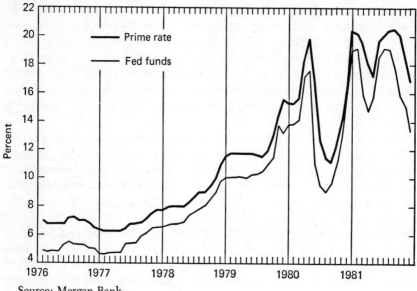

Source: Morgan Bank.

sense that the lending arrangement is not only open to negotiation initially, but also subject to renegotiation should the borrower's position change.

While banks have done much to increase the attractiveness of bank loans, it is also true that by moving to floating-rate loans, they have shifted much of the rate exposure involved in lending from their shoulders to those of the borrower. This may, depending on borrowers' risk preferences and rate views, make bank loans appear less attractive and thereby slow the growth of bank lending.

The prime rate, at which banks lend to their most credit worthy customers, is viewed by some as a collusive price-fixing device. This view is erroneous; the prime rate is, in fact, highly responsive to open-market conditions. A fall in open-market rates attracts bank customers to the open market and to other nonbank financing sources, and thus puts pressure on banks to lower the prime, whereas a rise in open-market rates increases the cost of bank funding and the demand for bank loans, and so tends to do the opposite.

When the Fed tightens credit, the resulting increases in the prime rate, particularly if they are frequent and sharp, make bankers unpopular with politicians and the public. So, gradually, bankers have moved away from what appeared to be an arbitrarily set prime to one that is based on money market rates and fluctuates up and down with them. Citibank began the trend in 1971 by linking its prime to the 90-day commercial paper rate. Specifically, Citi said that henceforth it would set its prime at the 90-day paper rate plus a spread, which has fluctuated from as little as ⅛ to as much as 1½ percentage points.[5]

While pricing loans at a flexible prime was supposed to eliminate a bank's interest rate exposure on loans by tying its lending rate to its cost of funds, banks still encounter difficulties during periods of tight money. In the United States, as in many other countries, the prime rate has been so politicized that, at times, it becomes impossible for the banks to raise it further. This happened, for example, in 1974. During such periods, banks can and have found themselves forced to make new loans at rates *below* their marginal cost of funds, that is, at rates below the cost of the extra money they had to buy to fund these loans.

When the economy is experiencing what economists would call the *normal* business cycle, interest rates are cyclically predictable—they rise when economic activity is expanding and fall as recession sets in; also, the *normal* slope of the yield curve is positive. As the economy moved into the 1980s, normality of this sort seemed to have vanished. The economy went through a whole business cycle in the single year 1980; interest rates reached historic highs with respect to both level and variability and the slope of the yield curve was negative most of the time. These and other conditions have forced further changes in bank lending practices.[6]

Competition from commercial paper.   For the commercial or industrial firm in need of short-term financing, the sale of commercial paper has always been an alternative to and competitive with short-term bank loans. In recent years, however, the volume of such paper outstanding has risen so rapidly that it seems to throw into question the banks' traditional role as suppliers of short-term finance, at least to all but their smaller and less credit worthy customers. One reason is that, except in times when political pressures hold the prime rate at an artificially low level, commercial paper rates are consistently lower than bank lending rates. Another factor is that, in recent years, the commercial paper market has matured; distribution facilities have improved and a growing number of investors have been attracted to the market—all of which makes it possible for more firms to borrow there and for them to borrow larger amounts.

Ironically, banks fostered the development of the commercial paper market by granting issuers backup lines of credit for their paper.

---

[5] This practice is not currently used.

[6] See Chapter 11.

Specifically, the banks promised, in exchange for balances or fees, to provide commercial paper issuers with money should they encounter difficulties in rolling their paper.[7] This commitment gave the issuers the liquidity required to make their paper salable.

At this point, there seems to be little banks can do to recapture the business that has moved to the commercial paper market. Reserve requirements, by forcing banks to buy more funds than they can lend, impose what amounts to a substantial tax on banking. Because of this, banks would be hard put to meet commercial paper rates even if they were willing to buy money and lend it out on a break-even basis. Another problem banks face is that most commercial paper has a maturity at issue of 30 days or less. The banks' prime rate, in contrast, is keyed off normally higher 90-day money market rates.[8]

Bankers' acceptances. The closest banks come to competing directly with the commercial paper market is by issuing loans in the form of bankers' acceptances. On certain types of transactions—financing exports, imports, and the storage and shipment of goods at home and abroad—the bank can take the borrower's note, accept it (guarantee payment at maturity), and then sell it in the open market without incurring a reserve requirement. The interest rate charged the borrower is determined by rates prevailing in the bankers' acceptance market. These are normally less than commercial paper rates, but the banks' standard acceptance fee—currently ½ to 1 percent—adds additional cost, so the *all-in cost* to the BA borrower exceeds rates on commercial paper. When loan demand is high, bankers normally sell the BAs they originate and take their spread, but when loan demand is slack, they may hold them as earning assets.

The real dilemma. While periods when loan demand is slack leave bankers feeling less than prosperous, some of the most difficult problems with respect to bank lending arise when money is tight. By accepting deposits from a firm and by building a customer relationship with it, a bank makes an often unwritten but nevertheless real commitment to lend to that firm when the latter needs funds. The bank, however, does not know when that need will occur or how large it will be. It can only be sure that the tighter money gets, the more loan seekers will be on its doorstep. To compound this problem, the one time that commercial paper issuers are likely to want to come or be forced to the banks for money is when money is tight. Thus, a question arises as to whether banks will be able to honor all their written and

---

[7] To *roll* paper means to repay maturing paper by selling new paper.

[8] To a limited degree, banks do compete with the paper market by offering fixed-rate, short-term advances priced from their cost of short-term money. See Chapter 11.

unwritten commitments to lend when money tightens. Also, if they do honor them, will they be thwarting Fed policy by raising their lending at a time when the Fed is trying to contain overall bank lending?

Leasing. Banks and bank holding companies entered the leasing business in the early 1960s. It was a natural adjunct to their normal lending activities since a financial lease is the functional equivalent of a loan. Under it, the lessee is obligated to make a stream of payments to the lessor, the amount of which equals or exceeds the price of the asset leased.

Leasing is attractive to a bank. First, because a bank can take advantage of the investment tax credit and of accelerated depreciation on equipment it leases, leasing provides a tax shelter that permits the bank to *defer* taxes on current income. Second, leasing gives a bank protection against inflation; presumably, the higher the rate of inflation, the greater the scrap value of the items leased will be at the end of the lease period.

Because many lease agreements entered into by banks run for years, sometimes even several decades, a natural question is how banks control the rate risk that would seem to be inherent in making such indirect long-term loans. The answer varies with the segment of the market considered.

The leasing of small-ticket, short-lived items—autos, postage meters, etc.—is normally not tax-shelter oriented, and the rates charged are high. In leasing big-ticket items, tax considerations are often of paramount importance. There are firms, not necessarily weak credits, that have such tremendous capital needs that they exhaust the tax benefits available to them under the investment tax credit and through accelerated depreciation before they make all the investments they require. If a bank that has taxable income leases equipment to such a firm, it can take advantage of tax benefits that the firm itself could not take on investment in the leased equipment.

Maturities on big-ticket, tax-oriented leases may run from 7 years on a computer to 25 years on a utility plant or oil loading dock. The agreements always contain a clause that requires the lessees to pay a substantial penalty if they break the lease. Surprisingly, a bank has little funding exposure on very long-term leases. The reason is that most are *leveraged leases.* The bank puts up 20 percent or more of the money required, enough to get the total tax benefits available; it then borrows the remaining funds required on a long-term basis from, say, an insurance company that has long-term funds available but, because of its low marginal tax rate, would not get the same tax benefits as a bank does from having the leased asset on its books. On a leveraged lease, the bank's funding exposure lasts only three to five years. After that, the rentals collected are used to repay the money borrowed and to build up a fund from which the taxes that the lease arrangement defers are eventually paid.

Balance sheet figures are misleading with respect to the importance of leasing to a bank or bank holding company. Only the lessor's equity in the item leased shows up as an asset, and in the case of leveraged leases, this equity drops to zero in a few years. However, the assets are still there, and even if the impact of leasing on the balance sheet is minimal, it may have a substantial effect on the bank's tax situation and on its return on equity.

The bank's portfolio

It used to be standard practice for a bank to invest some fraction of the funds deposited with it in government securities that could be sold to meet increases in loan demand or depositor withdrawals. In other words, the bank's portfolio provided liquidity and some earnings on the side.

For the nation's largest banks, with the possible exception of the deposit-rich B of A, this began to change in the early 1960s. At that time, many large banks, particularly those in New York, found that the secular uptrend in bank loans had eaten away most of the excess liquidity (bloated bond portfolios) with which they had emerged from World War II. At the same time, corporate treasurers began to manage their cash actively, taking idle deposit balances out of the banks and investing them in commercial paper and other money market instruments. This, too, created liquidity problems. To solve them, the banks turned to the newly invented negotiable CD and other methods of buying money. Liability management was born, and the big banks' liquidity became, in part, their ability to buy money.

A second factor that discouraged banks from holding bond portfolios primarily to provide liquidity was the ever-widening fluctuations that occurred in interest rates as a result of cyclical swings in economic activity and shifts in Fed policy. What the banks found was that, as loan demand slackened, interest rates would fall sharply, and as loan demand picked up, they would rise sharply. In this environment, using bonds as a source of liquidity meant buying bonds at high prices and selling them at low prices. Thus, a bank that viewed its bond portfolio as a source of liquidity found the latter to be an automatic money loser; over time, the portfolio provided some interest income and a lot of capital losses.

Today, since a large bank's government portfolio is financed in the RP market, it is a *use* of liquidity more than a *source*. Also, if such a bank sells securities, the RP borrowings used to finance them have to be repaid, so portfolio sales produce *no* money to fund loans or meet other cash needs.

Maturity choice. Because the yield curve normally slopes upward, the yield on a 2-year note typically exceeds the overnight RP rate by more than does the yield on a 90-day bill. Thus, a bank will get a better spread between the yield on its portfolio and its financing cost the longer it extends in buying governments along the maturity scale. This tempts a bank that is building up its portfolio to buy at least some governments and agencies with 2-year, 4-year, or even longer maturities, but doing so poses a risk.

An upturn in rates would cause not only a rise in financing costs, but also a fall in the value of the securities held, and the longer the maturity of these securities, the more dramatic that fall would be. Thus, a bank with governments extending out on the maturity scale might end up in a position where rising financing costs tell it to sell governments at a time when it can do so only at a substantial loss.

To avoid getting into such a bind, banks use several strategies. One is to minimize the damage that rising interest rates can do by holding securities with short current maturities. Another is to match the maturity of the securities purchased with the time span over which interest rates are expected to be down—a policy that will result in a runoff of the portfolio as rates start up again. A third strategy is to count on being smart enough to know when to buy and when to sell. Both of the latter strategies will be successful only to the extent that the bank succeeds in predicting interest rate trends. That, however, is difficult. Thus, it's not surprising that most large bank portfolios could have been managed better with hindsight than they were with foresight.

Portfolio management. Active portfolio management by a bank—a willingness to make judgments about interest rates trends and adjust maturities accordingly, to ride the yield curve, and to pursue other potentially profitable strategies—can significantly increase the return earned on the bank's portfolio. Nevertheless, many banks do not engage in such management.

Under federal tax laws, net capital gains earned by a bank on its portfolio used to be taxed at the capital gains rate, while net capital losses were deductible from ordinary income. This created an incentive for banks to bunch capital gains into one tax year and capital losses into another. Managing a bank's portfolio thus boiled down to deciding whether the current year was a gain or a loss year, which wasn't difficult. If the market was up, it was a gain year; if it was down, it was a loss year. During a loss year, a bank might find it had paper losses on securities it did not want to sell. That difficulty could be gotten around by selling these securities, taking the loss, and buying other securities that were similar but not so similar that the IRS would view the transaction as a "wash."

At the end of 1969, tax laws were changed; all bank capital gains on portfolio transactions are now treated as ordinary income and all capital losses as deductions from ordinary income. This tax change created, for the first time, a profit incentive for banks to actively manage their portfolios.

One reason many still do not has to do with bank accounting practices. Table 5–2 presents, in bare bones style, the format of a bank

Table 5–2
Typical format for a bank income statement

+ Interest income
    (including interest income on securities held)
− Interest expenses
+ Other operating income
    (including trading account profits)
− Noninterest operating expenses
    (including taxes other than those on capital gains)
= **Income before securities gains (losses)**
+ Securities gains (losses) net of tax effect
= **Net income**

---

income statement. Note that *two* profit figures are given, *Income before securities gains (losses)* and *Net income*. The first figure excludes capital gains and losses; the second reflects them as well as their effect on taxes due.

The special place given to securities gains and losses on a bank's income statement highlights them as an extraordinary item, and bank stockholders and stock analysts thus focus much attention on income before securities gains (losses). Since interest income on securities is included in this figure, but capital gains and losses on securities trades are not, bankers prefer interest income from their portfolio to capital gains. In addition, because stockholders and analysts like to see sustained earnings growth, bankers want this number to grow steadily on a year-to-year basis.

That desire can, at times discourage a bank from managing its portfolio. To illustrate, consider a bank that buys 3-year notes in a high-rate period, such as 1974. Two years later, interest rates have fallen substantially, and the 3-year notes, which have moved down the yield curve, are trading at a yield to maturity well below their coupon. At this point, the bank might feel that, to maximize profits over time, it should sell these notes and buy new issues that have a longer current maturity and therefore sell at a higher yield. The logic of such an *extension swap* is that the capital gains earned immediately on the sale of the old notes plus the interest earned on the new notes would, over time, amount to more income than the interest that would have been earned by holding the old notes to a maturity and then reinvesting. The swap, however, creates a capital gain in the current year and lowers interest income in the following year. To the banker who wants income before securities gains (losses) to rise steadily, such a redistribution of income oftens seems too great a price to pay for maximizing profits over time, so he doesn't do the swap.

A concern with steady earnings may also lead a bank to hold more governments or governments of longer maturity than caution would dictate. Conditions may suggest that loan demand is about to pick up, that interest rates are about to rise, and that the bank should therefore reduce its holdings of governments or the maturity of those holdings. Doing so in anticipation of the event would, however, mean a temporary earnings dip, a price a bank may be unwilling to pay.

A bank can put some of its portfolio into a *trading account*. The advantage in doing so is that capital gains realized in the trading account are included in the top-line income figure. The disadvantage is that securities in this account have to be valued on the bank's balance sheet at market value or cost, whichever is lower, whereas other securities in the bank's portfolio do not. At many banks, one finds an anomalous situation. The bank works hard to earn profits on the 10 to 30 percent of its portfolio in its trading account, while the rest of its portfolio is largely unmanaged.[9]

Municipal portfolio. State and local securities (*municipals* for short) offer banks the advantage that interest income on them is exempt from federal taxation. It is also often exempt from state and local taxation if the securities held are issued by or within the state in which the bank is located. However, some states and localities (New York State and New York City, in particular) impose a franchise tax on bank income that is based on total earnings, including tax-exempt income. Municipal securities, unlike governments, carry a credit risk. Thus, credit analysis plays a large role in a bank's decision about which municipals to buy.

While a bank's main objective in buying municipals is to obtain tax-exempt income, other motives may influence this decision. Banks receive large deposits from state and local governments, and these have to be collateralized. Sometimes the collateral used is governments, more often it is municipals. Also, a bank may invest in municipals because the issuer is a valued depositer.

The securities held in a bank's municipal portfolio typically range in maturity from short-term notes to bonds with a 10- to 15-year maturity. A bank often perceives its holdings of short-term muni notes as a

---

[9] For more on bank portfolio strategies, see Chapter 11.

true source of liquidity since their sale will, in fact, free funds for other uses.

A bank's incentive for buying long-term munis is to obtain a higher yield by taking advantage of the upward slope of the yield curve. Long-term munis, however, expose the holder to a substantial price risk. In investing in municipal securities, many banks seek to compromise between price risk and yield by *laddering* the maturity of their portfolios out to 10 or 15 years (i.e., by buying something in every maturity range). However, in munis as opposed to governments, the investor is normally paid to extend maturity virtually to the end of the maturity spectrum. As a result, some banks are willing to hold munis of very long maturity. In doing so, they follow what's called a *barbell* strategy, buying muni notes for liquidity and investing, when they like the market, in long-term munis for yield. This sounds risky, but practitioners argue that the supply of funds going into the far end of the market from fire and casualty insurance companies and from individuals is stable, whereas in the 10- to 15-year range dominated by the banks, it is highly cyclical. As a result, yields on medium-term munis go through large gyrations, and the medium-term investor who misplays his hand can be hurt as badly as the investor in long bonds.

Generally, banks do not actively trade their muni portfolios. One reason is tax considerations. A bank that buys tax-exempt issues when interest rates are high and later sells them at a capital gain when interest rates fall is trading future nontaxable interest payments for current taxable capital gains, a move that is often unattractive when evaluated in terms of its effect on aftertax income.[10]

Dealer operations

Most money market banks have extensive dealer operations. The biggest part of their activity is in Treasury and federal agency securities, but banks also deal heavily in and are underwriters of state and local general obligation securities. In addition, some banks deal in the CDs of other banks and in bankers' acceptances. Banks used to underwrite corporate issues, but since passage of the Glass-Steagall Act in 1933, they have been forbidden to do so.

Running a dealer operation makes sense for a large bank. Smaller banks often look to money market banks with whom they have a correspondent relationship to buy securities both for their own portfolio and for their customers. Also, large corporations, which are prime customers of money market banks and often have millions of dollars of short-term funds to invest, are ready customers for securities traded by bank dealerships. In this respect it should be noted that, while Glass-

---

[10] See also Chapter 11.

Steagall forbids banks from underwriting and dealing in corporate securities, banks can and do buy on behalf of customers commercial paper issued by corporations. The big direct issuers of commercial paper post rates with the banks, which, in turn, quote these rates to customers. If a customer wants $1 million of General Motors Acceptance Corporation (GMAC) paper, the bank carries out the transaction between the customer and GMAC and safekeeps the paper for the customer until it matures. Besides being a profit center, a bank's dealer department also provides it with useful, up-to-the-minute information on developments in the money and bond markets.[11]

Demand deposits

Demand deposits have traditionally been a key source of bank funding, and, as such, they are an important and valuable raw material to banks. Yet, in the United States, unlike many foreign countries, banks are not permitted to pay interest on demand deposits. A recent exception is NOW accounts which banks may offer to consumers.[12] So long as interest rates were low, forbidding the payment of interest on demand deposits caused bankers no problems; despite the fact that deposit balances offered a zero return, bank customers were willing to hold substantial amounts because the *opportunity cost* (forgone earnings opportunity) of doing so was negligible.

During the 1950s, however, things started to change. Interest rates began a secular climb, which, coupled with the periodic forays the economy made into the world of tight money and high interest rates in the 1960s, drove home to corporate treasurers, state and local financial officials, and other holders of large short-term balances a new fact of life: the cost of holding idle balances was high and growing. The response of these depositors was to trim their demand balances to the minimum level possible and invest excess short-term funds in interest-bearing instruments.

Because demand deposits are valuable to banks, and because holders of such deposits incur a substantial opportunity cost, an elaborate system of barter has developed in which banks trade services to customers in exchange for deposits. On small accounts, the barter involves imprecise calculations. It amounts to the bank giving free checking services to all customers or to those with some minimum balance.

On large accounts the barter is worked out more exactly; banks

---

[11] Many interesting things can be said about the positioning and financing strategies money market dealers, bank and nonbank, pursue to maximize profits. See Chapter 9 of Marcia Stigum, *The Money Market: Myth, Reality, and Practice* (Homewood, Ill.: Dow Jones-Irwin, 1978).

[12] See pages 27–28.

provide many services to corporate and other big customers: accepting deposits, clearing checks, wire transfers, safekeeping of securities, and others. In providing these services, banks incur costs that they could recover by charging fees. Instead, they ask customers to "pay" by holding demand deposits.

To determine the amount of compensating demand deposit balances appropriate for each customer, the bank first costs out each type of service it provides. It then sets up an activity analysis statement for each account, showing the types and volume of services provided and the costs incurred. Some of the demand deposits customers leave with a bank go to meet reserve requirements; the rest can be invested. Taking reserve requirements and current investment yields into account, the bank estimates the rate of return it earns on demand deposits. Finally, using that rate, it determines what dollar balances each account must hold so that the bank's earnings on the account cover the costs incurred in servicing it.

Banks also charge for credit lines by requiring compensating deposit balances; the standard formula used to be 10 percent of the unused portion of the line and 10 percent of any funds actually taken.[13] As might be expected in a barter situation, the compensation arrangements worked out between banks and customers are subject to negotiation and vary not only from bank to bank, but often from customer to customer at a given bank. Many customers obtain lines at less than the usual balance arrangement, and good customers may be able to get their banks to double-count balances for some purposes.

A bank that requires compensating balances on lines and loans is getting, at zero interest, deposits on which it can earn a return. An alternative way it could earn the same return would be to charge a fee for lines and higher rates on loans. Some customers prefer the latter approach, and in recent years, it has become more common for banks to grant fee lines and to quote two loan rates, a standard rate for loans with balances and a higher rate for loans without. For some public utility customers, this approach is mandatory since regulators will not permit them to hold large idle balances.

To the extent that banks obtain demand deposits either from retail customers by establishing extensive branch networks or from large depositors by exchanging services or reducing lending rates, they are paying some implicit rate of interest on such deposits even though the nominal rate is zero. The *all-in* cost, moreover, of demand deposits is still higher than this implicit rate because, as Table 5–3 shows, the reserve requirement on demand deposits, which was 16.25 percent for large banks prior to the phasing in of *new* reserve requirements for *all* institutions accepting deposits under the Depository Institutions De-

---

[13] These compensation arrangements have been significantly eroded by competition and by the practice of trading off compensating balances for higher lending rates.

Table 5–3
Depository institution reserve requirements (percent of deposits)

Type of deposit, and deposit interval in millions of dollars	Member bank requirements before implementation of the Monetary Control Act		Type of deposit, and deposit interval	Depository institution requirements after implementation of the Monetary Control Act[5]	
	Percent	Effective date		Percent	Effective date
Net demand[2]			*Net transaction accounts*[6]		
0–2	7	12/30/76	$0–$25 million	3	11/13/80
2–10	9½	12/30/76	Over $25 million	12	11/13/80
10–100	11¾	12/30/76			
100–400	12¾	12/30/76	*Nonpersonal time deposits*[7]		
Over 400	16¼	12/30/76	By original maturity		
			Less than 4 years	3	11/13/80
Time and savings[2,3]			4 years or more	0	11/13/80
Savings	3	3/16/67			
			Eurocurrency liabilities		
Time[4]			All types	3	11/13/80
0–5, by maturity					
30–179 days	3	3/16/67			
180 days to 4 years	2½	1/8/76			
4 years or more	1	10/30/75			
Over 5, by maturity					
30–179 days	6	12/12/74			
180 days to 4 years	2½	1/8/76			
4 years or more	1	10/30/75			

1. For changes in reserve requirements beginning 1963, see Board's *Annual Statistical Digest, 1971–1975* and for prior changes, see Board's *Annual Report* for 1976, table 13. Under provisions of the Monetary Control Act, depository institutions include commercial banks, mutual savings banks, savings and loan associations, credit unions, agencies and branches of foreign banks, and Edge Act corporations.

2. (a) Requirement schedules are graduated, and each deposit interval applies to that part of the deposits of each bank. Demand deposits subject to reserve requirements were gross demand deposits minus cash items in process of collection and demand balances due from domestic banks.

(b) The Federal Reserve Act as amended through 1978 specified different ranges of requirements for reserve city banks and for other banks. Reserve cities were designated under a criterion adopted effective Nov. 9, 1972, by which a bank having net demand deposits of more than $400 million was considered to have the character of business of a reserve city bank. The presence of the head office of such a bank constituted designation of that place as a reserve city. Cities in which there were Federal Reserve Banks or branches were also reserve cities. Any banks having net demand deposits of $400 million or less were considered to have the character of business of banks outside of reserve cities and were permitted to maintain reserves at ratios set for banks not in reserve cities.

(c) Effective Aug. 24, 1978, the Regulation M reserve requirements on net balances due from domestic banks to their foreign branches and on deposits that foreign branches lend to U.S residents were reduced to zero from 4 percent and 1 percent respectively. The Regulation D reserve requirement on borrowings from unrelated banks abroad was also reduced to zero from 4 percent.

(d) Effective with the reserve computation period beginning Nov. 16, 1978, domestic deposits of Edge corporations were subject to the same reserve requirements as deposits of member banks.

3. (a) Negotiable order of withdrawal (NOW) accounts and time deposits such as Christmas and vacation club accounts were subject to the same requirements as savings deposits.

(b) The average reserve requirement on savings and other time deposits before implementation of the Monetary Control Act had to be at least 3 percent, the minimum specified by law.

4. (a) A supplementary reserve requirement of 2 percent was imposed on large time deposits of $100,000 or more, obligations of affiliates, and ineligible acceptances. This supplementary requirement was eliminated with the maintenance period beginning July 24, 1980.

(b) Effective with the reserve maintenance period beginning Oct. 25, 1979, a marginal reserve requirement of 8 percent was added to managed liabilities in excess of a base amount. This marginal requirement was increased to 10 percent beginning Apr. 3, 1980, was decreased to 5 percent beginning June 12, 1980, and was reduced to zero beginning July 24, 1980. Managed liabilities are defined as large time deposits, Eurodollar borrowings, repurchase agreements against U.S. government and federal agency securities, federal funds borrowings from nonmember institutions, and certain other obligations. In general, the base for the marginal reserve requirement was originally the greater of (a) $100 million or (b) the average amount of the managed liabilities held by a member bank. Edge corporation, or family of U.S. branches and agencies of a foreign bank for the two statement weeks ending Sept. 26, 1979. For the computation period beginning Mar. 20, 1980, the base was lowered by (a) 7 percent or (b) the decrease in an institution's U.S. office gross loans to foreigners and gross balances due from foreign offices of other institutions between the base period (Sept. 13–26, 1979) and the week ending Mar. 12, 1980, whichever was greater. For the computation period beginning May 29, 1980, the base was increased by 7½ percent above the base used to calculate the marginal reserve in the statement week of May 14–21, 1980. In addition, beginning Mar. 19, 1980, the base was reduced to the extent that foreign loans and balances declined.

5. For existing nonmember banks and thrift institutions at the time of implementation of the Monetary Control Act, the phase-in period ends Sept. 3, 1987. For existing member banks the phase-in period is about three years, depending on whether their new reserve requirements are greater or less than the old requirements. For existing agencies and branches of foreign banks, the phase-in ends Aug. 12, 1982. All new institutions will have a two-year phase-in beginning with the date that they open for business.

6. Transaction accounts include all deposits on which the account holder is permitted to make withdrawals by negotiable or transferable instruments, payment orders of withdrawal, and telephone and preauthorized transfers (in excess of three per month) for the purpose of making payments to third persons or others.

7. In general, nonpersonal time deposits are time deposits, including savings deposits, that are not transaction accounts and in which the beneficial interest is held by a depositor that is not a natural person. Also included are certain transferable time deposits held by natural persons, and certain obligations issued to depository institution offices located outside the United States. For details, see section 204.2 of Regulation D.

NOTE. Required reserves must be held in the form of deposits with Federal Reserve Banks or vault cash. After implementation of the Monetary Control Act, nonmembers may maintain reserves on a pass-through basis with certain approved institutions.

Source: *Federal Reserve Bulletin.*

regulation and Monetary Control Act of 1980, will be 12 percent at the end of the phase in period. This means that such a bank can invest only $88.00 of every $100 it takes in. Also, a bank has to pay the Federal Deposit Insurance Corporation (FDIC) a fractional assessment on all deposits it accepts.

However high the all-in cost may be, banks are eager to obtain all the demand deposits they can. One reason is that the quantity of such funds supplied to a bank is quite stable over time, and a bank can thus count on these deposits being there regardless of what happens to economic conditions or interest rates. Banks also attach importance to demand and time deposits for other reasons: regulators like to see a lot of deposits, as opposed to bought money, on a bank's balance sheet; banks are typically ranked by deposit size rather than asset size; and bank analysts attach what is probably undue importance to the share of deposits in a bank's total liabilities.

While exchanging services for deposits has enabled banks to hold on to substantial amounts of demand deposits, banks have no way to bid for additional funds from this source. The demand deposits they get are limited to the amounts consumers choose to leave with them plus the amounts needed to cover the services large customers choose to buy from them. This contrasts sharply with the situation in the Euromarket where banks bid actively for deposits of all maturities, including call and overnight money (see Chapter 6).

Small-denomination time deposits

The all-in cost of time deposit money to a bank depends, in part, on the reserves the bank must hold against these deposits. As Table 5–3 shows, reserve requirements are much lower on savings and time deposits than on demand deposits, and on time deposits, they are lower the longer the maturity of the deposit.

The major competitors of banks in accepting time and savings deposits are savings and loan associations. When money becomes tight and interest rates soar, S&Ls are at a competitive disadvantage relative to banks. Because banks have many short-term and variable-rate assets on their books, they are able to capture rapidly rising interest rates on the asset side of their balance sheets. In contrast, the asset portfolios of S&Ls consist largely of fixed-rate, long-term mortgages. It thus takes considerable time for S&Ls to translate rising interest rates into rising revenues, and when money tightens, banks are therefore in a stronger position than S&Ls to bid for savings and time deposits by raising deposit rates.

To protect S&Ls from bank competition, the Fed, under Regulation Q, imposes lids on the rates that banks may pay on small-denomination savings and time deposits. These lids, which are periodically adjusted as economic conditions change, become higher as the maturity of the deposit lengthens (Table 5–4). The Federal Home Loan Bank Board, which regulates S&Ls, also establishes lids on the deposit rates S&Ls may pay; typically, these are set 0.25 percent above the rates banks can pay on the theory that, if S&Ls did not enjoy a rate advantage, consumers would, for convenience, opt to hold their savings accounts at commercial banks where they hold checking accounts. Other nonbank savings institutions enjoy the same rate advantage over banks that S&Ls do.

The Fed initially applied Reg Q lids to deposits of all sizes, but

Table 5-4
Maximum interest rates payable on time and savings deposits at federally insured institutions (percent per annum)

Type and maturity of deposit	Commercial banks				Savings and loan associations and mutual savings banks (thrift institutions)			
	In effect Feb. 28, 1982		Previous maximum		In effect Feb. 28, 1982		Previous maximum	
	Percent	Effective date	Percent	Effective date	Percent	Effective date	Percent	Effective date
1 Savings	5¼	7/1/79	5	7/1/73	5½	7/1/79	5¼	(¹)
2 Negotiable order of withdrawal accounts ²	5¼	12/31/80	5	1/1/74	5¼	12/31/80	5	1/1/74
Time accounts ³								
Fixed ceiling rates by maturity ⁴								
3 14–89 days ⁵	5¼	8/1/79	5	7/1/73	(⁶)	....	(⁶)	....
4 90 days to 1 year ⁷	5¾	1/1/80	5½	7/1/73	6	1/1/80	5¾	(¹)
5 1 to 2 years ⁷	6	7/1/73	5½	1/21/70	6½	(¹)	5¾	1/21/70
6 2 to 2½ years ⁷			5¾	1/21/70			6	1/21/70
7 2½ to 4 years ⁷	6½	7/1/73	5¾	1/21/70	6¾	(¹)	6	1/21/70
8 4 to 6 years ⁸	7¼	11/1/73	(⁹)	....	7½	11/1/73	(⁹)	....
9 6 to 8 years ⁸	7½	12/23/74	7¼	11/1/73	7¾	12/23/74	7½	11/1/73
10 8 years or more ⁸	7¾	6/1/78	(⁶)	....	8	6/1/78	(⁶)	....
11 Issued to governmental units (all maturities) ¹⁰	8	6/1/78	7¾	12/23/74	8	6/1/78	7¾	12/23/74
12 Individual retirement accounts and Keogh (H.R. 10) plans (3 years or more) ¹⁰,¹¹	8	6/1/78	7¾	7/6/77	8	6/1/78	7¾	7/6/77
Special variable ceiling rates by maturity								
13 6-month money market time deposits ¹²	(¹³)	(¹³)	(¹³)	(¹³)	(¹³)	(¹³)	(¹³)	(¹³)
14 12-month all savers certificates	(¹⁴)	(¹⁴)	(¹⁴)	(¹⁴)	(¹⁴)	(¹⁴)	(¹⁴)	(¹⁴)
15 2½ years to 4 years	(¹⁵)	(¹⁵)	(¹⁵)	(¹⁶)	(¹⁵)	(¹⁵)	(¹⁵)	(¹⁶)
Accounts with no ceiling rates								
16 Individual retirement accounts and Keogh (H.R. 10) plans (18 months or more)	(¹⁷)	(¹⁷)	(¹⁷)	(¹⁷)	(¹⁷)	(¹⁷)	(¹⁷)	(¹⁷)

1. July 1, 1973, for mutual savings banks; July 6, 1973, for savings and loan associations.

2. For authorized states only. Federally insured commercial banks, savings and loan associations, cooperative banks, and mutual savings banks in Massachusetts and New Hampshire were first permitted to offer negotiable order of withdrawal (NOW) accounts on Jan. 1, 1974. Authorization to issue NOW accounts was extended to similar institutions throughout New England on Feb. 27, 1976, in New York State on Nov. 10, 1978, and in New Jersey on Dec. 28, 1979. Authorization to issue NOW accounts was extended to similar institutions nationwide effective Dec. 31, 1980.

3. For exceptions with respect to certain foreign time deposits see the BULLETIN for October 1962 (p. 1279), August 1965 (p. 1084), and February 1968 (p. 167).

4. Effective Nov. 10, 1980, the minimum notice period for public unit accounts at savings and loan associations was decreased to 14 days and the minimum maturity period for time deposits at savings and loan associations in excess of $100,000 was decreased to 14 days. Effective Oct. 30, 1980, the minimum maturity or notice period for time deposits was decreased from 30 to 14 days at mutual savings banks.

5. Effective Oct. 30, 1980, the minimum maturity or notice period for time deposits was decreased from 30 to 14 days at commercial banks.

6. No separate account category.

7. No minimum denomination. Until July 1, 1979, a minimum of $1,000 was required for savings and loan associations, except in areas where mutual savings banks permitted lower minimum denominations. This restriction was removed for deposits maturing in less than 1 year, effective Nov. 1, 1973.

8. No minimum denomination. Until July 1, 1979, the minimum denomination was $1,000 except for deposits representing funds contributed to an individual retirement account (IRA) or a Keogh (H.R. 10) plan established pursuant to the Internal Revenue Code. The $1,000 minimum requirement was removed for such accounts in December 1975 and November 1976 respectively.

9. Between July 1, 1973, and Oct. 31, 1973, certificates maturing in 4 years or more with minimum denominations of $1,000 had no ceiling; however, the amount of such certificates that an institution could issue was limited to 5 percent of its total time and savings deposits. Sales in excess of that amount, as well as certificates of less than $1,000, were limited to the 6½ percent ceiling on time deposits maturing in 2½ years or more. Effective Nov. 1, 1973, ceilings were reimposed on certificates maturing in 4 years or more with minimum denomination of $1,000. There is no limitation on the amount of these certificates that banks can issue.

10. Accounts subject to fixed-rate ceilings. See footnote 8 for minimum denomination requirements.

11. Effective Jan. 1, 1980, commercial banks are permitted to pay the same rate as thrifts on IRA and Keogh accounts and accounts of governmental units when such accounts are placed in the new 2½-year or more variable-ceiling certificates or in 26-week money market certificates regardless of the level of the Treasury bill rate.

12. Must have a maturity of exactly 26 weeks and a minimum denomination of $10,000, and must be nonnegotiable.

13. Commercial banks and thrift institutions were authorized to offer money market time deposits effective June 1, 1978. These deposits have a minimum denomination requirement of $10,000 and a maturity of 26 weeks. The ceiling rate of interest on these certificates is indexed to the discount rate (auction average) on most recently issued 26-week U.S. Treasury bills. Interest on these certificates may not be compounded. Effective for all 6-month money market certificates issued beginning Nov. 1, 1981, depository institutions may pay rates of interest on these deposits indexed to the higher of (1) the rate for 26-week Treasury bills established immediately before the date of deposit (bill rate) or (2) the average of the four rates for 26-week Treasury bills established for the 4 weeks immediately prior to the date of deposit (4-week average bill rate). Rate ceilings are determined as follows:

Bill rate or 4-week average bill rate	Commercial bank ceiling
7.50 percent or below	7.75 percent
Above 7.50 percent	¼ of 1 percentage point plus the higher of the bill rate or 4-week average bill rate

Bill rate or 4-week average bill rate	Thrift ceiling
7.25 percent or below	7.75 percent
Above 7.25 percent, but below 8.50 percent	½ of 1 percentage point plus the higher of the bill rate or 4-week average bill rate
8.50 percent or above, but below 8.75 percent	9 percent
8.75 percent or above	¼ of 1 percentage point plus the higher of the bill rate or 4-week average bill rate

The maximum allowable rates in February for commercial banks and thrifts based on the bill rate were as follows: Jan. 26, 13.78; Feb. 2, 14.096; Feb. 9, 14.183; Feb. 17, 14.61; Feb. 23, 12.945. The maximum allowable rates in February for commercial banks and thrifts based on the 4-week average bill rate were as follows: Jan. 26, 13.18; Feb. 9, 13.571; Feb. 9, 13.853; Feb. 17, 14.167; Feb. 23, 13.958.

14. Effective Oct. 1, 1981, depository institutions are authorized to issue all savers certificates (ASCs) with a 1-year maturity and an annual investment yield equal to 70 percent of the average investment yield for 52-week U.S. Treasury bills as determined by the auction of 52-week Treasury bills held immediately before the calendar week in which the certificate is issued. A maximum lifetime exclusion of $1,000 ($2,000 on a joint return) from gross income is generally authorized for interest income from ASCs. The annual investment yields for ASCs issued in February (in percent) were as follows: Feb. 21, 10.79.

15. Effective Aug. 1, 1981, commercial banks may pay interest on any variable ceiling nonnegotiable time deposit with an original maturity of 2½ years to less than 4 years at a rate not to exceed ¼ of 1 percentage point below the average 2½-year yield for U.S. Treasury securities as determined and announced by the Treasury Department immediately before the date of deposit. Thrift institutions may pay interest on these certificates at a rate not to exceed the average 2½-year yield for Treasury securities as determined and announced by the Treasury Department immediately before the date of deposit. If the announced average 2½-year yield for Treasury securities is less than 9.50 percent, commercial banks may pay 9.25 percent and thrift institutions 9.50 percent for these deposits. These deposits have no required minimum denomination, and interest may be compounded on them. The ceiling rates of interest at which they may be offered vary biweekly. The maximum allowable rates in February (in percent) for commercial banks were as follows: Feb. 2, 14.3; Feb. 17, 14.80; and for thrift institutions: Feb. 2, 14.55; Feb. 17, 15.05.

16. Between Jan. 1, 1980, and Aug. 1, 1981, commercial banks, and thrift institutions were authorized to offer variable ceiling nonnegotiable time deposits with no required minimum denomination and with maturities of 2½ years or more. Effective Jan. 1, 1980, the maximum rate for commercial banks was ¾ percentage point below the average yield on 2½-year U.S. Treasury securities; the ceiling rate for thrift institutions was ¼ percentage point higher than that for commercial banks. Effective Mar. 1, 1980, a temporary ceiling of 11¾ percent was placed on these accounts at commercial banks and 12 percent on these accounts at savings and loan associations. Effective June 2, 1980, the ceiling rates for these deposits at commercial banks and savings and loans was increased ½ percentage point. The temporary ceiling was retained, and a minimum ceiling of 9.25 percent for commercial banks and 9.50 percent for thrift institutions was established.

17. Effective Dec. 1, 1981, depository institutions were authorized to offer time deposits not subject to interest rate ceilings when the funds are deposited to the credit of, or in which the entire beneficial interest is held by, an individual pursuant to an IRA agreement or Keogh (H.R. 10) plan. Such time deposits must have a minimum maturity of 18 months, and additions may be made to the time deposit at any time before its maturity without extending the maturity of all or a portion of the balance of the account.

NOTE. Before Mar. 31, 1980, the maximum rates that could be paid by federally insured commercial banks, mutual savings banks, and savings and loan associations were established by the Board of Governors of the Federal Reserve System, the Board of Directors of the Federal Deposit Insurance Corporation, and the Federal Home Loan Bank Board under the provisions of 12 CFR 217, 329, and 526 respectively. Title II of the Depository Institutions Deregulation and Monetary Control Act of 1980 (P.L. 96-221) transferred the authority of the agencies to establish maximum rates of interest payable on deposits to the Depository Institutions Deregulation Committee. The maximum rates on time deposits in denominations of $100,000 or more with maturities of 30–89 days were suspended in June 1970; such deposits maturing in 90 days or more were suspended in May 1973. For information regarding previous interest rate ceilings on all types of accounts, see earlier issues of the FEDERAL RESERVE BULLETIN, the *Federal Home Loan Bank Board Journal*, and the *Annual Report of the Federal Deposit Insurance Corporation*.

Source: Federal Reserve Bulletin.

since 1973 it has exempted all deposits of $100,000 or more. Thus, banks are currently free to bid whatever rate they choose for large time deposits, a freedom S&Ls also enjoy.

On June 1, 1978, the Fed authorized banks to pay on 6-month certificates with a minimum denomination of $10,000 the average return on T bills of the same maturity. S&Ls and savings banks were authorized to pay one quarter more on similar certificates. The purpose of the new savings certificate was to cushion the savings and loan industry against an outflow of funds into the money market, and thereby protect the supply of funds flowing into home mortgages. Unfortunately, these certificates failed to accomplish the purpose and, in addition, by 1981 were threatening to bankrupt many S&Ls and savings banks.

By 1980, lids on the rates banks and thrifts were permitted to pay depositors were making it increasingly difficult for these institutions to compete with money market funds and other nonbank institutions for monies that used to be regularly deposited with them. As a result, the Depository Institutions Deregulation and Monetary Control Act of 1980 provided for the gradual deregulation of the rates paid by banks and thrifts. Rate decontrol was welcomed by large banks which were long accustomed to buying money at market rates, but it was vehemently opposed by most thrifts and smaller banks which saw it either as a threat to their existing profits, if they were profitable, or as a threat to their continued viability if they were unprofitable. By the end of 1980, the fight against rate deregulation had become so intense as to throw into question when, and even whether, rate deregulation would be carried out.

Federal funds

Smaller banks typically receive more deposits than they need to fund loans, whereas large banks are in precisely the opposite position. The logical solution to this situation, in which small banks have excess reserves and large banks suffer reserve deficiencies, would be for large banks to accept the excess reserves of smaller correspondent banks as deposits and pay interest on them, a practice that used to be common before banks were forbidden to pay interest on demand deposits. To get around this prohibition, the Federal funds market, somnolent since the 1920s, was revived during the 1950s. In this market, banks buy Fed funds (reserve dollars) from and sell Fed funds to each other. Since purchases of Fed funds are technically borrowings instead of deposits, banks buying them are permitted to pay interest on these funds. The all-in cost of Fed funds to the purchasing bank is the rate paid plus any brokerage fee incurred. Because Fed funds purchased are not deposits, there is no FDIC assessment on them. They are also not subject to reserve requirements since the reserve requirement has been met by the bank that accepted as a deposit the funds sold.

Most sales of Fed funds are made on an overnight basis, but some are for longer periods. Overnight transactions in Fed funds provide the purchasing bank with a normally cheap source of money and a convenient way to make sizable day-to-day adjustments in its reserves. For the selling bank, Fed funds sold provide a convenient form of liquidity. Small banks, unlike large money center banks, cannot count on being able to buy funds whenever they need them. Therefore, they have to keep their liquidity resident in assets, and because overnight sales of Fed funds can be varied in amount from day to day, they give such banks flexibility to adjust to the daily swings that occur in their reserve positions.

Since the difficulties of the Franklin National were brought to light, banks have become acutely aware that, in selling Fed funds, they are making unsecured loans to other banks, and moreover they are often doing so at one of the lowest rates prevailing in the money market.[14] This being the case, banks carefully monitor the credit risks they assume by selling Fed funds. They will sell Fed funds only to banks to which they have established lines of credit, and they will sell to these banks only up to the amount of the lines granted. In establishing a line to another bank, the selling bank will consider the other bank's reputation in the market, its size, its capital structure, and any other factors that affect its credit worthiness. The selling bank may also consider whether the buying bank is, at times, also a seller of funds. A bank that is always a buyer is viewed less favorably than one that operates both ways in the market. Selling funds is also important for a would-be buyer because the Fed funds market is one into which some banks have to buy their way. They do this by selling funds to a bank for a time and then saying to that bank, "We sell funds to you, why don't you extend a line to us?"

Repos

The reemergence of the Fed funds market gave banks a back-door way of paying interest on demand deposits received from other banks. Corporations, state and local governments, and other big nonbank investors that have funds to invest for fewer than 30 days can't, however, sell that money directly in the Fed funds market because they are not banks. Partly to meet the needs of such investors, the RP market has developed into one of the largest and most active sectors of the money market. In it, banks and nonbank dealers each day create billions of dollars worth of what resembles interest-bearing demand deposits. In

---

[14] See Chapter 7.

fact, an investor that enters an RP transaction with a bank is making a loan secured by U.S. Treasury or other securities. Investing in RPs thus exposes the investor to less credit risk than depositing funds directly in the bank would.

A large percentage of all RPs done by banks are on an overnight basis, but open and term RPs are also common. Since the yield curve typically slopes upward, the rate on term RPs normally exceeds the overnight rate, with the spread being larger the longer the maturity of the term RP. Thus, from a cost point of view, an overnight RP tends to be more attractive. However, excessive reliance on overnight RPs and purchases of Fed funds may create a shorter book (a greater mismatch between asset and liability maturities) than a bank wants to run. If so, the bank can use term RPs to "snug up" its book.

Since the RP money a bank buys is not deposits, it pays no FDIC premiums on such funds. It also incurs no reserve requirements on money purchased in the RP market, provided that the collateral used is government or federal agency securities. However, on RPs done with other collateral, there is a reserve requirement. RP transactions always involve some paperwork, and if the buyer of the securities wants them safekept by another bank, there is a clearing charge. Banks doing a lot of RPs carefully track these costs, because they can significantly raise the all-in cost of RP money, especially if it is bought on an overnight basis. To avoid clearing charges, a bank prefers to do RPs with customers that will safekeep the securities "purchased with it."

The overnight RP rate is normally lower than the overnight Fed funds rate for two reasons. First, lenders in this market do not have direct access to the Fed funds market. Second, doing RP does not expose the lender to the same credit risk that selling Fed funds would. The banks' main alternative to buying funds in the term RP market is buying term Fed funds. The choice between the two is likely to be made strictly on the basis of which sells at the lower all-in cost. Normally, this will be term RP, which tends to trade below term Fed funds for the same reasons that overnight RP money is normally cheaper than overnight Fed funds.

Because RP money is cheap, and because a money market bank buys lots of it, such banks carefully search out and cultivate big investors in RPs. They make it a point to know the needs of their big customers—whether they can buy commercial paper, repos, or whatever—and they call these customers every day to get a feel for what monies they have available. The banks also keep track of who is issuing bonds and who is therefore going to get big money. For example, if New York State floats a $1 billion bond issue to obtain funds that it intends to pay out to school districts two months hence, every money market bank will know that the state has money to invest in RPs and they will all be calling the state to get some of it.

Doing RP with customers is the way banks get most of the RP money they buy. However, banks that are primary dealers in government securities also frequently do RP transactions with the Fed, and reverses as well. The Fed relies heavily on repos and reverses with dealers in governments to make short-term adjustments in bank reserves.

Negotiable CDs

In the early 1960s, the demand for funds at New York money market banks began to outstrip the banks' traditional sources. These banks, moreover, had no way to bid for funds outside their own geographic area, for example, to pull time deposits in from the West Coast. To solve this problem, Citibank introduced the negotiable Certificate of Deposit, an innovation that became an instant success and was widely copied. Today, CDs are a key funding instrument for every major bank.

The CD became important to domestic banks not only because it allowed them to tap the national market for funds, but also because it provided them with a means, really the only one available, to bid for longer-term funds in volume. In the domestic market, unlike the Euromarket, the supply of large-denomination time deposits offered by investors is thin, at best. Large corporations don't want to hear about time deposits; they want liquidity. State and local governments used to give large time deposits to banks, but they, too, have become increasingly interested in liquidity.

In buying longer maturity funds, the only alternatives a bank has to issuing CDs are to do term RPs or buy term Fed funds. Term RPs are a limited alternative, because, if a bank does RPs with any asset other than governments and agencies (banks have attempted to "RP" everything, including loans), it incurs a reserve requirement. Purchases of term Fed funds are a viable alternative to the sale of CDs, but the market for such funds has nowhere near the breadth of the CD market.

An issuing bank's all-in cost of CD money is the rate paid on the CD, FDIC insurance, the reserve cost, plus the commission paid to the issuing dealer, if one is used. At times, this all-in cost exceeds that of term Fed funds of comparable maturity. When it does, a bank will lean in the direction of buying term Fed funds, but within limits. All banks are conscious of their statements; for statement purposes, term Fed funds are classified as borrowed funds, CDs as deposits. Thus, cosmetic considerations guarantee that a bank will buy some multiple of the funds it buys in the term Fed funds market in the CD market.[15]

The major choice a bank faces in issuing CDs is what maturity

---

[15] Nationally-chartered banks are limited in the extent to which "borrowed funds" relate proportionally to their capital, whereas state-chartered banks are not. The latter, therefore, tend to be heavier users of this market.

money to take. If a bank thinks its book is running too short or that interest rates and loan demand are likely to rise sharply, it will be tempted to buy longer-dated funds, 6-month rather than 3-month money. Because of availability and risk considerations, however, most of the money banks buy in the CD market is purchased at the short end of the maturity spectrum.

When a bank opts to issue longer-term (say, 6-month) CDs, it is typically gambling that interest rates will rise. With an upward-sloping yield curve, this is an expensive bet because, in buying 6-month money, a bank forgoes the cheaper alternative of buying two consecutive batches of 3-month money. Thus, interest rates have to rise sharply for a purchase of long-term money in anticipation of rising interest rates to pay off. Banks therefore buy 6-month money in volume only if they believe strongly that the Fed is going to raise interest rates, or if the yield curve is relatively flat.

When a bank buys long-term money, it gambles not only that rates will rise, but also that it will have some use for the expensive money it is acquiring. Should loan demand be less than anticipated, a bank that had bought 6-month money would find itself holding high-cost funds for which it had no high-yield use.

Availability is also a consideration in a bank's choice of CD maturities. The real depth in the CD market is in the 1- to 3-month range. There is a market for 6-month paper, but it is thin, and the market for 1-year paper is still thinner. Thus, banks have little choice but to buy the bulk of their money in short maturities.

This, moreover, becomes increasingly true during periods of tight money. When interest rates are rising and a bank expects them to continue to rise, it will be tempted to increase the average maturity of the CDs it sells. It is selling its CDs, however, to sophisticated investors who are likely to share its view on rates and who therefore—just when the bank is trying to increase maturities—want to decrease the maturity of the CDs they buy. Generally, the investors get their way because banks can only sell paper that the market will accept. Thus, tight money and rising interest rates tend to force *down* the average maturity of CDs sold.

Issuing CDs. In issuing CDs, banks generally prefer to have these securities in the hands of investors who are likely to hold them for at least a substantial period, if not to maturity. That banks should attempt to sell an instrument, whose appeal, by design, is liquidity, to buyers who will rarely, if ever, trade it seems incongruous to the outside observer, but not to bankers. A banker doesn't mind an investor selling a CD because of an unexpected cash need, but sales by trading accounts are something else. As the banker sees it, paper bought by trading accounts and subsequently dumped on the street could provide unwanted competition for any new paper his bank might later choose to write. In their search for "warm-nosed" money, most banks prefer to sell as many of the CDs they issue as possible through their own sales forces to their own customers. However, a good portion of bank CDs are issued through dealers.

In the CD market, as in other sectors of the money market, a bank cannot buy unlimited quantities of funds. The reason is that not all investors in the money market are free to buy bank CDs because of either regulation or self-imposed investment parameters. And those that are, limit their purchases of paper to specific names and specific amounts for each name. Thus, at any time, there is some maximum amount of its paper that a bank can push into the market. That limit is one most banks have never approached and all banks attempt not to approach.

Several major banks have, however, breached this limit with unfortunate consequences. They suddenly found they could sell only small amounts of new paper to the market. Also, the excess supply of their paper on the street drove down its price, which, in turn soured investors who were holding that paper and raised questions on the bank's name. Such a situation takes time for a bank to remedy. The bank may have to cut back sharply on the CDs it issues for awhile and attempt to selectively place those CDs, perhaps at a premium rate, with investors who will hold rather than trade them.

Eurodollars

A final source of funding to which a bank may turn is the Euromarket, where it can bid for deposits (*take* money) of essentially any maturity from overnight on. A bank can also invest (*place*) money it has raised in the domestic market in Euro time deposits. The reserve requirement on Euros is established under *Regulation D*, it currently requires a domestic bank to hold reserves on any *net* borrowings (borrowings minus placements) of Euros that it makes for its domestic book over a 7-day averaging period. Because of Reg *D*, a bank that takes Euros of one maturity will often place Euros of some other maturity during the averaging period so that its reserve cost on the money borrowed is zero.

The head offices of money market banks are constantly alert to the opportunities for arbitrage between the domestic and Euromarkets that arise because of transitory rate discrepancies.[16] For example, if 6-month Euros are selling at 11.50 percent and 6-month money can be purchased at 10 percent in the domestic CD market, a bank will take

---

[16] Strictly defined, to arbitrage means to buy something where it is cheap and sell it where it is dear.

domestic 6-month money and place it in the Euromarket through its London or Nassau branch. Doing so, besides locking in a spread for the bank, permits the bank to bring back short-dated Euros at no reserve cost. Such intrabank arbitrages play an important role in holding Euro and U.S. rates in line.

Bank capital adequacy

In talking about bank capital adequacy, the first thing to note is that the essence of banking is to raise the return on equity earned by the bank through leverage. To illustrate leverage at work, let's use a simple example. Suppose an investor has $1,000 of capital to invest. He can borrow additional funds at 10 percent and he can invest at 15 percent. If he invests only his $1,000 of capital, he will earn $150 for a return of 15 percent on that capital. If, alternatively, he borrows $5,000 and invests a total of $6,000, he will have an investment income of $900, interest costs of $500, and profits of $400, which amounts to a 40 percent return on his $1,000 of capital (Table 5–5). By borrowing funds at a low rate and investing them along with his capital at a higher rate, our investor has raised the return on his capital.

In an uncertain world, leverage can work against as well as for the

Table 5–5
Leverage at work: Investor has $1,000 of capital

Case I: No borrowed funds used; investment returns 15%:
$$\text{Investment income} = 15\% \times \$1,000 = \$150$$
$$-\text{Interest cost} = 4\% \times 0 \qquad = \quad \underline{0}$$
$$\text{Profit} \qquad\qquad = \$150$$
$$\text{Rate of return on capital} = \frac{\$150}{\$1,000} = 15\%$$

Case II: $5,000 of borrowed funds costing 10% used; investment returns 15%:
$$\text{Investment income} = 15\% \times \$6,000 = \$900$$
$$-\text{Interest cost} = 10\% \times \$5,000 \quad = \$500$$
$$\text{Profit} \qquad\qquad = \$400$$
$$\text{Rate of return on capital} = \frac{\$400}{\$1,000} = 40\%$$

Case III: $5,000 of borrowed funds costing 10% used; investment returns 5%:
$$\text{Investment income} = 5\% \times \$6,000 \quad = \quad \$300$$
$$-\text{Interest cost} = 10\% \times \$5,000 \quad = \quad \underline{500}$$
$$\text{Loss} \qquad\qquad = -\$200$$
$$\text{Rate of return on capital} = \frac{-\$200}{\$1,000} = -20\%$$

---

investor. If, for example, our investor, who anticipated earning 15 percent on his investment, earned only 5 percent, then his profit would be −$200, for a rate of return on capital of −20 percent (Case III, Table 5–5).

Because bankers operate with borrowed funds that amount, in total, to a substantial multiple of their capital, they engage in leverage on a grand scale. Moreover, because assuming both a credit risk by lending and rate exposure by running a short book are fundamental elements of banking, the banker can never be sure of either what average return he will earn on his assets or what his cost of funds will be. The purpose of bank capital is to cushion bank depositors and other suppliers of debt capital to banks against any losses the bank might incur due to unfavorable leverage—borrowing costs higher than return earned.

While it's easy to see that a bank needs capital, the question of how much is difficult, perhaps unanswerable. In attempting to measure bank capital adequacy, the yardstick used to be the ratio of a bank's deposits to its loans, its major risk assets. As banks became active buyers of money, focus shifted to the ratio of equity to total risk assets. However well or poorly this ratio may measure bank capital adequacy, it in no way solves the question of what minimum value the ratio should have. For every $1 of capital, should a bank borrow at most $10, $20, or what? Any intelligent answer to this question should probably be based on a bank's earning power as measured by certain historical indexes and modified to allow for the bank's bad-debt experience. Such numbers, however, vary from bank to bank, suggesting that no absolute, industrywide standard can or should be set.

As a practical matter, the capital ratios currently prevailing in banking in no way reflect reasoned decisions by either bankers or regulators as to what these ratios should be. What they are at any point reflects historical evolution and prevailing economic conditions. In particular, during the post–World War II period, as loan demand surged and banks strove for continued earnings growth, bank capital ratios declined substantially. It is, moreover, not clear that an end to this downward trend is in sight.

The attitude of bankers toward the capital adequacy question is well illustrated by the words of one bank president: "Back in the credit crunch of 1974, because of inflation and an insatiable demand for credit, we got to the point where equity was about 4 percent of assets, so we had leverage of 25 to 1. At the peak, we and a lot of bankers asked how far can this go, and we decided we had better slow down and tighten up. So we set a leverage maximum of 25 to 1." In the next breath the same banker added: "We of course have to forget all about that standard when we deal with foreign banks. The leading Israeli banks have about 1 percent capital ratios, and in Japan the figure is 1 or 2 percent." In effect, this banker and other U.S. bankers, as well, measure capital adequacy in domestic and foreign banks by differing standards, a practice that suggests they have no absolute notion of what capital ratios should be.

Since the question of capital adequacy boils down to asking how much capital a bank needs to ensure its survival under unknown future conditions, it is not surprising that neither bankers nor regulators have a definitive answer to this question. The typical banker's motto in determining what minimum capital ratio his bank should maintain seems to be *stay with the herd.* A banker judges his leverage ratio to be high or low in terms of where he is vis-à-vis his peers. If the pack lets their capital ratios fall, he is comfortable in following, but he does not want to lead. This attitude makes sense for several reasons. First, the Fed tends to judge banks against the pattern of what their competitors are doing. Second, bank customers who watch leverage carefully will penalize a bank that gets out of line.[17]

Bank regulation. Banking in America is often referred to as a "dual" system because some banks operate under federal charters obtained from the Comptroller of the Currency, while others are chartered by the states. Banks operating under a federal charter are required to join the Federal Reserve System; state-chartered banks are not. State banks are more numerous than national banks, and the majority of them have not joined the Federal Reserve System, primarily because reserve requirements make Fed membership expensive; this attitude will change as the 1980 Banking Act is implemented and *all* banks are required to hold reserves at the Fed. National banks are larger than state banks on the average, and, as a result, banks that are members of the Fed, while fewer in number, accept over 70 percent of the deposits received by domestic banks. Almost all banks in the country have opted to insure their deposits with the Federal Deposit Insurance Corporation.

Bank regulation in the United States is layered. State banks are regulated by state banking authorities, national banks by the Comptroller of the Currency. In addition, banks that are members of the Fed are regulated by the Fed, and the FDIC regulates insured banks. The overlap in bank regulation has led to periodic calls for a single, unified system of bank regulation. Movement in this direction seems unlikely, however, because state banks, which are numerous and have considerable clout in Congress, are anxious to preserve a system in which the primary responsibility for regulating them rests with the local state banking authority; these banks fear being forced into a single national banking system.

Fortunately, the regulatory overlap is less than it appears on paper.

---

[17] For a further discussion of bank capital adequacy and capital needs, see Chapter 7.

Often the state regulators will focus on checking the accuracy of the bank's audited statements, whereas examiners from the Fed will be more concerned with whether the bank is being properly run.

The regulations under which U.S. banks, as opposed to British banks (see Chapter 6), operate are numerous, detailed, and complex, and they are becoming more so all the time. Perhaps one reason is the checkered history of the U.S. banking system, which periodically experienced waves of failures and suspensions of payments up to the 1930s. A second reason is that flexible regulation may be impractical in a country where there are 15,000 different banks, a situation unparalleled in any other major country.

Many people, particularly members of Congress, feel that if the regulators were doing their job, no bank would have problems, and that the existence of problem banks indicates the need for more or better regulation. Yet, as one regulator noted, the same member of Congress who says there should never be problem banks is also quick to complain, when wheat prices are low and there is a big overhang in the wheat market, that Nebraska farmers are having trouble getting bank credit.

The nature of banking is taking risks by lending and by doing some maturity arbitrage. Good regulators see their job as trying to keep these risks prudent. They also recognize that the regulatory structure should not be such that no bank ever fails. If it were, banking as a creative force would be stifled.

When a bank experiences such severe problems that it ceases to be a viable institution, the regulators will normally arrange some sort of merger between that bank and another strong bank. This salvage operation may involve, as it did in the case of Franklin National, first, substantial loans from the Fed to the ailing bank and, later, cash injections by the FDIC in exchange for some of the bank's less desirable assets.

The merger, if it occurs, is typically forced by events, not by the regulators. As one regulator noted:

> When a bank has problems, we try to save it so long as it's a viable institution. We will make suggestions to management, but it is their responsibility to right the situation. A bank ceases to be viable when public confidence in the bank weakens, usually due to some easily identifiable event. Before that occurs, we may look in the wings for potential marriage partners—act, if you will, as marriage brokers—but there is *no* shotgun for the marriage until public confidence is lost.

The fact that the Fed and the FDIC have not, in recent decades, permitted a major bank to fail with losses to depositors raises an interesting question: Would they ever? The answer, most observers (including some inside the Fed) believe, is no. The reason is that the economic consequences of permitting a major bank to fail with losses to depositors would be enormously more costly than acting to protect depositors. Still, there is what might be called the *political risk*, that is, the possibility that a large bank might, through its actions, so arouse the public's ire that the Fed and the FDIC would not be permitted to save it.

Bank holding companies

Almost all large banks and many smaller banks in the United States are owned by holding companies. Prior to the 1960s, bank holding companies were used primarily to surmount restrictions on intrastate branching by bringing a number of separately chartered banks under a single organization. Formation of multibank holding companies was brought under regulation by the Bank Holding Company Act in 1956. The purposes of this act, which is administered by the Federal Reserve Board, were twofold: to prevent the creation of monopoly power in banks and to prevent banks from entering, via their holding company, what were traditionally nonbank lines of activity.

In the late 1960s, many of the nation's largest banks formed one-bank holding companies which were not subject to the provisions of the 1956 act. One of the objectives in doing so was to create a vehicle through which they could indirectly enter activities that they could not carry out directly. The banks' ability to achieve such diversification was, however, severely limited by the Bank Holding Company Act of 1970. This act brought one-bank holding companies under regulation by the Federal Reserve Board, which is responsible for restricting their activities to those "which are so closely related to banking as to be a proper incident thereto."

A second reason banks formed one-bank holding companies was to achieve greater flexibility in liability management. During the late 1960s, open-market rates rose above the Reg Q ceiling on several occasions, and banks had difficulty selling CDs. To solve the resulting funding problem, the banks segregated certain loans on their books, put them in the holding company, and issued commercial paper, which was not subject to Regulation Q, to fund these loans. The Fed's response to this end run around Reg Q was to impose a reserve requirement on any paper sold to fund such loans. This reserve requirement does not apply to other assets sold by a bank to its holding company.

Today, bank holding companies use the proceeds from sales of commercial paper to fund various assets on their own books and on those of their nonbank subsidiaries (known as *subs*). These include bank credit card receivables purchased from the bank, assets leased, and loans extended through a nonbank sub of the holding company.

Edge Act corporations

A 1919 amendment to the Federal Reserve Act permits national banks and state banks that are members of the Federal Reserve System to establish international banking corporations, known familiarly as *Edge Act corporations.*

The operations of Edge Act corporations within the United States are restricted to activities that are incidental to the parent bank's international business—holding demand and time deposits received from foreign sources, issuing letters of credit, financing foreign trade, and creating bankers' acceptances. Edge Act corporations are also permitted to engage in overseas operations, to provide certain types of specialized financing—such as loan syndication—and to make equity investments in foreign financial institutions.

Today, all major U.S. banks have established one or more Edge Act corporations. The principal function of these subs is to carry out international banking business for the parent within the United States. The ability to set up an Edge Act sub, which, because of its federal charter, is exempt from state corporation and banking laws, gives banks a means to engage in interstate banking, albeit for limited purposes. This is particularly important to non–New York banks that use New York–based Edge Act subs to operate the equivalent of an international department in New York, the single most important domestic center for international banking. Edge Act corporations are also used by New York banks to participate in the regional markets for international banking that have developed in San Francisco, Chicago, Miami, and other commercial centers. For banks in high-tax states, Edge Act corporations offer an additional benefit—the ability to earn and book some income in lower-tax states.

With respect to the money market, Edge Act corporations are most prominent in the BA market. Currently, a substantial fraction of all BAs outstanding are Edge Act corporation paper.

Domestic banks carry out the bulk of their foreign activities not through Edge Act corporations, but through foreign branches. The extensive activities of these foreign branches in the Eurodollar market are the topic of the next chapter.

REGIONAL AND SMALL BANKS

In discussing bank management, our focus has been primarily on money market banks. In this concluding section, we shift to regional and small banks.

The first and most important point to be made is that our introductory remarks on profit and risk apply to *all* banks regardless of size:

Every bank seeks to maximize profits subject to the constraint that perceived risk be held to some acceptable level. Also, in making asset and funding choices, *every* bank seeks to choose a balance sheet that meets this goal.

Where money market banks and their smaller sisters differ is in the types of deposits and loan business they receive and in the funding options open to them.

Correspondent banking

Some of a large or regional bank's best customers are other smaller banks. Small banks look to a larger correspondent bank to provide them with various services: clearing checks, making wire transfers, buying and safekeeping securities, providing investment advice, offering participation in domestic and Euro loans, buying Fed funds in lots too small to be sold in the New York market, providing lines of credit, and buying and selling foreign exchange.

A bank using the services of a correspondent bank pays for many of these services by holding compensating balances at its correspondent bank. The correspondent bank relationship involves a form of barter, services for balances, that closely resembles the barter in which banks and their corporate clients engage. Both sorts of barter evolved because banks were forbidden by law from paying explicit interest on demand deposits.

Funding

Except in instances where it has done something to tarnish its good name, a money market bank has the option of buying huge sums of money in the Fed funds, repo, CD, and Euro markets, and money market banks liberally exercise this option. A typical money market bank may finance over 60 percent of its assets with money bought in these markets. The corresponding figure for a regional bank would be 30 to 40 percent, and for a small bank, 0 percent.

Regional and small banks rely less heavily than money market banks on bought money for several reasons. Money market banks have many major corporations as customers; the latter are often big borrowers but seek to hold the smallest possible deposit balances at the banks from which they borrow. As a result, money market banks, excepting the B of A with its huge branch network, are deposit poor and must buy outside money to finance their basic asset structure. Most regional and all small banks do a lot of consumer business and consequently receive large amounts of demand and time deposits from consumers. Net consumers tend to deposit in demand and time deposits at banks more than they borrow from banks. Thus, regional banks, and more especially small banks, are often deposit rich.

Being deposit rich is especially common for a small bank. In fact, the single most important difference between small banks and other banks is that small banks may well have resources comprising capital, *hard-core* (won't go away) demand deposits and savings money that exceed their loan assets. To pluck some numbers out of the air, a small bank might have $30 million in capital and deposits and only $20 million in loans, leaving it with a surplus of $10 million. The bank might invest these funds by placing $5 million through its correspondent bank in the Euromarket and selling another $5 million of Fed funds, also through its correspondent bank.

A second reason that regional and small banks rely less on bought money than money market banks do is *market access*. A bank's ability to tap the national money market for funds, credit problems excepted, is directly proportional to its size. Money market banks that have preserved their good name can essentially buy all of the money they want; for them, the binding constraint on buying money and ballooning their balance sheet is the need to maintain a respectable capital ratio. Large regional banks have fair access to the national money market. Small regionals have only *very* limited access to this market, and small banks have no access at all.

CD money. Technically, any bank can issue a large-denomination negotiable CD. However, a CD buyer desires liquidity and is therefore interested not just in negotiability, but also in *marketability*. He wants paper for which there is an active secondary market. Currently, there are only about 20 large domestic banks whose paper trades well in the secondary market. All other banks are shut out of the *national* market for CD money.

To sell CDs, banks that lack access to the national market—depending on their size—must look to regional or local customers in their economic sphere of interest. This means that smaller banks cannot balloon their CD borrowings as a major bank can. It does not mean that such banks cannot sell CDs to anyone except consumers. Smaller banks do sell CDs in varying sizes to corporate customers that have insufficient cash to buy a $1 million CD issued by a major bank.[18] The advantage of buying a CD that is not marketable because of size or name for a corporation that might instead make a time deposit is that, if the corporation experiences an unanticipated need for money, it can always use the CD it has purchased from one bank as collateral for

---

[18] Major banks can and sometimes do issue CDs with a face value below $1 million to corporate customers. The problem with such CDs is that they trade at a concession in the secondary market, which is essentially a market for $1 million pieces of paper.

borrowing from another bank. Thus by buying a CD, the corporation gets liquidity a time deposit would not afford it.

Small banks and other banks that do retail as well as corporate business also raise funds by issuing 6-month *money market certificates (MMCs)* and longer-term savings certificates. In 1978, the Fed gave banks authority to issue these consumer-oriented CDs so that they could compete more effectively for funds with money market funds and other instruments that offer consumers rates near or equal to the rates prevailing in the money market. MMCs now represent a substantial portion of the total time deposits received by banks doing a lot of retail business. The money banks raise by selling these certificates is expensive relative to the other deposits they receive; its high cost has forced small banks, and thrifts in particular, to make more sophisticated balance sheet choices and to look for arbitrages that will permit them to utilize this money profitably. An attractive use—from the point of view of risk and return—that small banks and *thrifts as well* can make of money raised through the sale of 6-month MMCs and not required to support their basic asset structure is to make Euro time deposits of similar maturity.

Federal funds. The market for Federal funds is so important for banks of all sizes that it seems appropriate to say a few words about the history of this market. During the early 1940s, banks purchased large amounts of the $400 billion of new government debt issued to finance World War II, and they adopted the practice of settling their reserve positions by trading short-term Treasury bills for cash settlement.

Gradually, it became clear that there was an easier way for the banks to settle—instead of selling bills among themselves, they began, in the early 1950s, to sell 1-day money among themselves. And as they did, the Fed funds market—dormant since the 1920s—was revived. Another reason for the revival of the funds market was that, as interest rates started to rise after the Treasury-Fed accord, which freed the Fed to pursue an independent monetary policy, everyone became more conscious of the value of money left idle. Banks, in particular, began to see the merit of keeping their excess funds fully invested. The revival of the Fed funds market was particularly attractive for retail banks with a customer base consisting largely of consumers. These banks needed an outlet for their surplus funds, and they took up the practice of selling Fed funds daily to their large-city correspondents.

By 1960, these developments led to a situation where the big New York and Chicago banks began to deliberately operate their basic money positions so that they were always short, on the ground that they needed room to buy all the Fed funds that were coming into them from smaller correspondents. This was an attractive situation for the large banks because Fed funds were the cheapest money around, and they naturally asked: Why not use it for 10 percent of our overall needs?

In the late 1950s, when the big banks sold to their correspondent banks the "service" of buying up the latter's excess funds, they said, "Of course, if you ever need Fed funds, we will be happy to sell them to you." This commitment came back to haunt them in 1963 when interest rates started to take off in the aftermath of the Kennedy tax cut. By then, the smaller correspondent banks had developed an insight into the money market; they began buying Treasury bills, which were then trading at a yield higher than the discount rate, and financing them first with their own surplus funds and then by purchasing Fed funds from the big banks.

At that time, Fed funds had *never* traded higher than the discount rate. The reason was that, since the banks bought Fed funds only to settle their reserve positions and then only as an alternative to borrowing at the discount window, any bank that was willing to pay more than the discount rate for Fed funds would naturally be subject to the accusation that, for one reason or another, it could not borrow at the window.

Gradually, the situation became critical for the big banks because all their correspondents were buying T bills at 4 percent, financing them with Fed funds purchased at 3.5 percent (the level of the discount rate), and raking in the spread. This continued for more than a year, during which time the big banks became huge net sellers of Fed funds. To fund the sales, these banks were issuing CDs at rates higher than the rate at which they were selling Fed funds to their "valued" correspondents.

Something had to give. Finally, in 1964, Morgan decided that if any bank could get away with paying more than the discount rate for Fed funds, it could, and on October 4 of that year it bid 3⅝ for funds at a time when the discount rate was 3½ and funds were trading at 3½. The $500 million estimated to have been traded at this higher rate that day was a small sum by today's standards, but the gambit succeeded and began a new era in the funds market. Rapidly, funds began to trade at a market rate that was determined by supply and demand and was affected by the discount rate only insofar as that rate influenced demand.

After funds began to trade at a market rate, the Fed funds market mushroomed and more and more banks got into it. Regional banks that, at the inception of the market, were selling funds to large banks began to operate their own regional markets. Before this development, most trading in Fed funds was done in New York and Chicago, with perhaps a little in San Francisco. Small outlying banks with only a little money to sell were excluded from the market, because it made no sense for a bank with $100,000 of overnight money to sell to telephone New York when the rate it would get was 3 or 3½ percent. However, when the regional banks began to buy Fed funds, it paid for a bank in Joplin, Missouri, to call St. Louis for $0.30 to sell even $50,000 of Fed funds. In the Fed funds market now, regional banks buy up funds from even tiny banks, use what they need, and resell the remainder in bulk amounts in the New York market. Thus, the Fed funds market resembles a river with tributaries; money is collected in many places and then flows through various channels into the New York market.

The national CD market, on the other hand, is open to only 20 or so banks in the country. The Fed funds market is broader, and many regional banks can and do buy Federal funds not only from their correspondents, but also in the New York market. All money market banks, with the exception of the deposit-rich B of A, are big net buyers of Fed funds; regional banks are smaller net buyers; and small banks are net sellers. Federal funds represent a source of liquidity both for banks that are net *buyers* of funds *and* for banks that are *sellers* of funds. For buyers, funds represent a source of liquidity because they are a liability that the buyer can expand at will. For sellers, funds also represent a source of liquidity because they are an asset the selling bank can liquidate without loss any time it needs money either to pay off deposit liabilities or to fund the purchase of a more attractive asset.

Euros. All money market banks, all regional banks, and some small banks participate in the Eurodollar market. Large banks are net takers of funds in this market and so are large regionals. Smaller banks, to the extent that they participate at all, tend to be net lenders of funds.

Assets

Loans. Banks, depending on their size, hold different types of loans on their books. A number of money market banks, the Irving Trust, Morgan, and Bankers Trust to name three restrict their business largely to commercial and industrial (C&I) customers and to other financial institutions.[19] Regional banks generally do at least some retail business, and all small banks do a lot of retail business.

Banks making domestic loans to corporate clients typically price these loans either at a floating-rate prime or a fixed rate tied to their cost of funds.[20] In contrast, banks that do retail business end up with a lot of 3- to 5-year *fixed-rate* paper that is financing car purchases and home improvements, and with long-term mortgages. The differences in maturities and pricing between C&I loans and consumer loans means

---

[19] Trust department business with wealthy customers is an exception.

[20] The above describes what might be called normal operating procedure for a bank in a normal world. In the historically unusual circumstances that prevailed as the 1980s dawned, banks lost, temporarily at least, *all* rational reason to hold investment portfolios of government securities. More about that in Chapter 11.

that funding the loan portfolio has quite different implications for small and large banks with respect to liquidity and interest rate exposure.

Size influences not only the types of borrowers that come to a bank, but also the size of the loan demand a bank faces relative to the total deposits it receives. Normally, loan demand at a money market bank far exceeds the bank's deposit base, and, as a result, the bank has to finance some portion of its loans with bought money. Small banks, in contrast, sometimes find themselves with more deposits than loans. Banks in that position, instead of having to solve a funding problem, have to seek out attractive earning assets.

One way in which smaller banks acquire additional loan paper is by buying participation in loans made by their larger correspondent banks. Large banks sometimes *participate out* loans to their smaller correspondents as an accommodation to the latter and sometimes as a means of solving their own funding problems. How attractive taking a participation in a loan will be for a given bank will depend not only on the national business situation—are business loans in the aggregate going up or down—but also on conditions in their locality. Regional and small banks have to look to borrowers in their own sphere of interest for loans, and demand for loans in that sphere may be sluggish even when loan demand on the national level is strong. Such sluggishness might reflect depressed farm prices for a country bank or a downturn in local industry for a city bank.

Besides participating in other banks' loans, banks with excess deposits formerly used some of their surplus funds to buy commercial paper. That has become less common as the cost of funds to such banks has risen through introduction of MMCs, and as the sophistication of such banks has increased. Many smaller banks now place funds in the Euromarket directly or through their correspondent. The spread between rates on short-term Eurodeposits and that on commercial paper is usually so wide that Euros are by far the more attractive investment.

Governments.   For reasons described in Chapter 11, it is becoming less attractive for banks across the board to invest in government securities, but most banks still have at least some governments and agency paper. Money market banks never invest in governments because they are looking for an interest-bearing asset in which to park spare cash. These banks, because they are deposit poor, always finance their holdings of governments in the repo market, and their government portfolio, to the extent that it yields them profit, does so because they are able to earn positive carry. Small banks, in contrast, often buy governments to absorb surplus funds. Regional banks, like large banks, are more likely to buy governments as an arbitrage.

Because a repo transaction is backed by securities, more banks have access to the national repo market than have access to the national CD market. Besides doing repo in the national market, regional banks also do repo with their local customers. Even a few small banks now get into the act by doing RPs with consumers; this innovation is a product of interest rates in the high teens.

The many differences that exist in the basic asset and liability options open to large and small banks have significant implications with respect to the liquidity risk and interest rate exposure these institutions face and the tactics and strategies appropriate for them. We will highlight these in later chapters.

6

Eurobanking

The Euromarket—born by trial, error, and accident in the years following World War II—is today a huge, highly efficient, highly competitive, and largely unregulated international capital market. Currently, U.S. money market banks do half or more of their total business in the Euromarket. The Euromarket is an international market, and, as one might expect, the smaller a bank, the less important its Euro operations are likely to be. Still even quite small U.S. banks participate in limited ways: by holding their liquidity in the form of Eurodollar call deposits or by buying participations in syndicated Euro loans.

In this chapter, we describe the broad outlines of this market and how banks participate in it. We say a great deal in later chapters about the Euro operations of U.S. and foreign banks. See in particular the discussion of running a Euro book in Chapters 9 and 11 and in Chapter 13, which talks about running a book in a non-native currency.

EURO TRANSACTIONS IN T-ACCOUNTS

The best way to start a discussion of the Euromarket is by explaining the mechanics of Eurodeposits and loans, about which there is much confusion. First, a definition: *Eurodollars are dollar-denominated deposits held at a bank or bank branch outside the United States or in an IBF.*[1] If a U.S. investor shifts $1 million of deposits from a New York bank to the London branch of a U.S. bank, to Barclays London, or to the London branch of any French, German, or other foreign bank and receives in exchange a deposit denominated in dollars, he has made a *Eurodollar deposit.* Such deposits came to be known as *Eurodollars* because, initially, banks in Europe were most active in seeking and accepting such deposits. Today, however, banks all over the globe are active in the Eurodollar market and the term Eurodollar is a misnomer.[2]

The first important point to make about Eurodollars is that, regardless of where they are deposited—London, Singapore, Tokyo, or Bahrain—they never leave the United States. Also, they never leave the United States regardless of where they are lent—to a multinational firm, to an underdeveloped country, or to an East European government. Let's work that out with T-accounts. As noted in Chapter 2, a *T-account* shows *changes in assets and liabilities* that result from a given financial transaction, as shown below.

T-Account	
Change in assets	Change in liabilities

Suppose, to get our example going, Exxon moves $10 million from its account at Morgan in New York to the London branch of Citibank. (You can think of Exxon as writing a check against Morgan New York and depositing it in Citi London, but the transaction is done by wire or telex.) Clearing of this transaction, which normally occurs on the day it is initiated, will result in several balance sheet changes (Table 6–1).

Before we look at these, two preliminary remarks are in order. First, Citi's London branch is an integral part of Citibank, and when the bank publishes statements, it consolidates the assets and liabilities of the head office and all foreign branches. However, on a day-to-day operating basis, Citi New York, Citi London, and Citi's other foreign branches all keep separate books. Second, Citibank has just one account at the Fed, that held by Citi New York, the head office.

Now let's look at Table 6–1. It shows that, as a result of the transaction, Exxon exchanges one asset, $10 million of demand deposits at

---

[1] International banking facilities (IBFs) are discussed in Chapter 11.

[2] Some people refer to dollar deposits accepted in Singapore and other Far East centers as *Asian dollars.* The natural extension of this practice would be to refer to dollar deposits accepted in Bahrain as Middle East dollars and dollar deposits accepted in Nassau as Caribbean dollars, that is, to use a multitude of terms to describe the same thing, an offshore deposit of dollars.

Table 6-1
A Euro deposit is made and cleared

Exxon	
	Demand deposits, Morgan N.Y. −10 million (Euro) time deposits, Citi London +10 million

Citi N.Y.		Citi London	
Reserves +10 million	London office dollar account (a "due to" item, Citi N.Y. to Citi London) +10 million	New York office dollar account (a "due from" item, Citi London to Citi N.Y.) +10 million	(Euro) time deposits +10 million

Morgan N.Y.		New York Fed	
Reserves −10 million	Demand deposits, Exxon −10 million		Reserves, Morgan −10 million Reserves, Citi +10 million

Morgan New York, for another, $10 million of Eurodeposits at Citi London. To make this exchange, Exxon withdrew funds from Morgan and deposited them at Citi. This means, of course, that when the transaction clears, Morgan has to pay Citi the funds Exxon has transferred from one bank to the other. Morgan does this in effect by transferring money from its reserve (checking) account at the Fed to Citi's reserve account at the Fed. Thus, the transaction causes Morgan to lose reserves and Citi New York to gain them. At Morgan, the loss of reserves is offset by a decrease in deposit liabilities.

At Citibank, the situation is more complicated, as Table 6-1 shows. Citi London has received the deposit, but Citi New York has received the extra reserves. So Citi New York, in effect, owes Citi London money. This is accounted for by adjusting the *New York office dollar account*, which can be thought of simply as a checking account that Citi London holds with Citi New York. To Citi London, as long as this account is in surplus, which it normally would be, the account is a *due from* item, and it shows up on Citi London's balance sheet as an asset. On Citi New York's balance sheet, the same account is a *due to* item, and consequently it shows up as any other deposit would. With this accounting framework in mind, it's easy to follow what happens on

Citibank's books as a result of Exxon's deposit. Citi London gets a new $10 million liability in the form of a time deposit, which is offset by an equal credit to its account with home office. Meanwhile, home office gets $10 million of extra reserves, which are offset by a like increase in its liability to its London branch.

Note several things about this example. First, the changes that occurred on every institution's balance sheet were offsetting; i.e., net worth never changes. This is *always* the case in any transaction the consequences of which can be illustrated with T-accounts.

A second and more important point is that, while Exxon now thinks of itself as holding dollars in London, the dollars actually never left the United States. In effect, the whole transaction simply caused $10 million of reserves to be moved from Morgan's reserve account at the New York Fed to Citi's account there (see Table 6–1). This, by the way, would have been the case in any Eurodeposit example we might have used. Regardless of who makes the deposit, who receives it, and where in the world it is made, the ultimate dollars never leave the United States.

A Euro loan

In our example, we left Citi London with a new time deposit on which it has to pay interest. To profit from that deposit, Citi London is naturally going to lend those dollars out. Suppose, for the sake of illustration, that Citi London lends the dollars to Electricité de France (EDF). Initially, this loan results in EDF's being credited with an extra $10 million in deposits at Citi London, as Table 6–2 shows. EDF,

Table 6–2
A Euro loan is granted to EDF

Citi London		EDF	
Loan, EDF +10 million	(Euro) deposits, EDF +10 million	(Euro) deposits, Citi London +10 million	Loan, Citi London +10 million

of course, has borrowed the money, so the $10 million will not sit idly in its account.

Let's assume that EDF uses the dollars it has borrowed to pay for oil purchased from an Arab seller who banks at Chase London. Table 6–3, which should be self-explanatory to anyone who has followed Table 6–1, shows the balance sheet changes that will result from this transaction. Note in particular that when EDF pulls $10 million out of Citi London, the latter, since it has no dollars other than a deposit balance

Table 6–3
EDF uses its borrowed dollars to pay for oil

EDF		Arab Oil Seller	
(Euro) deposits −10 million	Accounts payable −10 million	Accounts receivable −10 million (Euro) deposits, Chase London +10 million	

Citi London		Chase London	
New York office dollar account −10 million	(Euro) deposits, EDF −10 million	New York office dollar account +10 million	Time deposits, Arab oil seller +10 million

Citi N.Y.		Chase N.Y.	
Reserves −10 million	London office dollar account −10 million	Reserves +10 million	London office dollar account +10 million

New York Fed	
	Reserves, Citibank −10 million Reserves, Chase +10 million

with Citi New York, must ask Citi New York to pay out this money with dollars that Citi New York has in its reserve account at the Fed. As this is done, offsetting changes naturally occur in the New York and London office dollar accounts at Citibank. Meanwhile, opposite but similar changes are occurring on the books of Chase London and Chase New York.

It is important to note that in this Euro loan transaction, just as in the Eurodollar deposit transaction we worked through above, the dollars never leave New York. The transaction simply results in a movement of $10 million from Citi's reserve account at the New York Fed to that of the Chase. One might, of course, argue that we have not yet gone far enough—that the Arab oil seller is going to spend the dollars he has received and that they might then leave the United States. But that is not so. Whoever gets the dollars the Arab spends will have to deposit them somewhere, and thus the spending by the Arab of his dollars will simply shift them from one bank's reserve account to another's. In this respect, it might be useful to recall a point made in Chapter 2. The only way reserves at the Fed can be increased or decreased in the aggregate is through open-market operations initiated by the Fed itself. The one exception to this statement is withdrawals of cash from the banking system. If the Arab oil seller were to withdraw $10 million in cash from Chase London and lock it up in a safe there or elsewhere, the dollars would, in effect, have actually left the United States. However, no big depositor would do that because of opportunity cost; Eurodeposits yield interest, whereas cash in a vault would not.

A Euro placement with a foreign bank

In the Euromarket banks routinely lend dollars to other banks by making deposits with them and borrow dollars from other banks by taking deposits from them. People in the Euromarket and people in New York with international experience always refer to the depositing of Eurodollars with another bank as a *placement* of funds and to the receipt of Eurodollar deposits from another bank as a *taking* of funds.

Table 6–4
A Eurodollar interbank placement

Chase London		Crédit Lyonnais, London	
(Euro) time deposit, Crédit Lyonnais, London +20 million New York office dollar account −20 million		Deposit, Morgan N.Y. +20 million	Time deposit, Chase London +20 million

Chase N.Y.		Morgan N.Y.	
Reserves −20 million	London office dollar account −20 million	Reserves +20 million	Deposits, Crédit Lyonnais, London +20 million

New York Fed	
	Reserves, Chase −20 million Reserves, Morgan +20 million

Other people in the U.S. money market are likely to use the jargon of the Fed funds market, referring to placements of Euros as sales of funds and to takings of Euros as purchases of funds.

To illustrate what happens when a foreign bank ends up holding a Eurodollar deposit, let's work through the mechanics of a placement of Eurodollars with such a bank. Assume that Chase London places a $20 million deposit in the London Branch of Crédit Lyonnais.

The special feature of this example is that Crédit Lyonnais, unlike an American bank, is not a member of the Federal Reserve System and consequently does not have a reserve account at the Fed. Thus, it has to keep its dollars on deposit in a U.S. bank. Suppose that, in this case, the dollars are deposited in a Crédit Lyonnais account at Morgan New York. Then, as Table 6–4 shows, the net effect of the transaction will be that Crédit Lyonnais ends up with dollars on deposit in New York, and reserves move from Chase's account at the Fed to Morgan's account. Note again that the dollars remain in New York, even though they are now held by the London branch of a French bank.

HISTORY OF THE MARKET

Anyone following Tables 6–1 through 6–4 is likely to wonder what the rationale is for carrying on huge volumes of dollar deposit and loan transactions outside the United States in what seems to be a rather complicated fashion. The best way to answer is to describe briefly the stimuli that gave birth to the Euromarket.

Long before World War II it was not uncommon for banks outside the United States to accept deposits denominated in dollars. The volume of such deposits, however, was small and the market for them had little economic significance. During the 1950s, things began to change. One reason was the activities of the communist central banks. Since Russia and other communist countries imported certain goods that had to be paid for in dollars and exported others that could be sold for dollars, the central banks of these countries ended up holding dollar balances. Initially these balances were held on deposit in New York, but as cold war tensions heightened, this practice became less attractive to the communists, who feared that, at some point, the United States might block their New York balances. As a result, they transferred these balances to banks in London and other European centers. The value of the dollar goods the communist countries wanted to import often exceeded the amount of dollars they were earning on exports, so these countries became not only important lenders to the Eurodollar market but also important borrowers in this market.

While the cold war may have kicked off the Euromarket, there were other factors that stimulated its development. Historically, the pound sterling played a key role in world trade. A great deal of trade not only within the British Commonwealth but also between Commonwealth nations and the rest of the world or between non-Commonwealth countries was denominated in British currency, the pound sterling, and financed in London through borrowings of sterling. After World War II, this began to change. Britain ran big balance of payments deficits (that is, spent more abroad than it earned), and, as a result, devaluation of the British pound—a decrease in the amount of foreign exchange for which a pound could be traded—was a constant threat and, in fact, actually occurred several times during the period of pegged exchange rates. The chronic weakness of the pound made it a less attractive currency to earn and to hold, which, in turn, stimulated the trend for more and more international trade to be denominated in dollars. It also caused the British to impose restrictions on the use of sterling for financing international trade. Specifically, in 1957, the British government restricted the use of sterling in financing trade between non–sterling-area countries, and in 1976 it restricted the use of sterling in financing trade between Commonwealth countries and non–sterling-area countries. Because of the increased use of dollars as the availability of sterling financing decreased, importers began borrowing Eurodollars to finance trade, and the Euromarket emerged first as a nascent and then as a fast-growing and important international capital market.

In this respect it is important to note that British banks played a leading role. Historically, these banks had a dominant place in financing world trade, so they had expertise other banks lacked. Given that expertise, British banks shrewdly took the view that they could finance international trade in whatever currency was available and acceptable: beads or, as happened to be the case, dollars.

U.S. banks were *not* leaders in the development of the Euromarket. Quite the contrary, they entered it step by step and always *defensively*—their fear being that their London activities would undercut their domestic operations. One U.S. banker, who was in London during the market's formative years, noted: "The story of how the U.S. banks entered the Euromarket reflects rather poorly on us because we did not think out where the market was going. It just sort of grew up on us."

During the early 1950s, when the Russian and East European banks began depositing dollars outside the United States, the London branches of U.S. banks were *not* taking Eurodollar deposits. They began to do so very hesitantly several years later when some of their good U.S. customers said to them: "Can't you take our dollar deposits in London? The foreign banks do, and they give us better rates than you can in New York because of Reg Q." For several years this worked out satisfactorily because the head offices of the U.S. banks involved could profitably use the dollars deposited with their London branches in the United States; this was so because the structure of loan and other interest rates in the United States was such that U.S. banks could well afford to pay higher rates than those permitted under Reg Q.

Then the London branches of U.S. banks began getting 3- and 6-month money which the head offices of U.S. banks did not want because it did not fit their books (asset and liability structure). So, again very defensively, the London branches of U.S. banks began making Eurodollar loans to commercial customers and placements of deposits with foreign banks. In doing so they said: "We are giving you this money but don't count on our continuing to do so because we don't know how long we will continue getting this funny money called Eurodollars." For years, U.S. banks did not view their Eurodollar activities with customers as traditional, ongoing banking relationships.

In its initial stages, the growth of the Euromarket was hampered by the myriad of exchange control regulations that all nations except the United States imposed on their residents with respect to (1) the use of domestic currency to acquire foreign exchange, and (2) the disposition of foreign exchange earnings. This changed in 1958 when the major European countries, with the exception of the United Kingdom, substantially liberalized their foreign exchange controls as a first step toward making their currencies fully convertible.

A fourth factor that stimulated the growth of the Euromarket was the operation of Regulation Q during the tight money years of 1968 and 1969. At that time, U.S. money market rates rose above the rates that banks were permitted to pay under Reg Q on domestic large-denomination CDs. In order to finance loans, U.S. banks were forced to borrow money in the Euromarket. All this resulted in a sort of merry-go-round operation. A depositor who normally would have put his money in, say, a Chase New York CD gave his money (perhaps via a Canadian bank because of U.S. controls on the export of capital) to Chase London, which then lent the money back to Chase New York. In effect, Reg Q forced a portion of the supply of bought money that money market banks were coming to rely on in funding to move through London and other Euro centers. The operation of Regulation Q also encouraged foreign holders of dollars who would have deposited them in New York to put their dollars in London. Thus, for example, surplus German dollars borrowed by Italians ended up passing through London instead of New York.

Another important stimulus to the Euromarket were the various capital controls instituted during the 1960s to improve the U.S. balance of payments, which was in deficit. The first of these, the Interest Equalization Tax passed in 1964, was designed to discourage the issuance by foreign borrowers of debt obligations in the U.S. market.

This measure was followed, in 1965, by the Foreign Credit Restraint Program, which limited the amount of credit U.S. banks could extend to foreign borrowers. Finally, in 1968, the government passed the Foreign Investment Program, which restricted the amount of domestic dollars U.S. corporations could use to finance foreign investments. Whatever the wisdom and effectiveness of these programs (they were eliminated in 1974), there is no doubt that they substantially increased the demand for dollar financing outside the United States, that is, for Eurodollar loans.

The persistent balance of payments deficits in the United States have often been given substantial credit for the development of the Euromarket. By spending more abroad than it earned, the United States, in effect, put dollars into the hands of foreigners and thus created a natural supply of dollars for the Euromarket. There is some truth to this, but it should be noted that U.S. balance of payments deficits are neither a necessary nor a sufficient condition for a thriving and growing Euromarket. After all, foreigners can deposit dollars in New York *and* domestic holders of dollars can place them in London. Where dollars are held need not be a function of who owns them, it is quite often a function of the relative attractiveness of the domestic and the Euromarkets to depositors. What has made the Euromarket attractive to depositors and given it much of its vitality is the freedom from restrictions under which this market operates, in particular the absence of the implicit tax that exists on U.S. domestic banking activities because of the reserve requirements imposed by the Fed.

A final important stimulus was given to the Euromarket by the hike in the price of oil that occurred in 1974. Due to that price rise, the Organization of Petroleum Exporting Countries (OPEC) suddenly found member nations holding massive balances of dollars, which they deposited in the Euromarket. Meanwhile, many countries that were importers of oil experienced severe balance of payments difficulties and were forced to borrow dollars in the Euromarket to pay for their oil imports.

Just as dollars can be deposited in banks and bank branches outside the United States to create Eurodollars, the currencies of European countries can also be deposited outside their country of origin and thereby give rise to other types of *Eurocurrency deposits*. For example, German marks deposited in London in exchange for a mark balance are *Euromarks*. The major currencies other than dollars in which Eurocurrency deposits are held are German marks, British pounds, and Swiss francs (*Swissy* to the irreverent). There is also a limited market in Dutch guilders and rather difficult markets in other currencies. While the Euromarket is still primarily a dollar market, Eurodeposits of other currencies are an important and growing part of the total market.

THE MARKET TODAY

From the inception of the Eurodollar market, London has been its biggest and most important center. That this role fell to London is hardly surprising. London has a long history as a world center for a host of financial activities: international lending, trade financing, commodities trading, stock trading, foreign exchange trading, insurance, and others. In truth, that square mile of London known as the *City of London,* or more often as just the *City,* is and has been since the 19th century the financial capital of the world.

Some of the many factors that contributed to London's development as an international financial center were the freedom and flexibility with which financial institutions were permitted to operate there. That freedom and flexibility still prevail, and because they do, London—with its huge concentration of financial expertise—was the logical place for the nascent Euromarket to develop and flourish. Throughout London's history as a Euro center, foreign banks have been permitted to open London branches and subsidiaries with ease and operate these branches and subsidiaries with a minimum of regulation. The Bank of England has imposed no specific capital requirements on the London branches of foreign banks, and it has imposed no reserve requirements on the Eurocurrency deposits they accept. Britain taxes the profits earned by foreign bank branches and subsidiaries, but has imposed no withholding taxes on the interest banks pay to nonresident depositors.

While London has remained the preeminent center of the Euromarket, other centers have also developed over time. The Euromarket is, after all, a worldwide market. In the Far East in particular, Singapore and Hong Kong have both become important centers for Asian trading in Eurodollars. These centers suffer the disadvantage, however, that the natural sources of dollar supply and demand arising from trade and other activities in the Far East are not as great as those that focus on London, so their role remains a secondary one.

From the banks' point of view, one growing disadvantage of basing Euro operations in London is the high taxes that must be paid on profits earned there. Largely to avoid these taxes, *booking centers* have developed in several localities offering favorable tax treatment of profits—Bahrain in the Middle East, Nassau, and Grand Cayman, to name the most important. Banks that operate branches in these centers book there loans negotiated and made in London, New York, or elsewhere. They fund these loans either by having their branch buy money in its own name in the Eurodollar market or by funding the operation with dollars purchased in the name of their London branch. Nassau and Grand Cayman offer one important advantage over Bahrain; they are in the same time zone as New York and only one hour ahead of

Table 6-5
Eurocurrency market, based on foreign-currency liabilities of banks in major European countries, the Bahamas, Bahrain, Grand Cayman, Panama, Canada, Japan, Hong Kong, and Singapore ($ billions)

	1970	1971	1972	1973	1974	1975	1976	1977	1978	1979	1980	1981 March	1981 June
Estimated size:													
Gross	$110	$145	$210	$315	$395	$485	$595	$740	$950	$1,220	$1,515	$1,570	$1,575
Net	65	85	110	160	220	255	320	390	495	615	755	775	790
Eurodollars: as percent of all Euro-currencies—gross	81	76	78	74	76	78	80	76	74	72	74	75	77

Source: *World Financial Markets* (New York: Morgan Bank, 1981).

Chicago. Thus, it is easy for management in U.S. money market banks to direct their operations in these centers during normal working hours.

Next to London, the second most important center of the Euromarket is New York. Until the opening of international banking facilities (IBF), there, New York banks could not accept Eurodeposits, but New York still became an important center in Euro trading for several reasons.[3] First, the New York banks were active takers of Euros in the names of their Nassau and Cayman branches. There are also several foreign bank branches in New York that are active takers of Euros for the same reason. A second reason New York became an important trading center for Euros is that New York and other banks actively engaged in arbitrage between Euro and "domestic" dollars. A final reason for the prominence of New York as a Euro center is that many of the nation's largest banks direct their worldwide Euro operations from New York.

In addition to the major centers of the Euromarket we have described, there are numerous centers of lesser but growing importance, for example, Paris, Frankfurt, and Luxembourg in Europe. Many financial centers that would seem logical candidates to become Euro trading centers have, in fact, not done so. Generally, the reasons have to do with local exchange controls, bank regulations, taxation, or other inhibiting factors. Japanese banks, for example, are important participants in the Eurodollar market, but Tokyo has never become an important center of this market, in part because Japanese businesses have been restricted from incurring dollar-denominated liabilities.

From rather meager beginnings, the Euromarket has developed into a truly huge market. Unfortunately, it is impossible to say just how huge because there is no worldwide system for collecting data on the Eurocurrency market. The best figures available are probably the estimates made by Morgan Guaranty. Its figures (Table 6–5) cover Eurodeposits in all significant Euro centers. The *gross* figures in Table 6–5 include sizable amounts of interbank placements. Using estimates, Morgan eliminated these placements to get figures on the *net* amounts of Eurodollars and other Eurocurrencies that nonbank depositors have placed with banks in the reporting countries. From these net figures, it is evident that both Eurodollars and other Eurocurrency deposits have grown phenomenally over the last decade.

OVERVIEW OF BANK EURO OPERATIONS

In a very real sense, the Eurodollar market is a true international market without location, which means that for no bank is it a domestic

---

[3] For restrictions on deposit taking by IBFs, see Chapter 11.

market. Thus, every bank active in the market tends to compartmentalize its activities there, to think in terms of what Eurodollar assets and liabilities it has acquired. In the jargon of the market, every Eurobanker is running a *Eurodollar book.* In the case of foreign banks, the reason is obvious; they are dealing in a foreign currency, the dollar, which has limited availability to them at best. In the case of U.S. banks, the distinction between domestic and Euro operations arises from a less fundamental but still important consideration, namely, the fact that Fed reserve requirements and other factors create a real distinction between Eurodollars and domestic dollars, one that is of varying importance depending on economic conditions and on the maturities of the domestic and Eurodollar assets and liabilities compared.

Banking ground rules in the Euromarket are quite different from those that prevail on the U.S. banking scene, with the result that the character of U.S. bank operations in the Euromarket differs from that of their operations in the domestic money market. Thus, we will present a quick overview of bank Euro operations before we talk in detail about their deposit accepting and lending activities in this market.

The first important distinction between U.S. banks' domestic and Euro operations is in the character of their Euro liabilities. In the Euromarket all deposits, with the exception of call money, have a fixed maturity (*tenor* in British jargon) which may range anywhere from one day to five years. Also, interest is paid on all deposits, the rate being a function of prevailing economic conditions and the maturity of the deposit. While most bank Euro liabilities are straight time deposits, banks operating in the London market also issue Eurodollar CDs. Like domestic CDs, these instruments carry a fixed rate of interest, are issued for a fixed time span, and are negotiable.

A second important distinction between banks' domestic and Euro operations is that no reserve requirements are imposed against banks' Eurocurrency deposits. Thus, every dollar of deposits accepted can be invested.

Banks accepting Eurodollar deposits use these dollars to make two sorts of investments, loans and interbank placements. All placements, like other Eurodeposits, have fixed maturities and bear interest. The market for Eurodollar deposits, nonbank and interbank, is highly competitive, and the rates paid on deposits of different maturities are determined by market supply and demand. Since the Euromarket operates outside the control of any central bank, there are no Reg Q or other controls limiting or setting the rates that Eurodollars can command. As one might expect, Euro rates are volatile, rising when money is tight and falling when it is easy.

The rate at which banks in London offer Eurodollars in the placement market is referred to as the *London interbank offered rate,* or

LIBOR, for short. In pricing Euro loans, LIBOR is of crucial importance.

In the Euromarket, unlike the domestic market, all loans have fixed maturities, which can range anywhere from a few days to five years or longer. The general practice is to price all loans at *LIBOR plus a spread.* On some term loans, the lending rate is fixed for the life of the loan. By far the more usual practice, however, is to price term loans on a *rollover basis.* This means that every 3 or 6 months the loan is repriced at the then-prevailing LIBOR for 3- or 6-month money plus the fixed, agreed-upon spread. For example, a 1-year loan might be rolled after 6 months, which means that the first 6-month segment would be priced at the agreed-upon spread plus the 6-month LIBOR rate prevailing at the time the loan was granted, while the second 6-month segment would be priced at the same spread plus the 6-month LIBOR rate prevailing 6 months later. On Euro loans, banks never require the borrower to hold compensating balances.

Running a bank's Eurodollar book boils down to much the same thing as running its domestic book. The bank must decide what assets to hold and what liabilities to use to fund them. In making decisions with respect to its Euro assets and liabilities, the bank faces the same *risks* it does in its domestic operations—credit risk, liquidity risk, and rate risk. In its Euro operations, as in its domestic operations, a bank's objective is to maximize profits subject to the constraint that risks are held to an acceptable level.[4]

In a bank's Euro book, credit risk exists both on ordinary loans and on interbank placements, which—like sales of Fed funds—are unsecured loans. To control risk on ordinary loans, banks have credit standards for borrowers as well as limits on the amount they will lend to any one borrower. On placements with other banks, credit risk is controlled, as in the case of Fed funds sales, by setting up lines of credit that limit the amount the bank will lend to any other banking institution. As noted below, banks also use lines to limit what is called *country risk.*

Because most of a Eurobanker's assets and liabilities have fixed maturities, it would be possible for a Eurobanker, unlike a domestic banker, to run a *matched book,* that is, to fund every 3-month asset with 3-month money, every 6-month asset with 6-month money, and so on. If he did so, moreover, he would reduce his rate risk to zero because every asset would be financed for its duration at a locked-in positive spread. He would also minimize his liquidity risk, but he would not eliminate it, since on rollover loans he would still have to return periodically to the market to obtain new funding.

---

[4] The case for a bank running not a domestic *and* a Euro book, but rather a single *global* book, is made in Chapter 11.

While running a matched book would reduce risk, it would also limit the bank's opportunity to earn profits in an important and traditional way—by lending long and borrowing short. Eurobankers are aware of the profit opportunities that a mismatched book offers, and to varying degrees they all create a conscious mismatch in their Eurodollar books—one that is carefully monitored by the head office to prevent unacceptable risks. How great a maturity mismatch a given bank will permit in its Euro book depends on various factors: the shape of the yield curve, its view on interest rates, and its perception of its own particular liquidity risk. If a bank is running a global book, the size and nature of the mismatch it will want in its Euro book will depend in part on the nature of the interest rate exposure of its domestic book.

THE INTERBANK PLACEMENT MARKET

The pool of funds that forms the basis for the Eurodollar market is provided by a varied cast of depositors: large corporations (domestic, foreign, and multinational), central banks and other government bodies, supranational institutions such as the Bank for International Settlements (BIS), and wealthy individuals. Most of these funds are in the form of time deposits with fixed maturities. The banks, however, also receive substantial amounts of *call money,* which can be withdrawn by the depositor on a day's notice. Banks normally offer a fixed rate for call money, which they adjust periodically as market conditions change. To the holder, the major attraction of a call money deposit is liquidity. Time deposits pay more, but a penalty is incurred if such a deposit is withdrawn before maturity. From the point of view of the banks, call money is attractive because, with a positively sloped yield curve, it is cheap. Also, despite its short-term nature, call money turns out to be a fairly stable source of funds, so much so that a big bank might, in running its Euro book, feel comfortable viewing half of its call money deposits as essentially long-term funds.

Banks receiving Eurodeposits frequently choose, for reasons discussed below, to place some portion of the deposits given to them with other banks, often while simultaneously taking deposits of other maturities. As a result of all this buying and selling, a very active, high-volume market in interbank placements has developed. This market is worldwide. It also has a huge number of participants, which reflects two facts. First, banks from countries all over the world participate in the market. Second, every one of a bank's foreign branches (and many U.S., European, and Japanese banks have large numbers of them) participates in this market as a separate entity. This means, for example, that Citibank's foreign branches in London, Singapore, Nassau, and elsewhere all take and place Eurodollars in their own names.

Because there are so many players in the Eurodollar market and because they are scattered all over the globe, it would be difficult and costly for all of them to communicate their bids and offers for deposits directly to each other. To fill the gap, a number of firms have gone into the business of brokering Euro time deposits.

While the proportion of total Euro placements that is brokered is significant, not all such placements pass through the brokers' market. In particular, a fair amount of money is sold by continental banks to big London bidders on a direct basis, with the London bidder quoting rates based on those prevailing in the brokers' market. Also, a bank branch normally won't trade with another branch of the same bank through brokers, since the two communicate directly with each other.

A bank placing funds in the interbank market faces two risks. First, there is the *credit risk* which banks seek to control through the use of credit lines. In establishing lines to foreign banks, a U.S. bank will look at the normal criteria of credit worthiness such as size, capitalization, profitability, and reputation. In addition, a bank will be concerned about *country* or *sovereign risk*. Specifically, it will consider various factors about the bank's country of origin that might influence either the bank's viability or its ability to meet commitments denominated in a foreign currency. Of particular interest would be factors such as whether the country of origin was politically stable, whether nationalization on terms unfavorable to foreign depositors was a possibility, and whether the country's balance of payments was reasonably strong.

There's also a second aspect of sovereign risk that banks placing Eurocurrency deposits with other banks worry about. A bank selling Euros to, say, the London branch of the Bank of Tokyo must be concerned not only about the credit worthiness of that bank and the country risk, but also about the economic and political climate in London: Is it conceivable that by nationalizing foreign bank branches, freezing their assets, or some other action the British might render it impossible for these branches to honor their commitment to repay borrowed dollars? Questions of this sort are less of a concern with respect to London than with respect to smaller and newer Euro centers such as Bahrain and Nassau. Banks seek to limit the sovereign risk to which they are exposed by imposing limits on their lendings and interbank placements in a given country.[5]

The administration of these limits requires much painstaking work for several reasons. First, two sets of limits apply, country limits and limits on individual banks. Second, for Bank A to keep track of how much credit in the form of Eurodollar placements it has granted to Bank B, it has to track the Euro sales of *all* its branches to *all* Bank B's branches. Third, at the same time that Bank A is selling Euros to Bank

---

[5] On sovereign risk, also see Chapter 11.

B, it will also be granting credit to Bank B in other ways, for example, through the sale of Fed funds or via letters of credit.

Granting lines to buyers of Eurodollars used to be done more casually and less cautiously than it is now. In 1974, the Bankhaus I D Herstatt, a medium-sized German bank, failed under conditions that left several banks, along with other creditors, standing in line to get funds due them. This event, along with the difficulties experienced during the same year by the Franklin National Bank, sent shock waves through the Euromarket and caused banks to review with an air of increased caution the lines they had granted to other banks. The upshot was that many smaller banks lost the lines they had enjoyed, and they experienced difficulty buying Euros; some were even forced out of the market. *Tiering* also developed in market rates, with banks that were judged poorer credit risks being forced to pay up. In particular, the Japanese banks that are consistently big net takers of Euros had to pay up 1 to 2 percent, and so did the Italian banks because of unfavorable economic and political developments within Italy. [6] Several years after the Herstatt crisis, the Euromarket regained much of the confidence it lost in 1974 and lines were again enlarged. Tiering, however, has remained a phenomenon in the market, being more pronounced the tighter money gets and the higher rates rise.

Most banks, because of their size, home nation, and customer base, tend to be natural net sellers or buyers of Euros. However, it's important for a bank that wants to buy Euros to also sell them some of the time, since one way a bank gets lines from other banks is by placing deposits with them. In the Euromarket, as in the Fed funds market, some banks have to buy their way in.

EURO CERTIFICATES OF DEPOSIT

Because Eurodollar time deposits, with the exception of call money, have fixed maturities, from the point of view of many investors they have one serious disadvantage, namely, illiquidity. To satisfy investors who needed liquidity, Citibank began issuing *Eurodollar certificates of deposit* in London. Its example was quickly followed by other U.S. and foreign banks with London branches.

Because of the liquidity of Euro CDs, issuing banks are able to sell them at rates slightly below those offered on time deposits of equivalent maturity, ⅛ to ¼ percent less when the market is quiet. While Euro CDs were originally designed for corporations and other investors who wanted real liquidity, following the Herstatt incident an interesting development occurred. Many smaller banks and foreign

---

[6] For the flight of depositors to quality caused by failure of the Herstatt, see Chapter 14.

banks, as well, felt the need for the appearance of greater liquidity in their Eurodollar books. To get it, they sold Euro CDs to other banks with the understanding that the bank buying them would never trade those CDs, and the buyer would moreover permit the selling bank to safekeep the CDs to ensure that this understanding was honored. CDs sold on these terms, known as *lockup CDs,* are very close to time deposits from the point of view of the issuing bank, and normally the rate paid on them is very close to the time deposit rate. While no figures are available, it is estimated by some that as much as 50 percent of all Euro CDs sold are lockup CDs; others put the figure much lower. Some of the remaining Euro CDs are purchased by Swiss banks for investors whose funds they manage; these CDs, too, are rarely traded. Most of the rest of the Euro CDs issued in London are sold to investors in the United States: corporations, domestic banks, and others.

Since the major advantage to the issuing bank of writing Euro CDs is that CD money is cheaper than time deposit money, banks issuing such CDs carefully limit the amount they write so that the spread between the rates at which they can buy CD money and time deposit money is preserved. To issue CDs, the banks normally post daily rates, the attractiveness of which reflects both their eagerness to write and the maturities in which they want to take money. Occasionally, when the banks are anxious to write, they will also issue through either London CD brokers or U.S. money market dealers who have set up shop in London. These brokers and dealers also make a secondary market for Euro CDs, without which these instruments would have liquidity in name only. The Euro CD market is smaller than the domestic CD market, and Euro CDs are less liquid than domestic CDs.

EURO LENDING

Today the Eurodollar market is *the* international capital market of the world, which is very much reflected in the mix of borrowers that come to this market for loans. Their ranks include U.S. corporations funding foreign operations, foreign corporations funding foreign or domestic operations, foreign government agencies funding investment projects, and foreign governments funding development projects or general balance of payments deficits.

Lending terms

All Euro loans are, as we have said, priced at LIBOR plus a spread. Since different banks may be offering Eurodollars at not quite identical rates, the LIBO rate used in pricing a loan is usually the average of the 11:00 A.M. offering rates of three to five reference banks, the latter always being top banks in the market.

How great a spread over LIBOR a borrower is charged is a function of risk and market conditions. In a period of slack loan demand, a top borrower might be able to get funds at LIBOR plus as little as ½ percent. In contrast, a second-class credit shopping for a loan when money was tight might have to pay as much as LIBOR plus 2½ percent.

On rollover loans, which most Euro loans are today, a bank normally allows the borrower to choose whether to take 3-month or 6-month money each time a rollover date occurs. Banks will also grant a 1-year rollover option to good customers. However, they try to discourage the inclusion of this option in loan agreements because the thinness of the market in longer-term deposits means that match-funding maturities beyond six months can sometimes be difficult. What choice of maturity the borrower makes on a rollover date depends on whether he expects interest rates to rise or fall.

The bank may, at the borrower's request, also include in a loan agreement a *multicurrency clause* that permits the borrower to switch from one currency to another—say, from dollars to German marks—on a rollover date. Multicurrency clauses usually stipulate that nondollar funds will be made available to the borrower conditional upon "availability." This clause protects a bank from exchange control regulations and other factors which might dry up the market and prohibit the bank from acquiring the desired funds, even in the foreign exchange market.

While fixed-rate, fixed-term loans do occur in the Euromarket, they are uncommon. Banks are generally unwilling to make them unless they match fund, a policy which makes such loans so expensive that the borrower is likely to conclude his funding cost over the life of the loan would be less with a rollover loan. Also, a prime borrower willing to pay up to lock in a fixed borrowing rate may find a Euro bond issue cheaper than a fixed-rate term loan.

The maximum maturity that Eurobankers will grant on term loans generally is around 7 years, although some banks are willing to go to 10. In judging what maturity it will grant on a specific loan, a bank will consider the borrower's underlying need (what is he financing?), his ability to repay, and—if the loan is to be shared by several banks—what the market will accept. Typically, the more slack loan demand, the longer the maturity that is acceptable.

Often term loans extended to finance capital projects have an *availability period* during which the borrower receives funds according to some prearranged schedule based on his anticipated needs. The availability period may be followed by a grace period during which no repayment of principal is required. After that, the normal procedure is for the loan to be amortized over its remaining life. Some *bullet loans* with no amortization are granted, but they are the exception not the rule.

On Euro loans, the standard practice has been to disallow prepayment, but some agreements do permit it on rollover dates with, sometimes without, payment of a penalty. To gain greater flexibility, the borrower can negotiate a *revolving facility*, which during the life of the loan agreement, permits him to take down funds, repay them, and take them down again if he so chooses.

The fact that Euro loans are made to borrowers all over the world could create considerable legal complications for lenders, especially in the case of default. To minimize these, Euro loan agreements generally specify that the loan is subject to either U.S. or British law.

Many Euro loans granted to U.S. corporations by U.S. banks are negotiated at the bank's head office in the United States. This is particularly likely to be the case if the loan is granted to a foreign subsidiary that is kept financially anemic because it is operating in a weak-currency country, or if management of the overall firm is strongly centralized. If, on the other hand, the sub is financially strong and its management is largely autonomous, negotiation for a Euro loan will occur abroad, frequently in London.[7]

Loan syndication

Over time, syndication of Euro loans has become increasingly common. There are various reasons a bank might choose to syndicate a loan. On corporate loans for big projects (e.g., development of North Sea oil sources) the amount required might exceed a bank's legal lending limit, or the bank might not choose to go to that limit in the interests of diversifying risk. On country loans, the basic chip can be $1 billion or more, and there is no bank that could write that sort of business alone. Country loans often are for such huge amounts these days because certain borrowers, especially underdeveloped countries, are financing big development projects. Other countries with substantial borrowing needs are financing balance of payments deficits that they have incurred in part because the prices of oil and other raw material imports have risen sharply.

Big Euro loan syndication agreements are negotiated in London. Often the lead bank is a top U.S. bank, but in recent years German banks have become more aggressive in this area. While many of the banks that participate in a typical Euro syndication are based in London, it is not uncommon for continental banks and even domestic U.S. banks with no London branch to take a piece of such loans. Doing so

[7] For the impact of Euro lending on domestic lending practices, see Chapters 11 and 13.

may provide them with both a good rate and a chance to diversify their assets.

Loan syndication normally starts with the borrower accepting the loan terms proposed by a bank and giving that bank a mandate to put together a credit for it. Most such agreements are on a *fully underwritten basis,* which means the lead bank guarantees that the borrower will get all of the money stipulated in the loan proposal.

Since the amount guaranteed is more than the lead bank could come up with alone, it selects *comanagers* that help underwrite the loan. Once the lead bank and the comanagers have split up the loan into shares, they have about two weeks to sell off whatever portion of their underwriting share they do not want to take into portfolio. At the end of this selling period, the lead bank advises the borrower[8] as to what banks have participated in the syndication. Then the borrower and these banks attend a closing at which the final loan agreement is signed. Two days later, the borrower gets his money. From the point of view of the lender, participation in a syndicated loan carries a commitment to lend for the life of the loan, since such participations are rarely sold by one bank to another.

A number of different fees are charged on a loan syndication. First there is the management fee, which may run from as low as ⅜ percent to 1 percent or more, depending on market conditions and the borrower's name. Normally the lead bank shares some portion of this front-end fee with the banks that take significant portions of the total loan into portfolio.

A second fee the borrower pays is a spread over LIBOR on whatever funds he takes down. The borrower also pays a commitment fee, generally around .25 percent, on any monies committed but not drawn. Finally, there is an agency fee that goes to the bank responsible for interfacing between the lending banks and the borrower, that is, for the receipt and disbursement of loan proceeds and for general supervision of the operation of the credit agreement.

Merchant banks. A British bank can engage in a much wider range of activities than a U.S. bank can. There has, however, tended to be some degree of specialization between different British banks. In particular, the so-called *merchant banks* have specialized primarily in providing not loans of their own funds, but various financial services to their customers. These include accepting bills arising out of trade, underwriting new stock and bond issues, and advising corporate customers on acquisitions, mergers, foreign expansion, and portfolio management.

While loan syndication can be done directly by a bank, it has be-

---

[8] Borrowers frequently participate in this selection of participants.

come increasingly common for large U.S. banks to set up separate merchant banking subsidiaries with the principal function of syndicating loans. Loans are also syndicated by consortium banks, that is, by banks set up and jointly owned by several banks, frequently from different nations.

One reason that several top U.S. banks have opened merchant banking arms in London is that these subs can engage in activities, such as bond underwriting, that the branch itself could not because of the Glass-Steagall Act. Another reason is that some U.S. banks feel merchant banking activities, including loan syndication, are a different sort of business from commercial banking—one that requires deals-oriented money raisers and more continuity of personnel than is found in commercial banking. As one banker put it: "Merchant banking is using other people's assets and getting paid a fee for it; the other people in this case may include anyone in the market, including the parent bank. In loan syndications where we add value is by taking a view on price, terms, conditions, and amounts that can be done for a borrower and by then assembling the group which will manage and sell the issue."

Most U.S. banks' merchant banking subs do not keep substantial amounts of the loans they syndicate on their own books. Their objective is to provide the parent bank with the portion of the loan it wants and sell the rest to the market. One reason for this approach is that the parent bank has a comparative advantage over the sub in funding. It has a stronger name in which to buy funds, and it has experienced dealers and other funding personnel that the merchant bank could duplicate only at considerable expense, if at all.

Consortium banks.   A number of U.S. banks, in addition to or instead of setting up merchant banking subsidiaries, have joined with other banks to form consortium banks. These carry out many of the same activities as their merchant banking subs do. The objectives of U.S. banks in joining such groups have been mixed, depending on the size and experience of the bank. Some smaller banks joined to be able to participate in medium-term Euro financing. Other banks joined to gain experience in international financial markets in general, in specific geographic markets, or in new lines of business. Consortia formed by large banks provide a large standing capability for syndicating loans, and consortia are active in this area.

Euro lines

In addition to granting straight loans, Eurobankers grant lines of credit to a varied group of borrowers, including both domestic and foreign firms issuing commercial paper in the U.S. market.

Euro lines, unlike U.S. lines, are granted on a strict fee basis; no compensating balances are required. Many Euro lines are committed revolvers that legally commit the bank to provide the line holder with funds if he requests them. Eurobankers, however, have also granted Eurodollar and multicurrency lines on a more or less no-material-change-in-circumstances basis.

In the Euromarket and in foreign banking in general, some of the most important lines granted by banks are not lines to customers but lines to other banks. A French bank operating a dollar book in the London or New York market is running a book in a foreign currency, and so is a U.S. bank running a French franc book in Paris or a sterling book in London. All these banks worry with good reason about liquidity, that is, about their ability on a continuing basis to fund in a foreign currency the various assets they have acquired that are denominated in that currency.

To reduce the risks in running books denominated in foreign currencies, many of the major banks of the world have set up reciprocal line agreements. Under such agreements, a big French bank that naturally is going to have better access than a U.S. bank to the domestic French franc market would agree to provide a U.S. bank with francs in a time of crisis. In exchange, the U.S. bank would extend to the French bank a promise to supply it with dollars should its access to dollar funding be threatened.[9]

Euro loans for domestic purposes

While the bulk of Euro lending is to foreign borrowers or to U.S. corporations that are funding foreign operations, a growing number of U.S. corporations have been borrowing money in the Euromarket for domestic purposes. Their major reason for doing so is to reduce their borrowing costs. Frequently, the rate quoted on a Euro loan by a bank's London branch will be cheaper than the *all-in* cost (prime plus compensating balances) quoted by the same bank on a domestic loan, a situation that one top U.S. bank executive described as "sillier than hell."

There are several reasons for this price discrepancy. First, reserve requirements, which prevail in domestic banking but not in Eurobanking, constitute in effect a tax on domestic banking that tends to force domestic lending rates above Euro rates. Second, U.S. banks have only a single prime based on 90-day money market rates. With an upward-sloping yield curve from 1 day out to 90, this arrangement naturally penalizes borrowers who want very short-term money. In the Euromarket there is no such penalty. A 1-month loan is priced at

---

[9] For a more detailed discussion, see Chapter 13.

LIBOR for 1-month money plus a spread, an all-in rate that may be significantly less than LIBOR on 3-month money plus the same spread. In effect, Eurobankers charge *money market rates* on loans, while domestic bankers until recently did not.[10]

The potential advantages of borrowing in the Euromarket have led large U.S. corporations to exert pressure on their banks to grant them *either/or facilities,* that is, to permit them to borrow from their bank's head office or a foreign branch as they desire. Historically, the banks resisted, citing the importance of customer relationships, loyalty, and other factors. They had two reasons for doing so. First, their profit margin was likely to be larger on a domestic loan than on a Euro loan. Second, they knew they could not be competitive in the market for Euro loans. When a U.S. bank lends Eurodollars to a domestic borrower for domestic purposes, it incurs under Reg D a small reserve requirement, which forces it to raise the Euro rate it quotes to a domestic borrower a slight fraction above the rate it quotes to foreign borrowers. Foreign banks lending into the United States used to incur no such reserve requirement and thus were in a position to consistently underprice U.S. banks on such loans. Today foreign bank branches in the United States are subject to reserve requirements, and either/or facilities have become a common feature of U.S. bank lending agreements with large borrowers.

RUNNING A EURO BOOK

In running their Eurodollar books, the big U.S. banks have taken several decades to develop strategies that are sophisticated and with which they feel comfortable. One reason is that the top executives of money market banks were and often still are people with little experience in international business. Also, during the early years of the Euromarket, no one really understood the market or knew where it was going. Gradually, of course, market expertise developed in London, but that spread only slowly across the Atlantic. Thus, when the London branches of the big U.S. banks began running dollar books, the edict went out from home offices that asset and liability maturities were to be matched to minimize rate and liquidity risks.

The emphasis on matching continued for some time. In fact, it has only been since the early 1970s that U.S. banks have become willing to mismatch their Euro books aggressively to increase profits. Oddly enough, the Herstatt crisis probably contributed to their willingness to do so. As it blew over, bankers concluded that, if the Euromarket survived Herstatt, it was mature enough to survive anything.

---

[10] Recent changes in U.S. bank domestic lending practices, particularly the development of subprime lending and of short-term advances, are covered in Chapter 11.

Today, all the major U.S. banks have several foreign branches running Euro books, so their overall exposure to risk in the Euromarket is the sum of the risks associated with several separate branch books. So far as liability management is concerned, management's main concern is with the rate and liquidity risks that are created through the mismatch of the bank's consolidated Euro position. To control those risks, management sets up guidelines within which each branch is supposed to operate.

Obviously, there is no precise way to compare the risk associated with funding, say, a 3-month loan with overnight money versus lending 6-month money and funding the first 4 months with 4-month money. So head office guidelines take arbitrary and quite different forms. The purpose, however, is always the same—to limit the degree of mismatch the branch can practice.

Eurobankers often refer to the practice of lending long and borrowing short as running an *open book*. The head office might, for example, control the mismatch on a branch's book by setting limits on the open positions that the branch could assume beyond two months, four months, and six months. An alternative approach is to apply different weights to the mismatches in different maturity ranges (larger weights, the longer the maturity range) and then require that the weighted sum of all mismatches be less than some maximum dollar figure.

The job of operating the branch's book under these guidelines falls to local funding officers. In the London branch of a large U.S. bank, there will be several senior people responsible for making overall policy decisions and a number of dealers under them who actually buy and sell money. Much of the work of the senior people involves formulating a view of what is likely to happen to interest rates and then deciding, in light of that view and current market conditions, what strategies should be followed in taking and placing deposits.

In making decisions of this sort, the Euro liability manager is in a position quite different from that of his domestic counterpart. As a London Eurobanker who moved to the New York head office put it:

> In the United States a bank doesn't have to work very hard on liability management; if the cost of money goes up, the bank puts the prime up. Thus buying long money involves taking a view that the bank doesn't really have to,[11] and the typical practice is for the bank to fund the bulk of its domestic loans with short or very short money. In the Euromarket, in contrast, the only assets the bank can take on are fixed-rate, fixed-maturity assets. Thus, the Eurobanker who mismatches incurs a very real rate risk, and the existence of this risk forces him to constantly make interest rate predictions and to structure his asset and liability maturities accordingly.

[11] *Taking a view* is a London expression for forming an opinion as to where interest rates are going and acting on it.

If a Eurobanker expects interest rates to stay steady or fall, he will tend to lend long and borrow short, i.e., run a *short* book, assuming a normally shaped yield curve. How short depends in part on the slope of the yield curve. As one banker noted: "There's no incentive to take money at call and put it out for three or six months for a ¼ or ⅜ths spread. With a flat yield curve like that, you are taking a tremendous risk for little reward; if rates back up, you are left with a negative carry. But when the yield curve is steep, say a 1 percent spread between call and 1-year rates, there is a real incentive to overlend and take the spread."

As interest rates became high and highly volatile at the end of the 1970s, banks began imposing much tighter limits on the mismatch positions branch treasuries could assume. Also, the growing tendency for banks to globalize their world book led to a situation in which the head offices of a number of banks were dictating to their branches the positions the latter should run (see Chapter 11).

The dealers

Once a decision about the maturity structure of a branch's assets and liabilities is made, the responsibility for implementing this decision falls on the chief dealer and his assistants. The London dealing room of a large bank is a fascinating and busy place, populated during trading hours by a bevy of time deposit and foreign exchange traders engaged in rapid-fire, nonstop conversations with brokers and large customers.

The "book" that is thrust into the chief dealer's care is a sheet of data giving the current amounts and maturities of all the branch's assets and liabilities. The salient features of this book are something a good dealer keeps in his head—the mismatch in different maturities, the amounts of funds he is likely to have to buy or sell in coming days, and when and in what maturity ranges rate pressures from big rollovers might develop. On the basis of this information, the overall guidelines established for the branch, and the strategies set by local funding officers, the dealer's job is to do the necessary buying and placing of funds as profitably as possible for the bank. This may sound simple, but it leaves much room for the exercise of tactics and judgment.

On every Eurodollar loan a bank makes and funds, it has three potential sources of profit. First, there is the spread the bank gets over LIBOR, which compensates it for operating expenses and the credit risk it is assuming. Second, there is the extra $1/16$th or $1/8$th percent that the bank may be able to make if its dealers can pick up the needed funds a little below LIBOR, for example, through astute timing of the purchase. A third way a bank can profit from a loan is through mismatching its book.

While major decisions about mismatch are made by senior funding officers, the dealer has and needs some leeway in implementing them. When a big syndicated loan rolls over and a lot of banks are in the market trying to "match fund" their participation in the loan, a good dealer may find that he is forced to mismatch—buy funds in anticipation of need or pick them up later—if he does not want to overpay for his money.

In this respect it's worth noting that when the Eurodollar market was younger, a big rollover could cause a perceptible if temporary upward bulge in Euro rates. This is less true today because of banks' increasing willingness to mismatch and because of the market's increasing depth. In fact, today a $1 billion loan rollover can occur with minimal impact on market rates.

Eurobankers take time deposits from two sources, bank customers and the bank placement market. A major bank branch in London will have several people whose job is to contact major depositors, such as big corporate customers (e.g., the oil companies), certain central banks, and other big depositors. Unlike the time deposit dealers, these customer representatives have time to chat with depositors about market conditions and rates. The banks like to pick up money this way since it saves them brokerage. Also, at times, such money may be cheaper than what they could pick up in the interbank market. That depends on the sophistication of the depositor.

Banks that are large takers of funds also try to cultivate direct relationships with other banks. Banks, unlike corporations, can go into the brokers' market to take Eurodollars. Thus, a bank attempting to pick up money directly from other banks tries to save brokerage to post fair bid rates for different maturities and to suggest, indirectly at least, that sellers go elsewhere on days that it is posting noncompetitive rates because it does not need money. In this respect it's interesting to note that a major bank that posts noncompetitive rates may still pick up deposits either because the lender has lines to only a few banks or because his lines to other banks are full.

While large banks prefer to get money directly to save brokerage, brokers are extremely useful to them. For one thing, although brokers have to be paid, they save the banks money on both communications and personnel. A funding officer for one of the largest U.S. banks estimated offhand that without the brokers, he would need 200 telephone lines and 50 dealers to run his London dealing room. The brokers are also useful to a bank that suddenly discovers it has an hour to raise $200 million of short-dated funds, an amount that might take some time to dig out directly. A third advantage the brokers offer is the cloak of anonymity. As a funding officer at the London branch of one of the largest U.S. banks put it: "Suppose I want to sell $50 million and I call a bank direct, one which would have been prepared to do that transaction in the brokers' market. He sees that it is my bank on the other side and he gets nervous and wonders—what are they trying to do, $50 million or $200 million? So he does a $10 million deal and now not only have I not done the transaction, but also I have disclosed the amount I am trying to do." Anonymity in this respect is useful for all the top banks. They are a bit like bulls in a barnyard; whenever they move, their smaller companions get nervous.

Euro placements

One of the curious things about the Euromarket, at least to the uninitiated, is that many participants in the market are busily taking deposits with the right hand and placing them with the left. In the beginning, interbank placements may have been made partly out of a concern for balance sheet cosmetics. In domestic operations, it's not considered proper for a bank to loan out all the funds it takes in, the idea being that this would leave the bank with no liquid assets to sell and thus with a potential liquidity problem. For a money market bank, this notion makes little sense, but no U.S. bank, big or small, is going to get caught with no securities on its balance sheet. In their Euro operations, banks pick up few salable securities unless they run a Euro CD portfolio. Thus, especially in the early days of the Euromarket when matched funding was the rule, a book in which all assets were loans would have been logical and would have posed no great liquidity threat. It would, however, have looked bad according to the traditional criteria of bank management. Placements, which are not classed as loans but can be just as illiquid, do not present this difficulty. Thus, cosmetic considerations were one incentive for Euro placements. Once banks became willing to mismatch, *profits* became another incentive.

A domestic bank that has a strong view on where interest rates are going is hard put to place a big bet based on that view. If it expects interest rates to fall, there is no interbank market in which it can sell long-dated money in volume; since a savvy corporate treasurer is likely to have the same interest rate view that the bank does, his bank is not going to get him to take out a fixed-rate term loan at such a time. If, alternatively, a domestic banker expects rates to rise, he will want to buy long-dated money, but he has no place where he can do this in volume. Whatever his expectations, his options for structuring maturities are limited.

In the Euromarket things are different. A bank can't order its customers to take fixed-rate term loans whenever it would like them to, but in the placement market a bank can buy and sell funds in reasonable volume over a wide range of maturities. There are several reasons for the contrast in maturity options between the U.S. market and the Euromarket. First, the Euromarket is traditionally more accustomed to dealing in longer dates. On the deposit side in particular there have always been some suppliers of funds who were concerned primarily with preservation and safety of principal as opposed to maximizing return and were willing, for a spread, to supply long-dated funds to credit worthy banks. The ranks of such depositors have been joined in recent years by the Arabs, who are willing to offer top banks deposits with maturities as long as five years to stockpile oil income earmarked for financing planned investments.

The contrast in maturity options between the U.S. market and the Euromarket also reflects differences in the positions of banks operating there. The natural customer base of a foreign bank, for example, will include firms that don't have the same access to dollar financing that U.S. firms have in the domestic capital market, and that therefore may choose to borrow on terms different from those on which a large U.S. corporation would. Also, because the dollar is not their domestic currency, foreign banks are and should be more anxious to match fund than U.S. banks are. Smaller regional U.S. banks are in a somewhat similar position; they do not have the assurance that, say, Citi or Morgan has that they will be able to buy whatever money they need whenever they need it. Liquidity considerations are a final reason that a foreign bank might want to buy long-dated funds, whereas a top U.S. bank would not. Especially since the Herstatt crisis, foreign banks operating in the Euromarket have been concerned with liquidity, and one way they can get it is by buying, say, 1-year money and lending it out short term.

Placements are generally less profitable than loans are, because they don't offer the built-in spread over LIBOR. But because of the maturity options in the placement market, they at times offer attractive possibilities for speculating on interest rate changes. Assuming a positively sloped yield curve, such speculation is more attractive when interest rates are expected to fall than when they are expected to rise. A bank that expects interest rates to fall will lend long and borrow short. In doing so it gets paid for taking a view (the spread between the long lending rate and the lower short borrowing rate) *and,* if the bank is right, it earns something extra as the borrowing rate falls.

Alternatively, if a bank expects rates to rise, the natural strategy is for it to lend short and borrow long. Doing so will, however, cost the bank money, so it will come out ahead only if it is right and rates do rise sharply. Some banks, when they expect rates to rise will, instead of borrowing long and lending short, continue the pattern of lending long and funding short. Or they will fund in a barbell fashion, taking both very short and very long (six months and over) deposits. The success of this strategy depends on the speed and extent of the rate rise. A number of studies have shown that, during a period of rising rates, the barbell strategy provides funds at the cheapest cost because rates frequently do not rise quickly or sharply enough to offset the advantages of the cheap, short-dated funds used.

While there is a lot of variability, it would not be unusual to find the London branch of a large U.S. bank holding 50 percent of its Euro assets in placements and 50 percent in loans.

Mismatch strategies

Because of rollovers, most assets that a bank in the Euromarket is financing have original interest-rate maturities of three or six months, although some may go longer. In financing these, a bank can mismatch in various ways. The most extreme approach would be to rely on overnight money. Doing so would normally create the greatest positive spread from mismatch, but it would also expose the bank to the greatest rate risk. An alternative approach would be to fund a new asset for part of its life. For example, a bank might fund a 6-month asset with 4-month money (*buy 4s against 6s*, in the jargon of the trade) and then fund the remaining 2 months with overnight money or a purchase of 2-month Euros. One consideration in plotting this sort of strategy is the maturities that are most actively traded in the Euromarket. Funding a 6-month asset with, say, 1-month money would leave the bank, which planned to match fund the tail of the asset, in need of 5-month money, a maturity in which the market is thin.

If a bank buys 4s against 6s or pursues some similar strategy, it creates an open position in its book and thereby assumes a rate risk. One way it can seek to eliminate that risk while simultaneously locking in a profit from the mismatch is by entering into a *forward forward* contract, that is, *buying money of a fixed maturity for future delivery.* In the example above, the appropriate forward forward contract would be for 2-month money to be delivered 4 months hence. In the Euromarket, there is a certain amount of trading in forward forwards, but the market is thin.

The seller of a forward forward assumes rate exposure because he cannot be sure of how much it will cost him to fund that commitment. Therefore, he will not enter into such a contract unless he is compensated for his risk. In our example, the seller of 2-month money 4 months hence will want to get something more than the rate he expects to prevail on 2-month money 4 months hence. For his part, if the borrower is locking up a profit on his mismatch, he might well be willing to pay some premium on the forward forward contract. Another reason a buyer and seller might strike a forward forward deal is that they entertain diverse opinions with respect to where interest rates are headed.[12]

In an interesting book on Eurobanks, Steven Davis, a Eurobanker, statistically tested the results of several arbitrary strategies for mis-

---

[12] The recent development of Eurodollar futures trading certainly augments and may replace this activity.

matching over time. His conclusion was that, while mismatching is common in the Euromarket, it is not profitable over the long run.[13] This conclusion tends to surprise funding officers who have long experience in the Euromarket. Most of them claim that over time they can and have made money through mismatching. Perhaps one reason is that they follow more flexible strategies than those tested by Davis.

Another factor worth mentioning in this regard is that, in the game of mismatching, the big U.S. banks have a considerable advantage over their competitors in forecasting Euro rates. One reason is that Euro rates tend to track U.S. rates very closely, with U.S. rates generally doing the leading. This means that banks active in the U.S. money market with a close feel for developments there, i.e., domestic banks, have an edge over their foreign brethren in predicting Euro rates.

Also, the bigger the bank, the better the input it is likely to get from its head office and the more intimate the contact between London and the head office is likely to be. As the chief dealer in the London branch of a top U.S. bank put it:

> We get tremendous input from New York. I speak to people there two hours every afternoon on the phone. Also, the foreign exchange desk next to mine has a direct line open to New York at all times, and we have direct telex, too. All that information permits us to quickly build up a feel for conditions in the U.S. market. There's no way a smaller bank or a foreign bank can get access to the same information. They can read it tomorrow in the paper; we get it right away. That's important because in this market half an hour sometimes makes a big difference.

The information flow between London and New York is, of course, not only one-way. At times, London sees things New York does not, and the two have differing rate views. For example, when New York anticipated continued ease, a London dealer looking at his book might conclude that both Euro and domestic rates in a certain maturity range were likely to firm up, temporarily at least, due to a confluence of scheduled Euro rollovers. Alternatively, if New York foresaw an upturn in rates because domestic loan demand was beginning to revive, London might temper that view by arguing that no parallel increase in loan demand was occurring outside the United States.

Role of Euro CDs

In talking about bank funding in the Euromarket, we have relegated the issuance of Euro CDs to the end of our discussion. The reason is that CD money is much less important in Euro funding than in domestic funding. In the United States, large investors are not in the

---

[13] Steven I. Davis, *The Euro-Bank; Its Origins, Managements and Outlooks* (London: Macmillan Press, 1976).

habit of making time deposits, and the market for term Fed funds is thin. Thus, the domestic banker who wants to take 3-, 6-, or 9-month money is more or less forced to go to the CD market to get it. In the Euromarket, in contrast, a banker can obtain time deposits of any maturity either directly from nonbank depositors or in the interbank market.

Because of the availability of time deposit money, a bank will issue Euro CDs only if there is a distinct rate advantage in doing so. Also, because the overall market for such CDs is thin and the market for any one bank's CDs is thinner still, a bank will be cautious about the quantity of Euro CDs it writes, particularly if the CDs issued are likely to turn out to be *trading paper* as opposed to lockup CDs. The danger of overwriting is not only that the bank will lose its rate advantage in the CD market, but also that it may block actions it wants to take in the future. For example, if a bank writes a lot of 9-month CDs and then, 3 months later, wants to take 6-month money, it may find that it can't do so unless it pays up because there is so much of the old 9-month paper, which now has a 6-month current maturity, in the hands of dealers. A similar fear may also inhibit a bank from writing very short maturity Euro CDs. The treasurer reasons that writing a 1-month CD is not going to save his bank enough money to compensate for the fact that the presence of such securities in the market might, during their life, block his bank from seizing an attractive opportunity to write longer-term CDs. Investors, after all, are going to be willing to hold only so much of any one bank's paper in their portfolios.

Most Euro CDs have a maturity at issue of one year or less, but CDs with longer maturities—two, three, or even five years—are more commonly issued in the Euromarket than in the domestic market. While a bank will normally take any short-dated CD money offered to it by a nonbank customer, it may be unwilling to issue longer-term CDs unless it has a specific use for such funds, for example, to match fund a longer-term asset coming onto its book.

Particularly in the aftermath of Herstatt, buyers of Euro CDs have become highly selective. As a result, only major U.S. banks can today raise money in real volume in this market. Other banks, U.S. and foreign, do issue CDs to their customers, sometimes at the same rates as Citi or Morgan would pay. But were they to try to really write in volume, they would be forced to pay up, how much depending on the name, nation, and size of the bank. Tiering is pronounced in the secondary market for Euro CDs.

Arab dollars

In the Euromarket, the top U.S. banks, because of their size, reputation, and customer base, have always been the recipients of large deposits from nonbank depositors. Both because they could earn profits by laying off such deposits in the interbank market and because the maturity structure of the deposits they received was not necessarily what they desired for their Euro book, these banks became big sellers as well as takers of funds. In effect, they came to act as dealers in Eurodollar deposits.

After the OPEC nations dramatically increased the price of oil in 1974, the dealer banks rapidly became recipients of huge short-term deposits from Arab oil sellers. As they assumed this new responsibility of recycling petro dollars, their balance sheets changed dramatically, with placements becoming much more important relative to loans than previously.

Their new role as recyclers of petro dollars created problems for the big banks. One concerned liquidity. In taking a lot of short-term money from the Arabs, these banks were violating two basic rules of liability management: (1) a bank should not take a significant portion of its deposits from a single depositor or group of depositors, and (2) a bank should not accept big deposits of volatile short-term money. The one comfort to the big banks in this matter was that, regardless of what the Arabs did with their dollars, these dollars could not disappear altogether from the system. Thus, if the Arabs pulled a lot of money out of one bank, that bank could almost certainly buy back the lost dollars in the interbank market from the bank or banks in which the Arabs subsequently redeposited their dollars.

A second problem created by big Arab deposits was credit risk. By taking in huge amounts of Arab money and redepositing it with other banks, the dealer banks were forced to assume a credit risk that they thought properly belonged to the original depositor. To compensate for this risk, the dealer banks attempted to buy Arab money as cheaply as possible, a policy the Arabs seem to have understood. A final problem for a bank receiving big Arab deposits was that the resulting $2 or $3 billion increase in deposits and redeposits on its balance sheet tended to perceptibly erode the bank's capital ratios. Such erosion was something that a big bank might willingly have accepted to increase bread-and-butter loan business but not to earn a minuscule margin in the placement market. To cope with these problems, a few big banks sought to limit the size of their Eurodollar books, a policy that offered the side benefit of enabling them to buy money more cheaply than other banks could.

Over time, the problems created by Arab dollars have eased somewhat, partly because the Arabs gradually became more willing to place funds with the bottom end of the triple-A banks and the top end of the double-A banks. Whereas a decade ago 10 or 15 banks were receiving the bulk of Arab deposits, the list has now expanded to 50 or 60 banks and includes more non–U.S. names. In addition to expanding the number of banks with which they were willing to place money, the Arabs also became more willing to give top banks longer-term deposits, out to as long as five years. Thus, the price advantage to the top banks of buying Arab money has tended to slip from the shorter to the longer end of the maturity spectrum. This occurred, however, at a time when bank borrowers were loath to take down long-term, fixed-rate loans, so the development was of less immediate advantage to the big banks than might otherwise have been the case.

One fact that seems to surprise many people is that, as the Arabs acquired so many dollars, the Middle East did not expand into a major center for the Euromarket. (The "exception," Bahrain is primarily a booking center funded to a significant degree out of London.) Part of the explanation is that the Middle East has always been viewed as an area of political instability, so people there prefer to keep their funds elsewhere. Also, the Arabs have displayed little talent for the sort of cooperation that would be required to develop a major Middle East Euro center. In addition, unlike, say, the Chinese of Singapore, the Arabs have never displayed great interest in or aptitude for banking and finance.

Worldwide funding

As noted, the major U.S. and foreign banks participating in the Euromarket all have branches running their own separate Eurodollar books in each of the major centers of the market and in other newer, peripheral centers, as well. This proliferation of Euro activity naturally raises a question as to how centralized a bank's overall Euro activities should be.

In the past, it was typical for a bank's branches in different dealing centers to act in a highly independent way, each creating its own dollar book under guidelines set by the home office. Some banks now see benefits in greater coordination of the Euro activities of their different branches and are attempting to achieve it. Others, however, prefer to stick to decentralization. In this respect, Citibank and Chase are probably at extreme opposite poles; Citi having a reputation for decentralization and Chase for increasing coordination.

One argument for giving branches a high degree of autonomy is that funding at each is headed by senior and experienced officers who expect to accept responsibility and need it to develop. Also, if funding officers in some branches are bullish while others are bearish, letting each put his money where his mouth is has a pro side as well as a con. While it does mean that the bank will not make as much money as it would have if every branch had acted on a *correct* rate view promulgated by the head office, it also means the bank won't lose as much money as it would have if every branch had acted on an incorrect view.

Another argument for branch autonomy is that in a huge, worldwide organization, coordination of what everyone is doing is infeasible or, alternatively, if feasible, would be costly and might take so long that the bank would be handicapped in taking advantage of constantly changing opportunities.

One advantage of coordinating the activities of a bank's individual branches and thereby creating a worldwide Euro book for the bank is that doing so permits the bank to take its maximum open position in the most advantageous tax areas, for example, to run a very short book in Nassau and compensate by *snugging up* (decreasing the mismatch in) its London book. To the extent that the yield curve is upward sloping, this policy has the advantage of shifting the most expensive funding to the highest tax areas. A second argument for coordination is that a bank may feel so confident in its rate predictions that it wants to make all its bets in the same direction. A third and, by the 1980s, crucial reason for a bank to run a worldwide Euro book was that, because of interest rate volatility, head offices wanted to tightly control banks' overall interest rate exposure by running single global books in which worldwide Euro and domestic books were combined.

Another question with respect to the funding of a bank's worldwide Euro operations is the extent to which each branch should be expected to finance its operations by buying funds in its own name. This question arises for two reasons. First, the "natural" (local) supply of and demand for Eurodollars is not balanced in different Euro centers; Singapore, Bahrain, and the Caribbean centers, for example, all tend to be big net buyers of funds. Second, lenders of dollars perceive the risks associated with net buying centers outside London as being somewhat greater than those associated with London, and they are therefore not willing to lend as much to banks in these centers. Together, these two factors create a situation in which a bank's branches outside London may have to pay more for funds than the same bank's London branch would. For example, where the London branch might be able to buy in the middle of the market or at the bid side, the non-London branch might have to buy at the offered side of the market.

While this price differential does not amount to much, $1/16$ to $1/8$ percent typically, to the extent that it exists, there naturally is a temptation for a bank to have its London branch buy extra funds in its name and then relend them to its branches in other centers. The only real cost is that the British Inland Revenue requires the London branch to make some small taxable profit on such transactions. Currently, the minimum acceptable markup is $5/64$. Since this is a modest figure, many banks do fund—sometimes to a significant degree—the operations of their branches in other centers with funds purchased in London.

There are, however, banks that think every branch should stand on its own feet and do its own funding. One argument is that centers outside London will never be built up as meaningful entities in the global Euromarket unless they are seen to perform in the marketplace in their own names. A second argument is that "sourcing" huge quantities of funds in London which are destined to be used in other centers makes London appear to be a much bigger buyer of Euros than it really is which may thereby impinge on London's sovereign value.

Earlier we said that, in New York and elsewhere in the United States, there was a lot of dealing in Euros for funding the assets of bank branches located in the Caribbean. This funding is all done in the name of the branch, since, if a New York bank bought Euros in the name of the head office, these dollars would become "domestic" dollars and, as such, would be subject to a reserve requirement. The fact that the funding and lending operations of the Caribbean branches of U.S. banks are carried out mainly by personnel at the head office naturally raises the question of whether the profits of such branches should be treated as domestic income subject to domestic state taxation or as foreign income subject to taxation at lower foreign rates. This tax question is one reason New York banks establish IBFs.[14]

Eurocurrency swaps

The bulk of the Eurocurrency market consists of Eurodollar deposits, but it also includes Eurodeposits of German marks, pounds sterling, Swiss francs, Dutch guilders, Belgian francs, French francs, and other currencies. The uninitiated might think of a bank accepting deposits in all of these currencies as ending up with a mixed bag of different kinds of money. Not so the Eurobanker; he knows that he can turn one currency into another through the simple device of a *swap*. To him, money is money whatever its country or origin.

In the foreign exchange market, currencies are traded for each other on two bases, *spot* and *forward*. In a spot transaction, say, deutsche marks (DM) for dollars, the currencies exchanged are normally delivered two days after the trade is made. In a forward transaction, the exchange occurs at some specified date in the future, perhaps months later. *A swap is a pair of spot and forward transactions in which the forward transaction offsets or unwinds the spot transaction.* For example, if a holder of marks traded them for dollars in the spot market and simultaneously entered into a forward contract to sell these dollars for marks three months hence, he would have engaged in a swap. Note that the effect of this transaction is to permit the holder of marks to go into dollars for three months without assuming any *foreign exchange risk.* Specifically, by locking in a selling rate for the dollars he ac-

---

[14] See Chapter 11.

quires, the swapper eliminates any risk that he might suffer a loss due to a fall in the exchange value of the dollar against the mark while he holds dollars.

Most large banks act as dealers in foreign exchange. The individuals who run this part of the bank's operations take speculative positions, long and short, in various currencies as part of their normal dealing activities—making markets and servicing customers' buy and sell orders. In addition, based on their expectations of probable changes in exchange rates, they will assume speculative positions in foreign exchange designed to earn profits for the bank. Such activities expose the bank to foreign exchange risk. This risk, however, is one that the bank is prepared to assume within limits because the individuals running the foreign exchange department are experts in this area.

Funding officers, in contrast, have their greatest expertise in areas other than foreign exchange. As a result, in their Euro operations, banks normally confine speculation in foreign exchange to the foreign exchange department and require that funding officers match their Euro book in terms of currencies (e.g., use dollar liabilities to fund dollar assets). Thus, when a Eurobanker receives a deposit of a currency other than the dollar, he will either sell that deposit in the interbank market or swap it for dollars. Also, if he is asked to extend a loan denominated in a currency other than the dollar, he will fund that loan either by buying a deposit of that currency or by swapping dollars into that currency.

Most of the time, the spot and forward rates at which any currency trades against the dollar will *differ*. In particular, the dollar price that a foreign currency commands in the forward market will be higher than the spot rate if this currency can be borrowed more cheaply than the dollar or if it is expected to appreciate in value relative to the dollar. The opposite conditions will cause the currency to sell at a discount in the forward market.

If a currency is selling at a premium in the forward market, a swap out of the dollar into that currency will yield some gain, while a swap out of that currency into the dollar will produce some loss. If, alternatively, a currency is selling at a discount in the forward market, the result will be the reverse. The gain or loss inherent in any swap, the amount of which can be calculated at the time the transaction is arranged, can be expressed as an annualized percentage rate of gain or loss through the use of a simple formula.[15] This rate of gain or loss is a crucial element in a bank's decisions about what rates to charge on nondollar loans and to pay on nondollar deposits.

For example, suppose that a corporation offers a bank a 3-month DM

---

[15] See Chapter 16 of Marcia Stigum, *The Money Market: Myth, Reality, and Practice* (Homewood, Ill.: Dow Jones-Irwin, 1978).

deposit and that the mark is selling at a premium in the forward market. If the bank accepts the deposit, it will swap these marks into dollars and, in doing so, it will incur some loss. It will, however, also earn the going 3-month LIBOR on the dollars it obtains from the swap. Thus, the rate that the bank offers the depositor will roughly equal 3-month LIBOR minus the annualized rate of loss on the swap. In costing a nondollar loan, the bank follows a similar approach.

On such swap transactions, interest payments generate a residual foreign exchange exposure. For example, if a bank takes in a 3-month DM deposit and swaps it into dollars, the bank assumes a foreign exchange risk because it is committed to pay interest in DM on the DM deposit at maturity, while it will earn interest at maturity in dollars on the dollars it has placed or loaned. If the bank chooses to avoid this risk, it can lock in a fixed spread on the overall swap transaction by buying DM (selling dollars) *forward* in an amount equal to the interest to be paid in DM.

Several very large banks that receive many deposits of Euromarks and Swiss francs and also receive many requests for loans denominated in those currencies have departed somewhat from the swap-everything-into-dollars approach we have just described. Specifically, they have begun to run books in each of these currencies, matching deposits in these currencies against loans and placements in the same currencies. Doing so eliminates certain transaction costs associated with swaps into and out of dollars—the foreign exchange dealers' spreads between bid and asked in the spot and forward markets, and some bookkeeping and ticket costs. Banks running books in Euromarks and Euro Swissy feel that this reduction in costs permits them to offer depositors and borrowers of these currencies slightly better rates than they could if they consistently swapped all the *natural* DM and Swiss franc business they received into dollar assets and liabilities.

We have talked about banks using swaps to match their Euro books (in terms of currencies held and lent). Banks also use swaps in another way, to minimize funding costs. Suppose, for example, that a bank wants to fund a 6-month dollar loan. To any funding officer, every Eurocurrency deposit is nothing but a Eurodollar deposit with a swap tagged on. Thus, in shopping for 6-month money, a bank dealer will price out not only 6-month dollar deposits, but also 6-month dollars obtained by swapping deposits of other currencies into dollars. If 6-month dollars can be obtained more cheaply by buying 6-month Euromarks and swapping them into dollars than by buying straight dollars, the dealer will go the swap route.

Because all the banks in the Euromarket seize every opportunity available to reduce their borrowing costs through swaps, the all-in cost of dollars obtained by swapping any actively traded Eurocurrency into dollars tracks very closely the yield on straight dollar deposits of the same tenor. Thus, the rate savings that a bank can obtain by using a swap to obtain dollars usually amounts to no more than a very narrow spread. However, when the foreign exchange market starts moving dramatically, short-lived opportunities for saving ⅛th or ¼ percent through a swap do occur.

BANK OF ENGLAND REGULATION

Since London is the preeminent center of the Euromarket, it is important to ask who regulates what goes on in the London market, how they do it, and how well they do it.

The first important point to make is that regulation of domestic banking has always been much less formal in Britain than in the United States or on the Continent. Unlike many U.S. bank regulators, those of the Bank of England proceed on the assumption that bankers are prudent, honest people who know as much as, if not more than the regulators do about banking. Thus, their approach has not been to impose regulations and ratios; instead, they ask for periodic reports from the banks. On the basis of these, they discuss with each bank's top management in an informal way the quality of the bank's loans, their liquidity, any features of the bank's condition that the Bank of England views as unusual or out of line, and any suggestions that the Bank of England might make with respect to the bank's operations.

When foreign banks come to London, they are treated in much the same way as domestic British banks. If the Bank of England recognizes a bank as reputable in its home country, it will permit that bank to open a London branch with a minimum of red tape. The bank does not have to put in any capital; all it has to do to open an office is to agree to comply with certain regulations, and it is granted the same right to engage in banking that any other bank in the United Kingdom has. Foreign banks establishing independent entities, merchant banking subs or banking consortia, do have to put in capital, but again, if the parentage is reputable, the red tape is minimal. As an executive of a large U.S. bank noted: "When we went to the Bank of England for permission to open a merchant banking arm, they said: 'You need a foreign exchange trader, someone who knows British exchange control regulations, some capital, and since you are asking to be recognized as a bank, at least a window where you could take deposits whether you do or not. Oh, and one other thing. We'd like you to locate in the City of London. The rents are high which keeps out the riffraff.'"

In justification of the Bank of England's rather casual regulation of foreign banks, it might be added that the bank operates on the quite logical assumption that foreign bank branches are an inextricable part of the parent, which implies two things. First, it is difficult, if not impossible, to regulate these branches as independent entities. Second, it is also natural to assume that these branches are being regulated indirectly by banking authorities in the parent country, which regulate the activities of the parent bank as a whole.

The ease with which foreign banks can enter the London market and the minimal regulations imposed on their activities there have encouraged the entry of several hundred foreign banks in London. It has also permitted the rapid *growth* and constant *innovation* that have been characteristic of the Euromarket.

To a U.S. regulator, the British approach to bank regulation might seem like a time bomb guaranteed to create monumental difficulties at some time. Yet the record shows that the British approach to bank regulation has been at least as successful, if not more so, than the U.S. approach. One reason is that there is a lot of mutual respect between banks operating in Britain and the Bank of England. Because of this and because of the real powers the Bank of England possesses, banks don't fight "The Old Lady (of Threadneedle Street)"; instead, they take her suggestions seriously. Another reason the Bank of England approach has been so successful is that it is responsible for overseeing the operations of only a limited number of banks, about 100 domestic and 200 foreign banks. In contrast, U.S. regulators have to cope with over 15,000 banks. As one Bank of England official noted, the limited number of banks in Britain has permitted the Bank of England to know on an almost personal basis the managers of these institutions and, thus, whether they do or do not need closer supervision.

Naturally with the entry of so many foreign banks into London, it is becoming more and more difficult for the Bank of England to pursue this sort of personal regulation. As a result, in recent years the Bank of England has asked the banks to report to it with increasing frequency and it has visited them more often.

SOVEREIGN RISK

Investors, both bank and nonbank, depositing dollars in a bank or bank branch located in a foreign country are always concerned with *sovereign* or *country risk*. In the case of U.S. investors in particular, at least those with little experience in international business, there is real concern over the sovereign risk associated with making dollar deposits in London. As these investors saw it, at least before the United Kingdom's emergence as an oil producer, the periodic crises through which the pound sterling passed and the chronic weakness of the British economy both suggested that, at some time, the British might be tempted to block payment on the dollar liabilities of London banks.

While one cannot say this could never happen, there is only one conclusion that anyone who has studied the London market carefully can reach: the sovereign risk attached to dollar deposits in London is *very* close to zero.

One practical reason is that Britain would gain nothing from blocking payment of the Eurodollar liabilities of London banks during a sterling crisis. From the end of World War II until the United Kingdom became an oil producer, the pound sterling was a weak currency; to prop up its value, the British maintained tight controls on the use of sterling by domestic holders. Because of these controls, the Euromarket in London, which would in any case have been largely a market in offshore funds was *strictly* so. With the few exceptions permitted by the British exchange control authorities, all the Eurodollars that flowed into London were owned by foreign depositors and all the Eurodollars that flowed out went to foreign borrowers. In effect, London acted and still does act largely as a conduit through which dollars flow from foreigners to foreigners. Thus, inflows of Eurodollars to London do not add to British foreign exchange reserves and outflows do not subtract from them, which means, in turn, that blocking payment on the Eurodollar liabilities of London banks would do nothing to stem the loss by Britain of foreign reserves during a sterling crisis. Actually, in 1980 sterling seemed sufficiently strong so that the United Kingdom fully dismantled its exchange control apparatus.

The financial activities centered in the City of London, including Eurodollar transactions, earn Britain large amounts of foreign exchange, provide thousands of jobs, and add vitality to the whole economy. A second reason Britain would not block payment on Eurodollar deposits is that, if it did, it would lose these advantages. As a Bank of England official noted:

> If the British interfered with the payout of Eurodollars, nationalized foreign branches, or whatever, that would kill more than the Euromarket, it would kill London. Any action taken against Euro operations in London would immediately spread to London as a banking center; and if London is not a banking center, then it isn't a commodity market, it isn't an international insurance center, it isn't a stock or investment market generally. In London these things dovetail very closely, so if you damage one, you damage the lot. The game would not be worth the candle.

To the above it should perhaps be added that Britain could, of course, attempt to improve its reserve position by a two-pronged ploy: blocking payment on Eurodollar deposits in London banks *and* simultaneously seizing the dollar assets of these banks. However, this course of action, in addition to posing the difficult question of how Britain could, as a practical matter, seize the offshore assets of foreign banks, would be even more inconceivable than a mere blocking of Eurodollar deposits since its long-run consequences would, if anything, be still more disastrous for Britain as a financial center.

Had Britain, during a sterling crisis, been willing to do something dramatic and potentially dangerous to its economy, the logical step would have been to block the large sterling balances held by Commonwealth nations. That would have directly stemmed the loss by Britain of foreign exchange reserves by preventing conversion of these balances into foreign exchange. Blocking sterling balances is, it should be noted, a course of action that was open to Britain during every sterling crisis. Yet the British never took it, presumably in part because of the effect doing so would have had on London's role as a world financial center.

LENDER OF LAST RESORT

Another question that troubles some Euromarket watchers is: Who is to act as lender of last resort if some event much more shaking than the failure of the Herstatt hits it? This question really involves two separate questions: Who lends if the supply of Eurodollars dries up? Who lends if the solvency of a major bank or group of banks in the Euromarket is threatened through bad loans or other losses?

Dollars can't disappear, but they can move from place to place. Thus, it's conceivable, though unlikely, that the supply of dollars in the Euromarket could dry up because holders of dollars for some reason decided to move their deposits from banks in Euro centers to banks in New York or elsewhere in the United States. Such an eventuality would not cause U.S. banks severe liquidity problems with respect to their Euro operations; they could always buy back the dollars they had lost in the Euromarket in the U.S. market and use them to fund their Euro assets. To some extent, foreign banks could do the same thing, buy more dollars in New York and funnel them abroad, but they would face a crucial problem: Most of them would be able to buy in the U.S. market only a small fraction of the dollars they were accustomed to buying in the Euromarket. Thus, in the unlikely event of dollars drying up in the Euromarket, foreign banks could face a real liquidity problem.[16]

In meetings in Basel, Switzerland, central banks have discussed at length the question of lender of last resort to the Euromarket and have reached the conclusion that each one looks after his own. Thus, the Fed is the appropriate lender of last resort to a U.S. bank whether its troubles arise from its operations in New York or London, and the Bank

---

[16] Foreign banks negotiate standby lines with U.S. banks to protect against this risk. See Chapter 14.

of England stands behind the operations of its domestic banks both at home and abroad. The logical thrust of this philosophy is that, if foreign banks experienced liquidity problems with respect to their dollar operations, it would be up to their respective central banks to provide them with dollars, something that the central banks of major countries could certainly do either from their own reserves or by obtaining dollars through swaps from the Fed.

With respect to the second question concerning the possible failure by a major Eurobank or group of banks, the comment of a German banker is relevant. In speaking of the Herstatt failure, which sent shock waves through the Euromarket, he said: "The Bundesbank [German central bank] will never admit that they made a mistake, but in retrospect they know they did. They should not have permitted the Herstatt to fail; instead they should have merged it into one of the larger German banks. A bank failure on that scale will, I guarantee, never occur in Germany again."

The development of the Euromarket as an international capital market has made a significant contribution to the world economy over the last several decades, by providing financing for a huge expansion in international trade and investment. The development of this market has also tied, in ways hitherto unknown, the economies, capital markets, and fortunes of many free-world countries, including all of the major ones. Thus, to allow this market to falter or fail would create economic havoc on a worldwide scale. Central bankers know this and the almost universal opinion among bankers is thus that no central bank in a major country will again let one of its key banks fail. Moreover, if a group of banks were threatened, say, by defaults on loans to Poland, underdeveloped countries, or wherever, the central banks standing behind them would undoubtedly keep them afloat through individual or coordinated actions. As a top banker noted: "No central bank will ever commit itself publicly to keeping all domestic banks above size X afloat, but they know—and we know they know—that, should a major bank be threatened, the economic costs of inaction on their part would *far exceed* the cost of action. Therefore, they would act."

The question of who is the lender of last resort in the Euromarket has particularly troubled the Bank of England because of the extensive Euro operations carried out in London by foreign banks. The understanding under which foreign banks are permitted to open branches in London has always been that the parent would stand behind the branch, whatever difficulties it might encounter. In the case of merchant banking subs and consortium banks, this understanding was implicit but less formal. During the nervous and anxious period that prevailed after the Herstatt failure, the Bank of England acted to formalize this commitment by asking for "comfort letters" stating that each parent of a merchant banking sub or consortium bank would provide support, if required, to that entity up to its share of ownership.

Euro operations of small and regional banks

In this chapter we have focused largely on activities of money market banks in the Euromarket. Other U.S. banks, from major regionals down to small banks, also participate in this market in varying degrees and in varying ways. Whenever we discuss, in Parts III and IV, bank Euro operations, we make a point of discussing how banks of different size do and should use this market. The opportunities available to a bank in the Euromarket and the tactics and strategies it should use to exploit them vary widely depending on a bank's size. This is hardly surprising, since the same holds true with respect to the domestic operations of U.S. banks.

FOREIGN BANK OPERATIONS IN THE UNITED STATES

Foreign banks have used various organizational vehicles to enter the U.S. market. A few have set up wholly owned subsidiaries operated under a domestic banking charter. Of these, a handful are long-standing operations like Barclays' extensive banking system in California. Others are of recent origin.

A second way to enter the U.S. market commonly used by foreign banks is to set up *agencies* in U.S. financial centers. By far the largest agencies in the United States are those of Canadian banks. An agency cannot accept deposits in its own name and cannot hold loans on its own books. Instead, it acts as a loan production office and funding agent for the parent bank. It arranges loans and then books them at some branch of the parent, for example, Nassau or the head office. It also acts as an agent for the parent in the New York money market, buying and selling Fed funds and Euros for the head office's account. There are several advantages to a foreign bank in setting up an agency instead of a U.S. branch. Agencies are not subject to U.S. taxes on the loans they originate. In setting up an agency, a foreign bank also avoids a lot of overhead it would incur in setting up a branch with facilities for accepting deposits. Finally, prior to the passage in 1978 of the *International Banking Act (IBA)*, foreign bank agencies were subject neither to U.S. regulation nor to reserve requirements. Under the 1978 act, Congress took the view that these agencies were, in effect, branches and, as such, should be treated in a fashion similar to that specified for foreign bank branches.

A third way a foreign bank can enter the U.S. market is by setting up a branch. The growth of such branches in recent years has been explosive. Foreign bank branches operated, prior to the passage of the IBA in 1978, exclusively under state banking laws and were regulated solely by state banking authorities. Most are located in New York, California, and Illinois, which have specific legislation permitting the establishment of branches by foreign banks. Generally, such branches can engage in the full range of domestic banking activities.

Setting up a branch in the United States is expensive for a foreign bank not only in terms of overhead, but also in terms of taxation. Once a foreign bank establishes a U.S. branch, all of its income on loans into the United States becomes subject to U.S. taxation. Yet the U.S. market, and more particularly the New York market, acts as a magnet drawing in more and more foreign bank branches.

Foreign banks setting up U.S. branches do so for several reasons. First, they are attempting to follow their customers to the United States just as U.S. banks followed their customers abroad; the growth of international banking is, in part, a response to the emergence of multinational firms. Foreign banks are also attempting to develop relationships with large U.S. corporations; most of these have foreign operations and a foreign bank can therefore provide them with special services and expertise. A third reason foreign banks have set up New York branches is to obtain access to the huge domestic reservoir of dollars. Finally, New York is a convenient place for foreign banks to run and fund a Nassau or Grand Cayman Eurodollar book.

Most foreign bank branches are primarily wholesale operations servicing large, as opposed to retail accounts. For example, the customers of one big foreign bank branch in New York include a large proportion of the *Fortune* 500, big European corporations, Japanese trading corporations, large firms trading in commodities, and foreign banks for which the branch acts as a clearing agent. Foreign bank branches fund themselves much as domestic money market banks do, by accepting deposits and by purchasing monies in the Fed funds, Eurodollar, and CD markets. There are, however, differences. One is that CDs issued by foreign bank branches have only limited acceptance in the U.S. market. Another used to be that, for a foreign bank branch, there was no distinction between Eurodollars and "domestic" dollars, because foreign bank branches did not have to hold reserves against any of the funds they received in deposit or purchased. This changed with the passage of the IBA.

The position of a foreign bank operating in the New York market is much the same as the position of the London branch of the same bank in the Eurodollar market. It is acquiring assets and incurring liabilities in a foreign currency, the dollar, and it thinks of itself as running a dollar book. In running this book, moreover, the New York branch, like the London branch, is concerned about mismatch and is subject to guidelines from the home office with respect to the degree of mismatch it can run. One difference, however, is that foreign bank branches in New York, like domestic U.S. banks, make a lot of variable-rate loans, so mismatch in their books can't be measured or controlled in quite the same way in New York as in London.

The United States is the home of the dollar, so having a U.S. branch provides a foreign bank with additional funding and liquidity for its overall Eurodollar operation, because the U.S. branch can directly tap the vast domestic market for dollars. Setting up a U.S. branch also permits a foreign bank to establish an entity to which other branches in the bank's international network can turn to make adjustments in their dollar books; for example, if one of the bank's Middle Eastern branches was getting short-term dollar deposits but had to fund longer-term dollar loans, it might ask the New York branch to lay off its short-term deposits and buy it longer-term money.[17]

A final way in which foreign banks are currently entering the U.S. market is by buying U.S. banks. Two prominent examples are the purchase of Marine Midland Banks of Buffalo, N.Y., by the Hong Kong & Shanghai Banking Company of London and the purchase of Crocker National Corporation in San Francisco by Midland Bank of London. Acquisition of U.S. banks by foreign banks follows a trend common in other industries. Managers of large foreign firms and of large foreign pension and other funds view the United States as an attractive place in which to invest and diversify because—as compared to other countries—the United States ranks high in terms of economic and political stability and of potential for continued economic growth.

Competition with U.S. banks

When they were able to buy money without incurring a reserve requirement, foreign bank branches had a certain cost advantage over U.S. banks in making loans to domestic firms for domestic purposes. This cost advantage, which has now disappeared, was always partially offset by the fact that foreign bank branches have to pay up slightly for money they buy in the domestic market and by the fact that any Euros they buy are more expensive than domestic money of the same tenor. Despite this, for years foreign bank branches in major financial centers quoted loan rates to domestic corporations at LIBOR plus a spread, which worked out to a rate below the U.S. prime plus balances. This practice put pressure on domestic banks in these centers to make loans

---

[17] Chapter 13 covers the running of a book in a nonnative currency in depth.

to prime customers at below-prime rates and eventually to offer fixed-rate advances.[18]

Regulation of foreign branch operations

State regulation of the operations of foreign bank branches in the United States has always been much stricter and more detailed than the regulation to which foreign bank branches are subject in London. In New York State, for example, foreign banks are subject to all the detailed provisions of the state's banking law. In addition, they are required to hold qualifying assets equal to 108 percent of their total liabilities (intrabank deposits excepted); of this, 5 percent must be held in T bills or certain other instruments in a special account with a depository bank. Since the qualifying assets that a foreign bank branch may use to satisfy the 108 percent requirement include a wide range of instruments—loans on its New York book, CDs bought, deposits at other banks, Fed funds sold, bankers' acceptances held in its portfolio, and broker/dealer loans—this requirement does not impose a cost on foreign banks as do Fed reserve requirements. On the other hand, the 108 percent requirement does mean that a foreign bank's branch has to net borrow funds from the rest of the system—funds that constitute, in effect, the branch's U.S. capital base. The New York State 108 percent rule is designed to ensure that a foreign bank branch will always have sufficient assets to meet its deposit and other liabilities. As such, it has been viewed abroad as a model for foreign bank branch regulation and has been widely copied.

In the eyes of some foreign bankers, however, the New York State regulation is anything but a model. One British bank commented: "It's far too complex and to some extent outdated. In these days when funds can be moved rapidly, a foreign bank in trouble could rape its New York branch before the regulators smelled trouble. The only regulation that makes sense and that is going to be effective over the long run is to grant branch licenses only to banks that are credit and trust worthy."

One advantage that foreign banks used to enjoy over domestic banks is that they could open branches in several different states, whereas domestic banks were not permitted to engage in interstate banking. Because of this and other issues as well, considerable pressure was exerted on Congress to pass new foreign bank legislation putting foreign and domestic banks on an equal footing.

The International Banking Act of 1978. This pressure resulted in passage, in 1978, of the *International Banking Act (IBA)*. The major statutory changes provided by the act with respect to foreign banks

---

[18] See Chapter 11.

are: (1) foreign agencies and branches now have the option of federal licensing; (2) foreign branches and agencies engaged in retail banking are required to buy FDIC insurance; (3) foreign branches and agencies are subject to reserve requirements imposed by the Fed in exchange for which they now have access to the discount window and other services provided by the Fed to domestic banks; (4) foreign banks may no longer branch into more than one state; and (5) the Fed is authorized to act as an examining agency to police the activities of those foreign banks that established multistate branches prior to IBA passage and that were permitted, under a "grandfather clause" in IBA, to keep these branches.[19]

International banking facilities

As of December 1, 1981, banks in New York and 11 other states and foreign banks with U.S. branches in these states were permitted to participate directly in the Euromarket by forming International Banking Facilities (IBFs). Since IBFs are the answer of New York and other states to shell branches, we describe them in Chapter 11, where we discuss the operation by U.S. banks of huge shell branches abroad.

---

[19] The details of the International Banking Act are spelled out in a mimeographed report by the Board of Governors of the Federal Reserve System titled *The International Banking Act of 1978* and dated September 17, 1980.

PART III

Liquidity and
interest rate
exposure

7

The setting today

The topic of this book is how to run a bank; specifically, how a bank should make tactical and strategic decisions on structuring its balance sheet so as to maximize its profits subject to the constraints that liquidity risk be held to an acceptable level and interest rate exposure be assumed only on favorable risk-reward terms.

To understand the issues involved in successful management of a bank's balance sheet, one must know a good bit about banking and the environment in which it is conducted. Chapters 2 to 6 were intended to provide the reader lacking this knowledge with a survey of fundamentals. In this chapter, we discuss three other background topics; the first two are the stance of Federal Reserve policy since October 1979, and the question of bank capital adequacy. Our third topic is banks that made bad asset and liability choices; case histories of these banks provide instructive examples to which we will refer in later chapters.

RECENT FED POLICY

The Federal Reserve System, the nation's central bank, was established by act of Congress in 1913. The Federal Reserve Act divided the country into 12 districts and provided for the creation within each of a *district Federal Reserve bank*. Responsibility for coordinating the activities of the district banks lies with the Federal Reserve's *Board of Governors* in Washington, D.C. The board has seven members appointed by the president and confirmed by the Senate.

The main tools available to the Fed for implementing policy are open-market operations, reserve requirements, and the discount rate. On paper, authority for policymaking at the Fed is widely diffused throughout the system. In practice, however, this authority has gradually been centered in the *Federal Open Market Committee* (FOMC), which was established to oversee the Fed's open-market operations. Members of the FOMC include all seven governors of the system, the president of the New York Fed, and the presidents of 4 of the other 11 district banks; the latter serve on a rotating basis. Every member of the FOMC has one vote, but it has become tradition that the chairman of the Board of Governors plays a decisive role in formulating policy and acts as chief spokesman for the system.

In establishing policy, the Fed enjoys considerable independence on paper from both Congress and the executive branch. Members of the Board of Governors are appointed to 14-year terms so that the president has limited control over who serves during his term of office. The chairman of the board, who is designated as such by the president, serves in that capacity for only four years, but his term does not coincide with that of the president, and an incoming president must wait until well into his first term to appoint a new chairman.

Congress, like the president, has no lever by which it can directly influence Fed policy or its implementation. In creating the Fed, Congress endowed this institution with wide powers and granted it considerable leeway to exercise discretion and judgment. Having said that, one must hasten to add that the autonomy enjoyed by the Fed is, in reality, less than it appears. Presidents, concerned that the Fed was forcing interest rates too high, have attacked the Fed subtly and not so subtly from the White House. Also, the Fed is aware that Congress, should it become too distressed over high interest rates, might take away the autonomy it granted to the Fed.

Some history

The primary policy tool available to the Fed is open-market operations, the ability to create bank reserves in any desired quantity by monetizing some portion of the national debt.[1] The Fed could, in theory, monetize anything—scrap metal to soybeans—but it has stuck

---

[1] See Chapter 2 for an explanation of debt monetization.

largely to Treasury IOUs because there has never been any shortage of them in the market, and, in addition, they are highly liquid so the Fed can sell them with as much ease as it buys them. In formulating policy, the first question the Fed faces is what macroeconomic *targets* to pursue. There are various possibilities—full employment, price stability, or a stable exchange value for the dollar. The achievement of *all* of these targets is desirable. However, since the Fed has only *one* powerful string to its bow—the ability to control bank reserves and thereby money creation by the private banking system—it is often forced to make hard choices between targets, to choose, for example, to pursue policies that would promote price stability but might increase unemployment.

Once the Fed has chosen its policy targets, it faces a second difficult question: What policies should it use to achieve these targets? If it wants to pursue a tight money policy to curb inflation, does that mean it should force up interest rates, strictly control the growth of the money supply (if so, which money supply), or follow some other tactic?

Not surprisingly, the Fed's answers to the questions of what targets it should pursue and of how it should do so have changed considerably over time. External conditions—the state of the domestic and world economies—have been in constant flux. Also, central banking is an art form that is not fully understood, and the Fed's behavior at any time is therefore partly a function of its progress along the learning curve.

Before we look at how the Fed operates today, a few words on history are appropriate. During World War II, inflation was one extra disruption that the nation could do without. Thus, during the war, the appropriate stance for monetary and financial policy would have been for the federal government to raise taxes to cover as much war expenditures as possible and for the Fed to simultaneously pursue a policy of restraint to discourage private spending. This, however, was not done. Taxes were held down so that incentives would not be discouraged, and rationing and price controls were used to contain private spending and control prices. Meanwhile, the Fed pegged interest rates at the low levels that prevailed when the country entered the war. Its rationale was to encourage individuals and institutions to buy bonds by eliminating the price risk that would normally attach to holding them. This policy had the additional advantage of minimizing the cost to the Treasury of financing the burgeoning national debt.

In guaranteeing to buy whatever quantity of government securities was necessary to peg long- and short-term interest rates at low levels, the Fed lost all control over the money supply; its policy permitted a big buildup of private liquidity. In retrospect, this buildup was not totally undesirable because the liquid assets acquired by citizens during the war permitted them to finance, at the war's end, the purchase of cars and other goods that had been unavailable during the war. The resulting spending spree prevented a much-feared big postwar slump.

Inflation, however, did arrive on the scene. By 1948, the Fed was feeling uncomfortable about its obligation to peg bond prices, since that left it with no tool to fight inflation. The recession of 1949 provided some relief, but inflation again became a problem during 1950 when the Korean War broke out. Again, the Fed wanted to tighten but the Treasury resisted, arguing that higher interest rates would disrupt Treasury refundings, increase the cost of financing the national debt, and inflict capital losses on those patriotic individuals and institutions that had bought bonds during the war.

Finally, the Fed threw the gauntlet down to the Treasury in September 1950 by raising the discount rate. The Treasury retaliated by announcing a 1-year financing based on the old discount rate of 1.25 percent. Rather than allowing the financing to fail or rescinding the rate increase, the Fed bought the Treasury's new issue, stuck to its higher discount rate, and then resold the issue to the market at a slightly higher rate. This started a 6-month battle with the Treasury, ending in the famous March 1951 *accord* between the Fed and the Treasury, which read:

> The Treasury and the Federal Reserve System have reached full accord with respect to debt management and monetary policies to be pursued in furthering their common purpose to assure the successful financing of the government's requirements and, at the same time, to minimize monetization of the public debt.

This statement, despite the fact that it appears to be a prime example of "governmentese" that says nothing, was important. The key phrase, "to minimize monetization of the public debt," gave the Fed the right henceforth to pursue an independent monetary policy. The following year the Fed, to protect its flank, adopted a second policy of *bills only;* in the future, the Fed would confine its purchases of governments largely to bills. In adopting this policy, the Fed was saying to the market and the Treasury that, in the future, the market would set the yield curve and, in particular, the yields on long-term treasuries.

As a price for its accord with the Treasury, the Fed agreed to stabilize credit market conditions during Treasury financings. This policy, known as *even keeling,* was pursued until recently. The reason such stabilization was required was that the Treasury used to fix both the coupon and the price on Wednesdays when it announced a new issue. Thus, if anything important happened after the announcement of an issue but before it was sold the following week, this would kill the auction; that is, the Treasury would have been unable to sell its securities—something neither the Treasury nor the Fed could risk.

While even keeling prevailed, the Fed tried to plan major moves so that the market would have time to react to them before a Treasury financing. It also insisted, however, that Treasury financings meet the test of the market; the Treasury could not rely on direct support from the Fed.

In recent years, even keeling has gradually died an untolled death. One reason is that the Treasury adopted the policy of selling almost all of its coupon issues through yield auctions. Also, the Treasury's current policy of issuing notes of different maturities in a regular cycle has created a situation in which the Treasury is in the market so often with new coupon issues that, if the Fed were to even keel, it would have no "windows" during which it could decisively shift policy.

Before the accord, the Fed was forced to focus almost solely on interest rates. After the accord, the Fed's focus gradually shifted to *free reserves*—excess reserves minus borrowed reserves. The Fed reasoned that the stance of monetary policy would be sufficiently easy during a recession if free reserves were increased, thereby promoting additional bank lending and falling interest rates, and that during periods of excessive demand for output, the stance of monetary policy would be appropriately tight if free reserves were decreased, thereby promoting a fall in bank lending and a rise in interest rates.

This sounds reasonable, but it contained a fatal flaw. During a recession, interest rates are likely to fall by themselves as the demand for bank credit diminishes, so increases in free reserves may be consistent with a falling money supply and a tight monetary policy. In an overheated economy, in contrast, limiting free reserves to some small sum need not mean tight money. So long as the Fed continues to supply banks with reserves which the banks utilize, low free reserves are consistent with a rapid expansion of the money supply.

After a decade of obsession with free reserves the Fed shifted the focus of its policy, in the early 1960s, to interest rates. During this time, the economy was recovering sluggishly from a severe recession, and it therefore seemed appropriate to stimulate investment, which meant, in turn, that long-term interest rates should be lowered. However, the United States was also experiencing a disturbing balance of payments deficit, and the defense of the dollar therefore called for high short-term rates. In response to both needs, the Fed adopted *operation twist;* it started buying long bonds instead of bills in an attempt to force up short-term interest rates while simultaneously lowering long-term rates.

Whether operation twist was successful in altering the slope of the yield curve, in stimulating investment, or in decreasing the balance of payments deficit has been much debated. In any case, the policy died in 1965, a victim of the Vietnam War, which encouraged inflationary pressures in the economy and caused the Fed to switch the focus of its policy to curbing inflation. In 1966, the Fed introduced the first of several credit crunches that drove interest rates to historic highs.

As fighting inflation came to be a key target of Fed policy, another change was also occurring—a gradual shift in the focus of the Fed's attention away from interest rates and toward the growth of the money supply. One reason is that the level of interest rates does not necessarily indicate how tight or easy monetary policy is, because interest rates respond not only to what the Fed is doing but also to general economic conditions. During a recession, interest rates can fall, as occurred in early 1960, even though bank reserves and the money supply are shrinking. Similarly, during an expansionary period, rising interest rates are compatible with rapidly increasing bank reserves, bank credit, and the money supply. A second reason for the increased attention given to monetary aggregates by the Fed was the increasing popularity of monetarism—a view that the rate of growth of the money supply plays a dominant role in determining various macroeconomic variables, in particular the rate of inflation.

In the decade following 1966, during which the Fed continued to be concerned much of the time with controlling inflation, it gradually put more and more stress on measuring monetary tightness and ease in relation to the rate of growth of the money supply and, in doing so, abandoned its old concern with free reserves. This switch in focus was encouraged by Congress, which in a 1975 joint resolution, required that the Fed henceforth set and announce targets for monetary growth. In 1978, Congress passed the Humphrey-Hawkins Act which strengthened and formalized the requirement that Fed policy focus on controlling money supply growth.

Monetary policy in recent years

While from 1975 on, the Fed publicly described its policy as one of controlling the growth of the monetary aggregates, its method of seeking to do so was indirect, to say the least. At that time and even today, the FOMC's directives to the New York *open-market desk,* which implements Fed policy, contain two sets of targets: a target range for the Fed funds rate, and target ranges of growth for various measures of the money stock. To the uninitiated, an FOMC directive that says the desk shall carry out open-market operations so that Fed funds trade at X and money supply grows at rate Y sounds tidy and reasonable. As noted in Chapter 2, however, the Fed has only one policy tool, adjusting bank reserves—the impact of which it can augment by changes in the discount rate and in required reserve ratios. An institution charged with implementing policy that is given only one tool can, as economists have long noted, *hit only one target.* If it manages to hit two, the event is fortuitous.

Thus, Fed policymakers, whatever their public pronouncements may be, must view achieving one target—interest rate levels or money supply growth—as *the* binding constraint on how open-market operations shall be run; they must view achieving the second target as something which they hope—pray—will occur as a stroke of luck due to the well-intentioned. The alternative of foundering back and forth to achieve both goals is a recipe for achieving neither.

Prior to 1979, the Fed sought to control the growth of the monetary aggregates by controlling the Fed funds rate. If the monetary aggregates were growing too fast, the FOMC would instruct the open-market desk to raise the Fed funds rate and vice versa. At the time, the market was accustomed to having the Fed fine tune the rate at which funds traded, and the desk could, by making a few signals to the market, get funds to trade where it wanted them to. No highly precise adjustment of reserves was required.

During this period, Fed policy was not noticeably successful. A major problem was that the FOMC always moved the Fed funds target rate by only small amounts, ½ or ¼ percent. Moving the funds rate from 10 to 10¼ percent affected a few holders of securities but not much else. Fed policymakers were loath to move the funds rate by large amounts partly because they always took the view that things were *uncertain* and that maybe a month later they would know better where things stood, which they never did. Consequently, they never acted with the vigor necessary to control spending either by tightly controlling the growth of the money supply or by raising interest rates sharply. Whereas changing the Fed funds rate by ¼ percent had no major impact on either money supply growth or spending, raising it from 10 to 13 or even 15 percent might have. That experiment was one that the Fed was unwilling to make.

Prior to August 1979, William Miller was Chairman of the Fed, and Carter was in the White House. Miller, a team player, lacked strong convictions on what monetary policy should be, and Carter, elected by a party filled with populists, was not about to suggest that the play his monetary quarterback call be to control the growth of the money stock so tightly that monetary policy would slow spending and inflation, strengthen the exchange value of the dollar, and, in all probability, also induce a sharp rise in interest rates and a recession. By August of 1979, indirection in macro policymaking was becoming intolerable. The dollar was in crisis, and Carter, in choosing a new chairman for the Fed, had to pick a strong person who would command the respect of foreign central bankers and of the international financial community in general. His choice was Paul Volcker, then President of the New York Fed.

The "Saturday night special." In October 1979, Volcker instituted a dramatic change in Fed policy. Previously, the Fed attempted to control the supply of nonborrowed reserves so that Fed funds would track a target level that, in turn, was supposed to induce the money supply to grow within the Fed's target bands. Volcker switched gears 180°; he declared that henceforth the Fed would seek to control the growth of the monetary aggregates directly by holding the growth of nonborrowed reserves on a strict target path. To do so, the Fed necessarily had to relinquish its hitherto tight control over the Fed funds rate. In a nutshell, the new Volcker policy was to tightly control the growth of reserves which form the basis of the money supply, and let funds trade where they would.

In the same month, the Fed also sought to directly curtail the expansion of bank lending by imposing an 8 percent marginal reserve requirement on increases in the managed liabilities of large banks. The response of the market to these policy changes, dubbed Volcker's "Saturday night special" because it was announced on Saturday, October 6, was dramatic. Interest rates, which on October 5 had already risen in anticipation of further tightening by the Fed, moved sharply up again in response to the Fed announcement on the following day of changes in its policy, and the rates continued to move higher through March 1980 (Figure 7–1).

Figure 7–1
The yield curve before and after the Fed's "Saturday night special"

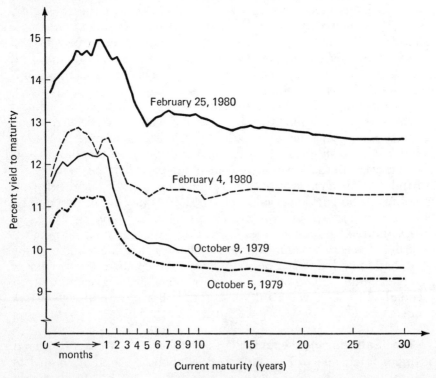

Ironically, the Fed, in the name of strictly controlling the money supply, began, for the first time, to experiment with the impact that tight money—in the form of high and sharply rising interest rates—would have on the economy. The new Fed policy is often described as a *reserves-oriented operating procedure*. The FOMC chooses a rate of growth for the monetary aggregates. Then the staff of the Washington Fed and the FOMC decide, in consultation with the manager of the system account in New York, what level of reserves is required by the banks to support the prescribed growth in the aggregates. The New York desk then supplies that level of reserves. The desk tends to take the current level of borrowed reserves as a given and focus on nonborrowed reserves, a residual variable. If the Fed's pursuit of its targets tightens credit-market conditions, borrowed reserves will rise, which will force up short-term interest rates. The Fed may seek to offset the effect of increased bank borrowings by reducing the nonborrowed reserves it supplies to the market, a move that will, in turn, reinforce the upward trend in short-term rates. Because of a number of technical considerations, it is difficult for the Fed in each operating week to precisely offset unanticipated changes in borrowed reserves by adjusting the nonborrowed reserves it supplies to the banks. Under the new system of pegging reserves rather than the funds rate, the Fed needs to and does, in fact, intervene much less frequently in the market than it did prior to October 1979.

Revolutions normally occur in steps, and the change in monetary policy instituted by Volcker was no exception. After October 1979, the Fed continued, as it still does, to set target bands for the rates at which Fed funds should trade. Until December 1980, the desk had to consult with the chairman if pursuit of the reserve target seemed likely to push the funds rate out of the enlarged band in which funds were permitted to trade. During the period from October to December, movements of the funds rate outside the prescribed bands put only temporary and modest constraints on the implementation of the board's new reserves operating procedure. In December, the desk was directed to continue to aim for its reserve objective regardless of where funds traded, with the proviso that the chairman be notified if funds traded outside their prescribed range. Currently that range, which has varied from 4 to over 8 percentage points, is so wide as to place no real constraint on the desk's efforts to achieve the reserve target.

What is money?

That the Fed's attempt, beginning in October 1979, to control the monetary aggregates *strictly* resulted in a policy any good Keynesian could have prescribed for controlling inflation—a sharp rise in interest rates—was not the only irony the Fed faced in the winter of 1980. It was simple for Congress to instruct the Fed to control the growth of the money supply. The difficult task was and is for the Fed to define precisely what money is, particularly in times such as the present, when the strains imposed on deposit-accepting institutions by various regulations, in particular by controls placed on the rates they may pay depositors, have spawned a variety of new and rapidly growing institutions and instruments: new NOW and ACT accounts, new time deposit certificates (including MMCs), money market funds, and further growth of the Eurodollar market.

In February 1980, the Fed abandoned its old definitions for a new, expanded set (Table 7–1). The new M-1B recognized the growing

Table 7–1
The Fed is changing definitions of money supply

Prior to February 1980
M-1: Money supply measured as the amount of demand deposits plus currency in circulation
M-2: M-1 plus small-denomination savings and time deposits at commercial banks
M-3: M-2 plus deposits at nonbank savings institutions
M-4: M-2 plus large-denomination CDs
M-5: M-3 plus large-denomination CDs

February 1980
M1-A: Currency plus demand deposits
M1-B: M1-A plus other checkable deposits, including NOW accounts
M-2: M1-B plus overnight RPs and money market funds and savings and small (less than $100,000) time deposits
M-3: M-2 plus large time deposits and term RPs
L: M-3 plus other liquid assets

January 1981
M-1: Currency plus demand deposits plus other checkable deposits, including NOW accounts
M-2: M-1 plus overnight RPs and money market funds and savings and small (less than $100,000) time deposits
M-3: M-2 plus large time deposits and term RPs
L: M-3 plus other liquid assets

---

importance of NOW accounts, which are, in effect, interest-bearing checking accounts. M-2 recognizes, in addition, that a lot of small-denomination time deposits (money market certificates in particular), Euro call deposits held by U.S. residents in the Caribbean, and money market fund shares are instruments that individuals and corporations currently use for holding what amount to money balances.

Finally, the large money supply measure, L, recognizes that individuals and corporations to a greater degree rely on a whole host of highly liquid instruments for holding their money balances. Contemplation of the scope of L and of the fact that even it is not all-inclusive is sobering. To theorize in the ivory towers of academia about the role of the money supply in economic activity is easy. To even measure, let alone control money supply in the real world may be impossible.[2]

A final irony is that granting permission to all deposit-accepting institutions to offer NOW accounts caused M1-A to start to decline in November 1981, as deposits shifted out of it into M1-B which consequently grew more rapidly than it would have otherwise (Figures 7–2

Figure 7–2

M1-A (discontinued in January 1981) grew erratically week to week and was rarely within the Fed's target bands

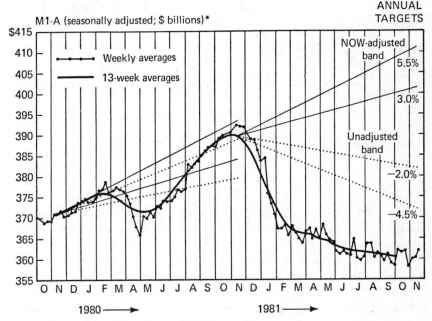

* Data not adjusted for effects of NOW accounts.
Source: The Morgan Bank.

---

[2] This prospect is not disturbing to all economic theorists. Many would argue that outsized increases in the money supply, however it is measured, are the *result* rather than the *cause* of excessive aggregate demand and of the inflation it induces. A hyperinflation, during which the government's presses print money literally full-time, seems to be one case in which monetarism's supposed causal chain works. But even in a hyperinflation the root cause of the problem is not the rolling of the presses but rather government spending, unmatched by tax revenues, that causes them to roll.

Figure 7–3

M-1B, which in January 1980, became simply M-1, has displayed erratic growth week to week and month to month

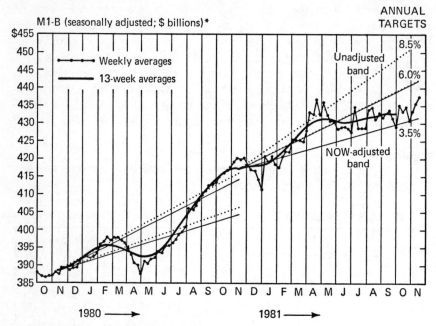

* Data not adjusted for effects of NOW accounts.
Source: The Morgan Bank.

and 7–3). In January 1982, the Fed, recognizing this, scrapped M-1A and dubbed what had been M-1B simply M-1. Definitions of money supply began the decade of the 1980s displaying a rapid rate of obsolescence.

The Fed's problem in measuring money is not only defining money, but also getting accurate numbers on whatever it has defined money to be. Every Friday afternoon, the Fed announces money supply figures. It is the dream of monetarists that these figures fall neatly along a prescribed growth path. In practice, they fall all over the lot. Weekly money supply numbers, which are always revised—often by substantial amounts—are full of "noise" and sometimes contain large errors. In addition, the seasonal adjustments the Fed makes in these numbers at times loom *very* large relative to week-to-week changes in the money supply; worse still, because of the rapidly changing way in which people hold their money balances, the validity of these adjustments is dubious, at best.

The upshot of all this is that there is a large random element in week-to-week changes in the money supply figures announced by the

Fed. Consequently, announcement of these figures, to which the market always reacts sharply, has become the basis for a weekly crap game on Wall Street. More important, the weekly money figures give the Fed a questionable yardstick for measuring what its policies have wrought. This is why the Fed always says it never bases policy on a single week's or on several week's money supply figures.

March 1980: Credit controls

By March 1980, interest rates had reached what were then regarded as astronomical levels, and the Carter administration directed the Fed to impose credit controls in an attempt to curb spending directly. At the same time, the Fed increased from 8 to 10 percent the marginal reserve requirement, imposed in October 1979, on the managed liabilities of large banks, and it reduced the base upon which this reserve requirement was calculated. The Fed also imposed a similar reserve requirement on monies bought by large nonmember banks, a new 15 percent reserve requirement on increases in the assets of money market funds, and a surcharge on borrowings by large banks at the discount window.

The Fed's actions in March 1980, threw the growth rates of M1-A and M1-B into a tailspin (Figures 7–2 and 7–3). Bank lending fell off because the Fed mandated that it do so. In addition, the economy slipped into a mini recession. At the same time, interest rates started to plummet, first because credit controls forced the banks to reduce the amount of funds for which they were bidding in the market, and second because the economy began to weaken (Figure 7–4). By June, short-term rates had fallen 1,000 basis points. In this environment, the Fed phased out credit controls between May and July.

In reaction to the sharp decline in money supply numbers, the Fed also pumped nonborrowed reserves into the system (Figure 7–5). It continued to do so until midsummer, at which time interest rates were again on the rise and M1-A and M1-B were back in their target ranges. At that point, money supply again began growing at outsized rates, the basis for this growth being the excessive reserves the Fed had pumped into the system in previous months.

In late 1980, interest rates hit historic new highs. Then, in January 1981, they fell off sharply but quickly rebounded to their previous peak levels and stayed there for four months, after which they began a gradual decline. During this period, the Fed first sopped up the excess reserves it had supplied to the banks and then allowed reserves to again expand (Figure 7–5).

By 1981, it was clear that interest rates were determined by the Fed's reaction function. The unanswered question was, to what was the Fed reacting? After all deposit-accepting institutions were per-

Figure 7–4

Since October 1979, the pursuit of monetarism by the Fed has created high and highly volatile short-term interest rates

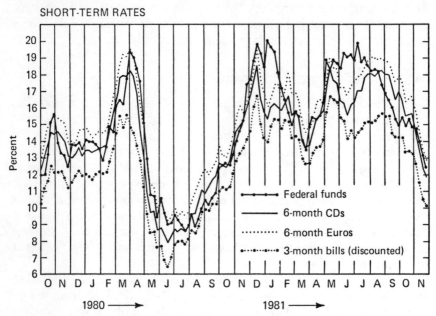

SHORT-TERM RATES

Source: The Morgan Bank.

mitted to offer NOW accounts in late 1980, M1-A plunged, as was to be expected. From then on, the Fed had to be focusing on M1-B (now M-1) and M-2. During much of 1981, M1-B, especially if looked at on the basis of a 13-week moving average, was behaving—moving within or below its prescribed growth bands—and thus providing no basis for historically high interest rates. At the same time, however, M-2 was growing much more vigorously (Figure 7–6). Finally, in the fall of 1981, as the economy showed signs of moving into a recession, the Fed eased by starting to supply more reserves to the banking system. Short-term interest rates declined rapidly, long-term rates more slowly; both, by historic standards, remained high in both absolute and real (i.e., nominal rate minus the rate of inflation) terms.

The major difference between the events of the fall of 1981 and those following the imposition of credit controls is that the Fed did not move so rapidly to expand bank reserves in the fall of 1981 as it did following the imposition of credit controls. Also, it permitted interest rates to fall more slowly and to bottom out at a higher level. Presumably the Fed had learned a lesson in the spring of 1980. This time around it was seeking not to repeat the mistake it had made then; it

Figure 7–5
The Fed's attempt to control the growth of M1-B (now M-1) has caused it to
widely vary the rate at which it increases the supply of reserves available to
the banking system

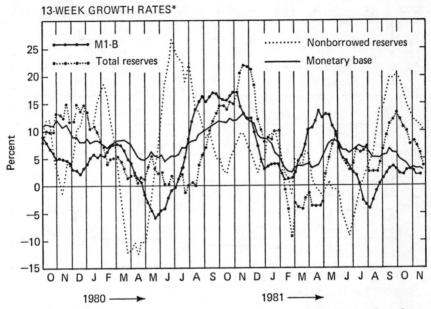

13-WEEK GROWTH RATES*

* Data as announced; any subsequent revisions (or restatements) not reflected.
Source: The Morgan Bank.

was trying to avoid pumping into the system reserves that would establish the basis for subsequent outsized growth of the money supply
and a new, sharp rise in interest rates.

What was/is the Fed really doing?

It is hard, in fact impossible, to find any informed person in the
money market who believes that someone who really understands the
money market and commercial banking could be a monetarist. That
raises the question of how monetarist the Fed truly is.

Since passage of the Humphrey-Hawkins Act and more especially
since the arrival in Washington of the Reagan administration with its
monetarists—including Beryl Sprinkel at the Treasury—the Fed has
had no choice but to publicly espouse monetarism. That in no way
means that the Fed may not be Keynesian in the closet. The Keynesian
prescription for a high rate of inflation is high real rates of interest;
during 1981, Fed policy had, in fact, a very Keynesian hue.

Figure 7–6

In recent years, M-2 has been growing much more rapidly than M1-B (now referred to simply as M-1): Money supply levels—M-2 versus M1-B ($ billions; monthly averages; data through November 1981)

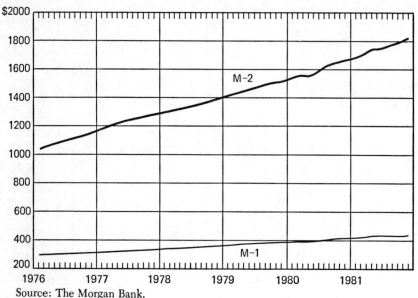

Source: The Morgan Bank.

A major goal of monetarism is to reduce—preferably to zero—the discretion the Fed has always exercised in implementing monetary policy. The great irony of the public espousal of monetarism by the Fed is that, by proclaiming itself to be monetarist, the Fed has vastly increased its range of discretion. As Arthur Burns realized some years ago, the Fed can—by picking and choosing among the various money growth rates and among the different periods over which these rates can be measured—justify almost any action it wants to take.

Moreover, since setting targets for the monetary aggregates is highly technical, the Fed can—without fear of dispute from Congress—set targets for whatever M it likes, even if those are targets that the Fed realizes will drive interest rates to historic peaks. If, alternatively, the Fed said to Congress, "Our objective is to have funds trade in the 18 to 19 percent range," a hue and cry would arise not only from Congress, but from one end of the land to the other.

As these observations suggest, it is possible that what the Fed was doing in 1981 was pursuing a tight money policy in the form of *high interest rates:* a policy that it justified by looking at whatever money figure justified its actions. Conceivably, Volcker felt that, with a strong

Republican administration in power—one dedicated to cutting government spending and slowing inflation—there was a chance, perhaps the last in a generation, to break the back of inflation by using high interest rates to brake the economy and to hold down the price indexes for a sufficiently long period to kill inflationary expectations; expectations that—so long as they persisted—were bound to reignite the fires of inflation.

The Bank of England, which over the last several decades has jounced interest rates up and down a good bit more than the Fed has, never espoused monetarism to the degree that the Fed has. In the Bank of England's view their job is to be central bankers, not ideologues. An interesting question: how many ideologues sit on the Fed's board? To the chagrin of monetarists, the number could be zero.

With this, we turn to the second of the three topics covered in this chapter, and another area of concern in managing a bank.

CAPITAL ADEQUACY

No bank or thrift can operate without capital. That capital serves crucial functions. First, it protects depositors and other bank creditors in the event of failure. How much capital a bank has and the resulting protection that capital affords a bank's creditors are important determinants both of a bank's ability to attract funds and of the rates it must pay for these funds. A second function of capital is that it permits a bank to withstand occasional losses. A third and related function of capital is that it enables a bank to assume risk. Delete from banking those elements that involve no risk and little is left; capital is the essential element that permits a bank to engage in banking.

No student of banking will argue with the proposition that a bank needs capital. The arguments about bank capital—and there are many—arise with respect to the question of *how much* capital a bank needs. No satisfactory answer has been given to this question, probably because none exists. Experience suggests only the observation—simple but sound—that a well-managed and profitable bank can get along with an extremely low capital ratio, whereas no amount of capital will suffice to guarantee the solvency either of a poorly managed bank that likes to play bet the bank or of an institution, such as a thrift, that is forced to operate under rules or in an environment that render it unviable.

This observation strikes regulators, bank credit analysts, and economic theoreticians as far too woolly. They desire that analysis produce some normative guideline—be it a rule, a magic ratio, or whatever—on capital adequacy.

Measuring capital adequacy

An approach to measuring bank capital adequacy favored by some theorists is: On the basis of past experience, the risk associated with different classes of assets held should be evaluated. Next, again on the basis of past experience, proper ratios of capital needed to support assets in each of these classes should be determined. Finally, a bank should allocate its capital among the different classes of risk assets it holds on the basis of these ratios to determine whether its capital is sufficient to support the amount and types of assets it holds.

This approach has the aura of being scientific because implementing it can be based on an elaborate massaging of all sorts of data. When the approach is scrutinized carefully, however, it emerges as neither scientific nor particularly useful. No amount of looking at the past or projecting the future can provide a definite, precise answer to the crucial questions: (a) how much riskier is one asset than another—a 3-year muni versus a 90-day Treasury bill, and (b) how much capital does a bank require to back each of these assets? Such questions can be answered only on the basis of *subjective* assumptions about what constitutes risk and how one kind of risk relates to another.

By definition, different people will answer these questions differently. More importantly, their answers will inevitably change—sometimes dramatically—as economic, political, and other conditions change. Any banker's perception of the risk associated with a municipal portfolio had to be changed by the New York City crisis, just as his perception of the risk associated with loans to Eastern European countries had to be changed by the 1981 rescheduling of loans to Poland. Except in well-defined games of chance, such as throwing dice, risk is not a *constant* that can be evaluated *a priori*.

Another problem with measuring capital adequacy by allocating capital to assets on a basis weighted to reflect differences in the risks associated with them is that, because this measure must be based on subjective judgments, it will never constrain a management that wants to play bet the bank. A risk-averse management will assign a much higher risk to buying long bonds in a volatile rate environment than will a go-go management that is convinced it knows where interest rates are going and wants to bet big and win big.

A more mundane answer to the capital adequacy question, one often expressed by bankers, is that, if all banks of a given size have the same capital ratio, then for banks of that size that ratio is adequate. The reasoning is that, since the banks in question are able to attract deposits, the public must perceive their capital as adequate.

A third answer to the question of bank capital adequacy is to argue that what should really count is not the absolute ratio of a bank's capital to its risk assets, but rather the size and consistency of its earnings. If a bank's earnings grow on average, and if it is consistently adding to its capital through retained earnings, then all functions of capital are fulfilled, and the bank therefore must be judged to have adequate capital.

Bank concern with capital adequacy

Since the question of what constitutes adequate bank capital reduces—the more one ponders it—to a conundrum that admits no definitive answer, a reasonable question is: Why don't bankers ignore the question and get on with the business of banking? The answer is that, to a large degree, they do precisely that.

Consider the major banks. Over the last two decades, their average ratios of risk assets to capital has risen from 10 to 1 to 25 to 1. As noted in Chapter 5, if one asked a thoughtful officer at such a bank what he believed his bank's capital ratio should be, his answer—however lengthy—would probably boil down to the statement: "The question really can't be answered. All I can say is that our bank is comfortable with its capital ratio so long as that ratio is in line with the capital ratios at banks of similar size." That is the herd-instinct answer to capital adequacy: stick with the pack and you are safe.

The attempt of banks to stick with the pack or even lag it a bit in an attempt to look "better" than their peers reflects several pressures to which banks are subject. As noted often in later chapters, banks—particularly large ones—are sensitive to the measures by which analysts rate banks. One reason is that the appraisal made by bank analysts will influence the bank's ability to buy money: the amount it can buy and the rates it must pay. The way bank analysts view a bank also influences the price at which the bank's stock trades. Every major bank would like to add to its capital by selling additional stock and therefore would like its stock to trade at a level where it could issue additional stock without diluting the equity of existing shareholders.

Bank analysts typically give kudos for high capital ratios and a high return on assets as opposed to equity. While the appropriateness of the importance bank analysts attach to these yardsticks is open to question, it is nevertheless true that their view inhibits banks from doing a lot of low-risk, low-margin business that would increase their return on equity at the price of decreasing their capital ratios and their return on assets.

Another source of pressure that inclines banks to stick with the herd on capital ratios is the Fed. After wrestling for several decades with how much capital is adequate for a bank, the Fed has yet to answer the question by promulgating an official yardstick. Nonetheless, the Fed does have an unofficial formula for estimating what a bank's capital ratio should be, and if the Fed does not like the ratio it sees at a bank during its annual examination, the Fed will make rumbling noises about how the bank's capital ratio is getting low.

Those are noises that an aggressive bank cannot ignore because such a bank is certain, down the road, to be asking the Fed to allow it to open a new Edge Act subsidiary, to permit its holding company to buy or enter a new business, or whatever. If a bank does make such a request, the Fed will, if it is concerned about that bank's capital ratio, turn down the request on the ground that the addition of new business would overly burden the bank's already inadequate capital.

Possible Fed action

While the Fed has yet to issue an official dictum on what constitutes adequate bank capital, the signs are that, if it does, it will use the capital allocation approach: measure the adequacy of a bank's capital by allocating its capital on a basis weighted to reflect the differences in risk associated with different classes of assets the bank holds. It is hard to find any reason for believing that it would be other than a mistake for the Fed to take this tack. Any measure of the risks associated with different classes of bank assets would necessarily be highly judgmental and therefore arbitrary. Moreover, if such risks are to be measured at all, that task could presumably be done better by practicing bankers than by regulators. The premise that bankers understand the business of banking better than regulators do is one on which the Bank of England, a highly effective regulator, has always operated.

The fact that a number of banks seek to allocate their capital in a more or less formal way among different classes of risk assets is no argument for the Fed to follow this approach in establishing guidelines for capital adequacy. Banks that assign capital to different classes of assets—e.g., 1 percent to their dealer operation, 3 percent to their muni portfolio, and so on—are seeking to establish some return-on-capital figures on which they can base the balance sheet decisions they must make when they seek to maximize their overall profit subject to the constraint that risk be controlled. Because judgments about risks are so subjective, this approach tends to turn into a time-consuming, convoluted, arbitrary, and unproductive exercise.

Instead of using the capital allocation approach, the Fed might seek to establish a standard for adequate capital by declaring some number to be the minimum acceptable capital ratio. This approach, too, would have its dangers. Specifically, if the Fed were to establish a rule that 3 or 4 percent was the minimum acceptable capital, attention would be focused on this number, and banks might face shareholder pressure to leverage themselves down to it. Worse still, a major bank, once it got to this limit or if it were already there, would find itself back in the same position it was in prior to 1960. At that time, major U.S. banks had only limited access to bought money and consequently had only a finite amount of resources they could employ. Today, in contrast, they are able to leverage themselves at will, a phenomenon reflected in the decline in the capital ratios of these banks over the last two decades.

As will be noted later, capital requirements are imposed on German banks; these requirements form a binding constraint on the ability of German banks to do Eurobusiness.[3] If similar constraints were placed on U.S. banks, they would be more likely to limit the growth of U.S. banks' international business than of their domestic business, because the margins banks earn are thinner on international business. It is debatable whether it would be in the best interest of the United States to impose capital constraints on its banks that would limit their ability to expand international business in step with the expansion of the international capital market.

Foreign banks, with the exception of German and Swiss banks, are generally not subject to specific capital requirements. Also, many foreign banks, particularly French and Japanese, are much more highly leveraged than are top U.S. banks. From the world point of view, U.S. banks do not lead the pack in the area of leverage.

The record

Table 7–2 shows how capital ratios vary among U.S. banks according to asset size. Note the dramatic increase in capital ratios as bank size decreases. Conventional wisdom being the more capital the better, the table seems to indicate that small bankers are highly conservative and responsible, large bankers the converse.

The conventional, obvious moral is, however, not always correct. Consider a major bank that has a capital ratio of 25 to 1 and that retains, in a middling year, $200 million of earnings. To maintain its existing level of leverage, such a bank must add $5 billion a year to its assets. For a major bank that has almost unlimited access to bought money, this is no problem. Consider next a small bank that, relative to its size, is likely to be as profitable as, if not given its natural advantages, more profitable than a large bank. It, too, retains earnings and must expand its assets to maintain its existing level of leverage. Whereas for a large bank funding the acquisition of additional assets is no problem, for a small bank with limited access to bought money, it can be. What the numbers in Table 7–2 probably reflect is not that the risk aversion of bank management is inversely correlated with bank size, but rather that the smaller a bank is, the harder it is for that bank to leverage its capital.

---

[3] Note that capital constraints did nothing to prevent German banks from getting heavily into risky international loans to Poland and other Eastern European countries. Ironically, their government encouraged them to do so as part of its *Ost politic.*

Table 7–2
Equity capital to risk assets*

Bank asset size ($ millions)	1970	1975	1979
$5,000	7.9%	6.1%	6.1%
$1,000–$5,000	8.5	8.0	7.6
$ 300–$ 500	9.7	8.6	8.2
$ 100–$ 300	9.8	9.3	9.0
$ 75–$ 100	9.6	9.4	9.3
$ 50–$ 75	9.7	9.7	9.5
$ 25–$ 50	9.8	9.8	10.0
$ 10–$ 25	10.8	10.5	11.0
$ 5–$ 10	12.5	12.6	13.2
Up to $ 5	19.1	19.5	20.8

* Risk assets are defined as net loans and lease financing receivables less FHA and VA loans, loans to U.S. banks, and loans to banks in foreign countries; plus obligations of state and political subdivisions, other bonds, notes and debentures, real estate other than bank premises, investments in unconsolidated subsidiaries, and customers' liability on acceptances outstanding.

Perhaps the greatest danger in imposing some minimum acceptable capital ratio on banks, and in particular on weak institutions like thrifts, is that to require an institution to have capital equal to a fixed percentage of its risk assets is to create a situation in which whatever portion of an institution's existing capital is needed to meet the requirement is, by definition, unavailable to serve a key function of capital, namely to enable the institution to withstand losses and thereby to provide a margin of safety for the institution's creditors. Required capital incorporates the same fallacy as required reserves. Requirements, whether on liquidity or capital, weaken rather than strengthen an institution because what is required is unavailable for use. An institution that uses a required resource automatically places itself in violation of an externally imposed rule on the standards its balance sheet must meet if the institution is not to be penalized by being fined, placed on a list of problem banks, or whatever.

The counterproductive nature of externally imposed capital constraints becomes particularly evident when a class of financial institutions begins, as the thrifts did, to lose significant amounts of capital as a result of prolonged industrywide operating losses. One response of the regulators is likely to be, as it was in the case of the thrifts, to permit new accounting practices, such as the deferred write-off of capital losses, that permit an institution to show a higher capital ratio that it would have had under what were previously considered to be prudent accounting practices. This is not to say that loss deferral accounting is not a good idea; it is. The point is that, when the chips are down, regulators will not permit capital rules they have created to bankrupt an industry. But if capital ratios are to be evaded or abnegated when they become binding, what is the justification for imposing them in the first place?

Opportunity cost of lagging the pack

Management at several of the largest and most respected U.S. banks consciously seeks to maintain slightly better capital ratios than their competitors on the theory that this will enhance their image in the eyes of bank analysts and investors and thereby marginally improve the terms on which they can obtain funds. It is difficult to discern whether such an edge exists for these banks and, if so, what it is worth to them in dollars and cents.

What is clear is that an opportunity cost attaches to a policy of limiting leverage to maintain a marginally better capital ratio unless doing so does, in fact, reduce a bank's funding costs. This opportunity cost grows, moreover, at a compound rate. A bank that forgoes low-risk, low-margin business (e.g., expanding its Euro placement book with minimal mismatch) will reduce the amount of earnings it can retain, which in turn, reduces the amount it can increase its assets in subsequent years without violating its self-imposed capital constraint. The cost of restricting leverage in a given year is not just the earnings forgone that year, but also the earnings forgone in future years, because the bank's decision to limit its leverage in one year reduces its retained earnings that year and, thereby, the size of the capital base from which it can leverage in subsequent years.

Capital notes

After Comptroller of the Currency James Saxon ruled that banks could use money raised through the sale of subordinated capital debentures as part of their capital, a number of banks issued such paper in the early and mid-1960s. At that time, capital notes were ballyhooed as a means for banks to increase capital without diluting equity.

Since debt is debt whatever the comptroller calls it, a bank must, in the context of asset/liability management, view the sale of capital notes as the assumption of a long-term, fixed-rate liability; as such, the sale of capital notes exposes a bank to interest rate risk.

In retrospect, in the 1960s, buying long-term money at a fixed rate was a good gambit for banks, because money bought then proved to be cheap over the long haul. As inflation became a problem and long-term rates rose, banks responded by tapering off their sale of capital debentures other than convertibles. Once the purchase of long-term money became unattractive to banks from a rate point of view, the major banks turned to a cheaper alternative for dealing with their capital ratio problem, namely, allowing that ratio to deteriorate slowly over time.

Capital at the stroke of a pen

It is the tradition in the United States for bank regulators to write detailed rules. While bank protests over such rules are often highly vocal, the truth is that banks find it easier to get around specific rules than to act in disrespect of the spirit of the Fed's request when it regulates by "jawboning."

A number of large depositors arbitrarily make it a rule to deposit funds only with banks having a billion or more in assets; consequently, there is a big incentive for an $800 or $900 million dollar bank to reach the billion-dollar mark. A number of such banks do so on statement dates by depositing with each other hundreds of millions of dollars, thereby increasing both sides of their balance sheets.

Should the Fed impose explicit capital requirements, a similar game could be played by the banks. For a bank, any debt maturing in over five years can be treated as capital. This being the case, should capital become a binding constraint on the expansion of big banks, a simple and expeditious remedy would be for these banks to engage in bilateral lending: two banks each agree to lend each other $100 million for X years under a contract that gives the right of offset. At the stroke of a pen, these banks would have created an extra $100 million of bank capital and, in the process, have made a joke of capital requirements.

Ironically, central banks, the Fed included, have created a precedent for this. A common way central banks obtain foreign exchange reserves is to create them at the stroke of a pen—by doing swaps of domestic currency for foreign currency with other central banks.

De facto government guarantees

Institutions that operate in the international capital market are concerned with the capital adequacy not only of top U.S. banks, but of major foreign banks. The endless attention devoted by analysts to making fine gradations with respect to the credit worthiness of the world's top banks on the basis of capital ratios and other data is probably largely a waste of time. The failure of the Bankhaus Herstatt taught central banks one lesson: The cost of permitting a major bank to fail far exceeds the cost of bailing it out through an assisted merger with a healthy bank. The upshot is that, today, all of the top free world banks—whether they are American, British, Japanese, or whatever—have, in effect, the de facto backing of their central banks.

This suggests that central banks as lenders of last resort ought to be, if anything, even more concerned than they are about bank capital adequacy. However, if one looks at banks that got into trouble, the Herstatt included, the problem was not that any of these banks initially had too little capital, but rather that management controls were too loose or that management decided to bet the bank. For no bank is capital, however large, a substitute for either good management or an economic environment in which the institution can be economically viable. In this respect, the experience of the thrifts is instructive. What got the thrifts into trouble was not inadequate capital, but rather the fact that regulators and legislators failed to permit the thrifts to make a timely and graceful exit from their traditional and no-longer-viable line of business: using short-term deposits to fund long-term, fixed-rate assets.

This said, we will now examine a few large banks that got it wrong.

BANKS THAT GOT IT WRONG

In discussing how one ought to run a bank—the topic of the rest of this book—it is often helpful to reinforce a point being made by describing the difficulties into which violating some fundamental, frequently simple principle of asset and liability management got a particular bank. To provide background for such references, we will briefly tell the stories of three prominent banks that got it wrong.

A survey of problem banks and thrifts suggests that the root of difficulties at such an institution is always one or some combination of three factors. First, the institution has inept management that—often in attempting to achieve over-rapid growth of the bank—plays bet the bank and commits other management sins. Second, the institution is the victim of dishonesty. Third—the case of many thrifts—the institution is forced, largely by misregulation, into a position in which its economic viability is threatened.

In selecting case studies of banks that got it wrong, we have limited our choices to banks that were victims of inept management. The problems that the thrifts got into by borrowing short at regulated rates and investing long in fixed-rate assets are so well known that no case study is required for us to refer, as we often do in later chapters, to the difficulties facing these institutions.

The Franklin National Bank[4]

On October 8, 1974, the Franklin National Bank of New York made history by becoming the largest bank ever to have failed in the United States. Nine months before its demise, Franklin, with $3.7 billion of deposits, was the nation's 20th largest bank.

History. Franklin, incorporated in 1926, remained for almost four decades a Long Island retail bank. In the 1950s, Arthur Roth, Franklin's chairman, pursued an aggressive growth and liberal loan policy. Since Franklin operated in a rich and growing area and was protected by state law from the competition of New York City banks, Roth was able to attain rapid growth at Franklin. Between 1950 and 1961, Franklin's assets rose from $71 million to $1.2 billion.

In 1960, the New York State legislature passed the Omnibus Banking Act that permitted New York City banks to establish branches in Nassau, the county where, along with Suffolk, Franklin was the dominant retail bank. The resulting competitive threat led Roth to conclude that, if Franklin's rapid growth were to continue, it would have to enter wholesale banking in New York City. In 1961, Franklin applied to the Comptroller of the Currency for permission to establish a New York City branch. Permission was promptly granted, and after some delays, Franklin opened its first New York City branch in 1964. In 1967, Franklin acquired, via a merger with the Federation Bank and Trust Company, 13 additional city branches.

To establish a base and then to grow in the highly competitive New York market, Franklin made loans to companies whose low credit ratings made it difficult for them to borrow from major New York banks. Because of its liberal lending policies, Franklin was able to expand its assets from $1.5 billion in 1964 to $3 billion in 1969.

Having experienced a decline in earnings subsequent to its move into the New York market, Franklin decided to move abroad. In June 1968, Franklin's international division held less than $12 million of foreign deposits and had outstanding loans and acceptances of $48.7 million. To expand its small international base and to participate in the growing Eurodollar market, Franklin decided to open a foreign branch. Costs in London being high, Franklin began by opening a shell branch in Nassau and a representative office in London; in 1972, Franklin upgraded its London office to a full branch. Between 1969 and 1973, Franklin's foreign branch deposits as a percentage of total deposits soared from 7.7 to 30.5 percent, its foreign branch loans as a

---

[4] Two long and useful descriptions of the Franklin's downfall are: Joan Edelman Spero, *The Failure of the Franklin National Bank* (New York: Columbia University Press, 1980), and Joseph F. Sinkey, Jr., *Franklin National Bank of New York: A Portfolio and Performance Analysis of our Largest Bank Failure*, FDIC, Division of Research, Working Paper, no. 75-10.

percentage of total loans from 2 to 19.8 percent. At this point, foreign operations had become a major element in Franklin's overall operations.

In expanding its domestic loan portfolio, Franklin lent to poorer credits on terms no better than its larger New York competitors were charging on loans to good credits. On its Euro loans—most of which consisted of syndications—Franklin got only the usual, normally small, spread, but in most cases it was at least making loans in which other established banks participated.

In 1972, the management picture at Franklin was somewhat complicated and clouded by the entry on the scene of the Italian financier, Michele Sindona, who purchased 21.6 percent of the common stock of the holding company which owned the Franklin. Shortly thereafter, Sindona and a close associate, Carlo Bordoni, were elected to the Franklin board of directors. Sindona, who had ownership interests in a number of Italian banks, took the view that, in the new floating exchange rates era—begun in March 1973—speculating in foreign exchange was an attractive and appropriate way for a bank to seek to earn big profits.

Presumably, his view influenced the decision of Franklin's management to try bolstering its weakening profits by becoming a highly speculative dealer in foreign exchange. On May 17, 1971, Franklin traded $19 million of foreign exchange; on May 14, three years later, it traded $3.3 billion.

Problems at the time of failure. By 1974, a decade of rapid growth and poor management had left Franklin with a number of problems. In searching for growth and profits, the bank had made a number of bets, each of which turned out to be ill conceived or ill timed.

To achieve its growth targets, Franklin consistently lent to poor credits in its domestic operations. As a result, by May 14, 1974, classified loans represented 58.7 percent of Franklin's capital while its loans criticized by national bank examiners totaled 62 percent of capital.[5] Franklin's gamble that loans to poor credits would be paid off resulted, by the spring of 1974, in massive losses when the impact of tight money and an economic slowdown further weakened the ability of Franklin's borrowers to meet their loan commitments.

At the same time, Franklin's earnings were also suffering because it had bet in a number of ways that interest rates would fall in in 1974. Specifically, in 1973, the Franklin's president, Paul Luftig, believ-

---

[5] A classified loan is one cited by examiners as being at risk to some degree. A classified loan may or may not be nonperforming. A nonperforming loan is a loan on which interest is not paid when due. Since banks are examined only periodically, a loan may become nonperforming before it is classified.

ing that interest rates would decline in 1974, shortened the bank's domestic book which was already characterized by high reliance on short-term borrowings and, in particular, by large purchases of Fed funds. Luftig's 1973 forecast of lower rates in 1974 also led the Franklin to balloon the bond holdings in its trading account. Both its short book and its bond holdings hurt Franklin's earnings when rates, including those on Federal funds, rose to unprecedented heights in 1974. An additional drain on earnings was Franklin's quarter-of-a-billion municipal portfolio which, in 1974, was yielding an average of only 4 percent while the bank's average cost of funds was 7.5 percent.

Franklin's decision to speculate in foreign exchange, like the other bets it made, cost it dearly. From October 1973 to January 1974, the dollar appreciated over 10 percent against European currencies and the Japanese yen. Anticipating that this trend would continue, in January 1974, Franklin's traders began speculating heavily in favor of the dollar by shorting foreign currencies. Precisely at this moment, the termination of U.S. controls on capital outflows and the easing of foreign restraints on capital inflows caused the exchange value of the dollar to slide sharply. By May 1974, Franklin's net short position in the steadily appreciating dollar was $232.6 million.

Part of Franklin's massive speculation in the foreign exchange market reflected a decision by bank management to seek to profit from such speculation. Part resulted from unauthorized trading which Franklin's traders were able to carry out because they had the cooperation of clerks in the foreign exchange department, of Peter Shaddick, whom Sindona had hired to head Franklin's international division, and of Bordoni.

The trading losses Franklin took on its foreign exchange positions, which far exceeded the limits set by management, became so large that Shaddick and Bordoni felt compelled to hide them. One way they did so was to enter into sham transactions with two Sindona-owned banks: At the end of an unprofitable quarter, Franklin would buy or sell currencies with these banks at rates that enabled Franklin's foreign exchange activities to show a profit; subsequently, these transactions were reversed at the same price.

The downfall. While Franklin's various ill-conceived gambits were apparent and a source of concern to both regulators and astute members of the banking community, public perception of the Franklin's difficulties did not become widespread until May 1, 1974. On that date, the Federal Reserve Board denied Franklin's parent holding company its request to acquire Talcott National Corporation, a U.S. finance and factoring company that Sindona had purchased with the intent of selling it to Franklin. The Fed's basis for denying the acquisition was that it would be "a complication and diversionary factor" in Franklin's efforts to undertake an until-then unpublicized $1 billion retrenchement program that the Comptroller's office had recommended after a 4-month examination of the bank ending in March 1974.

The Talcott decision triggered concern about the Franklin's viability. One immediate result was that Franklin, with purchases of Fed funds totaling one sixth of its liabilities, suddenly faced a liquidity crisis. A number of banks that had been selling to Franklin Fed funds (such sales are unsecured loans) became unwilling to do so. As a result, on May 8, 1974, Franklin was forced to borrow $110 million at the discount window of the New York Fed.

On May 10, the Franklin announced that it would omit its regular quarterly dividend; three days later it announced that it had suffered a $14 million loss due to "unauthorized foreign exchange trading," that it had undertaken a shake-up of top management, and that its president had been removed. On May 14, the FDIC listed Franklin as a "potential payoff," which meant that there was a 50 percent chance that Franklin would need FDIC assistance in the near future. These announcements precipitated a further crisis in confidence in the Franklin which, in turn, exacerbated its liquidity problem. By May 15, Franklin's borrowings at the discount window had risen to $750 million—the retrenchment in the Franklin's borrowings from private sources sought by the Comptroller had almost been achieved but hardly in the orderly fashion hoped for by that agency.

At this point, the Franklin was no longer viable, and its fate fell into the hands of federal regulatory bodies. Any time after May 12, the Comptroller's office could have forced the Franklin to close by declaring it insolvent. The Fed, after fulfilling its initial lender of last resort function, could also have forced the bank to close by cutting off its access to the discount window. Instead, it allowed the Franklin's borrowing at the window to rise, by the date it was finally closed (October 8, 1974), to $1.7 billion.

Responsibility for solving the Franklin problem ultimately fell to the FDIC, which opted for a deposit assumption solution. As in similar cases, the FDIC sought competitive bids for the Franklin from possible merger candidates. Of the bids submitted by four banks, the European American Bank and Trust Company's was highest, and on October 8, the Franklin was merged into EAB&T. For its bid, EAB&T was required to accept $1,487 million of Franklin's assets, an amount equal to $1,612 million of deposits remaining at the Franklin plus certain other liabilities minus its purchase bid of $125 million. For its part, the FDIC assumed the Franklin's loans at the discount window, $314 million of other liabilities, and assets equal roughly to the sum of these two figures.

Dishonesty played a role in the failure of the Franklin, but only a minor one. Even in its absence, the bank would have failed due to inept management. What led the bank to ruin was the determination of management to take a small, successful retail bank and turn it almost overnight into a major national bank that was active in both wholesale and international banking. This obsession with growth and earning profits commensurate with the bank's growing size, led the bank to make one gamble after another, each of which failed and left management yet more desperate to make still another gamble that would pay off big.

The experience of the Franklin illustrates a point made later: The time to really watch a bank's management is when things are going badly. At some point, management comes to the realization that they are going to lose either their jobs or, worse still, their bank unless they make a high-stake gamble and win. That stark reality—nothing to lose on a gamble and everything to win—is bound to dampen whatever natural risk aversion management may have.

The First Pennsylvania Bank

The story of the First Pennsylvania Bank, or First Pennsy as it is known familiarly on the street, bears strong similarities to that of the Franklin. Fundamentally, the bank's problems arose from its attempt to pursue an aggressive growth strategy that would bring it, in a decade, from a small but successful regional bank to a competitor with national money center banks.

In 1968 John Bunting, Jr., was named chief executive officer of First Pennsylvania Corporation. Bunting, an outspoken and controversial banker, immediately began to convert a conservative regional bank into an aggressive financial conglomerate. His moves to accomplish this, which were bold and characterized by a heavy emphasis on innovation, expanded Philadelphia's largest bank into bond trading, consumer finance, and mortgage banking. Initially, Bunting's strategies turned First Pennsy into one of the most profitable banks in the country; the growing pains came later.

Surfacing problems. In 1979, First Pennsy began to attract attention as a bank that perhaps had got it wrong in a big way. On September 11, 1979, First Pennsylvania Corporation reported that its earnings were down 11 percent from 1978 in the second quarter, making it the third consecutive quarter that the holding company had posted a year-to-year decline. Six days later, Bunting resigned and was immediately replaced by George Butler, a more conservative figure who, it was hoped, would reverse, over a short transition period, the downward trend in the bank's profits.

Shortly before resigning, Bunting stated publicly "banking isn't fun any more." Presumably for him it was not; by 1979, most of Bunting's strategies for growth—each of which individually incorporated a bet on the level and direction of interest rates, and all of which together constituted betting the bank—had gone sour.

One big gamble that was hurting First Pennsy's earnings in 1979 was its decision to buy a huge—$1.2 billion—bond portfolio and short fund it to earn carry profits. Initially, this strategy earned substantial profits for the bank. However, when rates again began to rise in 1978, this position became a nightmare. Carry on the position turned negative and became a drain on bank earnings that the bank could cut only by taking a huge ($124 million) capital loss on selling its bonds that, because of rising interest rates, were trading well below their book value.

In 1971, Bunting formed a bond trading subsidiary, First Pennco. Initially, this operation was successful and highly profitable; its traders were regarded on Wall Street as sharp and knowledgeable professionals. In 1979, however, First Pennco, which had made the same bet on rates that the bank had—buying long bonds and funding them with short-dated money—was contributing red ink to the income statement of the holding company. So, too, was First Pennsylvania's once-profitable mortgage banking operation, Pennamco Incorporated. High interest rates were even putting First Pennsylvania's previously profitable consumer finance operation under stress.

Not every bet a bank makes on rates is obvious as such. The outcome of a loan to a grade B credit often depends not only on the management skills of the borrower, but on the economic environment—including interest rates—in which the firm operates. First Pennsy, while more conservative than Franklin, made, as part of its aggressive growth strategy, its share of loans to lesser credits. In 1979 and subsequent years, these loans led to substantial losses partly because the borrowers were further weakened by high and unpredictable interest rates.

By mid-1979, First Pennsy was showing the obvious signs of a bank in trouble. Not only were its profits declining, but its return on assets—26 cents for each $100 of assets—was low even for a large bank. And its capital had fallen to 3.35 percent of total assets—a capital ratio of roughly 30 to 1.

Retrenchment.   When Butler took over the helm of First Pennsylvania, he began a policy of retrenchment. In October, the holding company sold to Manufacturers Hanover Corporation a half-dozen profitable consumer finance subsidiaries and its unprofitable mortgage service subsidiary, Pennamco.

The retrenchment, which netted First Pennsylvania a gain of almost $45 million, was to be the first of many. In October of 1979, First

Pennsy, like every other participant in the financial markets, was hit by the Fed's "Saturday night special" (noted in Figure 7–1), which led to a dramatic upsurge in interest rates that carried into the spring of 1980 when credit controls were imposed. The unpredictable and very sharp upturn in rates that began in October compounded the woes of First Pennsy. Every interest rate gamble it had on the book, including its still huge bond portfolio, became a yet more costly mistake.

Bail out at a price.   By April 1980, First Pennsy had not only an earnings, but also a severe liquidity problem. It was losing deposits, it could no longer sell its CDs in the national market, and it was experiencing difficulties in buying money from other banks. Partly at the insistence of Volcker at the Fed, the FDIC mounted a rescue operation. Together with 22 private banks, the FDIC put together a $1.5 billion aid infusion comprising $500 million in loans and a $1 billion line of credit.

The bail-out package, which was designed to ward off the possible collapse of First Pennsylvania, the nation's 23d largest bank, came at a stiff price. While granted the right to continue to fight for survival, First Pennsy was required by its creditors to sell off enough of its low-yielding bonds to realize a $75 million loss for the year. Ironically, as First Pennsy began the forced sale of upwards of a half billion of long bonds, the value of these securities began to rise due to sharp declines in credit market rates.

At the beginning of 1980, First Pennsy's rate-sensitive liabilities exceeded its rate-sensitive earning assets by around $1.25 billion, or 15 percent of its earning assets. Over the year, reductions in First Pennsy's holdings of fixed-rate assets and its acquisition of a $175 million 5-year loan as part of the bail-out package put together for it by the FDIC reduced this gap to about one fourth of that size.

Butler began 1981 professing to see, as he had before, some light at the end of the tunnel. First willingly and then in response to conditions laid down by the banks who provided it with a bail-out package, First Pennsy was becoming a much slimmer organization, one that Butler hoped, ironically, would become what it had started out as, namely a respectable, profitable regional bank.

Unfortunately, 1981 was not slated to be an easy year for First Pennsy. Interest rates that were declining—albeit slowly—permitted the bank, after losing money for five straight quarters, to post an $8 million profit for the first half of the year. Then rising interest rates hit First Pennsy with a vengeance. In May, the rate on its 5-year loan, pegged once a year to the going 1-year CD rate, shot from 11.5 to 18.25 percent. This cost First Pennsy an extra $1 million a month. In addition, the company had to pay interest on another part of the $325 million loan it received from the FDIC; for the first year, this loan was interest-free.

Also at midyear, First Pennsy found itself having to pay 17 percent to support a $254.6 million portfolio of fixed-rate assets (mostly bonds) that were yielding on average only 9.25 percent. At that point, First Pennsy's mismatch or gap was costing it between $1.5 and $2 million a month. By the end of 1981, First Pennsylvania Corporation, which once had assets of over $10 billion, had shrunk to a $5.5 billion institution due to the sale of its mortgage and consumer finance subsidiaries, the discontinuance of First Pennco, and the forced sale of much of its bond portfolio. The corporation still had $255 million in fixed-rate assets, but it was determined to regain a full balance between its interest-sensitive liabilities and its interest-sensitive assets. Like a lot of financial institutions, First Pennsy entered 1982 needing—to solve its remaining problems—a healthy drop in interest rates but was not certain it would get one.

Whereas Franklin's problems reflected some measure of dishonesty and in the end truly reckless speculation, First Pennsy's troubles resulted in large part from a single fatal, but at the time not so obvious mistake: To achieve an accelerated rate of growth, Bunting made a series of rate bets that together constituted betting the whole bank. That, as we note later, is a mistake that a bank is likely to make only if it is guided by the views of a *single* strong-minded individual. Bunting was such a man, and his views prevailed at First Pennsy until he resigned.

The First National Bank of Chicago

From its founding in 1863, conservatism was a hallmark of the First National Bank of Chicago. That changed in 1969 when Gaylord Freeman became chairman. In five years, he transformed First Chicago from a regional bank into a holding company with offices around the country and branches and affiliates in Euro centers around the globe.

Freeman's emphasis on growth resulted in a near tripling of the bank's loans outstanding between 1969 and 1974. As hindsight was to show, that go-go growth cost First Chicago a stiff price: a breakdown of internal controls and the extending of loans to numerous poorer credits.

A point constantly stressed in later chapters is that, in a world characterized by high and highly volatile interest rates and by far-reaching changes in the structure of financial institutions and in the regulations under which they operate, it is crucial that a bank be managed by a competent team: one that is characterized by good internal communications and cooperation and that has a clear view of the direction in which it wants the institution to move. It is also crucial that all of the different strategies undertaken in different areas of the bank be well controlled and mesh with management's overall objectives.

Such management goals were not accomplished at First Chicago under Freeman. Instead of picking a successor, Freeman announced in 1972 that four officers were in the running for the top job. This created, until 1975, when Robert Abboud won the position, an atmosphere in which people tended to take sides and then take swipes at those they viewed as being on other teams. While Freeman's intent was to let the best man win, the competition he opened up for the top slot at the bank created tensions and frictions that made it impossible for First Chicago's management to develop and follow tightly controlled and closely coordinated strategies for growth.

The Abboud era. The lack of control that characterized growth Freeman style was most evident in the bank's loan portfolio. When Abboud became chairman in 1975, he inherited an appallingly risky loan portfolio that included $850 million of bad REIT (real estate investment trust) loans. In 1976, when federal examiners went over First Chicago's books, they concluded that classified loans totaled 191 percent of bank capital. Had 50 percent of the bank's doubtful loans and 25 percent of its substandard loans been written off, virtually all of First Chicago's capital would have disappeared.

Abboud stated in an interview after he left the bank that the Comptroller of the Currency did not force First Chicago out of business, as it had the Franklin, or arrange a bail out, as it had for First Pennsy, because First Chicago was just too big. Fear existed that, if the bank's condition were made public, havoc would result in both the domestic and international credit markets. Declaring the ninth largest bank in the United States insolvent was perhaps more than the financial system could tolerate.

According to Abboud, during the Freeman years, 1971–74, when the bank's assets rose from $8 to $17 billion, normal controls on lending vanished. Proper records were not kept; the bank had no way of knowing what its total commitments were. Loan officers were not getting proper documentation, and they were allowing customers to favorably alter the standard terms of loan notes.

To pull back First Chicago from the edge of bankruptcy, Abboud instituted a program to regain control over lending at the bank and to improve the quality of its loan portfolio. The job was difficult because the bank, due to its rapid expansion at home and abroad, was short on experienced lending officers. Abboud, who became known for his abrasive style of management and who used fear and intimidation freely, did nothing to ease the shortage of skilled personnel. Under his reign, infighting continued, and the bank lost good officers—including some whom it sorely needed to retain a number of long-standing good and hitherto loyal customers that the bank eventually lost.

The upshot of Abboud's accent on caution in lending was that First Chicago did succeed in improving the quality of its loan portfolio but only at the price of seeing its loan growth lag during 1978 and 1979 when other banks were enjoying strong loan demand. Under Abboud, First Chicago seemed to be losing its ability to compete in the corporate market for high-quality credits.

By 1979, another problem, short funding, was beginning to have a severe impact on First Chicago's earnings. Part of the problem's origin was outside the bank's control. As interest rates continued to rise from their lows at the end of 1977, the bank lost many low-cost consumer deposits to money market funds and other higher-yielding investments. This forced First Chicago to buy increasing amounts of short-term money in the money market to fund, among other things, a lot of bad loans the bank could not get off its books.

During 1979, the bank continued to make fixed-rate loans which it short funded. As interest rates went through the roof at the end of 1979 and in early 1980, First Chicago's earnings suffered visibly. Earnings in 1979 were off by 12 percent from the previous year, and on a quarter-to-quarter basis, earnings in the first quarter of 1980 were off by 44 percent.

These dismal earnings reflected not only the residual impact of previous bad loans, but misplaced bets on interest rates: short funding of fixed-rate loans, a short position in the bank's large Euro book at a time of rising rates, and a $3 million loss on bond trading in the first quarter of 1980.

The corner turned.   On April 28, 1980, the board of First Chicago fired Abboud and hired, after a two-month search, Barry F. Sullivan, a 49-year-old executive vice president of Chase Manhattan Bank, as its new chairman and chief executive officer. In sharp contrast to his predecessor, Sullivan has built a reputation for having an unassuming manner, an almost unfailing sense of humor, and—of crucial importance—an ability to listen and to tolerate dissent.

By the end of 1980, Sullivan had made discernable and encouraging improvements in First Chicago's performance. Nonperforming loans, which equaled a horrendous 11.5 percent of total loans when Abboud took over in 1975 and which Abboud brought down to 5 percent, fell still further under Sullivan. At the same time, First Chicago's return on assets, still well below that of its major competitors, jumped sharply during 1981.

One weakness Sullivan still must battle is the slow rate at which First Chicago is acquiring desirable new loans. The infighting which characterized First Chicago under Freeman and continued under Abboud, took its toll in many ways including the continued attrition of experienced loan officers. By bringing in a number of outsiders, Sullivan caused the exit of yet more officers, some of whom the bank would have done well to keep. However, on the credit side, Sullivan has made a point of personally courting good corporate clients which First Chicago lost during the period of internal turmoil under Abboud.

A point already stressed is the importance to a bank of having a top management team that communicates and cooperates to implement carefully chosen strategies. The failure of First Chicago to achieve this under either Freeman or Abboud was a major source of its problems. The bank's officers were demoralized; they also could not get together on strategy. For example, because of lack of cooperation and understanding between First Chicago's lending and funding officers, it was the last bank of its stature to offer its customers subprime loans priced off money market rates. With his more collegial style of management, Sullivan seems to have a chance to change this and to create a successful management team.

8

Liquidity management

In the 1960s and 1970s, banking became progressively tougher and more sophisticated. One message of Chapter 7 is that the pace of this trend has sharply accelerated thanks to a variety of factors: lofty and volatile interest rates, unpredictable and destabilizing changes in Fed policy, dramatic shifts in the regulatory environment, and the penchant of corporate treasurers for developing pencils as sharp as those of their friendly banker to whom they used to look for financial guidance.

Today, a good banker has to be someone who can read sheets of numbers and immediately comprehend their implications. He must engage in a constant and sophisticated analysis of his balance sheet, asking: What is my liquidity? What is my interest rate exposure? Are the levels of both appropriate for today? for the economic environment I anticipate tomorrow? If not, what must I do?

Unfortunately, liquidity and interest rate exposure are *not* separate properties of a balance sheet that can be dealt with one at a time. If they were, a banker's job would be less taxing. In practice, *a bank's liquidity and interest rate exposure are inextricably intertwined; changing one always alters the other.*

To illustrate, suppose a bank that is funding variable-rate loans decides it needs more liquidity; to get it, the bank buys a lot of

6-month CD money. By doing so, it increases its liquidity; also, wittingly or unwittingly, it increases its interest rate exposure. Should interest rates now fall, the bank may find itself funding with high-cost, long-term money loans on which yields are floating, even tumbling, down.

However intertwined liquidity and interest rate exposure may be, the crucial *first* step a banker must make in managing his balance sheet is to separate the two. Specifically, he must ask, given his present balance sheet, what is his liquidity *and* what is his interest rate exposure? This exercise will do three things for him: (1) tell him precisely where he stands now; (2) clarify the implications, with respect to both liquidity and interest rate exposure, of any move he might make; and (3) by implication, prevent him from falling into the trap of making an interest rate exposure decision when he thinks he is making a liquidity decision or vice versa.

From what we have said, it follows that our discussion of managing a bank's balance sheet must begin with an in-depth look at liquidity and interest rate exposure: what are they, how can they be measured, and why are they important?

We begin with liquidity for several reasons. First, liquidity problems tend to surface in the short run, and, while an adroit banker can live with an interest rate gamble gone sour for some time, he cannot survive even in the short-run without liquidity. Liquidity is what keeps the doors open in the short run. Second, if a banker feels that he has satisfied his minimum liquidity needs—that he can carry on his normal business without fear that he might be forced in a panic to bid at the worst moment for funds—he may decide to take chances to produce extra profits. However he does so, perhaps by increasing the mismatch in his book, his action will almost certainly raise his minimum liquidity needs. Thus, a banker can't make a reasoned decision to alter his interest rate exposure before he knows his liquidity position.

DEFINITION AND FUNCTIONS OF LIQUIDITY

Put tersely, *liquidity is having money when you need it.* More formally, *it is the ability to ensure the availability of funds to meet commitments at a reasonable price at all times.* To highlight the implications of this definition, we will examine the functions of liquidity.

Reassurance to creditors

Banks would make little money and be economically unimportant if all they did was to lend their capital. What banking is all about is *leverage.* A bank starts with some capital and then seeks to increase the return on that capital (1) by taking deposits and borrowing money, and (2) by then investing its total capital, deposits and borrowings, at an average rate it hopes will exceed the average rate at which it has accepted deposits and borrowed.[1]

A bank, depending on its size and position, will have various creditors: people who give it demand deposits, savings deposits, CD money, Fed funds, and repo money. *All* those suppliers of funds, whether they are small savers, major corporations buying million-dollar CDs, or other financial institutions lending millions of dollars in the Fed funds market, are, with respect to their investing of short-term balances, extremely *risk averse.* Their first concern is *not* return; it is *safety of principal.* Specifically, they want to know that they will be able to get the money they have deposited with or lent to their bank when due or on demand. Only when that concern is satisfied will lenders consider and compare rates offered by different banks.

A first and crucial function of liquidity is that it provides reassurance to a bank's creditors that deposits or other monies they have given the bank can be repaid. So long as a bank is perceived as having adequate liquidity, lenders will not worry about placing money with it. However, once lenders start to question, even in the slightest degree, a bank's liquidity, they will think twice about giving it money. This, in turn, will result in the bank having to *pay up* to buy CD money, Eurodeposits, or Fed funds. Rate tiering is a fact of life in every one of the non–rate-regulated markets in which banks buy money, and for most large banks these markets are the ones that count because they buy so much money there.

It is painful for a bank to pay up for money during the initial stage when people perceive it as *perhaps* having a liquidity problem. If that problem persists and if the perception of it becomes widespread and strongly held, something worse occurs; a bank may suddenly find it cannot buy money anywhere at any price. The reason is that, even under rate tiering, the differentials between the rates different banks pay are typically so minute that, from the investor's viewpoint, there is no penalty for not lending to a bank that is perceived as having a liquidity problem. If the perception that a bank has a liquidity problem closes off its access to the market for funds, then, at that point, a problem, which may have been minor, short-run, and soluble, becomes a major problem that can be dealt with only by a drastic restructuring of the bank's balance sheet, most typically one that involves a shrinking of the bank's footings.[2]

---

[1] See Chapter 2.

[2] Bankers have imported from London and often use the British expression *footings.* On any balance sheet, footings are total assets which, by definition, equal total liabilities plus net worth.

Examples of this are provided by the Franklin National in 1974 and First Pennsy in 1979. Each rapidly went from a position where it had access to the national market and could sell its CDs at almost the same rate as Morgan or Citi to a situation in which it was suddenly not only not in the national market but not even in the regional market any longer. As their short-term liabilities began to run off, these banks could not replace their maturing funds at any price. The problems they faced occurred initially not so much because people knew that the mismatch between their assets and liabilities was bad, but rather because people realized the unfavorable impact on their earnings that this mismatch would have unless rates fell sharply. The market viewed these banks as having a potential liquidity problem, and the market's reaction to this perception—ceasing to lend to these banks—created the contingency feared.

Ensures ability to repay borrowings

One function of liquidity is to assure a bank's *creditors* that the bank will be able to pay off its debts so that they will continue to lend it funds. A related, but different, function of liquidity is to ensure *the bank itself* that it will always be able to repay its outstanding borrowings as they come due without necessarily having to seek to roll them.

To illustrate in an oversimplified way, note that, so long as a bank is funding 3-month assets with 3-month liabilities, by definition it can't have a liquidity problem because the funds it needs to pay off its borrowings will always be produced by maturing assets. This situation contrasts sharply with that of a bank that is financing 6-month, fixed-rate loans by rolling 3-month CDs or, worse still, overnight Fed funds.

Ensures ability to lend to meet prior commitments

A bank extends two sorts of lines of credit to its customers. One is called a *committed facility:* the customer pays a fee for this, and the agreement legally binds the bank to lend to the customer if the latter chooses to take down funds. The more usual line of credit extended by a bank is *not* a legal commitment to lend. However, a bank typically treats it as if it were.

A bank is in business to do business with its customers. If it refused to make a loan to a customer to whom it had extended a line of credit, it would probably lose that customer. Worse still, if word got around that it had done so, the bank would probably lose other customers. For reasons of building customer relationships, any line of credit is treated by a bank for all practical purposes like a legal commitment to lend unless the customer happens to be tottering on the edge of bankruptcy; then the bank may get away with turning down a loan request.

A major bank may have outstanding lines of credit equal to some multiple of its outstanding loans. This means that it never knows when it may be hit by a big demand for new loans. Since customer relationships require that such demand be met, a bank must be prepared to fund unanticipated increases in its loans. To do so, it must maintain adequate liquidity, and the only way it can is by ensuring that the size of its current takings from the market and its good name are such that it can go to the market and buy more money as it needs to.

Avoids forced sale of assets

If a bank gets into a terribly illiquid position and is unable to roll its outstanding borrowings as they mature, one of its options is to sell securities on a *forced* basis. Generally speaking, this would occur against a background of high interest rates, and consequently, the securities would have to be sold at substantial losses. In the worst case, these losses could be so large that they would impair the bank's capital. For example, a severe liquidity problem forced First Pennsy to sell off governments in its portfolio at far less than the value at which it had booked these securities. As a result, the bank lost roughly one third of its capital and emerged from the exercise not only a chastened, but also a much smaller institution.

A similar situation may obtain with the sale of loans. Major banks sell participations in loans to their correspondents as a service to the latter or sometimes to improve their own liquidity. When major banks do this, normally for reasons of customer relations, they stand ready to buy back those participations at a market price if the correspondent chooses to sell them. Except for such transactions, little secondary trading occurs in bank loans. Therefore, a bank with a liquidity problem will look first to the sale of securities as a source of funds. But if its problem is extreme, it may also go to other banks and try to sell them loans on its books. Unfortunately, the background for such sales is typically, as in the case of the forced sale of securities, that interest rates are high. Consequently, when the loan is priced to reflect not only the name of the borrower, but the rate and conditions of the loan, the name of the game is fire sale; that is, the loan is sold at a *market price* that is inevitably well below the face value, and the selling bank takes a substantial loss.

The above scenario is precisely what happened to First Pennsy. Its liquidity situation was so severe in 1979 that it had to come hat in hand to its big New York correspondents and say, "Look, we really have a liquidity problem. In fact we have a survival problem. Would you care to take some of our loans off our hands?" The outcome was that First Pennsy did get rid of some of its loans; it also sustained substantial losses doing so.

Precludes having to pay up in the market

As noted, if the market perceives that a bank has a liquidity problem, the minimum penalty the market will impose on that bank is to force it to pay up for funds. An equally important eventuality for a bank to avoid is to have to go into the market to bid for funds when it doesn't want to, for example, when rates are peaking. Having adequate liquidity can ensure that a bank is not forced to do this.

To illustrate, consider two banks operating in the following environment: the yield curve is sharply inverted, interest rates are high and about to peak, for example, as in the fall of 1980. One bank, having correctly anticipated a possible peak in rates, has protected itself by buying long-term funds and can stay out of the market for some time. The second bank, counting on a downturn in rates that failed to materialize, has relied too much on purchases of overnight funds and is finally forced to add to its liquidity by buying longer-term funds at the worst possible moment, when rates are at or near their peak.

Avoids nonvolitional use of the discount window

Often a large bank will reason that it has not been to the discount window for a while, Fed funds are 19 percent, the discount rate is 14 percent, so why not borrow a hefty amount at the window for a weekend to take the edge off its cost of funds? A bank can get away with this, although under the Fed's current policy on borrowing at the window, a bank will be unable to do this often. This sort of borrowing is done not because the bank has a liquidity problem, but because it is trying to shave its borrowing costs.

The situation is totally different if a bank gets into a serious liquidity problem: it can't buy money in the market and has to crawl to the discount officer on its knees saying, "I need money." The Franklin National did this when it was a basket case, literally bankrupt. First Pennsy did it when it was still viable but getting poorer by the day.

When a severe liquidity problem forces a bank to go to the discount window on a *nonvolitional* basis, that bank puts itself literally at the mercy of the Fed. Once it does this, the Fed can and will dictate to bank management how, in the Fed's view, the bank should and must restructure its balance sheet to regain financial health. To cite a case in point, it was the Fed and the FDIC which forced First Pennsy to sell off securities and loans at fire sale prices. In effect, the Fed and the

FDIC said to that bank, "We will help you, but when you have taken our medicine, you will be a viable but much smaller institution." In the case of the Franklin National, the Fed and the FDIC forced the demise of this bank via an assisted merger with the European American Bank.

Illiquidity has many prices. The highest by far is to be forced to borrow nonvolitionally from the Fed because a bank that does so hands over control of its destiny to the Fed.

SOURCES OF LIQUIDITY

Liquidity—having money when it's needed—is vital to a bank. The sources of liquidity to which a bank may turn are varied.

Assets maturing in the near term

"Assets maturing in the near term" is a bit of a catchall; what it includes will vary depending of the size and position of a bank.

Any bank's loan portfolio will throw off cash in several ways. Some of a bank's loans may be about to mature and will not be renewed. Others may be on an installment basis and consequently throw off cash periodically as installments come due. Finally, all of a bank's accruing loans throw off cash in the form of periodic interest payments.

Most banks will have some securities and money market instruments—such as Treasury bills, BAs (own held in portfolio or purchased paper), other banks' CDs, and perhaps Euro placements or sales of term Fed funds—that are near maturity and can be viewed as an immediate or near immediate source of liquidity. For a small bank, Fed funds sold are a *key* source of liquidity, since a bank can vary the amount it sells from day to day. In fact, for a small bank, the sale of Fed funds or, if the bank has sufficient funds, the sale of Euro call money is probably the most attractive means available of storing liquidity.[3] The liquidity of a small bank is necessarily resident almost exclusively in its assets, whereas that of a major bank resides to a large degree in its ability to buy money.

Many of the C&I loans a large bank makes have no definite maturity because they are often rolled; also, they cannot be called. However, large banks do make several special classes of loans, the outstanding amounts of which they can vary at will by altering the rates they charge. Specifically, money market banks can reduce the overnight loans they make to brokers and dealers simply by posting a higher loan

---

[3] Normally major U.S. banks decline to accept Euro call deposits in amounts less than some high minimum, such as $5 million.

rate. Also, such banks can reduce loans in the form of short-term advances simply by raising the rates they charge on non–prime-priced loans. These short-term advances, the volume of which a bank feels free to control through pricing, are often closer to "arm's length deals" than are regular loans made to firms with which the bank is cultivating a customer relationship.

Readily salable short-term assets

A second source of liquidity for a bank is assets that are near maturity and for which a bid can be counted on. Such assets will typically include a few longer-term securities nearing maturity and a lot of money market instruments.

In a world of relatively stable interest rates, this second source of liquidity is attractive because a bank can count on being able to sell such securities at or near book value. In the conditions that prevailed at the end of the 1970s and the beginning of the 1980s, this was typically not the case. When interest rates move 300 basis points in a week, as they occasionally did during this period, buying short-term securities to store liquidity and then promptly reselling these securities to meet a liquidity need can easily result in substantial losses: 1 or 2 percent of the amount invested depending on the maturity of the security. No longer can a bank buying money market instruments assume they are a riskless store of liquidity.

A bank's ability or willingness to view liquid assets as being immediately convertible to cash depends, in part, on its willingness to accept possible losses from the sale of these securities and the resulting impact of such losses on its income statement. Thus, what sorts of funds a bank thinks of itself as being able to realize from the sale of short-term assets depends on three things: (1) the size of its holdings, (2) the volatility of interest rates, and (3) its willingness to absorb losses to raise cash. To this it should be added that, when a bank is listing the assets it can sell to raise cash, there is no reason to limit its list to short-term liquid assets. Depending on what the bank is willing to sell and on its willingness to absorb losses or take gains, anything for which there is a bid is a liquid asset. Even the president's desk is a liquid asset if there is a bid for it, and if Napoleon once used it, there probably is.

A final note: in textbooks on banking, a bank's total government portfolio is often listed as its first and foremost source of liquidity; according to textbooks, gaining liquidity is why banks buy governments. For large banks, this view is incorrect. All such banks hock their government and federal agency portfolios in the repo market. If they sell these securities, they do realize cash, *but* they must immediately use most or all of that cash to pay off the repo borrowings which they used to finance these securities. Small banks that do not borrow in the repo market could realize cash by selling off governments and agencies, but their disinclination to take capital losses may prevent them from doing so when money tightens and they need cash.

Access to purchasable funds

A third source of bank liquidity is *access to purchasable funds:* the ability to write CDs, domestic or Euro; to buy Fed funds; to take (buy) Euro time deposits; and, if the bank's money needs arises from an expansion of its government portfolio, its agency portfolio, or its dealer position, to do more repo.

Wide discrepancies exist among banks in their access to bought money. These discrepancies reflect the fact that *an individual bank's access to bought money is directly and positively correlated with its size and with the market's perception of how good a name the bank has, that is, its credit worthiness.*

Money market banks and major regional banks all have extensive Euro operations and, unless they have blemished their good name, can buy huge amounts of money in the national and Euromarkets in any of the ways enumerated above. Some smaller regionals run a Euro placement book; others lack facilities for taking Eurodollars.[4] Also small regionals can sell their CDs and buy money in other ways only within their local sphere of influence, that is, from the business firms, other financial institutions, and consumers who form their natural customer base. Small banks have little or no access to bought money for two reasons. First, they can buy money only from customers in a severely restricted geographic area. Second, Regulation Q, while being phased out, still restricts their ability to compete for demand and time deposits by offering higher rates.

Major investors lending large amounts of money to banks are *extremely* sensitive in selecting the banks to which they will give money—to bank credit worthiness. Investors evaluate a bank's credit worthiness in terms of the level and consistency of its earnings, the quality of its assets (how high its loan loss ratio is), the bank's reputation for sound management, and the strength of its capital position. Because of the sensitivity of investors to bank credit worthiness, there is a tiering among major banks not only in the rates they pay to buy money, but also in the amounts of money they can buy.

Once a major bank does anything to sully its name, it will find that, even if it is still a large and viable institution, its access to bought money has noticeably diminished. Investors will want only so much of its paper, and if it tries to sell more, it will have to pay up sharply.

---

[4] Euro placement books run out of shell branches are described in Chapter 11.

Paying up a little is acceptable; paying up a lot is not, because doing so casts still more doubt on the borrower's name. An example is the First of Chicago. No one could seriously argue that, because of that bank's losses and retrenchment in 1980, it was in imminent danger of bankruptcy. Nonetheless, those events not only forced First Chicago to pay up for money, but limited its ability to buy money until it reestablished its good name.

The access to purchasable funds that money market banks with good names enjoy means that they could expand their size almost without limit were it not for their need to maintain capital ratios that are respectable in the view of bank management, bank regulators, and investors. As noted in Chapter 7, what is respectable boils down to staying in line with the herd. While capital is often the binding constraint on the expansion of well-managed money market and large regional banks, the same is not true of smaller banks; their limited access to purchasable funds sets a second constraint on their ability to expand their footings and to change their liability structure.

Loan participations.   One of the ways in which money market and major regional banks can buy money is by participating out loans. Large banks that participate in syndicated Euro or domestic loans or that make large loans themselves often sell off pieces of these loans to their correspondents to cultivate a relationship with them.[5] A second reason a large bank does this is to build a network of correspondents to which it may, when money is tight, be able to sell off either pieces of new loans it can't or does not want to fund entirely itself, or even pieces of existing loans in its portfolio. A money center bank that has built a network of correspondents that regularly buy loans from it has, in effect, created an extra means by which it may be able to raise funds when money is tight.

Liquidity cushion.   In buying money, it is a good rule for a bank that cannot always immediately buy whatever amount of new money it may need to buy more money than it needs to support its present asset structure. A bank that does this acquires a useful *liquidity cushion.*

A bank lacking such a cushion can see the greatest deal in the world come down the pike and be unable to take advantage of it because it

---

[5] *Loan participations* for this purpose should be distinguished from *syndicated loans.* In both the domestic and the Euromarkets, very large loans to a single credit are syndicated, because both in terms of funding and of the credit risk exposure to a single name, the loans are too large to be handled by a single bank. There is no magic number to tell how much a bank should lend to a single credit. In the United States, banks are not permitted to lend to a single credit an amount exceeding 10 percent of their capital. Canadian banks are subject to no such restriction and make much larger loans to a given name—often to the consternation of their American competitors. Euro loan syndication was discussed in Chapter 6. Syndication of domestic loans is carried out in a similar fashion.

presently has no money to do so and can't raise that money either rapidly enough or at all. Example: a small regional is suddenly approached by its big city correspondent which says, "We have a terrific loan and thought that as a favor we would allow you to participate in it. You can lock in 1 percent over a prime for a year." For such a bank, a safe loan at that rate is a terrific opportunity. The minimum participation in the loan is, however, $5 million. If the bank does not have $5 million in liquidity, it just has to watch the deal go by. Alternatively, if it has been selling MMCs and laying off the money at a positive spread in the Fed funds market awaiting just such an opportunity, it can snap up the deal.

A second reason a liquidity cushion is useful is that it ensures failure of a present source of funds will not force the liquidation of desirable assets. An example is thrifts; they start losing even MMC money to money funds when short-term rates drop because a dive in the latter causes the maximum rate thrifts may pay on MMCs to fall faster than do yields on money funds. If a thrift faced with this situation has used the money raised through the sale of MMCs to invest in 6-month Euros (i.e., offset high-cost money by doing a profitable arbitrage with matched maturities), it can respond to the drop in its MMC deposits by letting its holdings of Euros run off. Alternatively, if the thrift has been using MMC money to fund its basic mortgage portfolio, any drop in its MMC deposits may mean a fire sale; a thrift's last resort sources of funds are loans from the FHLB, which—because they are priced at market rates—are expensive and loans from the Fed, of which it can get only a limited amount.

Last resort borrowing

Every bank should have some last resort source from which it can raise funds on a temporary basis. One source most banks use is lines of credit from other banks. Banks that have a correspondent bank will ask that bank for a standby line of credit. Such lines are almost like the lines issuers of commercial paper use to back their paper. A small bank will come to its larger correspondent and say, "We do not really expect to ever have to borrow from you, but if we do, will you accommodate us?" The correspondent gives them what amounts to a standby line, which the small bank may use if it really needs to. Some regional banks will ask money market banks for similar standby lines. The largest regionals, however, view money market banks as competitors and consequently are more likely to ask a foreign bank for a dollar standby line. Foreign banks, in turn, establish dollar lines of credit with top U.S. banks. Regardless of their size and name, foreign banks feel an extra liquidity risk when they deal in dollars because they lack access to purchasable dollars that a top U.S. bank has. Top U.S. money market banks will, for similar reasons, ask French banks for French franc lines of credit to back their franc operations, German banks for DM lines of credit to back their DM operations, and so on.[6]

The Fed used to be a lender of last resort for just member banks. Under the 1980 Banking Act, it will be a lender of last resort for all banks and thrifts as well. It is appropriate and normal for a bank experiencing a *temporary* liquidity problem to ask the Fed for aid while it rebuilds its liquidity position in one way or another. The bank's liquidity problems may have arisen because of some mistake in bank management or because of some development beyond the bank's control, such as a downturn in the local economy. A bank that asks the Fed for temporary aid may get some uncomfortable calls and free advice from the Fed while it is solving its problems. However, this sort of borrowing should in no way be confused with a Franklin National or a First Pennsy situation in which the borrowing bank in effect asks the Fed to bail it out and, by doing so, gives the Fed and the FDIC limited or full control over its fate.

It is normal that small banks in farm states borrow from the Fed every year on a seasonal basis. These banks lend to farmers and therefore need seasonal accommodation from the Fed during the period it takes for the crops being financed to grow and be sold. Such borrowing, while seasonal, is also as rate sensitive as other Fed accommodation credit.

MEASURING LIQUIDITY

We have described the importance of liquidity and its sources. A trickier and more subtle question is: How should a bank measure the liquidity of its balance sheet?

The short run

In measuring liquidity, a bank must ask what its liquidity is at the current moment and over appropriately chosen longer periods, for example, one and three months.

The logical place for a bank to begin assessing liquidity is with respect to the *very* short run, because it is in the short run that liquidity problems tend to surface. This point, mentioned before, is crucial and deserves elaboration.

A bank would be *technically illiquid* if, for example, it had a book composed of 6-month assets and 1-month liabilities. Moreover, it could maintain such a position for some time without experiencing any

---

[6] See Chapter 13.

liquidity problem if it were always able to keep its balance sheet in precisely this shape. However, as a matter of practice, a bank won't be able to do so because the environment in which it operates changes constantly. For example, a shift in the yield curve from a positive to a negative slope coupled with a rise in interest rates might occur and force the bank to drastically alter the mismatch in its book to protect its profitability.

A second, more subtle danger that a bank with a technically illiquid balance sheet faces is that, anticipating a decline in interest rates, it may be tempted to further whittle down the average maturity of its liabilities: i.e., start buying a lot of overnight Fed funds. That strategy will yield the bank profits if its interest rate forecast is correct. On the other hand, the strategy of financing long-term assets with Fed funds will put the bank in a position where the least upset will cause a liquidity problem. That upset might come in various forms. The bank's interest rate forecast might prove erroneous, or other uncontrollable factors may come into play. For example, a money market bank may find that suddenly a bunch of big customers to whom it has extended lines of credit all come in at the same time and each write checks on it for $100 million. And then for some reason, seasonal or accidental, deposits dip; the next day the bank needs an extra billion dollars of Fed funds, and the same turns out to be true the day after; suddenly, the bank wakes up to the fact that its basic liquidity position has undergone a shift; the bank is less liquid that it was.

At this point, various scenarios may occur. The bank may find that, because of some phenomenon it did not perceive, the banking system is less liquid that it was. Then the bank has to scratch for funds and finds that everyone else is scratching too. This can lead to a panic in which each bank is trying to outbid the others for funds.

A second possibility is that the bank, which suddenly has a liquidity problem, is in a unique position because it was taking a rate gamble that its major competitors were not. In that situation, there will be funds in the market, but the question is whether the bank will be able to buy them. A bank that has stretched its short-run liquidity position may find that, whereas its Fed funds borrowings used to average $1 billion a day, they have now crept up to $2 billion. Worse still, borrowing that money may get harder every day because suddenly people ask why this bank is borrowing so much in the short market. Once this happens, prudent lenders start pulling back from offering funds to the bank. If this snowballs, the bank will find that it can't maintain its outstandings. It has a severe liquidity problem which will force it either to liquidate assets or, if it can, to buy longer-term money. If the bank can do neither, it will be forced to the discount window on bended knee.

Not all banks experience severe liquidity problems that surface in the short run. In fact, relatively few do. A sine qua non for getting into such a position is *overreliance on very short funding,* a degree of overreliance so severe that the least upset—often caused by nonvolitional factors—will throw the bank into a liquidity bind. A bank that has *not* relied too heavily on short-term funds will have time to adjust even to changes in Fed policy that force all banks to scramble for money. In contrast, a bank that has overrelied on short-dated funds must, in the same situation, throw itself at the mercy of the market and say, "I will pay anything." Once it does this, no one will give it money except the Fed.

Basic surplus

Because a severe liquidity problem can surface rapidly in the short run, a first and crucial liquidity measure every bank should calculate is *basic surplus* or some variant of this.

A bank's basic surplus equals its liquid assets minus its day-to-day liabilities. The calculation is:

$$\text{Liquid assets} - \text{Day-to-day liabilities} = \text{Basic surplus}$$

Liquid assets include all assets that can be sharply reduced or gotten off the books rapidly without incurring unacceptable capital losses and without impairing customer relationships. Examples would be cash, excess reserves, loans to brokers and dealers, short-term advances, lendings of Fed funds, and money market investments maturing within 30 days. Day-to-day liabilities are short-dated forms of bought money: overnight Fed funds (excluding hard-core purchases),[7] repo borrowings, borrowings from the Fed, and time deposits with maturities of less than 30 days.

In interpreting basic surplus, note that, by definition, a *positive* number means that the bank is using longer-term liabilities to support liquid assets; this gives the bank extra liquidity to meet all the functions of liquidity described above. Conversely, if a bank's basic surplus is *negative,* some portion of its longer-term illiquid assets are being supported by day-to-day borrowings.

A well-managed bank will view its basic surplus as a tactical variable; depending on its size and perception of possible liquidity problems, it will want to maintain its basic surplus at or above some minimum amount. The latter might, for example, be in the range of half a billion dollars for a money market bank.

Basic surplus is a snapshot of where the bank is today. It relates most directly to the bank's position over the next week. A bank wants a positive basic surplus because that surplus gives it a *liquidity cushion*

---

[7] A bank that regularly buys Fed funds from its smaller correspondents will view some proportion of these overnight funds as *hard-core,* i.e., funds that won't go away.

which it can use for making adjustments to any volitional change or nonvolitional shock that threatens to impair its short-run liquidity.

To illustrate the concept of basic surplus, we give some sample figures in Table 8–1 showing what the basic surplus calculation of a

Table 8–1
How the calculation of basic surplus at a money market bank might look ($ millions)

Cash and balances with foreign banks	$ 27
FRB balance net of reserve requirements	61
U.S. government and agency securities (investment)	768
U.S. government bond dealer position	201
Municipal bond dealer position	27
Federal funds sold and dealer loans	457
Advances to foreign branches*	267
Advances to subsidiaries*	45
Acceptances held	34
Short-term fixed advances*	612
Brokers' loans	732
Term federal funds sold*	212
A: Total liquid assets	$3,443
Federal Reserve Bank	$ 0
Federal funds purchased (excluding hard-core)	1,489
Repurchase agreements	912
Time deposits (excluding savings)*	419
Term Federal funds purchased*	254
Foreign branch redeposits at head office*	171
B: Total day-to-day liabilities	$3,245
Basic surplus (A − B)...................................	$ 198

* Remaining maturity less than 30 days.

money market bank might look like. In a table of this sort, the items included and their relative magnitudes will vary widely with a bank's size and its mix of business. Figure 8–1 pictures the big week-to-week swings that typically occur in the basic surplus of a major bank.

Liquidity ratios

Once a bank has ascertained that it has a comfortable basic surplus, it must determine its liquidity position over longer periods, e.g., one, three, and six months. Here, the focus must not only be on the current state of the balance sheet, but also on how the latter might change due to outside shocks (loan demand jumps) or volitional factors (the bank

Figure 8–1

Week-to-week swings in basic surplus at a major bank typically follow a highly variable pattern

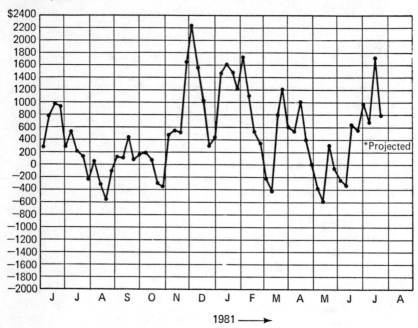

decides to alter its interest rate exposure by adjusting its assets or liabilities).

A good way to evaluate a bank's liquidity position over a time horizon of one or more months is to calculate the ratio of the new money the bank will have to buy over this period to its total outstanding interest-sensitive borrowings excluding hard-core deposits and purchases of Fed funds. The *liquidity ratio* is:

$$\text{Liquidity ratio} = \frac{\text{New money required to be bought}}{\text{Total interest-sensitive funds required}}$$

Determining the numerators and denominators of this ratio for several periods calls for work and many judgments. Starting with the denominator, the bank has to predict what will happen to loan demand in various categories and also what changes, if any, it will want to make in its investment and dealer portfolios. This calculation permits the bank to determine what change, if any, will occur in the total assets it must finance and in the total amount of interest-sensitive funds it will therefore require.

Comparing the latter figure with its current holdings of interest-sensitive funds, the bank can calculate the *net* amount of new money it must raise. To get a *gross* figure, which is what is needed for the numerator in the liquidity ratio, the bank must adjust the net amount of new money needed for any change it anticipates in deposits; it also must add to this net figure all maturing CDs, term Fed funds, and other bought monies that are scheduled to go off its books and must be replaced (see Table 8–2).

Table 8–2
Constructing a liquidity ratio: Numbers illustrative of a money market bank ($ millions)

	Actual (June 2, 1982)	*Forecast for change*	*June 30, 1982 level*
Assets			
Basic surplus	$ 562	$– 62	$ 500
Loans	5,236	+ 83	5,319
Advances to branches	2,637	– 112	2,525
Portfolio	2,332	– 26	2,306
All other	1,567	– 62	1,505
Total assets:	12,334	– 179	12,155
Liabilities and Capital			
Demand deposits	$ 2,816	$+ 137	$ 2,953
Hard core Fed funds	1,125	–1,125	—
TT&L note*	105	– 105	—
Long-term funds	6,365	–3,132	3,233
Capital, trust deposits and other	1,923	+ 193	2,116
Total liabilities:	12,334	–4,032	8,302
Net funding requirements ...		$ 3,853	$ 3,853

$$\text{Liquidity ratio} = \frac{\text{Net funding requirements}}{\text{Total interest-sensitive funds required}}$$

$$= \frac{3,853}{12,155} = 31.7\%$$

* TT & L: Treasury Tax and Loan account.

Later we will discuss how a bank should approach making the difficult predictions that are incorporated in its liquidity index. Here, we focus on what the percentage figures produced by the liquidity ratio mean and what ratios are appropriate or comfortable for a bank.

If, over the next month, a bank's liquidity ratio is 30 percent, this means that in this period the bank must buy an amount of interest-sensitive funds equal to 30 percent of the total amount of such funds it will require. Is 30 percent high or low? That depends on the position of the bank. A small bank could not do it; a regional bank, depending on its size, might be able to live comfortably with such a number; a money market bank would probably view such a number as par for the course. In fact, money market banks with broad access to bought money might be comfortable letting this number run up to 50 percent. The higher the number, the greater the liquidity exposure the bank accepts.

With respect to the 3-month liquidity ratio, an acceptable range at a money market bank might be between 50 percent and 85 percent. The 85 percent figure calls for buying a lot of new money and, therefore, represents substantial liquidity exposure. As Figure 8–2 indi-

Figure 8–2
Week-to-week swings in liquidity ratios at a major bank follow a variable pattern (1-, 3-, and 6-month horizons)

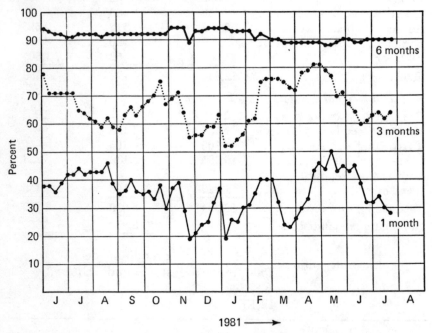

cates, a large bank's liquidity ratios are likely to display a lot of variability over time.

For a bank that can control the average maturity of its assets or its liabilities, a liquidity ratio can be used as a decision variable. The value of this ratio can be reduced through the purchase of longer-term liabilities.

Where within the range that it considers acceptable, a bank will seek to establish its liquidity ratios will depend largely on whether it expects money to tighten or ease. A money market bank that sets a 50 percent maximum on its 1-month liquidity ratio and an 85 percent limit on its 3-month liquidity ratio might strive to achieve these limits if it were convinced that money would ease and rates therefore decline. Alternatively, if the same bank anticipated a tightening of money, it would want to build liquidity immediately by buying all the 6-month money it could, and consequently, its ratios would fall.

Two additional and important comments should be made about liquidity ratios. First, just calculating the numerator gives management a feel for the art of the possible. If the numerator turns out to be $6 billion, management may say, "Well, the liquidity ratio looks OK, but can we really raise $6 billion of money over three months?" That's a useful insight.

A second point is that any step a bank takes to alter its liquidity exposure will necessarily affect its interest rate exposure. In this chapter our focus is on liquidity. When we get to strategies in Part IV, we will integrate liquidity and interest rate exposure considerations.

Liquidity index

The liquidity ratios introduced above give a bank a measure of the quantities of money it must buy relative to its total needs for bought money over varying periods. A different and equally interesting exercise is to put some number on the overall *maturity mismatch* or *gap*, as it is widely called, in the bank's balance sheet.

The idea of measuring the match or mismatch in a bank's balance sheet is in itself simple. Consider, for example, a hypothetical bank that has only 3-month assets on its book and funds them with 3-month liabilities. Dividing total liabilities by the total matched-maturity assets would yield an index of 1, indicating that the bank's book was perfectly matched.

Constructing such a *liquidity index* for an actual bank is more complex. Banks have assets and liabilities in widely varying maturity ranges, so to construct a single liquidity index, an arbitrary system for weighting different maturities must be introduced. Also, the nominal maturity of an asset or liability may differ sharply from its stated maturity. Consequently, a banker, in constructing a liquidity index, must make subjective judgments in assigning maturities to certain assets and liabilities.

To get an idea of what is involved in constructing a liquidity index, look at Table 8–3 which gives an example for a hypothetical money market bank. Note first that constructing the table requires that assets and liabilities be grouped into meaningful maturity categories. Second, numbers must be assigned for weighting assets and liabilities in different maturity categories. In choosing these weights, it is important

Table 8–3
Constructing a liquidity index for a hypothetical money market bank*

Nominal maturity	Assets ($ millions)	Liabilities ($ millions)	Weight to be applied†	Weighted value of assets ($ millions)	Weighted value of liabilities ($ millions)
Current	$ 5.350	$ 6.375	1	$ 5.350	$ 6.375
1-month	15.500	16.225	2	31.000	32.450
3-month	3.525	4.125	3	10.575	12.375
6-month	6.230	4.535	4	24.920	18.140
Beyond 6 months	8.520	7.865	5	42.600	39.325
Total weighted values of assets and liabilities				$114.445	$108.665

$$\text{Liquidity index} = \frac{\text{Weighted value of total liabilities}}{\text{Weighted value of total assets}} = \frac{108.665}{114.445} = .9494$$

* Assets and liability numbers used are those that might be appropriate for a money market bank.
† Weights are arbitrarily assigned.

that they *rise with nominal maturity.* The liquidity index is constructed (bottom of Table 8–3) by dividing a weighted total of liabilities by a weighted total of assets. A figure of 1 for the index would indicate that the bank's book was roughly matched. A number significantly less than 1 would indicated that the bank was *gapping,* i.e., *financing its assets with liabilities of shorter average maturity.*

Gapping with the interest rate exposure it implies is a strategy for making above-normal profits. Calculating the liquidity index offers a measure of the gap and an idea of how the gap is affecting the bank's liquidity. Once this is understood, it is clear why the weights used in constructing the liquidity index, whatever they may be, must ascend with nominal maturity. Adding long liabilities—buying 6-month money—decreases the gap and adds to liquidity, so such monies should be given a higher weight in constructing the liquidity index than are purchases of Fed funds. Similarly, long assets deserve a high weight because buying them increases the gap in the bank's book and decreases its liquidity, which should be reflected in a fall in the liquidity index.[8]

---

[8] Some banks argue that no weights should be assigned to the gap in different maturity ranges because manipulating a liquidity index constructed using arbitrary weights can lead to distorted and suboptimal funding strategies. Such banks prefer to eyeball their gaps in different maturity ranges and may well set an absolute limit on the gap permitted in each range.

Assigning maturities. For some liabilities, nominal maturity equals actual maturity, e.g., for a CD that will mature three months hence. For other liabilities on a bank's balance sheet, assigning nominal maturity requires judgment. Capital, which has no maturity, belongs in the beyond-six-months category. Demand deposits and savings deposits withdrawable on demand technically should be classed as current liabilities, but in fact, a bank can be certain that some portion of such deposits is hard-core; they won't go away and should therefore be included in the beyond-six-months category. Example: a bank that has $2.5 billion of demand deposits and has never had less than $2 billion on average during any month over the last two years might conservatively decide to place only one-half billion of its demand deposits in current liabilities, the other $2 billion in the beyond-six-months category. For a bank, the important thing in making this judgment is not to kid itself. A bank that buys Fed funds daily, particularly from a correspondent network, can carry out a similar analysis; some portion of such funds is going to come to it regardless, and that hard-core portion belongs in the beyond-six-months category.

Similar ambiguities are found on the asset side of the balance sheet. Many loans that have a stated maturity of three months will be rolled so their nominal maturity is longer. A bank with $1 billion in governments, agencies, and municipals would be kidding itself if it thought it could sell off all of these at the snap of a finger, especially if the portfolio contained long bonds. Maybe one week the bank could easily get off $300 million of long bonds; maybe the next week there would be no bid for such securities. This points up two things: (1) the liquidity index should be reworked frequently and honestly, and (2) just the exercise of assigning nominal maturities to various assets and liabilities gives the bank useful information about its true liquidity position.

Once the assets and liabilities have been entered into a form such as Table 8–3, constructing the liquidity index is simple math. Weighted values are calculated for assets and liabilities in each maturity category. These are summed, and then the weighted value of total liabilities is divided by the weighted value of the total assets.

Usefulness. A liquidity index of the sort proposed, imperfect as it may be, will, if constructed regularly and honestly, give a bank a good idea not only of what its current mismatch is, but also of how that mismatch with its implications for liquidity is evolving over time in response either to changes in the outside environment—no bid for long bonds—or in response to changes the bank chooses to make in its asset/liability structure. In addition, constructing a liquidity index forces a bank to evaluate the liquidity characteristic of any assets or liabilities it acquires, something that can easily be overlooked when the bank is focusing on adjusting interest rate exposure.

A liquidity index is also extremely useful for engaging in *what if* exercises: What if we put on some long-term, fixed-rate loans and finance them with 1-month paper? The weight applied to the terms loans will be 5, that applied to the CDs used to fund them will be 2. Clearly this maneuver, if carried out on a large scale, would increase the mismatch in the bank's book, and that will show up in the deterioration it would cause in the bank's liquidity index.

The time horizon for which the liquidity index provides useful information is much longer than that presented by the liquidity ratios proposed above. Therefore, a bank may find this index useful as a third decision variable to be considered when it makes long-range strategic decisions. Note that a bank can move the index up by adding long liabilities, down by adding long assets.

Because a bank's Euro book contains—with the exception of call money—only fixed-term assets and liabilities, it is simpler to measure the liquidity of its Euro book than that of its domestic book. The liquidity index we have constructed is most useful for measuring the mismatch in a bank's domestic book. It is also useful for measuring the mismatch in the book of a bank that has a foreign branch that holds assets and liabilities denominated in a foreign currency. That job can be difficult: one money market bank counted 16 different French franc assets its Paris office could hold.

Calculating the ratio of current liabilities to current assets as recorded in the construction of a liquidity index is a rough measure of basic surplus as an index or quick ratio. A bank may gain additional insight into its current liquidity position by comparing these two numbers and tracking how they vary against each other over time. In making this comparison, the bank should bear in mind that the assets and liabilities included in calculating basic surplus are not precisely those classed as current assets and liabilities in constructing the liquidity index. In particular, in calculating the liquidity index, some portion of demand deposits is included in current liabilities.

DETERMINING LIQUIDITY NEEDS

To determine its liquidity needs, a bank requires three sorts of information: (1) it must project its absolute future liquidity requirements, which means forecasting loan demand, deposit levels, and shifts in customer loan and deposit preferences; (2) it must forecast interest rates (will they be low and will money be easy to buy in the future or vice versa?); and (3) it must determine how confident it is in its liquidity projections; the less confident, the more liquidity needed as a cushion against uncertainty.

Forecasting loan demand

Forecasting loan demand is probably the toughest nut for a banker to crack. Basically, there are two ways to do it. One sounds scientific and sophisticated; it also doesn't work. The second method is ad hoc and gives only short-run predictions; yet, despite its inelegance, it produces useful numbers.

The econometric approach. The first and seemingly most sophisticated way for a banker to predict loan demand is to start with an econometric forecast based on a macroeconomic model. The banker can use an in-house model or buy predictions from any one of a number of forecasting services.

Assume our banker is at a New York money market bank. Once he has his macro forecast in hand, he will reason: historically, under the conditions projected, the banking system's share of financing the level of economic activity forecast is X; of this, New York banks' share is typically Y; finally, of that share, his bank's slice is Z. Let's say that this leads our banker to conclude that loans at his bank will rise by $2 billion over the year. That's useful but insufficiently precise information, since a bank makes tactical asset and liability choices with respect to a much shorter time horizon. So our banker goes back to the forecast and observes that the first quarter is supposed to be good, the second quarter great, the third quarter fair, and the fourth quarter a tailoff. Knowing this, he reuses the XYZ approach to predict what loans at his bank will be quarter by quarter.

This approach can hardly be faulted for lack of effort. At a major bank, the loan forecast figures produced will be based on the best predictions the best econometricians in the country can make using the most elaborate macroeconomic models ever constructed, models that can be run only on sophisticated computers. Unfortunately, the econometric macro model approach to predicting loan demand *almost never works*. The reason is that even the most sophisticated predictions of economic activity year by year are unreliable, and on a quarter-to-quarter basis, which is what a banker needs, they are frequently useless.

The building block approach. Since macro approaches are of little help to a banker in forecasting loan demand, he is forced to fall back on his own devices. He assesses what the economy looks like now and what his big customers are doing. Then he goes to his lending officers who know their customers well and asks what they anticipate from those customers in the way of additional loan demand over the next month or so. Then he adds in loans he knows are coming up due to special circumstances; e.g., his customers are making four large acquisition loans over the next two months for $200 million each.

With this information—where loans are now, what new loans are anticipated customer by customer in the short run, and what special loans (such as for acquisitions) are in the pipeline—a banker can accurately estimate where loans will be a month from now.

Unfortunately, beyond the coming month, he is again in the land of ignorance. So he must fall back on the notion, rightly or wrongly, that high interest rates will usually mean relatively tight credit conditions. Thus, if he is predicting that the prime will go from 15 to 18 percent over the next nine months, that almost certainly implies loans are going to be a lot higher nine months hence. This tells him that, on all counts—liquidity exposure, ability to accommodate additional loan demand, and interest rate exposure—he should buy some 6-month money *now*, i.e., build liquidity.

The building block approach to projecting loan demand is not without problems. First, the banker may get his interest rate forecast wrong. (Actually big banks get it right more often than wrong, at least with respect to major moves in rates.) Second, our banker may find himself operating in an atypical situation of the sort that prevailed in the late 1970s and early 1980s. The yield curve, defying all notions of what was "normal," remained inverted most of the time—not only month after month, but also year after year. And interest rates were frequently high during periods when money was easy. In forecasting, there's no sure thing!

Another problem that has recently developed in forecasting bank loan demand is the spread of either/or loan provisions described in Chapter 11. Today, even if a banker gets it right—he thinks loans are going up half a billion in the current quarter and they do—he can't be sure where his big customers will decide to take down their loans, in the domestic or in the Eurodollar market. In the former case, the loans go on the book of the head office, while in the latter, they may go on the bank's London or Caribbean book.

Loans on the head office's book are often made at a floating prime while Euro loans are always made for fixed periods at a fixed rate (LIBOR plus a spread). This means that the bank must, from the point of view of both liquidity exposure and interest rate exposure, fund these two types of loans differently. Today, a banker must forecast not only what amount of loans his customers will demand but in what form, domestic or Euro, they will take down these loans.[9]

---

[9] For changes in bank lending practices see Chapter 11.

Forecasting deposits

Ask a small banker to forecast what his average daily demand deposits will be over the next week or two, and he will probably answer, "That's a cinch. They'll be what they are now give or take a few percentage points for growth, seasonal factors, and random variations." Ask the liability manager of a major bank the same question, and he's likely to reply, "We can't do it."

All of the demand deposits a major bank receives from commercial customers are on a quid pro quo basis. The bank promises to provide the customer with certain free services in exchange for which the customer gives the bank demand deposits that average out *over the month* to some minimum amount per day. That gives the depositor wide leeway in the amount he will deposit with his bank at any time. He can hold deposits near zero one week and make up for that by ballooning them the next week. The depositor's bogey is an average daily figure over a month; balances held during individual weeks don't count.

A bank's commercial customers exercise with a vengeance their freedom to vary the compensating balances they give their bank. As a result, a major bank that has a daily average of $3 billion of demand deposits over the month may find that those average daily deposits vary from week to week by as much as $500 million (Figure 8-3).

The week-to-week variability money market banks experience in demand deposits creates *no* liquidity problems for them. On a monthly basis, a large bank's average daily demand deposits display considerable stability; the same banker who says he can't predict next week's demand deposits within half a billion will give a confident prediction of what his daily demand deposits will average over a period three or six months hence. Also, a major bank can easily compensate for wide swings in demand deposits on a week-to-week basis. If demand deposits are down during a week, the bank takes more Fed funds; if they are up, it takes less.

Predicting shifts in customer preferences

At any time, apart from marginal differences in the timing with which market participants adopt a new rate forecast, there will almost always be a general view on the outlook for interest rates. Suppose people think that rates will be lower several months hence. Once that expectation becomes general, a bank's borrowers will all want short loans, while its depositors will be demanding 6-month CDs. The

226

Figure 8–3

Week-to-week swings in demand deposits at a major bank follow a highly variable pattern

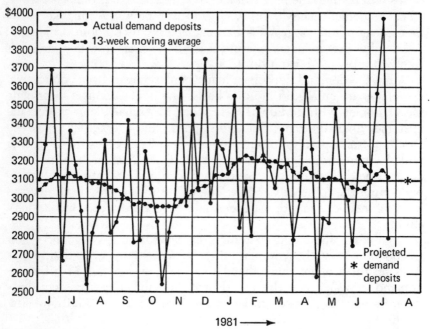

bank's customers, acting in self-interest, will force the bank to borrow long and lend short just at the moment when the bank, from the point of view of its own liquidity and interest rate exposure, would choose to do the opposite. The converse is also true, if a bank's customers expect rates to rise, they will want to borrow long and lend short, precisely the opposite of what the bank would like them to do.

The moral, short and sweet, is that a bank must seek to perceive the trend in interest rates *before* its customers do and predict how its customers will react to this trend. To illustrate, suppose that the bank sees early on that rates are going to rise. Then it knows that sooner or later its borrowers are going to hit it for longer-term maturities, because they want to lock in rates. To prepare for this, the bank must buy longer-term money *now* to accommodate the anticipated later demand for longer-term loans. If the bank does not, its customers' preferences will dictate the average maturity of the bank's assets and liabilities. This will adversely affect not only the bank's liquidity, but its interest rate exposure.

Assessing the outlook for interest rates

When a bank seeks to measure its liquidity needs, a crucial factor will be its outlook on interest rates. What the bank really wants to know is whether rates are likely to rise or fall; getting the forecast right down to the last 10 basis points is unnecessary.

As noted, the general assumption is that higher rates will mean tighter money and vice versa. Tight money means not only that loan demand will rise and deposits will become harder to hold, but also that bought money in general will become more expensive and *harder to get*. A prediction of higher interest rates gives a banker several reasons for stocking up on liquidity: He anticipates greater loan demand, fewer deposits, *and* a lessened availability of purchasable funds. If his anticipation is correct and he waits to buy the funds he expects to need for accommodating additional loan demand, he may find that he must pay more for such funds and that he has difficulty getting them.

In making his interest rate prediction, a banker will typically look closely at the shape of the yield curve and what it discloses about the general expectation on interest rates. If, for example, the banker anticipates a rise in rates and the yield curve is steeply positive, this tells him that his expectation on rates coincides with the general expectation and he had better act quickly to acquire additional liquidity. Conversely, a negatively sloped yield curve would, in the same situation suggest that the world, rightly or wrongly, disagrees with his view.

In forecasting the availability of funds, as in forecasting loan demand, the banker must beware of anomalous situations. In the late winter of 1980, interest rates were at historic highs and money was easy. Then the Fed imposed credit controls which sharply limited the growth of bank lending. As a result, money became truly tight for would-be bank borrowers. At the same time, nominal interest rates fell because banks, constrained in their ability to lend, demanded fewer purchasable funds. A year later, interest rates were again at historic highs, but credit controls were a thing of the past and money was easy. Unfortunately for the forecaster of interest rates and of funds availability, the Fed's current monetarist policies have created a world in which the anomalous has almost become the norm.

Degree of conviction in a rate forecast

A bank may purchase liquidity for future use for two purposes. One is to ensure that it will be able to accommodate loan demand given its forecasts about interest rates, loans, deposits, and the availability of purchasable funds. A second reason for purchasing liquidity is to provide a *margin against error* in the bank's forecasts. A banker may feel confident about his predictions, or he may put little faith in them. The less confident he feels, the farther from the mark he will fear his forecasts may be, *and* the greater the need he will feel for a liquidity cushion to protect against the unforeseen. Thus, it is a basic truism that *a bank's need for liquidity will always be inversely correlated with the degree of certainty it feels about the future.* Every banker should bear this in mind.

LIQUID: TO BE OR NOT TO BE?

So far we have been talking about general determinants of a bank's liquidity. Here, we want to make a crucial point. If a banker feels a high degree of confidence in his prediction with respect to rates, there are times that he should go out on a limb.

Specifically, *if a banker is convinced that interest rates, however lofty they may be, are about to tumble, that is the moment to take a chance: to be as illiquid as he dares.* In particular, it is the moment to lend long at peak rates, to let CD borrowings run off, and to borrow heavily in the overnight market. If the yield curve is inverted, this policy may produce negative carry in the short run, but if the banker is right on interest rates, the market will bail him out handsomely as rates come down.

Conversely, *the best time for a bank to be as liquid as possible, even to the point of being overly liquid, is when interest rates have been low and are about to rise.* A banker convinced that this will occur will buy 6-month money at rates that may look terribly expensive. Again, however, if his rate forecast is correct and rates rise, the market will reward him for acting on his conviction. To illustrate, in November 1980, the yield curve was inverted and 6-month money at 14 percent looked exorbitant. Yet a money market banker who strongly believed that rates were about to shoot back up and who consequently bought several billion of such money would have had the satisfaction, not long after, of seeing those funds being lent at a prime of 20 to 21 percent.

In both cases we have cited as moments to go out on a limb, by getting either overly illiquid or overly liquid, the market imposed a cost on the initial position assumed. This need not be the case. For example, a banker might strongly disagree with the general view on interest rates, be convinced that they were about to rise when the yield curve was negatively sloped. In that case, he could borrow long, lend short, and be paid by the market to do so. All this looks like a free ride; the banker is adding to liquidity and being paid to do so. However, the ride has a cost, namely the assumption of additional interest rate exposure. If rates fall, as the yield curve predicts they will, the ploy will cost the bank money. This caveat notwithstanding, it has been the case, in recent years characterized by a constantly inverted yield curve, that people who chose to buck the trend at the right moment have made good money. This circumstance is, however, unusual. Normally, the yield curve proves correct sooner or later.

Implications of too much or too little liquidity

When a banker decides how much liquidity to buy, it is important that he get it right, because having too much or too little over a long period will cost his bank money. Liquidity costs money because a bank literally has to buy it. What form that cost takes depends on market conditions. If the yield curve is positively sloped, liquidity costs money because the bank must pay more for long-dated funds than for short money. If the yield curve is negatively sloped, the cost of liquidity—buying 6-month money—is assuming the risk that the yield curve will prove correct and rates will drop.

Having too little liquidity can also be very costly. A bank that allows its balance sheet to become illiquid may be forced into the market for funds at a time when rates are high and peaking. A bank with too little liquidity forgoes the option of coming to the market when it wants to. A bank with adequate liquidity has the luxury of waiting to buy liquidity until rates come its way.

When to purchase liquidity and how much to pay

A bank should buy liquidity in accordance with the expectations outlined above. In doing so, it should pay particular attention to beating its customers to the draw because, if it does not, they will change the nature of the bank's book in a way opposite to what the bank desires.

Often, buying liquidity, which for a domestic bank means buying 6-month money, will be a costly option. Whether a bank should do it is a decision that must be made on the basis of *managements's propensity to accept the cost of avoiding a risk in the form of liquidity exposure.* A case in point: 6-month money costs 18 percent and the bank's interest rate forecast is that 3-month money three months hence will be 17.5 percent. The bank's predictions imply that buying 6-month money instead of buying 3-month money with the intent to roll it once will cost 50 basis points. Should the bank's liability manager buy 6-month money to minimize liquidity exposure or should he buy 3-month money and roll it? The answer depends on management's risk aversion, which can't be quantified. So the liability manager's only choice is to walk up to his chairman and say, "Look, according to our interest rate forecasts, buying liquidity is going to cost us around 50 basis points. Do you want to do it?" If the chairman says yes, the liability manager has his clue as to what to do.

The bank in our example correctly recognizes that buying liquidity in the situation described will cost money. Also, the chairman's choice, which time may prove to have been correct or overcautious, is made, as it should be, on the basis of the most accurate estimate the bank can make of the cost of liquidity.

Nonchoices. Sometimes, in buying liquidity, a bank faces non-questions that appear to be real questions. Take the case of a bank that is trying to settle its reserve position on a Wednesday. If funds go to 25 percent, should it buy Fed funds in the market to settle or should it borrow at the Fed? The basic implication of borrowing at the Fed is that the more a bank does so now, the less it will be able to do so later; that is the way the rules are currently set up. Thus, the question of whether the bank should pay 25 percent for funds or borrow at the Fed at 14 percent, i.e., of whether it should pay an 11 percent penalty for staying out of the window, is no question at all. Paying an extra 11 percent for $50 or $100 million for one day is nothing relative to the cost of what the bank, by going to the window, would give up in terms of its ability to return later if it needed to. In this sort of situation, people too often take their eye off the ball. They say, "There is no way I am going to pay 25 percent. I am going to the Fed."

The above choice, which is really no choice, is an example of one of many money market trade-offs in which the correct action appears at first glance to be counterintuitive. Yet when the numbers are worked out, no choice exists because only one option makes sense. In our example, a banker would always pay up for Fed funds rather than go to the discount window, at least until and unless Fed policy shifts.

The cost of too much liquidity

Having too much liquidity, like having too little, imposes costs on a bank. If the yield curve is positively sloped, this means almost auto-matically that liquidity purchased in the form of 6-month money can be used only at rates lower than the rate the bank pays for it. Thus, in the short run, the cost of too much liquidity is negative spreads.

In the long run, the problem with having too much liquidity is that it leads to a compulsion to invest in longer maturities, to stretch for yields which turn out all too frequently to be historically low. Nor-mally when the banking system is overly liquid, the yield curve is positively sloped because all this liquidity is pressing on short rates. So, in an attempt to improve earnings on liquidity, banks start buying assets with longer maturities. Usually, the outcome is that they buy treasuries at rates that turn out to be horribly low when the secular trend in interest rates reasserts itself, or they make fixed-rate term loans, an equally no-win proposition. Having too much liquidity leads banks to make decisions that will almost certainly come back to haunt them. To avoid this trap, a banker wallowing in liquidity should think twice when he finds himself saying, "We have got to invest in something that will give us a positive spread."

Consequences of too little liquidity

The consequences for a bank of having too little liquidity is a topic on which we need not dwell. Earlier we outlined the many functions of liquidity. If a bank has too little liquidity, some or all of those functions will not be fulfilled. Specifically, a bank with too little liquidity may be unable to take advantage of opportunities for profitable asset acquisitions; it may have to pay historically high rates to restore its liquidity; it may be forced to sell assets at significant losses; it may be unable to lend under prior commitments; it may, if its condition is publicized, be unable to renew maturing purchased liabilities; and, worst of all, it may be forced to make excessive use of the discount window, which in turn may lead to surrendering control of the bank to the Fed.

Euros

In this chapter, we have not specifically mentioned Eurodollar assets and liabilities. The vast majority of the 15,000 odd banks in the United States do not operate a Euro book and, therefore, need not be concerned about including Euro assets and liabilities in their liquidity calculations.

For a bank that does have a Euro book, including Euro assets and liabilities in its liquidity measures is simple because such assets and liabilities all have, with the exception of Euro call deposits, fixed maturities. Thus, a bank can—in calculating basic surplus, liquidity indexes, and any other liquidity measures—easily add to the appropriate numbers for its domestic assets and liabilities similar numbers for its Euro assets and liabilities. Classifying the latter with respect to maturity calls for only one judgment: estimating what portion of the bank's Euro call deposits should be classified as hard-core.

All the general points we have made about liquidity—its importance, the need to track it, and the risks and possible rewards that accrue to a bank from being, at an appropriate moment, overly liquid or illiquid—are equally valid whether applied to a bank that runs only a domestic book or to one that runs a global book comprising a domestic book and a Euro book.

CONCLUDING THOUGHTS

A bank should always bear in mind that its ability to maintain its outstanding liabilities is totally dependent upon maintaining a good image in the market. In fact, *the secret of liability management is to have the person who is giving the bank money think that the bank is doing him a favor by taking it.*

There is no magic formula to dictate the amount of liquidity a bank should maintain in all economic situations. As we have tried to show, the amount of liquidity a bank holds should be closely related to its expectations of future developments that will affect the demand for credit.

There are times for a bank to be overly liquid, even though doing so is costly. There are times for a bank to be illiquid even though this entails risks. Only when its actions are based not only on the lessons of past experience, but on a *firm* projection of the future, should a bank incur risk to produce the rewards that can accrue from managing—actively and imaginatively—its liquidity position.

9

Interest rate exposure

Interest rate exposure is the uncertainty introduced into a bank's earnings by possible changes in interest rates.

In the never-never land of theory, a bank could conceivably operate with *no* interest rate exposure. To illustrate, consider a bank that has *no* capital. Its sole activity is to intermediate as follows: It accepts 3-month deposits at the going rate and invests at a ⅛ markup all monies received in instruments of the same maturity. This institution's sole source of income is the ⅛ spread it earns for being an intermediary, and its profits—assuming no change in volume—will be the same whether interest rates are 2 percent or 20 percent.

So much for theory. *All* real-world banks face interest rate exposure because their balance sheets are structured so as to give rise to *natural* causes of such exposure. Also, many banks, when the moment seems propitious, consciously adjust the structure of their balance sheets to increase their interest rate exposure in an attempt to earn profits higher than those that would accrue from simple intermediation.

CAUSES OF INTEREST RATE EXPOSURE

"Free funds"

Every bank must have capital, and in addition, it will have some hard-core demand deposits, deposits that will stick with it through thick and thin. Neglecting transaction costs, capital and hard-core demand deposits are *free* funds for a bank. Purchased funds, in contrast, cost a bank money, how much depending on the general level of interest rates, the shape of the yield curve, and the extent to which rates on certain classes of liabilities are limited by regulation.

For every bank, free funds are a natural cause of interest rate exposure. To illustrate, consider a bank that had no funds other than capital and hard-core demand deposits; it would earn twice as much if the prime rate were 20 percent than it would if the prime were 10 percent. This point, obvious when made, is all too often unrealized or ignored.

If a bank's free resources comprise the bulk of its total resources, its earnings will be more vulnerable to changes in interest rates than they would be if those resources comprised a small proportion of its total. Most small banks have large amounts of free resources. They do not have to go out and buy money and could not if they chose to. As a result, their earnings are highly sensitive to the rise and fall of interest rates over the business cycle, and they can do little about this.

Large banks also have resources in the form of capital and hard-core deposits that subject them to interest rate exposure. However, unlike small banks, large banks have long been in a position where they must buy every dollar they need to support incremental increases in assets. Consequently, the proportion of their total resources comprising free funds is much smaller than it is for small banks. As a result, free funds are a less important natural cause of interest rate exposure for large banks than for small ones. Regional banks fall in between.

Loan composition

The types of loans that predominate on a bank's book depend in large part on its size, on its geographic position, and, in some cases, on past strategic commitments to go after certain types of business. What sorts of loans a bank books will strongly influence (1) how large that bank's natural interest rate exposure is, and (2) how acutely the bank feels the need to willingly accept additional interest rate exposure to increase earnings.

Small banks. Small banks make a lot of loans at rates related to prime. In addition, they make many loans to consumers for home improvements, car purchases, and the like. Generally speaking, competition in the markets in which small banks operate is such that they can charge attractive rates; their competitors in the business all want a good return. Since a small bank has lots of either free or cheap funds, it can, when rates are high, earn enormous spreads on this sort of loan business. And even when rates are down, its spreads are—compared to those a money market bank earns on its natural business—attractive.

The fact that a small bank's natural loan business involves lending out significant amounts of free or low-cost funds in markets where competition permits charging attractive rates and, consequently, garnering attractive spreads, has two implications for interest rate exposure at such a bank. First, because such a bank's lending rates will rise and fall with the general level of rates in the economy, its earnings are subject to a high degree of unavoidable interest rate exposure. Second, the attractive spreads small banks earn on their natural business, even when rates are down, means that they are not under constant pressure, as are larger banks, to volitionally accept additional interest rate exposure to raise earnings.

Large banks. In bygone days when interest rates were marked by relative stability and a gentle secular trend upward, banks typically made fixed-rate term loans. However, as interest rates become increasingly volatile, making fixed-rate loans that had to be funded with floating-rate purchased monies created an unacceptable level of interest rate exposure for large banks. Consequently, they switched almost exclusively to lending at a floating-rate prime.

The natural concomitance to this strategy for minimizing interest rate exposure would have been for these banks to fund their floating-rate loans largely with liabilities whose maturity coincided with that of the assets supported. Unfortunately, this overall strategy, while limiting the interest rate exposure that would otherwise have resulted from commercial lending at major banks, would have impinged painfully on their profits. The larger a bank, the more competitive it must be in setting lending terms because its borrowers will shop rates at other banks and also have sources of funds other than bank borrowing, in particular, the commercial paper market. Consequently, a major bank can't charge a would-be borrower an 01 more than the rate at which a competitor would provide funds to that borrower. This keen competition keeps *lending rates at large banks low relative to their cost of funds, and the spreads they earn on intermediation are miniscule.* If a major bank attempted to live on the normal spreads it earned from commercial lending, it would be lucky to pay its overhead.

To make money on commercial business, a major bank *must* structure its assets and liabilities so as to assume additional interest rate exposure. Commercial loans, whatever their stated maturity, often stay on a bank's books for long periods because they begin as term loans or they are rolled. In contrast, the longest-dated money a bank can buy in meaningful size in the *domestic* market is 6-month money. This means that for a commercial bank *six months is the long run* when it makes decisions with respect to accepting or creating interest rate exposure. Also, the asymmetry of maximum loan life and maximum liability life means *liability management automatically becomes the prime tool a major bank must use to create and control interest rate exposure.*

Neutral strategy. A small bank faces much natural interest rate exposure it can do little about. On the other hand, its spreads are large enough so that it can live with this exposure and still, on average, be highly profitable over time. In contrast, a large bank has less natural interest rate exposure, but its spreads on commercial business are so small that it is forced to seek out additional interest rate exposure to earn acceptable profits.

In between are some banks that could take a view on interest rates and act on it but prefer not to. They reason, "Our margins are sufficient so that, if we always make 3-month, floating-rate loans, and fund them with 3-month liabilities or follow some other *neutral* policy, we will, over the long run, make adequate profits despite our natural interest rate exposure." A bank that believes this is taking a long view and makes no attempt to influence its earnings in the short run, quarter by quarter.

To many who look at cases such as First Pennsy, which bought—on the incorrect view that interest rates were about to fall—long bonds using short money, it seems that banks should get out of the business of making and acting on interest rate predictions and stick to intermediation plain and simple.

However, the alternative of following a neutral strategy that promises to be profitable on average over the cycle has its own dangers. The Continental Bank is a case in point. Its geographic position in the Midwest made it easy, even natural, for this bank to become a huge buyer of Federal funds from the vast number of regional and smaller banks that surround it. Among major banks, the Continental is the largest buyer of Fed funds, picking up as much as $8 or $9 billion of them every day. Over the ebb and flow of the business cycle, relying heavily on purchases of hard-core Fed funds ought to be profitable because the yield curve normally slopes upward, and Fed funds are the cheapest money around. However, when abnormal conditions prevail over a long period, as they did from 1979 to late 1981, a strategy of using Fed funds liberally can, as it did in the case of Continental, adversely affect earnings not just over a quarter or two, but over a period sufficiently long to become a source of concern to management.

Predicting interest rates.   There is a case to be made for pursuing a neutral strategy if a bank can afford it. Major banks typically can't, but fortunately they manage to correctly predict the wide swings that occur in interest rates more often than not. It is only when they make an occasional egregious error that it gets into the newspapers. It is not news that Citibank gets its right and earnings are up. It is news when Citi's London office loses, as it did in the fourth quarter of 1980, $73 million on a bad bet on interest rates, a loss sufficiently large to severely affect the bank's earnings for the quarter.

Management's focus.   A bank that is deciding whether to actively manage its assets and liabilities—funding short at times and long at others in an attempt to maximize short-run profits—must make that choice on the basis of management's time horizon with respect to measuring performance. Does management seek to maximize short-run earnings or does it focus on the long run? If management's focus is on short-run earnings, it must bear in mind that, while a short-run focus on maximizing earnings may pay off handsomely for many quarters, it will always lead to an occasional bad decision because no bank gets its interest rate forecast right every time. Seeking to win by being fast footed should be chosen only by those who are prepared to stumble occasionally.

Portfolio securities and mortgages

The holding of both long bonds and mortgages is another natural cause of interest rate exposure for banks. Acquiring either involves devoting resources to assets that will produce a long-term, fixed-rate flow of income. If a bank acquires such assets when interest rates are at a peak, this will enhance its earnings over time. If, alternatively, it acquires such assets at rates that, in retrospect, prove low, its earnings over time will suffer. One need go no further than the thrifts to observe what happens when a financial institution gets into a position where fixed-rate, long-term assets put on at *low* rates comprise the bulk of its assets. Some banks are in a position similar to that of the thrifts with respect to both their mortgage portfolios and their securities portfoliios.

For a bank or thrift contemplating the acquisition of long-term, fixed-rate assets, the decision often involves a trade-off between the short and long run. Whatever the size or exact nature of the institution making the decision, buying such assets will frequently adversely affect short-term earnings. The attraction of such assets is that they offer an opportunity for maintaining high and stable earnings over some longer period, particularly when interest rates appear likely to fall.

Consequently, the decision to buy long-term, fixed-rate assets should always be made on the basis of the long-run implications of doing so.

Small banks. A bank's motives for acquiring long bonds or mortgages and the impact of doing so on its earnings over time vary considerably with bank size. A small bank is naturally exposed to a decline in interest rates because it has substantial free funds it must put to use. To such an institution, buying long-term, fixed-rate assets looks like an appealing way to sustain earnings when it fears a slow-down in economic activity and a fall in interest rates.

In acquiring such assets, a small bank uses its own money, as op-posed to bought money. Therefore, it is not crucial that such a bank perfectly time portfolio acquisitions. If a small bank—fearing that interest rates are about to peak and loan demand to slacken—gets into long bonds at 14 percent, but such bonds, in fact peak at 16 percent, the bank loses no real money. By buying at 14 percent, the bank, over time, may well get an attractive spread between its cost of funds and its yield on assets, which is what it wanted. At worst, the bank's failure to time its purchase perfectly, that is, to buy at 16 percent, imposes on it an opportunity cost: the extra 2 percent it forgoes because using free resources to buy long bonds at 14 percent precludes investing these resources at 16%.

Large banks. In discussing portfolio acquisition, a crucial distinc-tion is that, whereas small banks are tempted to buy long-term securi-ties because they have funds that must be put to use, large banks buy long bonds to make a bet on interest rates. To finance their purchases, large banks use someone else's money—most often very short-dated money bought in the RP market.

For a large bank, as for a small bank, the best time to buy long bonds is when interest rates are peaking. The payoff a large bank seeks is not to lock in a high rate on funds with which it must do something, but rather to position itself so it can earn positive carry and possibly capital gains as bond yields fall. If a large bank succeeds in buying bonds as rates are peaking, it will often be buying at a time when the yield curve is inverted, and initially, the carry on its position will be nega-tive. This is no cause for major concern, because if the bank's view that interest rates are about to fall is correct, the market will bail out the bank; as rates fall, carry on its position will turn positive.

For a large bank, the importance of carry in earning portfolio profits means that timing and the correctness of its rate projections are more crucial for it than for a small bank. A small bank that buys long bonds at 14 percent and watches bond yields peak at 16 percent incurs an opportunity cost. A large bank making the same timing mistake will, because it is using someone else's money, suffer real losses that run through its income statement to the bottom line. Worse still, if the bank's mistake is not a minor error in timing but rather a major error about the direction of rates, rising negative carry and the real dollar losses it entails may eventually force the bank to sell the bonds at a substantial capital loss, as did First Pennsy.

Tax considerations. In addition to buying taxable governments and agencies, banks of all sizes invest in municipal securities. Their objective is to maximize aftertax profits by earning tax-exempt income.

For a large bank, carry is not an issue in the purchase of tax-exempt securities. Banks never finance these securities with repo money because the interest paid on such borrowings to finance a municipal portfolio would not be a deductible expense. In deciding what amount of municipals to buy, the biggest problem large banks face is accurately forecasting their taxable income for the fiscal year and their resulting need for tax-exempt income. Because of the amount of foreign-source income large banks earn, and because of the amount of foreign taxes they pay, most major banks that work at it are able to hold their federal taxes to a minimal amount regardless of how large their published income statements show their profits to be.

Customer preferences

Bank customers form expectations on interest rates based upon any changes they project in economic activity, in Fed policy, and in the trend in inflation. If their expectation is that interest rates will rise, they will seek to invest short-dated money and borrow long-dated funds; if they believe rates will fall, they will do the opposite. In discussing liquidity, we noted that a bank must anticipate shifts in customer preferences and take a position against what it expects its customers to do. Otherwise, its customers will dictate the bank's liquidity position. The same applies with equal force to interest rate exposure. To control it, a bank must anticipate shifts in customer preferences and act to pre-position itself accordingly. This is a central point, whether the bank's concern is liquidity or interest rate exposure.

Resiliency of markets for bank paper

The way a bank changes the structure of its liabilities is to sell its own paper into the market. A bank's ability to do this is directly and positively correlated with its size.

For large banks and, to a lesser degree, for smaller regional banks, the ability to sell CDs, commercial paper, BAs, and other paper can—depending on market conditions—be either a natural cause of interest rate exposure or a means of altering that exposure at will. It is the latter if conditions are such that the market can readily absorb large quantities of whatever paper a bank or its holding company chooses to sell. That, however, is frequently not the case.

To illustrate, suppose that a bank is convinced loan demand and interest rates are about to rise and, consequently, that a good gamble would be to buy a lot of currently expensive 6-month money. The bank's ability to do so might be impeded for one of several reasons. First, the dealers through which it would normally sell such paper may be in such a terrible *technical* position that they just won't take it. In July 1981, for example, dealers, having made the incorrect gamble that rates were coming down, were loaded with long paper on which they had a tremendous negative carry. In that environment, there was no way a liability manager at a major bank would have been able to sell $1 billion of 6-month CDs. Second, even if dealers are in good technical shape, a bank may be prevented from selling long paper because both investors and the dealers also anticipate a rise in interest rates and thus won't buy such paper.

If a bank has failed to pre-position itself against a predicted rise in loan demand which materializes and—because of market conditions—can't sell long-dated paper, it will be forced to accept additional interest rate risk. In this case, the lack of resiliency in the market for bank liabilities becomes a natural cause of interest rate exposure.

As the above suggests, a key part of a bank liability manager's job is to continually examine market conditions, assessing his ability to sell various types of paper in different maturity ranges. The liability manager who fails to do so may end up kidding himself into believing that his options for controlling interest rate exposure include what are, in fact, infeasible tactics in the prevailing market environment.

Temptations of the yield curve

Most banks focus on short-run earnings—quarter-to-quarter changes in profits. Bank managers are aware of this, and they are under constant pressure to make money. In terms of earnings, small banks enjoy numerous natural advantages. As a bank grows in size, these diminish. Large banks enjoy almost no natural advantage they can exploit to increase short-term earnings. Because of this and because management in large banks is always operating under pressure to increase earnings quarter by quarter and year by year, they are constantly tempted to assume interest rate exposure, because doing so is almost the only means they have to increase earnings. This simple statement is the key to the motivation behind active bank liability management.

A positively sloped yield curve. The assumption of interest rate exposure involves taking positions in the cash market along the yield curve. If the yield curve is positively sloped—short rates low, long rates high—a bank is sorely tempted to lend long and borrow short to maximize spreads. That tactic enhances short-term profits but increases the bank's interest rate exposure. If the yield curve is correct and rates eventually rise, short rates will change most; the yield curve, as it rises, may flatten or even invert, and the bank will end up financing long-term, fixed-rate assets with short-term, variable-rate liabilities at an ever-widening negative spread. This is more likely to occur in the long run than in the short run, so the bank manager finds himself faced in the short run with a trade-off between increasing short-run profits and threatening long-run profits. Concentration on increasing short-run earnings, unless astutely done, will almost always redound adversely on a bank in the long run, because, sooner or later, rates will change in a way that hurts the bank's profits.

A negatively sloped yield curve. If the yield curve is inverted, at first glance, things look more attractive to the active liability manager. He can increase spreads and short-run profits by buying long-dated money and lending short; to boot, he increases his liquidity. The liability manager also increases his interest rate exposure, the risk again being that the yield curve will prove correct, which it almost always is in the long run. If rates fall, the bank, instead of making a positive spread on reinvesting its long money, will find itself making a negative spread on the long money with which it is stuck. The bank will still have liquidity, but now it will be paying for that liquidity instead of having the market pay for it.

Relationship of liquidity to interest rate exposure. Earlier we said that liquidity and interest rate exposure are inextricably intertwined. The above remarks spotlight this. When the yield curve is positively sloped, accepting additional interest rate exposure (borrowing short and lending long) to increase short-run profits also imposes a second cost or risk on a bank, namely, a decrease in the bank's liquidity.

If, alternatively, the bank, faced with an inverted yield curve, borrows long and lends short to raise short-term earnings, it increases its liquidity and is paid by the market for doing so. The liquidity may, however, prove costly in the long run because part of its price is an increase in interest rate exposure.

No bank that is under pressure to increase short-run earnings can escape the temptations of the yield curve. Moreover, the steeper the yield curve, the more alluring it is for a bank to seek to position its assets and liabilities along the yield curve in a way that promises increased short-term earnings at the price of accepting additional interest rate exposure.

The essential point to make here is not that banks should never succumb to the temptations of the yield curve; many do so successfully much of the time. What should be stressed is that the attempt to maximize short-run profits can and sometimes does get a bank into deep long-run trouble for one or more of several reasons: the bank fails to assess the full risk it is assuming; it willingly assumes more risk than it should; or the bank, when it makes a bad gamble, refuses to act with dispatch to cut its losses. First Pennsy, which did so, literally was told by the regulators that it *must* staunch the flow of red ink to its bottom line by staging a fire sale of its assets. An interesting sidelight on this fire sale is that it was held just weeks before interest rates began a staggering drop of 1,000 basis points; that bit of timing cost First Pennsy a big chunk of its capital.

MEASURING INTEREST RATE EXPOSURE

For reasons outlined above, all banks face some natural and therefore unavoidable interest rate exposure. In addition, many banks seek to actively adjust their interest rate exposure to enhance earnings by taking advantage of forecasted changes in interest rates. The upshot is that, for all banks, a key part of managing a bank—or to put it more strongly, *what banking is all about*—is managing interest rate exposure, natural or contrived.

Measuring interest rate exposure is simple; essentially, there is only one way to do it. One starts by recognizing that, if interest rates are rising, the bank's profits will rise if it is able to reprice its assets at higher rates before it reprices its liabilities. Alternatively, if rates are falling, the bank's profits will rise if it is able to reprice its liabilities at lower rates before it reprices its assets.

ARBL

To measure its interest rate exposure, a bank needs a figure that will show it what amount of assets will be repriced before liabilities. For brevity, we refer to this number as ARBL (*assets repriced before liabilities*).[1]

Two points must be made about the construction of ARBL. First, judgments incorporated in constructing this number are minimal. The

---

[1] The first major bank to use this term was the Morgan Bank.

only important one is recognizing that hard-core demand deposits, like capital, must be regarded as infinite liabilities, since neither will go away over any reasonable planning horizon. Hard-core purchases of Fed funds, while regarded as *long-term* funds in measuring liquidity, are regarded as what they are—overnight or very short-term funds—in measuring interest rate exposure. Hard-core Fed funds purchased are not going to go away, but they are repriced each time they are rolled, and repricing is what counts in measuring interest rate exposure. A similar point should be made with respect to variable-rate CDs. A six-by-one CD (a CD that matures in six months but is repriced each month) is regarded as 6-month money in a liquidity measure, but as 1-month money when interest rate exposure is being measured. From the point of view of interest rate exposure, it is not the maturity of the CD that counts but how often it is repriced. As cannot be stressed too often, a banker, in examining an asset or a liability, must be careful to correctly distinguish liquidity characteristics from interest rate exposure characteristics; often the two differ sharply.

Setting ARBL to enhance profits. If a banker is convinced that interest rates are about to rise, he will want to build up ARBL to some large *positive* number. Positive ARBL means that, as interest rates rise, his assets, to reflect higher rates, will be repriced more rapidly than his liabilities, and, consequently, the spread between his yield on assets and his cost of funds will widen.

Conversely, if a banker is convinced that interest rates are about to fall, he will want lower ARBL. Normally, a bank, no matter how strong its conviction that interest rates are about to fall, will be unable to achieve negative ARBL. A bank has a lot of infinite liabilities in the form of hard-core demand deposits and capital on its balance sheet, and these cannot be offset by assets of equal maturity. Thirty-year bonds are about the longest fixed-rate asset a bank can acquire. Therefore, a bank will always be exposed to some *very* long-run interest rate exposure due to the possibility, however unlikely, that interest rates might take a steep, secular drop.

How many ARBLs? A banker will almost always entertain not one, but several views on where interest rates are headed over time. He might think that rates are likely to rise sharply over the next three months, level off for some period, and then drop as the economy turns into recession. For this reason, he will want to construct ARBLs for different periods (Figures 9–1 to 9–3). Regardless of the number of ARBL figures he constructs, the most important from a policy point of view will be the 1-month, 3-month, 6-month, and 1-year or more figures.

Figure 9–1

ARBL: Hypothetical worldwide interest rate exposure positions of a money market bank ($ billions)*

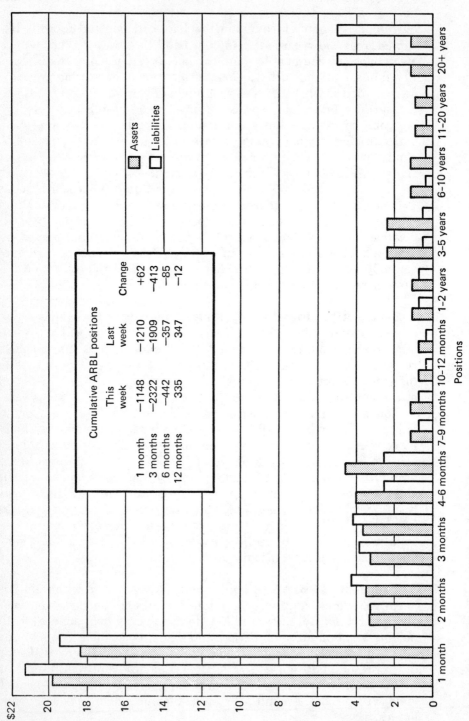

* Figure 9–1 is constructed by summing the numbers in Figures 9–2 and 9–3. In each category, the first two columns show the preced-

Figure 9-2
The domestic component of the bank's ARBL: Hypothetical domestic interest rate exposure positions ($ billions)*

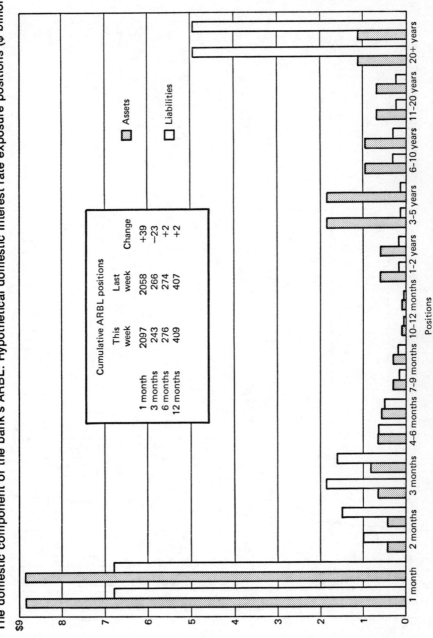

Cumulative ARBL positions			
	This week	Last week	Change
1 month	2097	2058	+39
3 months	243	266	−23
6 months	276	274	+2
12 months	409	407	+2

* In each category, the first two columns show the preceding week's position, the second two columns the current week's position.

Figure 9-3

The Euro component of the bank's ARBL: Eurodollar interest rate exposure positions ($ billions)*

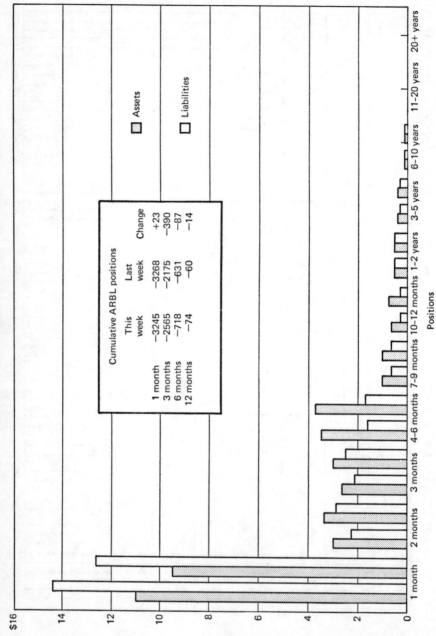

Cumulative ARBL positions			
	This week	Last week	Change
1 month	−3245	−3268	+23
3 months	−2565	−2175	−390
6 months	−718	−631	−87
12 months	−74	−60	−14

* In each category, the first two columns show the preceding week's position, the second two columns the current week's position.

Altering ARBL.   A bank's ARBL figures are not fixed in stone. They can, to some degree, be manipulated by a bank: up if it anticipates higher interest rates, down if it anticipates lower interest rates. Generally, it is easy for a bank to lower ARBL; it simply ceases to write new CDs and picks up the monies thus lost in the Fed funds market. Increasing ARBL is more difficult. Shortening the interest-rate maturity of assets may not be easy; also, a bank's ability to sell longer-dated paper, say 6-month CDs, may be constrained by the resiliency of the secondary market for bank liabilities which, in turn, depends on the technical condition of the dealers and on customer preferences.

ARBL as a tactical variable.   Generally, for a bank, overnight out to three months is the short run, six months the long run. With interest rates as volatile as they have been in recent years, it is crucial that a bank concentrate first on its short-run ARBL positions to protect current earnings.

Normally, a bank will impose some limit on how high or low it will allow ARBL in a given maturity range to go. In doing so, the bank seeks to limit the interest rate exposure it will accept. There are times, however, when a bank holds such a strong conviction on where interest rates are headed that it may want to temporarily violate its limits in a given maturity range. If its limit on 1-month ARBL is $3 billion, the bank's liability manager may say, "I am absolutely convinced that interest rates are going up. Therefore, I want a $4 billion ARBL." As noted, market conditions may constrain both his ability to reach this number and the speed with which he can do so. An equally important constraint is the possible consequences of his being wrong. No liability manager should create a big *gap*—a large positive or negative ARBL number in a given maturity range—without (1) consciously recognizing it is making a bet on interest rates, and (2) fully evaluating not only the profits it will earn if it wins its bet, but also the losses it will sustain if it loses.

The short run versus the long run

Bankers pay a lot of attention to short-run ARBL or similar measures of short-term interest rate exposure for several reasons: often their principal focus is on short-term earnings; recently, short rates have been extremely volatile; and, generally, bankers have greater confidence in their short-run interest rate forecasts than in the long-run forecasts.

Despite the good reasons for actively managing short-run ARBL (a tactical variable) to enhance current earnings, it is important that a bank not lose sight of the long run. Against the background of operating in the short run, a banker—to the extent he can—must also think in strategic terms about the secular outlook for interest rates and maintain his long-run measures of ARBL (a strategic variable) at levels that offer adequate protection against whatever he foresees as the most likely long-term trend in interest rates. Because the current volatility of interest rates forces bankers to focus on short-term tactical decisions with respect to ARBL—decisions that have to be made to protect and enhance current earnings—management often loses sight of the long-term implications of unbalancing its ARBL position and thus of its vulnerability to secular changes in interest rates.

Often critics say to bankers, "You can't take the risks you do by gapping [running ARBL way up or down]. Look at what happened to First Pennsy, First Chicago, and Citi. To avoid that, you should get into a fully matched position." This advice is a natural reaction to the problems that have surfaced at these and other banks, and *the critics of gapping have a point*. The problem with their advice is that, if a bank acted strictly in accordance with the long-term strategic view—match everything—that would alter its short-run ARBL. In structuring ARBL over the full maturity range, there frequently arises an easily identifiable trade-off between long-term and short-term earnings. It again raises a basic question: Should management's focus be on maximizing short-run or long-run earnings?

The Euro book

Most U.S. banks run only a domestic book. However, all large and many regional banks also run a Euro book. For a bank that runs one, it is crucial that assets and liabilities in this book be included in the overall calculation of ARBL. Note that Figure 9–1, which pictures one money market bank's worldwide ARBL position was constructed by combining the numbers in Figures 9–2 and 9–3, which show, respectively, ARBL in the bank's domestic book and in its Euro book. In the situation shown, the bank's short-run positive ARBL in the domestic book is more than offset by short-term negative ARBL in its Euro book. The huge figure for assets in the 1-month category on the New York book reflects the fact that the bank has made a large amount of variable-rate, prime loans that are subject to repricing at any time.

Including the Euro book in the calculation of ARBL is crucial for several reasons. First, for large banks, the Euro book will often be bigger than the domestic book. Second, a bank with a large Euro operation will find that it has a greater flexibility in changing the maturity of its assets and liabilities in its Euro book than it has in its domestic book. The flexibility in the Euro book arises from the bank's ability to borrow and lend large amounts of fixed-rate, fixed-term money in the vast interbank market for placements of Eurodollars. If a bank has involuntarily slipped into a position where its domestic book is geared for higher interest rates and it expects lower interest rates, it can use the placement market to create a natural offset to this by gearing its Euro book in the opposite way.

A bank's Eurobusiness is not all making and taking placements. It also involves making customer loans. Here, again, the Euromarket offers an advantage in adjusting ARBL. All Euro loans, whatever their ultimate maturity, are priced, on each roll date, for some fixed period at a fixed price that equals the quoted LIBO rate for the term chosen by the borrower plus some spread. Usually it is possible for a bank to guess what term—say one, three, or six months—the customer will pick on a roll date. This permits the bank to beat its customer to the draw. The bank anticipates what interest rate maturity the customer will choose and buys the money it will need beforehand. The attempt by banks to pre-position themselves on the basis of their perception of customer preferences explains why, whenever there is a big agglomeration of loans being repriced around the end of the month, LIBOR tends to rise for the time period favored by borrowers. Most people think this occurs because bank dealers bid up the market to get the highest rate possible when loans are repriced. The real reason is that banks do a lot of prefunding: buying money of the maturity they anticipate their customers will demand before the roll date.

Controlling offshore position risk

Some banks take the position that, since it is hard for bank management to get interest rate forecasts right, the best tactic is to let the managers of each of its books—the domestic book and Euro books in various foreign branches—set their ARBLs in accordance with their view of interest rates. The price of this tactic is that, since some liability managers will get it right while others get it wrong, except in the unusual circumstance where every manager gets it right, the bank will make less money than if all managers had followed a policy dictated by head office that turned out to be based on a correct view of interest rates. The offset is that, if every manager acts independently, earnings will not be as disastrous as they would have been if every manager were instructed to act on a view that was promulgated by top management and later proved incorrect.

The position that decision making with respect to gapping should be decentralized is not shared by many other top banks. There is a strong case for the position that a bank's global book should be managed by the bank's top management. Such a policy implies several things. First, top management should establish parameters that limit the size of the bets each of their foreign branches may make. Second, the people at the head office who are most closely associated with determining the outlook for dollar interest rates should communicate their view to branch managers running Euro books and should expect those managers to take advantage of that guidance.

In a tightly managed bank, head office will closely examine each foreign branch's Euro book weekly, and, if the book deviates too far from the guidelines top management has set with respect to liquidity and interest rates exposure, the message will go out, "Tidy up your position because it is diametrically opposed to our outlook."

A bank that does not operate this way may end up in a position where it has structured its domestic book to take advantage of an anticipated rise in interest rates only to find that its London book is structured exactly the opposite way. Suddenly, the bank has a *hedge,* perhaps one large enough to wipe out the bet head office is making. There is no way a hedged bet can enhance short-term earnings. Quite to the contrary, losses on one side of the Atlantic will be offset by profits on the other, and the net effect on earnings, if the hedge is perfect, will be a wash: *zero.*

Having top management coordinate a bank's worldwide book does not mean that the liability manager of an offshore branch should have no freedom. Suppose the general instruction from head office is, "We expect interest rates to fall and everyone should run a short book." Suddenly, a big depositor comes into the bank's London office and says, "I have $200 million I want to place with you for a year." If the London office manager takes that money, he will change the structure of his book. Whether he does so will depend on whether he thinks there is a good reason to do so. Eurobusiness, as opposed to domestic business, is done much more at arms length. In particular, deals in an attempt to build customer relationships are struck less frequently than they are in the domestic market. The London manager may decide to take the $200 million of 1-year money because he believes that the dip of interest rates will be temporary and that, over the life of the deposit, earnings will benefit from this deposit on his book. Or he may feel that, because the yield curve is inverted and is likely to stay that way for awhile, his initial gains on the deposit will offset his later losses. Finally, he may take the money because he knows of a pocket where he can lay it off—someone else on the other side who will be looking for 1-year money.

If the manager took the $200 million of 1-year money, head office would pick that up in its weekly review of his position. If the bank, understanding his reasons for taking the position, still wanted to stay say $3 billion short, it could easily do so by going short $200 million elsewhere in its global Euro book.

Foreign currency operations

A handful of *very* large banks have significant local currency operations abroad: Paris, Frankfurt, or other foreign offices that accept deposits and make loans in the local currency. Since interest rates in foreign countries live a life distinct from that of dollar interest rates, the manager of a branch dealing in a foreign currency is pretty much left to exercise his own judgment with respect to running his book: i.e., managing the liquidity position and assuming interest rate exposure. Also, his assets and liabilities should be excluded from the bank's overall liquidity and interest rate exposure calculations.

There is, however, one small exception. Usually a U.S. bank cannot produce large amounts of dollars by swapping local currency held in a foreign branch for dollars. However, in some countries, a foreign branch can swap dollars into the local currency. This occurs, for example, in the Brussels branches of some U.S. banks because Belgian francs are hard to come by. Recognizing this, Belgian authorities permit foreign banks with local branches to borrow limited amounts of Eurodollars and swap them into Belgian francs. A branch that does this creates a dollar liability that is vulnerable to nonreplacement. Such borrowings should, therefore, be included in the bank's liquidity position. However, since the liability is a swap, it need not be included in the calculation of interest rate exposure. Questions on this level are sophisticated; few banks face them, and even for these banks the amounts involved are small.

RELATIONSHIP OF INTEREST RATE EXPOSURE TO LIQUIDITY RISK

While we have sought, in this and the preceding chapter, to focus separately on liquidity and interest rate exposure, the two are inextricably intertwined. To change one almost always implies a change in the other; thus, a good bank liability manager must always keep his eye on both.

Sacrificing liquidity to accept interest rate exposure

Whenever the yield curve is positively sloped, a banker is tempted to enhance current profits by lending long and borrowing short. In doing so, he necessarily sacrifices liquidity because the maturity of his assets has now become greater than that of his liabilities. Consequently, he must worry about being able to replace his liabilities as they mature. If a bank has to worry about liquidity, which all but the giant banks do, its inability to accept liquidity risk will limit its ability to accept interest rate exposure. This is a *critical* point. A banker might be absolutely certain about his interest rate forecast: the yield curve is upward sloping and rates are going nowhere. Consequently, he might say, "I am going to lend all my money for as long as I can and cover that by buying money in the day-to-day market." In practice, however, he can't do this because his ability to accept liquidity risk is limited. Over the long haul, he might find that one day he just can't buy that much day-to-day money. He is suddenly faced, in the short run, with a liquidity problem, one that might force him to close his doors.

Even if a bank does not fear a liquidity problem (it is Morgan or Citi and can get all the short money it wants, if not in the domestic market, then in the Euromarket), it still must place some limit on the interest rates bet it will place, no matter how steeply positive the yield curve is, and no matter how strong its conviction that rates are not going to change. No interest rate gamble is ever a sure thing, and if a bank makes a bet that is sufficiently large and things go wrong, its losses may be so staggering that it will be forced out of business. That almost happened to First Pennsy.

Liquidity, interest rate exposure, and profits

If a liability manager seeks to increase liquidity when the yield curve is positively sloped, he can only do so by buying long-term money and lending it short; by doing that, he effectively eliminates liquidity risk *and* decreases short-run profits. If, alternatively, the yield curve is negatively sloped, buying liquidity will enhance short-run profits but at the price of producing additional interest rate exposure, since a negatively-sloped yield curve is always predicting that rates will go down. The one saving grace of buying liquidity when the yield curve is negatively sloped is that, in this situation, the market pays the liability manager for adding to liquidity. By buying liquidity, the liability manager is storing up treasures in heaven in the form of short-run profits, which, if the yield curve stays inverted for a long period, may amount to a significant sum, one that provides him with a comfortable cushion against the losses he may later incur due to the interest rate exposure he assumes in buying liquidity.

A bank's decision as to when and whether to buy liquidity should be influenced not only by the shape of the yield curve and expectations of how that curve will change, but by the bank's conviction as to *how quickly rates will rise or fall*. Buying liquidity may cost a bank dearly if the yield curve is steeply sloped, but even so, that purchase may prove highly profitable if rates move quickly. Buying liquidity when the yield curve is inverted is immediately profitable but risky. However, this, too, may contribute to long-term earnings if rates stay put for a prolonged period. The yield curve is always correct but sometimes only in the very long run.

Long-run considerations. Short-run considerations limit a bank's ability to accept interest rates exposure; so, too, do long-run considerations. A banker never knows what attractive opportunity might come down the pike in the long run. If, to accept interest rate exposure, he has stretched his liquidity to the limit, then liquidity considerations will become a binding constraint on his ability to take on additional attractive assets or to take advantage of new and even more attractive opportunities to assume interest rate exposure.

The foregoing centered on a bank having sufficient confidence in its interest rate forecast to choose to assume interest rate exposure. A bank may form a view in which it has confidence by relying on in-house expertise or, if it is small, by following what economists at the major banks and dealers are saying. How much risk a bank should assume on the basis of a given level of confidence is an individual decision that must be a function of management's propensity to assume risk to produce return.

No one can tell a bank chairman what propensity to assume risk he should have because his risk preference is presumably one of the reasons he was hired. The most one can say is that no banker should make interest rate bets so large that he is betting the bank. Bets that large are typically made only when a bank is headed by a strong individual who imposes his view of interest rates on other bank officers—an extremely dangerous practice.

PROBLEMS WITH AVOIDING INTEREST RATE EXPOSURE

The prescription often given to banks—avoid risk by matching the bank's book—has a sound ring and is often voiced by people who do not understand commercial banking. Avoiding interest rate exposure can cause a bank problems.

SPREADS MAY BE INADEQUATE TO SUPPORT EARNINGS

A bank that seeks to avoid interest rate exposure will, to the extent possible, run a matched book. In doing so, all it will earn is the natural spread it gets as an intermediary because it buys funds at the bid side of the market and sells at the offered side. It bears repeating that spreads on intermediation tend to vary inversely with the size of the bank and, in particular, to be miniscule for a large bank. A decision by a large bank to match its book would have a severe negative impact on its earnings, would limit its ability to add to capital and thus to grow, and in the worst case, might ultimately put the bank out of business.

Complying with customers' desires

If a bank's policy is to avoid interest rate exposure, that means that, if a good customer wants long-term money, the bank can give it to him only if it can borrow money of equal maturity. If it can't, the bank will lose the unsatisfied customer who will go elsewhere. Similarly, if a depositor wants to place 3-year money with a bank at an attractive rate, a bank that is determined to run a matched book will be able to accept that deposit only if it uncovers an acceptable 3-year asset at a fixed rate. If it can't, it loses the depositor.

To stay in business, a bank has to maintain a loyal customer base, and time and time again, its ability to do so will depend on its willingness to accept at least some interest rate exposure.

Prevents developing long-term strategies

The avoidance of interest rate exposure involves a commitment to match the interest rate maturity of every asset (liability) a bank acquires voluntarily or involuntarily with a liability (asset) of the same maturity. Once a bank commits itself to doing this, it has lost the ability to develop long-term strategies.

Suppose the bank says, "We are worried that the secular trend in interest rates is down. How are we going to cope with the fact that over the long haul, interest rates are likely to fall to 10 percent from 18 percent where they have been the last couple of years? How are we going to sustain earnings?" If the bank has a strong conviction that rates will fall secularly, instituting a strategy to offset the impact of this on earnings is a necessity. But if the bank is also determined to match asset and liability maturities, this necessity will run smack into its ongoing policy of allowing *no* asset-liability mismatch. Trying to implement a long-term strategy—buying long assets and financing them with short money at the margin—will automatically violate the policy of matching the interest rate maturities of assets and liabilities. A bank with a policy of avoiding mismatch, can, in this situation, do nothing.

Inhibits ability to leverage capital

The heart of banking is leveraging capital and to do this, a bank needs customers. If it loses customers because its policy is to avoid any mismatch between the interest rate maturities of assets and liabilities, it will automatically limit its ability to grow and to leverage capital.

The decision to run a matched book will also create other sticky problems. If the bank is accreting capital, accepting additional hard-core demand deposits, or happens to sell a long-term capital note issue when rates are at a cyclical low, what should it do with the money? Insisting on running a matched book means that the bank should use its money to buy 30-year bonds, a decision that might prevent the bank from going into other, more attractive positions.

When all is said and done, *it is impossible to run a bank without accepting interest rate exposure.* The fact that such exposure can lead to problems is not an argument for eliminating it. Rather, it is an argument for accepting interest rate exposure only in a balanced and methodical way, for asking, every time the bank makes a bet, not only what it stands to win if it is correct, but also what it stands to lose if it is incorrect, and, in particular, how prepared it is to accept that loss.

LONG-TERM CONSIDERATIONS

Short-term measures of ARBL are a *tactical* variable, long-term measures a *strategic* variable for affecting long-term profits. There are essentially three ways a bank can adjust long-term ARBL: altering its securities holdings, making fixed-rate term loans, and issuing capital notes.

Adjusting the securities portfolio

As we will note in Chapter 11, it is difficult for a bank to make portfolio profits, particularly on long bonds. Yet there is a case to be made for buying such securities at times.

Case for buying bonds. For a bank, large or small, with a strong conviction that interest rates are going to drop sharply and remain low for a prolonged period, buying long bonds while yields are high offers the best means available to sustain earnings as the business cycle ebbs and rates drop. The danger is that the unforeseen occurs and rates go the other way.

For a small bank, the danger in buying long bonds is somewhat less than for a large bank. A large bank always buys bonds with other people's money which it garners by doing repo. A small bank typically uses its own money to buy bonds. This distinction is crucial. Should rates rise instead of fall, the large bank is faced with negative carry that it can eliminate only by selling its bonds at a loss. For a small bank, its portfolio is truly a source of liquidity; by doing RP against it, the bank can produce funds to relend. Moreover, if the anticipated fall in rates that caused the bank to add to its holdings of governments fails to materialize and rates rise steeply, the bank may be able to earn an attractive spread when it lends out the funds it obtains by repoing its portfolio.

Another long-term consideration for a bank in buying tax-exempt securities is maximizing aftertax earnings over the long run. We will cover this topic in Chapter 11.

Case against buying securities. If, at the margin, a bank has a balance sheet constraint—it is concerned about its capital ratio—it will want to take on, at the margin, assets that will provide the greatest return in an overall sense. A bank that buys governments does not get anything in the way of improved customer relationship with the Treasury, whereas by making a loan to a customer it wants to cultivate, it does. So on that count, loans would be the wiser use of the money.

Also, over the life of the loans, the bank will probably make a greater spread with loans than if it held governments. For any maturity range, governments pay the lowest yield, since they offer the investor the lowest credit risk *and* high liquidity. It will *never* happen that a bank can buy a government and simultaneously buy money to finance that security to maturity at a positive spread.

The case against governments is that buying them is usually a sub-optimal use of resources compared to whatever other asset the bank could acquire if other long-term, fixed-rate assets were available, which they may not be at times, especially for a small bank. A second reason for a large bank not to buy long bonds is that, if yields move up, the bank may be forced by the effect of negative carry on profits to sell these securities at a loss. If this loss is large, it may not only lower current earnings, but actually invade capital.

Fixed-rate term loans

As a strategy to sustain earnings in the face of a predicted secular downturn in interest rates, making fixed-rate term loans is an even worse bet than buying governments. At least in the past, it has been a *no-win* proposition, no matter how interest rates move. Banks are in the business of attempting to avoid undue risk, so it stands to reason that they will, if leaned upon, consent to make fixed-rate term loans only to their best customers. This does happen. Subsequently, if rates fall as predicted, the same good customers come back to their bank and say, "I am getting killed by having to pay this high rate. Can we please renegotiate?" And the bank has usually renegotiated because it wanted to keep the customer. That is why fixed-rate term loans have been a no-win proposition. If the bank is right in its interest rate forecast and rates do fall, the high-yielding asset will be taken away from it. If the bank is wrong and rates rise, the bank will have the privilege of enjoying negative carry on that asset. To the above it should be added that this is beginning to change. The increasing tendency of large corporate treasurers to shop loan rates and terms among banks has led banks to be more hard-nosed about renegotiating loan terms and imposing prepayment penalties.

Making fixed-rate term loans has usually turned out to be the wrong thing for a bank to do. In some cases, the bank's motive was not to insulate earnings from a downturn in rates, but to grow by giving other banks' customers loans on terms more favorable than those these customers' banks would give them. First of Chicago used this ploy to lure customers from the Continental and other Chicago banks. As rates subsequently rose, it lived to rue the day it did so.

Capital note issues

It's hard to find a good argument for banks in general to issue capital notes. Occasionally, a bank may feel that rates are at an attractive cyclical low and that issuing long-term capital notes will provide cheap funds over the long run. An example is the 5s of 95 which Morgan issued in 1965. For a major bank to issue 30-year notes in the high-rate environment prevailing in recent times would be a disaster; it would also be a very visible vote of no confidence in government policy.

A stronger case for issuing capital notes of shorter maturities can be made for banks that do a lot of consumer lending—short-term car loans and long-term mortgages. If, for this reason, a bank builds up a large block of fixed-yield assets on its book, the proper way to finance them is to use short-term funds when the yield curve is positively sloped but look for the occasional moment when rates bottom out and longer-term notes can be sold at rates sufficiently attractive to lock in a positive carry on such assets. This is essentially the tactic that finance companies use, especially those financing purchases of autos, farm equipment, and other durable goods for which the borrower will take years to pay.

One problem with using capital notes to finance blocks of longer-term consumer loans, is that, when those loans begin to look like a bad bet because rates are rising, the market is typically not receptive to long-term bank paper. What is really called for to make a capital-note strategy work is *prefinancing*. The bank issues its notes before rates start to rise and while the yield curve is still positively sloped. Prefinancing is costly initially, so a bank that practices it must take a long view—be willing to sacrifice current earnings to improve future earnings.

INTEREST RATE EXPOSURE
AND PROFITS

Risk versus reward

In making strategic decisions on interest rate exposure, as in making tactical decisions, it is crucial that a bank, each time it examines a strategy, measure the potential profit or loss against its need for profit and its ability to withstand losses. This is self-evident but bears repeating because failure to do so has been the root cause of severe problems at more than one bank.

If one wants to examine what happened at First Pennsy or First of Chicago, one cannot criticize the interest rate judgments the banks made. Anyone can make that kind of mistake. The misdeed in every case was that *the bet made was too big.* Management could not live with the losses that were incurred. If those banks had played *what if* games—asked not only how happy they would be if they got extra earnings, but also how well they could sustain the losses if their interest rate forecasts proved wrong—then, in each case, the bet probably would have been much smaller. This leads to the notion that each bank must develop for itself some measure—perhaps quantifiable—of how much risk it is willing to assume to produce a given return. Is the risk of losing $100 million on an interest rate play worth the possibility of winning the same amount? If those are the outside parameters of the bet and the answer is no, the bet is too big.

The danger of growth targets for profits

Annual percentage targets for profit growth are dangerous because they become a justification for assuming unacceptable risk positions. A good example is Citi. Some years ago, Walter Wriston, its chairman, said, "Citibank's earnings will grow 15 percent per year indefinitely." And for about a decade they did. Then earnings growth slackened. This leads one to hazard the guess that Citi may well have entered the fourth quarter of 1980 saying, "It's make or break. Unless we make a big bet, we are not going to make our 15 percent." So they made a big bet and earned nothing in the fourth quarter.

The chief executive's job. Economists always talk about firm's seeking to maximize profits over time. If you spoke to them about a bank's "need" to make profits, they would not know what you meant, but some bankers do. Consider a bank that has made bad rate or credit gambles, as did the First of Chicago. Earnings are down, and it is evident to at least some members of top management that, if things don't improve, they are going to lose their jobs. A situation of this sort is dangerous and calls for the bank board to keep a close eye on what the bank is doing.

The risk preference of a banker who is in danger of losing his job undergoes a strange transformation. He argues, "If I make a big bet and earnings improve, I will keep my job. If, on the other hand, the bet costs the bank a ton of money, I will lose my job, which would have happened anyway." To the bank manager, there is no penalty in making a losing bet; to him personally, the payoff on the bet is asymmetric: heads he keeps his job, tails he loses nothing. Therein lies the danger when a banker says, "We *need* to earn more profit." It's a danger that leads to many bad decisions.

The danger of having nothing to do

To survive and grow, a major bank must make bets on interest rates. If the yield curve has a sharp positive slope, it will lend long and borrow short. Presumably, at some point, short rates will rise, but if it takes time for that to occur, the bank will have made some extra profit. If, alternatively, the yield curve is inverted, the bank will lend short and borrow long. Again, if rates are slow to fall, the bank will have earned extra profits. Of course, in each of the above cases, rates might move so swiftly that the bank incurs a loss on its gamble. The point, however, is that in either case the bank at least has an opportunity to accept interest rate risk to produce return.

The third and perhaps most dangerous situation is when the yield curve is *flat* and remains so for some time. With a flat yield curve, a bank cannot make any extra profits by taking positions along the curve. What can it do to augment the meager profits it makes on commercial lending? *Nothing.* In that situation, it is important that management does not start getting fancy ideas about doing crazy things, such as taking big positions in foreign exchange, bonds, money market instruments, or whatever it trades, in an attempt to bolster its earnings on its natural business.

It is the environment within which a bank operates that gives it the opportunity to accept interest rate exposure. If the environment offers no such opportunity, there is nothing to do, no game in town to play. A bank's earnings, reflecting this, will be limited to the small spread it earns on its natural business.

There is a moral to be drawn from this. There are times when there is no opportunity to do anything but sit there and subsist until an opportunity presents itself. Were the yield curve to stay flat for the next 10 years, no major bank would be able to raise its profits above the 40 to 75 basis points they earn now. Even accepting interest rate exposure, banks' return on equity typically ranges from 12 to 20 percent, which, for highly leveraged institutions engaged in risky activities, is hardly attractive.

A concluding thought

Throughout this chapter we have forcused on the standard sources and measures of a bank's interest rate exposure—the mismatch in different periods between the interest rate maturities of its assets and liabilities.

Depending on the time and on the bank, focusing solely on gaps may lead a bank to make significant omissions in calculating its overall interest rate exposure. Three additional factors that some banks should consider in measuring such exposure are the following: (1) During a period, such as the present, when foreign exchange rates are strongly influenced by differentials among interest rates in different countries, a big position in a bank's foreign exchange trading operation, which is nominally a bet on exchange rates, may, in fact, be a bet on the direction in which U.S. interest rates will move relative to rates in one or more foreign countries. (2) High interest rates may significantly reduce the survival prospects of firms to which a bank has loans outstanding. If so, these loans become part of the bank's overall interest rate exposure. Examples of firms whose prospects in 1981 were strongly dependent on interest rates were International Harvester and Chrysler. Both firms had big debts to service and both had products the sale of which was strongly affected by credit conditions. (3) In today's markets, the price of gold is highly sensitive to dollar interest rates. Consequently, for the few banks that actively trade in it, uncovered positions in gold are an additional source of interest rate exposure.

PART IV

Tactics and strategies

10

Forecasting interest rates

No bank can avoid accepting at least some natural interest rate exposure. In addition, most larger banks operate under such highly competitive conditions that they are forced to assume additional exposure to maintain adequate earnings.

Interest rate exposure, natural or volitionally accepted, must be managed; the only way a bank can do this is on the basis of a view on interest rates. Thus, to operate, bank management must devise some way to forecast interest rates.

THE BLACK BOX APPROACH

Many brilliant economists and econometricians have labored long and hard to produce mathematical models of the economy. The premise underlying all such models is that changes in certain economic variables will have predictable effects on other variables, effects that can be determined by careful analysis of the economy's past behavior. All econometric models contain two sorts of variables, *exogenous* and *endogenous.* The values of exogenous variables are produced outside the model, perhaps by government decision makers setting fiscal and monetary policy. Endogenous variables, in contrast, are variables whose values are predicted by the model.

The model itself is a complex set of equations which incorporates all the econometrician has learned from the past behavior of the economy about how economic variables interact. Using his model, the econometrician predicts the values of those variables that are endogenous to his model given information on the current state of the economy— GNP is X, interest rates are Y, and so forth—and what he knows or expects the values of those variables exogenous to his model to be.

Building an econometric model of the economy is a huge and expensive undertaking, the end product of which is an impressive array of equations comprehensible to only an elite few. To obtain predictions from the model, the econometrician first puts in the latest data on the current state of the economy and values for the exogenous variables; he then runs the model on a computer.

Both the procedures and the end results of econometric forecasting are so impressive and even intimidating to most people that every year business firms spend millions of dollars to buy economic predictions put out by firms that have developed major macroeconomic models. Any economist worth his salt would tell a banker looking for a way to establish a view on interest rates to go to one of the so-called black box firms and buy its rate forecasts. After all, this is the age of science, and the econometrician's black box forecasts are "scientific" predictions.

Unfortunately, while macro models may be useful for forecasting certain things, those that purport to forecast interest rates have a *disastrous* record. As one banker who follows interest rates closely noted, "Any time a guy with a black box wants to trade bonds with me on the basis of his model's predictions of interest rates, I'll take him on *and* clean him out."

So much for black boxes. At one point, even the Fed, which has its own black box model and presumably a goodly bit of inside information, admitted that the interest rate predictions produced by its model were poorer than those produced by the yield curve.[1] It may be true

---

[1] In defense of econometric models, a point akin to the one made in Chapter 1 about optimization models should be added. Many people are *overly* critical of the results produced by econometric models because they begin by expecting too much. Constructing an in-house econometric model can be highly useful for a bank whose management lacks a good understanding of how the different sectors of the economy interact and of how various outside forces affect the economy.

The value of building an in-house model is not that it will produce more accurate forecasts than those produced by other models, but that it will force consistency into management's views of the future. A management that pays attention to its model would not have forecast, in the fall of 1981, as did the management of a major New York bank, that the federal deficit would be larger than Washington's worst predictions, but that simultaneously inflation would abate faster and unemployment would rise more slowly

that yield curve predictions of the direction in which interest rates are headed are almost always correct in the long run. However, the yield curve is notoriously inaccurate in forecasting short-run interest rate trends. One piece of supporting evidence for this statement is that in 1981, the yield curve had been inverted for so long that a whole generation of bond traders had grown up thinking that an inverted curve was "normal."

FORECASTS INCORPORATING SUBJECTIVE ELEMENTS

For a banker, six months is the long run. Consequently, to manage his interest rate exposure, he needs to be able to forecast correctly, more often than not, very short-run shifts in the *direction* of interest rates. To predict where interest rates will be tomorrow, two weeks from now, or two months from now, one must (1) take into account a lot of subjective information that can't be incorporated into a black box model, and (2) then make some careful judgments.

To illustrate, we describe the thought process that one banker—a pro with a good track record at predicting interest rates—goes through in coming up with his predictions. The setting is early August 1981. Interest rates have been wallowing around for several months. Where are they headed next? Our banker reasons:

> There is a whole litany of arguments that can be made for interest rates being lower right now or in the near future. The economy is slowing down. Businesses are being hurt worse and worse by high interest rates, and there is a question of how much longer this can go on. The thrifts are in terrible shape; something has to be done for them. Some government bond dealers, who bought bonds on the conviction that rates had to drop, are experiencing such terrible negative carry that they are in danger of going under. The cost of financing the Treasury debt is astronomical, so much so that for the first time in decades the Treasury considered omitting a long bond from the quarterly financing announced in July, to avoid locking themselves into very high-cost, long-term debt service.
>
> I tick off all of these fundamental reasons why interest rates have to come down. Then I think about what Chairman Volcker of the Fed said about high rates unfortunately having an inhibiting effect on economic activity and about what Undersecretary of the Treasury Sprinkel said about the money supply showing recent growth rates below the FOMC

---

than predicted by the administration. The virtue of a model is that it forces consistency into management's macro projections. Management cannot be predicting that X and Y will both rise, when a premise of their model—one to which they have presumably agreed—is that a rise in X will cause Y to fall.

[Federal Open Market Committee] targets, and at some point things reach a critical mass: I say interest rates are going to drop.

Then, depending on the intensity of my feeling, I ask by how much they could change. What kind of room is there, given the problems that the Fed has? I believe that, if the economy were flat and the Fed had its druthers, it would like to hold interest rates in the high teens, maybe around the 20 percent level, through the end of the year. The Fed knows that that is the cutting edge in the inflation fight. They have been getting good numbers on the wholesale and consumer prices indexes. In my judgment, the Fed is trying to put together a string of good inflation numbers for practically a whole year. If the string comes out around the 7 or 8 percent level, it will represent a major victory against inflation, and more importantly, it will change expectations. That is what the Fed is after, a change in expectations.

Next I ask what will happen if the Fed eases up now as it did in the spring of 1980 and lets rates drop by 1,000 basis points. They would probably lose all credibility and be back to square one in terms of changing inflationary expectations. That means to me that the Fed can let interest rates come off some but not much; they might let funds drop from say the 18 to 19 percent range to 16.5 to 17 percent.

That is the sort of thinking process I go through. I put in a lot of subjective elements. The problem for the guy with the black box is that, while he may perceive the same subjective elements I do, he can't get the proportions right with respect to the kind of effect they are going to have on rates.

Hindsight shows that that was not a bad premise on which to operate for a month or two, and every good banker should be constantly revising his outlook on rates as changes occur in the economy and on the political scene.

What should and what may happen

In forecasting interest rates, it is important to distinguish between what one thinks *should* happen to interest rates and what one thinks *may*, in fact, happen. This is crucial.

The banker quoted above went on to note:

A lot of people have been going around now for two months saying that there is no reason on the fundamental side for interest rates to be as high as they are. The key fundamentals that usually dictate the level of interest rates—the rate of inflation, the pace of economic activity, and the value of the dollar—are all at levels such that they constitute major reasons why interest rates should be lower than they are. But interest rates are not lower.

So you have to look for an extraneous idea, one that does not usually apply. One theory is that the Fed may recognize that this is their last clear chance with a compatible administration to put inflation to bed. The Fed's perception may be that, in the long historic perspective, this is the last shot they will get for changing inflationary expectations. You cannot put that into a black box.

The above rundown of one banker's thought process shows how many important, constantly changing, and often subjective factors that can't be incorporated into an economist's model need to be considered in a well-thought-out interest rate forecast.

Models come in various flavors

It also points out something else of interest. Without saying so, the banker quoted clearly implied that he thinks Volcker is a closet Keynesian who believes that high interest rates, not some magic money supply number, is what is needed to change inflationary expectations.

That observation raises yet another problem with black box models. Economists do not now, never have, and probably never will agree on what theory best explains how the economy ticks at the macro level. Thus, black box models come in various flavors—Keynesian, monetarist, and, now, supply side. Not surprisingly, black box predictions based on different macroeconomic models yield different predictions. So a banker who buys a black box prediction not only must put his faith in black box forecasts, but must also pick the brand of forecast he wants.

HOW TO BUILD A VIEW ON INTEREST RATES

If bankers can't rely on economists to guide them on where interest rates are headed, they have to come up with a view on their own. Generally, in major banks, there are a number of people who carefully track all the obvious and not so obvious factors—political and economic, domestic and international—that may impinge on dollar interest rates and who produce, using the sort of reasoning illustrated in the comments quoted above, a view on the direction in which interest rates are going.

It's useful for a bank to have five sharp people, all with their own carefully formed ideas as to where interest rates are headed, but to manage its interest rate exposure, a bank needs a management point of view on rates. To illustrate the problem, suppose two bank officers are sitting in a room; one says interest rates are going down, the other says they are going up. Unless the two work at defining how strongly each holds his respective view, they can leave the room thinking that their views are diametrically opposed. Alternatively, if they talk about the intensity of their conviction, they may find that one assigns a 55 percent probability to rates going down and a 45 percent probability to rates going up, whereas the other assigns exactly the opposite probabilities to these outcomes. If so, the two are, in fact, really quite close in their interest rate outlooks.

For a bank to use the views of its in-house experts to form a bank view on interest rates, one on which the bank can—as it must—act, some tool is required for (1) measuring the intensity of its experts' convictions on rates, and (2) molding these convictions into a single bank view on interest rates. A method for doing this that is simple and produces good results is the histogram.

The histogram approach

Here is how one bank uses this approach. Each week, it gives its experts a sheet (Figure 10–1, Part A) which shows an array of potential values for changes in the 30-day CD rate. The experts know what that rate is now, and they independently apportion 100 percent of their confidence along the array of possible changes. Each participant assigns various *subjective* probabilities (expressed as percentages) to certain values along the array and, by implication, zero to the others.

Next, the experts meet to compare their assignments of probabilities. Each participant tries to convince the others of the validity of his view. Often, some will change their views because a potentially key factor, disregarded in his projections, is introduced in another.

Suppose that the five participants, Adams through Wolf, assign— after considered discussion—the probabilities for changes in the 30-day CD rate displayed in Figure 10–1, Part A. The next step in constructing a bank view of interest rates is to average these probabilities for each interval in the array to get the average figures (percentage probabilities) shown in the bottom line of the table.

From these average numbers, a histogram (Figure 10–1, Part B) is constructed. This histogram is a bar chart displaying a probability distribution in which the assigned probabilities add up to 100 percent. Note this histogram shows graphically that the bank's experts have a lot of confidence that the 30-day CD rate will fall over the next month. Their ideas as to how much it will fall vary considerably, but as a group they assign a great deal of confidence to a drop on the order of 100 to 200 basis points.

The histogram approach does not give a single-valued prediction of where the 30-day CD rate will be one month hence. It gives something better: a range of possible changes in value and the confidence that the experts as a group attach to each of these changes in value. As noted in earlier chapters, it is crucial for a bank in deciding (1) whether to place a bet on interest rates, and (2) how large a bet to place, to know how confident it is in its rate prediction. The histogram gives bank man-

Figure 10–1
Sample histogram: 1-month horizon (part A: the data—assigned subjective probabilities and best guesses)

Sources and uses of funds committee
Item: 30-day CD rate
Date: 7/27/81
Horizon: 1 month hence

Committee member	Best guess Change in basis points	Assigned subjective probabilities of changes in the 30-day CD rate (basis points)											
		-800	-700	-600	-500	-400	-300	-200	-100	0	100	200	300
Adams	-100							25%	45%	30%			
Brown	-100						10%	25%	30%	25%	10%		
Jones	-90							30%	45%	15%	10%		
Smith	-50					10%	10%	10%	35%	35%			
Wolf	-190						20%	40%	20%	10%	10%		
Average	-106					2%	8%	26%	35%	23%	6%		

Range of best guesses: -190 to -50 basis points
Expected value of rate change: -113 basis points
Current rate: 17.90%
Expected rate: 16.77%

Figure 10–1 (*continued*)
(part B: histogram displaying the average subjective probabilities the group assigns to various possible changes in the 30-day CD rate 1 month hence)

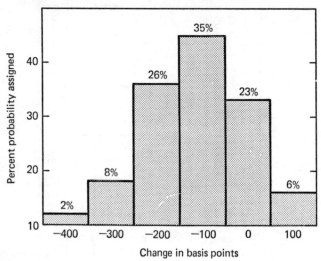

Change in basis points

agement not only the experts' view on the direction in rates, but their confidence in that view.

To determine what funding strategy it should pursue, bank management needs a histogram not only for a 1-month horizon, but for longer periods. Figures 10–2 and 10–3 show sample histograms for the 30-day CD rate three and six months hence. Note that, as the time horizon of the prediction increases, the conviction on the part of the participants that rates will fall increases, but the range of the outcomes they consider possible and, concomitantly, their degree of confidence in just how much the 30-day rate will fall, decreases.

This is not surprising. It shows what one would expect; the longer the time horizon of the prediction, the greater the uncertainty the participants feel.

Assigning a best guess

A second part of the histogram exercise is to ask each participant to assign a best guess as to where the 30-day CD rate will be at the end of the time horizon under consideration. One would expect each participant's best guess to be close to the expected value of the probability distribution he assigns to the array of possible changes in the 30-day

Figure 10–2
Sample histogram: 3-month horizon (part A: the data—assigned subjective probabilities and best guesses)

Sources and uses of funds committee
Item: 30-day CD rate
Date: 7/27/81
Horizon: 3 months hence

Committee member	Best guess Change in basis points	Assigned subjective probabilities of changes in the 30-day CD rate (basis points)											
		-800	-700	-600	-500	-400	-300	-200	-100	0	100	200	300
Adams	-350		10%	10%	15%	20%	20%	15%	10%				
Brown	-300				15%	20%	30%	20%	10%	5%			
Jones	-340				15%	25%	25%	20%	10%	5%			
Smith	-200					10%	20%	40%	20%	10%			
Wolf	-290				10%	20%	30%	20%	10%	10%			
Average	-296		2%	2%	11%	19%	25%	23%	12%	6%			

Range of best guesses: -350 to -200 basis points
Expected value of rate change: -290 basis points
Current rate: 17.90%
Expected rate: 15.00%

Figure 10–2 (continued)
(part B: histogram displaying the average subjective probabilities the group
assigns to various possible changes in the 30-day CD rate 3 months hence)

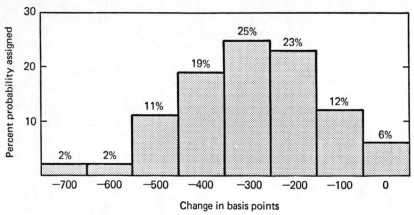

rate.[2] However, that may not be the case when the time horizon of the
prediction is long, and the participants consequently feel a high degree
of uncertainty.

Look, for example, at Figure 10–3, which shows a histogram with a
6-month time horizon. The participants' high degree of uncertainty
causes the histogram to be flat. In this situation, a participant making
his best guess as to where the 30-day CD rate will be six months hence
has to come down on one side or the other, and his best guess may
diverge considerably from the expected value of the probabilities he
assigns to different ranges of change in the 30-day rate.

On histograms with longer time horizons, there are two measures

---

[2] The calculation of expected value:
Let

E = Expected value.
x = A value to which a probability is assigned.
y = The probability assigned as a decimal.
Σ is a symbol denoting "sum over."

Then

$$E = \Sigma xy$$

Applying this formula to the average probabilities assigned in Part A of Figure 10–1 to
possible rate changes in basis points, we get

$$E = 0.02(-400) + 0.08(-300) + 0.26(-200)$$
$$+ 0.35(-100) + 0.23(0) + 0.06(100)$$
$$= -113$$

which coincides with the number given for "expected value of rate change" given below
the table.

Figure 10–3
Sample histogram: 6-month horizon (part A: the data—assigned subjective probabilities and best guesses)

Sources and uses of funds committee
Item: 30-day CD rate
Date: 7/27/81
Horizon: 6 months hence

Committee member	Best guess Change in basis points	Assigned subjective probabilities of changes in the 30-day CD rate (basis points)											
		−800	−700	−600	−500	−400	−300	−200	−100	0	100	200	300
Adams	−650	10%	15%	15%	10%	10%	10%				10%	10%	10%
Brown	−400	5%	10%	10%	15%	20%	15%	10%	10%	5%			
Jones	−490		10%	15%	20%	20%	15%	10%	10%				
Smith	−500		10%	10%	20%	20%	20%	10%	10%				
Wolf	−490			10%	25%	25%	20%	10%	10%				
Average	−506	3%	9%	12%	18%	19%	16%	8%	8%	1%	2%	2%	2%

Range of best guesses: − 650 to − 400 basis points
Expected value of rate change: −385 basis points
Current rate: 17.90%
Expected rate: 14.05%

Figure 10–3 (continued)
(part B: histogram displaying the average subjective probabilities the group
assigns to various possible changes in the 30-day CD rate 6 months hence)

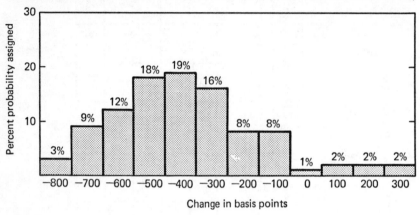

Change in basis points

that are useful to management. Consider again Figure 10–3. The best
guess number tells management that its experts feel the most likely
outcome six months hence is that the 30-day CD rate will be down 500
basis points. However, the *flat* nature of the histogram indicates that
the expert's conviction in this prediction is weak. Therefore, the bank
should not make any big bets on the experts' best guess of the long-run
trend in the 30-day CD rate.

Making tactical funding decisions

Histograms of the sort illustrated in Figures 10–1 to 10–3 form an
ideal basis for determining the bank's optimal tactics and strategies for
funding itself over the next six months. Usually, once the committee
participants have discussed their views, they are able to accept the
expected value forecasts of the 30-day CD rate for one, three, and six
months in the future. Assuming that rate changes between benchmark
points (e.g., one and three months) will occur on a straight-line basis,
the committee calculates—grossing up for reserve costs, FDIC insurance, and the impact of compounding—what the bank's funding costs
would be if it rolled 1-month CDs over the next six months, if it rolled
3-month CDs over this period, or if it bought 6-month money outright
(Table 10–1).

In our example, this calculation indicates that the cheapest tactic for
the bank would be to roll 1-month CDs. Note that this tactic would be
compatible with selling, to increase liquidity, 6-by-1 CDs, that is,
6-month, variable-rate CDs that are repriced monthly.

Table 10–1
Six-month funding options report derived from expected rate values in
Figures 10–1 to 10–3

Option		Effective rate* (percent)	Previous rate (percent)	Previous rank
1-month rollover strategy		16.81	17.06	1
3-month rollover strategy		17.15	17.38	2
Sell 6-month CD outright		17.92	18.25	3
Current high/low spread	1.11			
Previous high/low spread	1.19			
			This week (percent)	Previous week (percent)
Current rates used to calculate funding options	1-month CD		17.90	18.00
	3-month CD		17.75	17.85
	6-month CD		17.38	17.70

* Effective rate reflects nominal rate adjusted for 3 percent reserve requirement and, where appropriate, the effects of compounding.

The final decision

The single most important decision-making body in a major bank is the sources and uses of funds (S&U) or assets and liabilities committee (ALCO). This committee, comprised of the bank's top officers, makes short-run tactical and long-run strategic decisions about how the bank should structure its balance sheet over time: what assets it should acquire, what funding strategies it should pursue, and, by implication, what liquidity position and interest rate exposure it should adopt.

Typically, the interest rate predictions—in histogram or other form—produced by the bank's in-house committee on interest rate forecasts will be presented to the S&U or ALCO committee whose membership often overlaps, to some extent, that of the interest rate committee. In the example we have used, the interest rate experts will present to the S&U committee their histograms, the reasoning behind these histograms, and their implications for funding. Specifically, in our example, the interest rate experts would conclude by saying, "Our prediction is that the cost of funds is going to be around 16.75 percent over the next six months which implies a prime of something like 18.5 percent."

Management at this point has the opportunity of asking itself whether it really believes this. Management may disagree and say,

"We think rates will fall more slowly and that we should do 6-months outright." Or they may accept the interest rate committee's conclusion.

The sort of exercise we have described should be done in all top banks and in regionals, as well. Also, the exercise should be repeated to catch, as quickly as economic and political signs permit, mistakes such as the one the bank was making in its 6-month forecast of the 30-day CD rate.

SMALL BANKS

It is as crucial for a small bank, as for a large bank, to have a view on interest rates and to formulate policy on the basis of that view. A small bank, however, often lacks the in-house expertise to form its own view on rates. If so, it should form a view by listening to people whose views it respects: experts at its correspondent bank and economists at major banks and money market dealerships. Such people are quoted daily in financial publications and frequently speak at seminars arranged for their corporate and banking clients.

In choosing the views they will value, one caveat small bankers should respect is: do *not* listen to the views of politicians and government officials. There are two reasons. First, some officials, such as the chairman of the Council of Economic Advisors, may purposely choose not to predict in public what they believe in private is likely to occur in the future. A case in point: a high government official who fears that inflation will worsen and that interest rates will therefore rise will publicly paint the rosiest picture of the future possible because he knows that his act of predicting more inflation and higher interest rates may—*by influencing the public's expectations*—become self-fulfilling. A second and equally important reason that a small banker should be wary of listening to government officials is that people who lack a deep understanding of how financial markets operate are often appointed to important economic positions in government. William Miller, who acted as both chairman of the Fed and Secretary of the Treasury, is an example. His background was such that he did not know the money market well, and consequently, in public pronouncements, he so constantly contradicted himself and reversed position that eventually he lost all credibility with the financial community.

A small bank, even more than a large bank, might be tempted to buy the output of various forecasting services. However, since such a bank lacks the in-house expertise to critically examine the rate forecasts made by such services, doing so might be a waste of money.

Whomever a small bank ultimately decides to listen to, the bank should never act to alter either its liquidity position or interest rate exposure unless that move is consistent with an interest rate view with which the bank itself is satisfied. A small banker must hunt among experts until he finds someone or some group with a good track record that seem to be saying things that make sense to him.

MEASURING FUNDING PERFORMANCES

The profits a bank earns over the short and long run derive directly from how successfully it structures its balance sheet. In this structuring, by far the most important single element is liability management. Therefore, every bank should attempt to measure the performance of its liability manager.

Because of the sharp differences that exist between the types of assets and liabilities a bank has in its domestic and Euro books (all Euro assets and liabilities have fixed interest rate maturities), performance in the two books should be measured separately.

What numbers a bank should look at in measuring the performance of its liability manager will depend on the mix of business it does and on how it funds itself. For purposes of illustration, we consider measuring performance in a money market bank that specialized in wholesale business and whose principal business is, therefore, making loans to commercial and industrial customers. Such a bank would want to track the spread it achieves over time between the prime rate and the cost of the interest-sensitive funds it buys in the money market (Figure 10–4). Obviously, the more successful the bank's liability manager is in minimizing the bank's cost of bought money, the wider this spread and the greater the bank's profits will be.

Comparing prime to the bank's cost of bought money, however, tells only part of the story of how successful the bank's liability manager has been. A second question or set of questions that should be asked are *what if* questions that compare the cost of funds achieved by the bank to the cost that could have been achieved had the bank pursued some other funding strategy.

One approach, illustrated in Figure 10–4, is to compare the bank's cost of funds to what it would have been had the bank pursued a neutral strategy of rolling 3-month CDs. In that case, the bank's cost of funds would have been approximately that represented by the "13-week proxy" (13-week moving average of the cost of 3-month CD money) plotted in Figure 10–4.

If market conditions are such that there are no good funding bets to be made, the bank's actual costs of funds should closely track the 13-week proxy. Note, during the period pictured in Figure 10–4, that the bank's cost of interest-sensitive funds fell well below the 13-week proxy from mid-December 1980 through April 1981, indicating that

Figure 10-4

Measuring funding performance in a hypothetical domestic book: Weekly average interest rates (rates, not compounded, on 365-day basis ex prime)

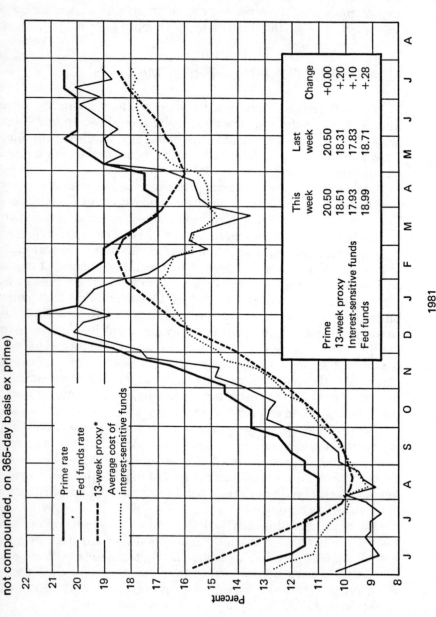

	This week	Last week	Change
Prime	20.50	20.50	+0.00
13-week proxy	18.51	18.31	+.20
Interest-sensitive funds	17.93	17.83	+.10
Fed funds	18.99	18.71	+.28

Legend:
- Prime rate
- Fed funds rate
- 13-week proxy*
- Average cost of interest-sensitive funds

1981

* The 13-week proxy is a 13-week moving average of the cost of 3-month CD money.

the bank, by active liability management, had reduced its cost of funds substantially below the rate it would have paid had it pursued a neutral strategy. What occurred during this period is that the bank's liability manager correctly predicted in November that interest rates were about to rise sharply and bought substantial amounts of 6-month money at a time when the yield curve was upward sloping in the 3- to 6-month area. Initially, this raised the bank's cost of funds above what it would have been had the bank pursued a neutral strategy. However, as Figure 10–4 shows, this extra cost was insignificant compared to the saving in funding costs that this strategy produced in subsequent months.

A more telling measure of how well the bank's liability manager performs would be to compare his actual cost of funds to what he could have achieved had he had perfect foresight on where rates were headed. A handful of highly sophisticated managers of short-term money market portfolios measure the return they achieve against precisely such a measure. However, there are several questions and problems associated with constructing a number for the cost of funds that a bank could have achieved with perfect foreight. First, does one want to assume that the liability manager also had perfect foresight about future loan demand and the size of the bank's funding needs? Second, however one answers that question, generating a cost-of-funds-with-perfect-foresight number requires a sophisticated optimization model. For a small bank with limited funding options, constructing such a model would be of limited value and probably a waste of money.

For a large bank, the extra *insight produced* by a perfect-foresight measure of funding costs might well justify the cost of doing so. A bank constructing such a measure should, however, realize that a lot of judgmental information must constantly be fed into such a model if it is to reflect what the liability manager could, in fact, have done. For example, at a given point, the optimal strategy for the bank might well be to sell $2 billion of 6-month CDs whereas the market could absorb no more than $1 billion of the bank's 6-month paper. The liability manager always faces several constraints: (1) internally imposed constraints on how liquid or illiquid management will permit the bank to be, and (2) constraints imposed by the market on what funding options are, in fact, open to the bank at a given time. Any measure of the liability manager's actual performance against some optimum must take both constraints into account to provide a realistic measure of how well he performed, of where he made mistakes, and of how much better he could have done had he always operated from a correct rate view.

11

Strategic decision making

No bank can avoid interest rate exposure.[1] Therefore, to be well managed, a bank must organize a framework for making strategic decisions about what long-run interest rate exposure it will accept. Also, because banking involves many different sorts of business and because it is evolving exponentially, a bank will often be called upon to make strategic decisions about other complex issues: How do we react to some outside shock such as the changes in bank lending practices being forced on banks by their customers? How do we better coordinate our domestic and offshore tactics? Given the changing economy, should we reconsider our portfolio strategy? Do we want to get into new ventures or new lines of business?

This chapter examines how a bank should organize strategic decision making, the sorts of decisions it is likely to face, and key considerations on which it should base its decisions.[2]

---

[1] See Chapter 9.

[2] A conspicious omission in our list of issues calling for strategic decisions is *liquidity*. Normally, a bank's liquidity decisions are *tactical*.

THE SOURCES AND USES (S&U) OR ASSETS AND LIABILITIES COMMITTEE (ALCO)

The tactical and strategic decisions that a bank, whatever its size, makes with respect to its sources and uses of funds or—which amounts to the same thing—its liabilities and assets, should be made by a committee. These decisions are crucial to the profitability and future of the bank and therefore should be made by a group comprising people who will bring to bear on the decision-making process differing points of view, expertise, and insights.

As a basis for routine decisions about managing liquidity and interest rate exposure, a bank's S&U committee will need five basic types of information: an economic forecast, data on the bank's internal cost of funds, a measure of the mismatch in the bank's book, an interest rate forecast, and a projection of the bank's future funding needs. In a large bank, a staff of experts will produce this information; in a small bank, a single person may do it all.

The economic forecast. A large bank has staff economists who make its economic forecast. A small bank has to rely on publicly published forecasts by various experts, or it may purchase them from services, such as DRI (Data Resources Inc.), that sell projections based on a proprietary econometric model. As noted previously, economic forecasts—even those produced using sophisticated econometric models—have a poor track record with respect to accuracy. All too often, an unanticipated change in one or more variables exogenous to the model—e.g., a war, a crop failure, or whatever—upset a model's predictions. Nonetheless, a bank, whatever its size, must have some forecast on which to hang its hat; it should not develop strategies as if the economy were headed into a boom if most forecasters are predicting a recession. Fortunately, a bank need not put great faith in the specific numerical predictions contained in its forecast, e.g., that GNP will rise or fall X percent. What a bank must get a handle on is the *general direction,* up or down, in which the economy is likely to head over the time horizon covered by the strategy being devised.

The internal cost of funds. Measuring a bank's internal cost of funds calls for measuring two things: (1) the ongoing cost of funds on the bank's book, and (2) the cost of funds to the bank at the margin. In measuring the former, it is important that each source of funds on the bank's book be fully costed out. For example, the cost of passbook savings to a bank equals the explicit 5.25 percent rate it pays *plus* a realistic estimate of the overhead costs associated with garnering and holding such deposits. The same goes for demand deposits.

It is important that a bank not confuse the cost of funds it has booked with its marginal cost of funds. If the bank is thinking about acquiring a new asset, the worst mistake it can make is to measure its potential profit on the new asset by subtracting from its yield the cost of funds on its book. To fund the new asset, the bank must acquire *funds at the margin,* and the difference between their cost and the cost of funds on its book can be huge. A bank that fails to distinguish between the cost of funds it has booked and its cost of funds at the margin may unintentionally kid itself into thinking it can use its existing resources to fund, at a profit, *both* existing and new assets.

A mistake many banks have made over the past 10 years is to rationalize making fixed-rate loans as follows: "We'll take a portion of our demand deposits, which are essentially free money, and pool them with some funds purchased at the margin. The cost of the resulting pool of funds will be such that we can earn a profit on making some fixed-rate loans." This is nonsense because the bank lent out its last free demand deposit years ago, and it isn't going to get any more.

Measuring the mismatch in a bank's book. In Chapter 9, we introduced the concept of ARBL (assets repriced before liabilities) and described how a bank should use this to measure the mismatch in its book. A key point made there was that a bank should measure ARBL over different time horizons; short-run ARBL is a tactical variable, long-run ARBL a strategic variable. Also, a bank with offshore operations should measure ARBL on the basis of its worldwide position, because a mismatch in a bank's domestic book may be offset by an opposite mismatch in its Euro book.

The interest rate forecast. The critical nature of the interest rate forecast in bank planning is something we have stressed frequently. It bears repeating that this forecast should be consistent with the bank's economic forecast. If a bank is predicting higher economic activity, it should be expecting interest rates to be, if anything, higher; the converse is also true. Exceptions may, however, occur if interest rates are being affected by some extraneous factor: a noble experiment by the Fed in monetarist policy or an acceleration of the inflation rate during an economic downturn.

However a bank makes its interest rate forecast, it is crucial that the bank seek to measure the *confidence* it places in its forecast. The direction of the forecast determines the nature of the bet on rates the bank should make; the confidence the bank has in its forecast determines how big the bet should be. If a bank is almost certain (99 percent confident) that the next move in interest rates will be up or down, making a large bet is not that risky. If, alternatively, a bank puts only marginal faith in its prediction (assigns 60 to 40 percent probabilities), it should bet small, because a big bet will entail a big risk.

Projecting funds needs. In Chapter 8, we talked about how a bank projects its funds needs and, in particular, how it projects future loan demand. In making a long-term projection of funds needs, two key factors are (1) the direction in which the bank thinks the economy will move, and (2) where the bank thinks it will fit into this move. The latter will depend on different factors for banks of different size. A small bank must ask whether local business is likely to move in the same direction and at the same pace as the overall economy. It also must be concerned with local demographics: is the population in its sphere of influence expanding or contracting? A wholesale money market bank, such as Bankers Trust, cares little about what is happening locally, because its business is spread over the whole country, in fact, over the whole world. A money market bank that is a big lender in the Euromarket should base its funds needs forecast on a projection not of domestic economic activity, but of economic activity worldwide.

THE SHORT-RUN/LONG-RUN TRADE-OFF

The data needed by the S&U committee will be supplied by staff members of varying seniority. The S&U committee itself should, however, comprise the bank's top management, because making the crucial decisions that fall to this committee is top management's responsibility. It bears repeating that the decisions the committee makes in a given situation will depend, in part, on management's propensity to trade risk for return. Also, a total dedication by management to near-term earnings will almost always redound to the bank's disadvantage in the long run.

At times, management's propensity to assume risk for reward may be affected by the state of its current earnings relative to its long-term earnings objectives. A risk-averse management faced with poor current-quarter earnings may choose to prop up short-run earnings at the expense of accepting a possible drag on long-run earnings. This need not be a bad decision; the important thing is that, if management wants to make this decision, they had better make it consciously.

A management that wants consistency of earnings should always focus on the long run, that is, year-by-year profits, rather than on the short run, quarter-by-quarter results. Any bank that focuses on quarter-by-quarter results, as *most banks do*, is probably maximizing short-run profits at the expense of long-run profits. A big problem for management is that, whatever its natural inclination may be, it faces strong outside pressure to emphasize quarter-by-quarter results. A source of much of this pressure is, as we will see, bank stock analysts.

An ongoing concern of banks, because they need to grow with their customers, is to increase capital.[3] To do so, in addition to retaining earnings, banks would like to be able to sell new stock. So as not to dilute the equity of existing shareholders, a bank that wants to sell new stock must get the value of its shares above book value. To do so, a bank needs the cooperation—in the form of favorable reviews of its performance—of bank stock analysts. Unfortunately, bank stock analysts focus, to the point of myopia, on short-run results. Thus, a bank that wants to maximize long-run profits *and* add to capital by stock issues faces a problem: by doing the former, it may impair its ability to do the latter.

METAMORPHOSIS OF BANK LENDING

The widespread attention commanded for decades by the prime rate might lead the unattentive observer of banking to assume that bank lending practices are set in stone; what changes is simply the rate. Nothing could be further from the truth. In Chapter 5 we described the evolution of bank lending practices during and after World War II: the shift by banks from supplying short-term to medium-term C&I financing; the growth of competition to bank C&I lending from the commercial paper market; and the introduction by banks of loans at a variable-rate prime, a move that shifted interest rate risk—in a climate of increasing rate volatility—from the banks to their corporate clients.

In recent years, the pace of change in bank lending practices has, if anything, accelerated. The world still keeps its eye glued on prime, but as one banker succinctly noted, "Prime is dead."

The passing of prime

Bank lending terms used to be "10 plus 10." To get a line of credit, the customer had to put up 10 percent compensating balances; if he took down funds under the line—in addition to paying prime—he had to put up another 10 percent compensating balances on the amount of the loan. In those days, *prime was close to the banks' cost of funds, and what the banks really made money on was the free balances that granting lines and loans generated.* Then, competition began to whittle away at the balances. Instead of 10 plus 10, the terms became a

---

[3] See Chapter 7.

straight 10 percent for the existence of the facility, and competition gradually cut that to 5 percent. By 1980, line and loan agreements for major loans were being written with no balance provisions.

As compensating balances vanished, banks found themselves earning on lines and loans just the rate charged on the funds taken down. Consequently, *banks had to administratively widen the spread between prime and their cost of funds so they could make some money.* Treasurers at major corporations, who push ever faster pens, reacted to a prime rate that floated at an increasing spread to banks' cost of funds by saying, "We won't borrow any more at prime except in circumstances where it is to *our* advantage to do so. The spread between prime and other money market rates is so high that prime has become unrealistic. Worse still, we are being forced to accept the interest rate risk our bank used to take. And to top things off, banks always raise prime in step with money market rates, but when they misjudge the direction of rates and mistakenly fund loans with high-cost, long-term funds, banks are slow to lower prime as money market rates drop."

Either/or facilities. In bygone days, it was the practice that the terms on which major corporations could borrow from U.S. banks were as follows: they could get Eurodollar loans on Euro terms—LIBOR plus a small, fixed spread—to fund foreign operations, *but* they were supposed to borrow at prime to fund domestic operations. The Euromarket is near perfect and, consequently, *very* efficient. Corporate treasurers, eyeing the terms they were getting from domestic banks on Euro loans booked outside the United States and, on prime rate loans booked at the bank's head office, were quick to conclude that a Euro loan was often the better deal. So they literally forced their banks to agree on large loans, particularly large syndicated loans, with line agreements that provided an *either/or facility:* when the time came to take down funds, the corporate treasurer could choose— regardless of where the funds were to be spent—whether he wanted a Euro loan priced off LIBOR or a loan priced at prime. Since roughly 1980, every large-term loan negotiated by a major corporation with a money market bank has contained an either/or option.

The either/or option gives a borrower two advantages: (1) he can, at times, use it to lower his funding cost by getting money in the market where the bank's spread is lower, and (2) he can use it to place his own bet on rates. If rates are on a plateau, the borrower may find that a Euro loan is cheaper than a prime loan and opt for the former on that ground. Alternatively, the borrower may anticipate a rise in rates and decide that his cheapest option is to fix his borrowing rate. In that case, he might take down 6-month money in the Euromarket even though the rate he pays, 6-month LIBOR plus a spread, exceeds prime. Finally, the borrower might ask for a loan at prime because he anticipates that money market rates will fall and wants to position himself so that his borrowing cost will fall with those rates.

Advances.   After the advent of either/or facilities, the next change in bank lending practices was the introduction by major banks in the domestic market of short-term, fixed-rate loans priced off a bank's marginal cost of funds. On such loans, dubbed *advances,* a bank would price overnight funds at a spread over the Fed funds rate, 30-day money against 30-day CDs or 30-day term funds, and a 6-month advance against 6-month money. Advances in the domestic market are priced in much the same way as Euro loans are priced in the Euromarket, against money market rates.

It is a misconception that banks began making advances in the domestic market solely to compete with the commercial paper market. Another motive was to keep business that they could not have kept had they insisted that borrowers pay prime at a time when borrowers felt that prime was unrealistically high. Big banks felt compelled to devise some pricing mechanism that would give the borrower a rate he would view as a realistic; that is what really pushed banks into making loans at *subprime* rates.[4]

Initially, banks made only short-term advances, but pricing against a bank's cost of funds soon crept into longer-term agreements. Today, no corporate treasurer would sign an agreement saying that for the next seven years his bank stands ready to lend him money but that, if he borrows, he must always pay prime. He wants the option of paying prime or having a loan priced on an advance basis. Pricing of longer-term advances resembles Euro pricing. The borrower can choose the time period for which he wants to fix a rate, and over that period, the rate he is charged will be some fixed spread over the bank's cost of funds for money of that maturity.

Since Euros in any maturity range generally trade at a rate that equals the all-in cost—grossed up for reserve requirements and FDIC insurance—of money of the same maturity in the domestic money market, a borrower will get about the same deal from Euro pricing that he will on a domestic loan priced off money market rates. Only when U.S. and Euro rates are temporarily out of synchronization would he find that taking one option rather than the other will save him many basis points.

As would be expected, in choosing between a loan at prime and an advance, the borrower will take into account his rate expectations. If

---

[4] Traditionally, prime rate loans were considered, implicitly, to be 90-day working capital loans. As corporate treasurers' borrowing needs began to be identified with greater precision (because of major advances in cash-flow projection techniques), the underlying rationale for traditional prime rate lending eroded.

he believes rates are about to fall, rather than borrow at a fixed rate for 60, 90, or 180 days, he will take a prime loan on the expectation that prime will float down with other rates and that he will quickly realize the benefit of falling rates. Conversely, a borrower who thinks rates are going up will want to lock in a fixed rate on a 6-month advance. To illustrate, suppose the yield curve has a steep positive slope—from 12 to 16 percent—and prime is 13 percent; a borrower who is convinced that the yield curve is right and rates are about to rise sharply might well opt for a 6-month advance priced off the current 16 percent cost of 6-month money rather than take a prime rate loan at 13 percent.

Not surprisingly, as corporate treasurers have been forcing their will upon banks with respect to lending terms, C&I lending at major banks has become more and more of an arms-length transaction. The relationships that these banks carefully cultivated with their customers are diminishing in importance.

Impact on funding

Advances characterized by cost-plus pricing—short-term advances and floating-rate term loans that are priced at some fixed spread over the bank's marginal cost of funds—already represent 10 to 15 percent of the total C&I loans made by large banks, and the amount is constantly increasing. With each day that passes, the domestic market for C&I loans comes to resemble Euro lending more closely.

This change in domestic lending practices promises to have significant effects on banking. First, it is already forcing large banks to rethink and restructure their funding strategies. Second, it is creating pressure for a change in the structure of the banking industry because it places regional and smaller banks at a disadvantage.

Almost all banks used to (and most banks still do) think of themselves as financing most of their assets with a single, large, amorphous pool of funds. When a lot of bank assets were floating-rate prime loans, this concept was workable. If rates rose unexpectedly, banks quickly brought their lending rates into line with their funding costs by raising prime. Alternatively, if banks as a group bought long-term money on the expectation that rates were going to rise and rates, in fact, fell, banks could and did respond by lowering prime slowly. It was, in part, against this asymmetry of changes in money market rates and changes in prime that corporate treasurers rebelled.

The growing trend toward cost-plus pricing of loans is forcing banks to abandon the pool concept of funding. To protect against the interest rate exposure implied by booking a lot of loans at rates that are tied at a narrow spread to floating money market rates in different maturity ranges, banks are being forced to think in terms of allocating specific pools of funds of specific maturities to support pools of assets of similar maturity. Within that framework, there remains room for a bank to choose to assume interest rate exposure. A bank that faces a positively sloped yield curve and is convinced that rates are going nowhere might opt to fund 30-day advances by rolling Fed funds. Or a bank that thought rates were about to rise might buy extra longer-term money in anticipation of making such loans at an attractive spread.

A second reason that cost-plus pricing is forcing a breakdown of the pool concept of funding is that a bank using this concept does not know how to price advances properly. A bank's current cost of funds depends on how successful it has been in the past in anticipating changes in interest rates. If the bank has taken a wrong view on rates, its cost of funds will be high; and if it then attempts to price fixed-rate advances off its current cost of funds, it will price itself out of the market. If, alternatively, the bank's cost of funds is low relative to market rates (the bank correctly forecasted rising rates and funded long), then if the bank prices fixed-rate advances off its current cost of funds, it will be competitive in getting loans and it will make money on them. The problem in this case is that, if the bank prices its loans off its current cost of funds, it will be charging rates so low as to give away to its borrowers, instead of to its shareholders, the rewards of its past success at predicting rates.

Impact on the structure of banking

Cost-plus pricing has never caused a big interest rate exposure problem for banks that are active lenders in the Euromarket. In the vast interbank market for Euros, banks of all sizes can freely bid for and get at the same or almost the same rate, funds in various maturity categories. In its Euro book, a bank always has the option of funding a matched position and thereby avoiding interest rate exposure, provided it respects a caveat laid down earlier: a bank's presence in the market as a taker of funds must exceed that needed to support its present asset structure.

In the domestic market there exists no interbank market for funds over a wide range of maturities. Overnight Fed funds are traded actively among banks, but there is only a limited market for term Fed funds. A limiting factor on the demand side of the market for term Fed funds is that national banks must treat purchases of term Fed funds as borrowings rather than deposits.

The truly binding constraint on the growth of the market for term Fed funds lies, however, on the supply side of the market. The only way U.S. banks can get on their domestic books large deposits of money with a 1-month, 3-month, or longer maturity is by selling certificates of deposit to domestic institutional investors. Domestic certificates of deposit must, however, compete for investors' monies with a host of other short-term instruments: bankers' acceptances, commercial paper, repo, Treasury bills, municipal notes, and Europaper. In foreign countries, the menu of short-term, liquid securities available to institutional investors is much narrower than it is in the United States. Consequently, foreign banks get more large time deposits on their domestic books than do U.S. banks. These large time deposits form the basis of foreign deposit markets for funds over a range of maturities. Another relevant factor is that foreign banks are generally not required, as are U.S. banks, to hold reserves against demand and time deposits. The absence of reserve requirements abroad permits foreign banks to compete more effectively than U.S. banks can for large domestic deposits. It also inhibits the growth of alternative methods of finance, such as the sale by corporations of commercial paper.

The lack of domestic interbank markets for funds of differing maturities means that, if cost-plus pricing of loans grows and creeps down to loans of smaller size made by smaller borrowers, banks excluded from the national CD market—which means almost all banks—will be at a disadvantage vis-à-vis the elite few that can borrow in this market. The only source of funds a domestic bank can tap nationwide is the CD market. A bank that is excluded from this market and wants to participate in a large syndicated loan or itself make a loan that is priced off CD rates will find that there is no spread in the deal for it.

A small bank with a $5 million lending limit can participate in a syndicated Euro loan because, if that bank goes to one of the brokers in the Euromarket and says it wants to bid for $5 million of 1-, 3-, or 6-month money, some bank or banks that have extended lines to this small bank will give it the money it wants in the maturity range it wants. If the same small bank chooses to participate in or itself extends a loan priced off domestic CD rates, it will find that it cannot buy funds in that amount in the domestic market. It could use Euros to fund domestic loans, but since they trade at a price grossed up for reserve requirements and FDIC premiums, it would, if it used Euros, earn no spread and under the new Reg D would also incur additional reserves.

A large regional bank with access to the domestic CD market might find that it could buy in the domestic CD market monies necessary to fund cost-plus priced advances, but only if it paid an extra 50 basis points above the rate money center banks were paying. Again, no spread.

The few small banks that might be able to deal in cost-plus priced loans at a profit are those banks that loom so large in their geographic sphere of influence that they have the advantages of a monopoly position working in their favor, one of those advantages presumably being the ability to sell small-denomination CDs to local businesses at submarket rates.

The trend toward cost-plus pricing of loans is forcing money market banks to rethink their funding concepts. It is also giving them a competitive advantage that is likely to cause a long-term shift of business toward them. Because of this, cost-plus pricing will add one more incentive to the host that already exist for bank mergers and some rationalization of the U.S. banking system.

Bank competition with commercial paper

Back in the 1930s, banks basically financed the working capital of corporate America. Today, the commercial paper market does so. While bankers once viewed the growing commercial paper market as threatening and unwanted competition, they no longer do so. Bankers realize that, if the $170-odd billion of business done in the commercial paper market were added to the $373 billion of C&I lending currently on their books, the impact on their capital ratios would be disastrous.[5] Also, bankers now perceive the commercial paper market as providing them with a tidy and steady flow of fee income for providing lines to paper issuers, lines that—because they are largely unused—have little or no impact on bank liquidity or interest rate exposure. In effect, the commercial paper market provides banks with fees for doing next to nothing.

To create the appearance of liquidity necessary to sell commercial paper, almost all issuers back a very high percentage of their outstanding paper with *committed* facilities. Initially, banks granting such lines tended to say to the issuer, "You can have the lines, but only if you promise to pay 1 percent over prime if you take down funds under it." The issuer responded by saying, "We'll give you 2 percent over prime." That was rational since, as the banks soon learned, most paper issuers make it a policy never to use their bank lines as a last resort source of funds if they can avoid doing so. When money is tight, commercial paper issuers would pay up rather than come into their banks for funds. This being the case, bankers said, "OK you can have the lines, but we want a fee," which they got and still get.

Two trends threaten the rather cozy income-for-doing-nothing situation that banks have gotten themselves into vis-à-vis the commercial paper market. First, the introduction and proliferation of short-term advances priced off short-term money market rates enabled banks to quote rates that are competitive or nearly competitive with short-term commercial paper rates, especially the all-in rates on dealer paper. Second, the Fed is reducing reserve requirements on time deposits and shortening their minimum length. This trend may well culminate in a situation where there are *no* reserves against time deposits and *no*

---

[5] Figures are as of early 1982.

minimum length on such deposits. If this happens, banks will be able to lend on truly competitive terms to corporations selling commercial paper. Should competition among banks drive banks to do so, the result will be a ballooning of banks' balance sheets and a concomitant deterioration of their capital ratios.

Concluding comments

We have noted several significant changes that are occurring in the nature of bank lending. The pace of change in this area is, if anything, likely to accelerate. This means that a bank's S&U committee must now face and is going to continue to face a host of critical, strategic decisions about the kinds of business the bank wants to do and about how the bank is going to fund this business and control its interest rate exposure.

As noted in Chapter 12, one of the issues that is certain to crop up is: should the bank—using financial futures to hedge its funding cost—go back to making 2- to 4-year, fixed-rate term loans?

PORTFOLIO STRATEGIES: TAXABLE SECURITIES

Because banks invest in *taxable* securities issued by the Treasury and federal agencies, and in *tax-exempt* securities issued by states and municipalities, for totally different reasons, a discussion of bank portfolio strategies must deal separately with the two.

Traditionally, banks held large portfolios of governments and agencies. In recent years, however, the trend has been for banks to sharply pare their holdings of these securities. This is hardly surprising. In today's environment of high and highly volatile rates, *no valid argument can be made for a bank to invest in taxable securities.*

The old portfolio game

From 1950 through roughly 1978, the economy experienced a series of mild and predictable cyclical ups and downs; it was subject to what people refer to as the *normal* business cycle. During that period, interest rates, following the business cycle, tended to decline to a trough over roughly a two-year period and then turn back up again and stay high for three years or so. This rate pattern made buying governments a sensible strategy for banks that could correctly call the turns in interest rates.

As noted in Chapter 9, every bank faces natural interest rate exposure because of the free funds in the form of capital and hard-core demand deposits that are on its book. A plunge in interest rates, for example, from 20 to 10 percent will halve a bank's earnings on its free funds.

One way a bank can seek to protect its earnings against this natural interest rate exposure is to buy—when it takes the view that interest rates are peaking—high-yield, long-term securities and hold them as rates fall. A large bank following this strategy will finance the securities acquired in the RP market and profit from the *positive carry* it earns once rates turn down. A small bank buying governments with its own funds will profit from having tied up funds in high-yield, long-term assets.

In an economy subject to the normal business cycle, the old rule for weighty bodies—what goes up must come down—applies equally well to bond prices. A bank that buys governments to maintain earnings when a downturn in rates appears imminent must, if this strategy is not to impair its long-term earnings, succeed at calling the trough in rates and get out of its governments before rates begin to move to new cyclical highs and bond prices to new lows. We say new cyclical highs for rates and lows for bond prices, because the secular trend in interest rates over the last 35 years has been up.

The above strategy sounds simple, but in practice it involves substantial risks and costs that a bank should fully recognize before making a strategic decision to buy governments. Consider a money market or regional bank that decides rates are about to peak. At the time it reaches this conclusion, two conditions are likely to prevail: (1) loan demand has been high for some period and the bank—measured against whatever internal constraint it imposes on its capital ratio—is fully leveraged; and (2) other market participants probably share the bank's expectation that rates are nearing a peak; if so, the yield curve will be inverted.

The first condition means a bank that acquires additional assets to protect against the natural interest rate exposure to which its free funds expose it, will be forced to temporarily balloon its balance sheet and, more particularly, to *violate* its capital constraint. The second condition, a negatively sloped yield curve, means that a bank which— in anticipation of a rate decline—buys fixed-rate, long-term assets and finances them with day-to-day money, will, until the anticipated decline in rates occurs, experience *negative* carry. That negative carry can be a *staggering* drain on earnings. Moreover, it cannot be avoided because *the best time to acquire a portfolio of taxable securities is almost always when the negative spread between yield on the portfolio and the RP rate is greatest.*

Initial negative carry means a bank that considers buying governments almost always faces a trade-off between short-term earnings and long-term earnings: The first must be sacrificed to improve the latter.

Also, because of initial negative carry, the longer it takes for the bank to be right in its decision to buy governments—i.e., for rates to fall—the less the bank will make on the whole transaction. Besides decreasing current earnings, buying governments also exposes a bank to the risk that, if its forecast that rates are peaking proves incorrect and rates, in fact, rise, the bank will, at some point, be forced to sell its bonds at a loss to cut the earnings drain imposed by negative carry. As the experience of First Pennsy well illustrates, capital losses resulting from a poorly timed decision to buy bonds and a later decision, after rates have risen, to sell those bonds can severely erode a bank's capital.

No capital gains, please

A large bank that buys bonds to protect against the natural interest rate exposure to which its free funds expose it—and that is the *only* reason for a bank to buy bonds—will, if it is right on rates, watch the carry on its bonds turn from negative to positive as rates drop. Simultaneously, the value of its bonds will rise. However, selling bonds at a capital gain is never an objective of a bank's portfolio strategy. Bank stock analysts focus solely on *net operating earnings, which include carry but exclude capital gains and losses.*[6] This leads large banks to milk the last dollar of positive carry possible out of any bonds they buy. If a bank has unrealized profits on its governments, carry on these securities is probably still positive. Only when carry has dropped to zero will a bank sell its governments, and by then, it will usually find that it is getting out of its bonds even—at a price near where it bought them.

Because of the obsession of bank stock analysts with net operating income, banks *never* sell governments held in portfolio directly to produce gains. They will, however, sell governments at a loss to rid their balance sheet of low-yielding assets on which carry is negative; the bank made the wrong bet on interest rates, and its expectation is continuing negative carry. An asymmetry exists: from time to time a bank will find a good reason to take a capital loss on governments; it will never find a good reason to take a gain.

A bank that seeks to maximize net operating income may not be maximizing its *total* earnings, including capital gains, over time. Selling bonds while carry on them is still positive might, in some instances, produce more profit than the bank could reasonably expect to earn by holding its bonds until carry on them dropped to zero. Because gains and losses on a bank's dealer account, if it has one, run though the income statement to net operating earnings, a bank perceiving the above might reason, "We want to be able to sell governments we hold

---

[6] See Chapter 5.

as an investment at a gain if that seems to be the right thing to do, so we'll stash them in our dealer account." In practice, banks never do this because securities in a dealer account must be marked to market monthly, and the resulting gains and losses are included in current income.

When a bank buys governments to protect against interest rate exposure, it does so with the idea of holding them over some longer period and does not want its current income figures swung all over the lot by the fluctuations that are bound to occur in rates even if the bank is correct in its view that the trend in rates will be down. It is the instability of earnings that would come from marking its bonds to market every month that prevents banks from carrying in its dealer account securities other than those it actually acquires through its dealing activities.

For portfolio purposes, larger banks always buy governments to get positive carry, small banks to lock in high yields; neither ever buys governments for capital gains.

A suboptimal use of resources

If a bank is concerned about its capital ratio, which most large banks are, it will face a balance sheet constraint and, consequently, want to ensure that the assets it takes on at the margin provide it with the greatest overall return available. For any maturity range, governments are the lowest-yielding, taxable instrument in which a bank can invest, and a bank gets no credit in the way of customer relationship by buying governments.

A bank that adds to its holdings of governments will normally begin by accepting a loss in the form of negative carry, and at the same time, it is expanding its balance sheet. Neither is a thing a bank wants to do. Therefore, the only time a bank should buy governments is if it feels highly confident that over the life of the investment, it will earn a positive carry on the financing that stacks up well against its alternative uses of funds and also compensates it for having ballooned its balance sheet. The latter is a nonquantifiable cost, but a bank should seek to develop a feel about it. For a bank, the trouble with expanding its balance sheet is that this may limit its ability to take advantage of something attractive that comes down the pike.

The moral of the above is that a bank should carefully examine its rate forecast and all alternative investments before it buys governments. If a bank takes a relatively short view on rates—concludes that interest rates are likely to be down over the next three or six months—it should seek protection against natural interest rate exposure not by investing in governments, but by lending in the Euromarket and covering with day-to-day money. A short view calls for a tactical play, and the play that pays best is to lend Euros because Euro rates are much higher than yields on governments.

If a bank takes a longer-term view on rates—thinks they will be cyclically down for several years—it should consider buying governments in the bank range, 4- to 7-year maturities. An alternative would be to make fixed-rate term loans. The pros of doing so are that loans yield more than governments and contribute to customer relationships. The con is that, if the bank is correct on rates, the customer who takes fixed-rate money may, after rates have dropped, ask that the rate on his loan be renegotiated; that happens frequently.[7] In some situations, a bank may not have a choice; if there is no loan demand, it may be forced to buy governments.

The rewards of getting it right.   The best and only valid reason for a bank to buy governments is to protect against interest rate exposure. A bank that pursued this strategy from 1950 to 1975—buying governments as rates peaked and holding them until rates bottomed out and started up again—would have done *very well*. In fact, most banks during this period managed their government portfolios poorly. Part of the problem was the difficulty banks had in making correct rate forecasts. Equally important, bankers do not adequately understand the running of a government portfolio; in particular, they fail to appreciate that, in buying governments, a bank assumes a more than normal risk.

The secular case for governments

The strongest case that can be made for buying governments is on the basis of a confident and very long view: a bank strongly believes that rates are headed into a long-term secular decline. In that situation, a bank would want to create a negative long-term ARBL, and the best, perhaps only, way for it to do so would be to buy governments. Suppose, for example, that 7-year governments yield 14 percent and that day-to-day money costs 18 percent. A bank that buys governments will lose 44 percent until interest rates fall, suffer the burden of ballooning its balance sheet, and watch its capital ratio deteriorate. On the other hand, it is making a long-term bet, and it can always get its balance sheet back into shape by letting other marginal assets run off. This is a strategic choice. The bank is betting that, on average, over the next seven years the cost of financing its portfolio will be, say, 8 percent and that, over this period, it will earn a long-term profit. If the bank is correct, its strategy will pay off handsomely.

---

[7] This situation is changing on loans negotiated by large borrowers with big banks. The trend, noted earlier in the chapter, toward more arms-length relationships between such customers and their banks has made these banks feel less vulnerable than they did in the past about enforcing no prepayment clauses on long loan contracts.

To the above we should add that at no time since World War II would the view that interest rates were headed into a secular decline have been correct. Moreover, to bet heavily on this rate view in the high and highly volatile rate environment prevailing in the early 1980s would be to bet the bank on a long shot. What happened at First Chicago and First Pennsy attests to this.

No case for governments now

We began our discussion of bank portfolio strategies by saying that, in the early 1980s, *no* valid case could be made for a bank to hold governments. Since the end of World War II, the one good reason for a bank to buy governments was to protect its earnings against temporary, *cyclically predictable* declines in interest rates. Prior to 1980, interest rates were cyclically predictable; since then, they have become cyclically unpredictable. In 1980, rates took off on a roller coaster ride. Until that recent phenomenon is replaced by a clear return of the normal business cycle, a *big* portfolio move by a bank would be extremely dangerous. That is what we meant by saying that currently *no* case exists for a bank to buy governments.

Liquidity. Governments are not a source of liquidity to large banks that finance them with RP. They are a poor source of liquidity for small banks that buy governments with their own money. Banks that thought otherwise had a rude awakening in August of 1966. The economy was then passing through the worst credit crunch in decades, and there was *no* bid in the dealer market for Treasury bills. Banks that thought they had liquidity because they held bills found they had none.

A small bank, to the extent that it wants liquidity resident in its assets, should not buy bills. Instead, it should sell overnight Fed funds or Euros. The rate is always better than that on bills, and the bank has no risk of ownership. A bank that sells funds can change the amount it invests not only day to day, but during a day if it needs to. More and more banks have come to appreciate this.

THE FED'S PROPOSED RESERVES ON RP

A few years ago, the Fed proposed reserve requirements on all RP banks did against governments and other money market instruments. The Fed argued that this step was necessary to prevent banks from raising funds in the RP market during a period when Fed policy was to limit the expansion of bank lending. As often occurs, the Fed, in making this proposal, displayed a conspicuous lack of understanding of commercial banking. RPing governments is a potential source of liquidity only to small banks that buy securities with their own money. The major consequences of imposing reserve requirements on RP done by banks would have been (1) to remove the last justification large banks have for holding governments, and (2) to put bank dealers at such a competitive disadvantage with respect to nonbank dealers that the former would have been forced to close up shop. The first consequence would have narrowed the market for governments; the second would have removed from the government market some of the best capitalized dealers acting as market makers there. Once the Fed understood this, it withdrew its proposal.

Don't fall in love

We have stressed that the one reason for a bank to buy governments is to mitigate against the vulnerability of its earnings to a decline in rates; that is the only reason. Moreover, a decision to buy governments is highly risky because it entails for all but small banks two significant upfront costs: negative carry and a ballooning of the bank's balance sheet. Thus, a bank should decide to buy governments only when it has a high degree of confidence in its forecast that rates will fall and when the size of the bet it is making is based on a realistic appraisal of the risks this strategy will entail.

To the above, one caveat should be added: *don't fall in love.* For better, but more usually for worse, portfolio managers often fall in love with their portfolios or with individual issues in it. Unfortunately, such love is unrequited; a portfolio does not love its owner. People frequently hold on to bonds because they really love the bonds they own, or more correctly, they love what they thought was the correctness of their decision to buy certain issues in the first place. A portfolio manager who feels this way won't give up his securities easily; he keeps waiting for the market to vindicate the correctness of his judgment. As some portfolio managers who fell in love with the long-term 2½s issued during World War II can attest, the wait for vindication can be long and expensive.

MUNICIPAL SECURITIES

A bank's objective should be to maximize not pretax profits, but *after tax* profits. As noted later in this chapter, the desire to enhance aftertax income has a considerable effect on where banks book and fund their international business.

With respect to domestic operations, there are several ploys a bank may use to decrease its tax bill. The cleanest and simplest is for a bank to realize any unrealized losses it may have in its securities portfolio.

For a bank, capital gains and losses are taxed at the same rate as ordinary income, so every dollar of capital losses offsets a dollar of ordinary income for federal tax purposes. The disadvantage to a bank is that taking losses reduces its capital.

Another way banks seek to earn income sheltered for some period from taxation is by doing in the holding company, which owns the bank, or in the bank itself, leasing deals. Leasing can be highly profitable on an aftertax basis because of fast write-offs permitted on the items leased. A third ploy that a few banks have begun to use to postpone taxes is issuing zero coupon bonds. Issuing zero coupon bonds is a form of tax shelter to the issuing bank because this bank, despite the fact that it pays no interest on its bonds until they mature, may write off as an interest expense each year the amount by which its bonds would have to accrete in value to reach par at maturity.

A fourth, important way in which banks seek to maximize aftertax income is by investing in municipal securities. Interest income on such securities is exempt from federal taxes and also from state and local taxes if the securities are issued within the bank's state of domicile.

Muni notes and bonds

To a bank, the major tax advantage in—and reason for buying—municipal securities is that interest income on them is tax-exempt whereas any interest costs incurred to carry them are tax deductible. This tax advantage is unique to banks.

In buying municipals, as in buying taxable securities, a bank should consider both liquidity and interest rate exposure. As noted in Chapter 5, many banks follow a *barbell* strategy in buying munis: They buy some muni notes for liquidity and some long-term munis for high yield. An alternative is *scaling,* buying maturities along the full maturity program.

Studies suggest that, of the two approaches, the barbell approach produces a higher aftertax yield. A major motive for a bank in buying long-term munis, as in buying long-term governments, should be to counter the natural interest rate exposure it faces because it has free funds in the form of capital and hard-core demand deposits. Long-term munis have the advantage over governments that interest income on them is tax-free but, like governments, they expose the holder to an interest rate risk.

When a bank buys long-term munis, it should realize that rates may at some future time exceed those prevailing when it buys these securities and even that rates may continue their secular upward trend. A profitable bank can offset some of the risk this possibility implies by determining that its strategy will be to do tax swaps whenever rates rise. For example, if a bank buys long-term munis at 10 percent and yields on such securities rise to 12 percent, the bank's strategy will be to sell its 10s and buy 12s. Doing such swaps will reduce the bank's taxes in the year the swaps are done and will also usually increase the income the bank earns over the life of the securities.

In this respect, it is interesting to note that, at times in recent years, the potential gain in income over time from swapping out of low-coupon into current-coupon securities has been so attractive that many money-losing thrifts could have vastly improved their situation by doing such swaps even though, because of their negative earnings, they would have received no immediate tax benefits. What deterred thrifts from making such swaps was the fact that taking the huge resulting capital losses would, in many cases, have wiped out their capital. In 1981, the Federal Home Loan Bank Board finally gave federally chartered thrifts that swapped out of low-coupon bonds into high-coupon bonds the right to amortize the resulting capital loss over the remaining life of the investment, i.e., to use loss deferral accounting. State-chartered S&Ls and savings banks were prevented by the FDIC from using this accounting practice and therefore were barred, de facto, from doing such swaps.

Liquidity.   Because of the potential importance of doing tax swaps, a bank buying munis should ensure that the securities it acquires have liquidity in the sense of being marketable. One mistake made by many small banks and some large banks (especially banks buying scaled maturities) is to buy strips of serial municipal issues: $10,000, $20,000, or whatever of each maturity. A typical municipal serial issue is a borrowing for $50 million, comprising $1 million of securities maturing in each of the first 25 years and $25 million of bonds maturing in 40 years. An investor who buys a strip of such an issue has no liquidity since such securities just don't trade. In addition, an institution that buys strips of this and that municipal issue ends up with a portfolio on which it has excessive and costly paperwork; just to do the interest bookkeeping alone is an expensive nuisance.

Munis as collateral.   States commonly require that banks collateralize public deposits with governments or appropriate state bonds. In a state such as Texas that has a lot of cash, it is attractive for local banks to buy state bonds for this purpose. The resulting arbitrage is profitable; the bank underbids for the deposits (i.e., pays nonmarket rates) and earns tax-exempt income on the bonds held as collateral.

Industrial development bonds and loans.   For years, states and municipalities have been permitted to issue tax-free bonds to finance various projects designed to promote the local economy. It is also possible for a private borrower to obtain a ruling from the Treasury that interest paid on a loan that will promote the economy of a particular area will be tax-free to the lender. Since banks began making floating-rate loans, industrial development loans have grown sharply in volume and provided stiff competition to the purchase by banks of municipal securities.

For a bank, buying a bond is an arms-length transaction; the bond never knows who owns it. In contrast, a bank that makes an industrial development loan to a private borrower can expect to improve its relationship with that borrower and, as a result, to receive profitable balances and fee income.

Limit on muni holdings. Industrial development loans are a substitute for municipal securities because there is some limit on the quantity of tax-exempt income a bank will want to earn. Buying municipals or making tax-free loans cuts a bank's effective tax rate on its total income. If a bank succeeds in getting that rate down to zero, then any additional tax-exempt investments it makes will yield it just the coupon, not the taxable equivalent of the coupon. Consequently, the carry on these investments will probably be negative.

RUNNING A EUROCURRENCY BOOK

A large proportion of the growth, over the last 15 years, in the balance sheets of money market and major regional banks was made possible by the decisions of these banks to diversify out of domestic business into international business. U.S. banks do the bulk of their international business in the Euromarket.[8] The largest of these banks also run local-currency books at their foreign branches, for example, a French franc book at Paris office and a yen book at Tokyo office. For a U.S. bank, running a Eurocurrency book and running a local currency book at a foreign branch are totally different operations. Local governments usually impose on the local-currency operations of foreign banks a range of restrictions that have no counterpart in the largely unregulated and highly competitive Euromarket. Also, economic conditions in a local capital market often diverge sharply from those prevailing in the broad international market for capital. We consider here a U.S. bank's *Eurocurrency book;* in Chapter 14, we turn to a U.S. bank's foreign operations in local currencies and to foreign bank operations in dollars.

---

[8] Chapter 6 describes the structure of the Euromarket and how banks operate in it.

Assets and liabilities

The Euro liabilities of U.S. banks are almost solely deposits. Some are made by international corporations and other nonbank customers; the remainder represent *redeposits* of funds by banks with other banks. As Table 6–5 shows, redeposits or placements—as they are more typically called—equal a large proportion, approximately 75 percent of gross Eurocurrency deposits.

U.S. banks hold three classes of assets in their Eurocurrency books: loans, placements, and bonds denominated in foreign currencies. The last of these is becoming increasingly important.

U.S. banks have two motives for adding foreign-currency-denominated bonds to their Eurocurrency books: (1) to adjust their interest rate exposure in this book, and (2) to place a bet on exchange rates. On regular syndicated Euro loans, the maximum period for which a borrower may fix his rate is typically six months. Euro placements are made and accepted for longer periods, but the interbank market for deposits with a maturity of more than six months is thin. Consequently, a bank that anticipates a sharp decline in interest rates and wants, for this reason, to build up a large, positive, long-term ARBL in its Euro book cannot do so by lengthening the maturity of its loans and placements. It must buy bonds.

For a U.S. bank, it would make no sense to book low-yield, U.S. Treasuries, which it can fund in the domestic RP market, in its Euro book. Many U.S. money market banks can buy only governments and rated private issues. Euro bond issues are rarely rated; also, individual Euro issues are small and, for this reason, illiquid. Consequently, U.S. banks do not invest in Euro bonds. Because of these considerations, normally the only bonds it makes sense for a U.S. bank to put on its Eurocurrency book are medium-term, foreign-currency-denominated bonds—either foreign government bonds, such as UK gilts, or foreign corporate bonds that are rated and reasonably liquid.

The forward market in foreign exchange is thin to nonexistent for long maturities. Therefore, medium-term bonds denominated in a currency other than the currency used to purchase them cannot usually be hedged to maturity. A bank will thus never use one currency to buy bonds denominated in another unless the bet on foreign exchange rates to which the purchase exposes it is a bet it wants to make. Also a bank will make this play at a specific branch only if the exchange controls, if any, imposed by the country in which that branch is located permit the branch to do so.

To illustrate, suppose that the Paris office of a U.S. bank wants to invest deposits of Euro French francs in bonds to hedge its earnings against an anticipated fall in interest rates. It could buy bonds denominated in French francs. However, it observes that German paper in the 5- to 8-year range is paying 12 percent; since Germany has a better track record than France at controlling inflation, using French francs to buy DM-denominated bonds look like a good long-term bet. If Germany is more successful than France at controlling inflation, the bank will get a double payoff by investing francs in DM-bonds: a high current yield on the asset acquired *and* some extra return because the mark appreciates relative to the franc.

A bank making this sort of play might put on and take off a hedge against its foreign exchange position many times in response to short-term fluctuations in the mark-franc exchange rate. However, in assuming the position, it would expect to be naked long DM and short French francs most of the time.

A bank that buys foreign-currency-denominated bonds to hold in its Eurocurrency book must track both its interest rate exposure and its foreign exchange risk day by day, even hour by hour in turbulent markets.

Choosing the mix of assets

In choosing what mix of assets to hold in its Euro book, a bank has to consider its needs for liquidity, flexibility, and adequate market presence. To meet these, a bank must be an active buyer and seller in all maturity ranges in the interbank market for Eurocurrency deposits. A bank that actively trades Eurodeposits will have liquidity in the sense that it can, at any point, bid in this market for extra deposits either to replace lost customer deposits or to expand its footings. The growth of either/or lending facilities has increased the need for such liquidity by allowing bank customers to convert domestic loans to Euro loans at will. Being an active participant in the interbank market also gives a bank flexibility to alter the maturity composition of its Euro book by taking and making additional deposits of different maturities. For example, it permits a bank that anticipates a rise in interest rates to establish a positive ARBL by taking 6-month deposits and making overnight or 1-month placements. A final reason a bank must be active in the interbank market for Euros is that *it is as important in the Euromarket as in the domestic market for a bank to establish a market presence that exceeds that needed to support its basic asset structure.*

Return on assets (ROA). A bank's needs for liquidity, flexibility, and adequate market presence all give it good reasons for running a large placement book. However, another concern—return on assets—may constrain the size of its placement book. All banks worry about their leverage against capital, and some even fix a limit on it. The closer a bank comes to being as leveraged as it is willing to be, the more selective it will be in taking on assets. At the margin, when capital becomes a binding constraint on asset growth, a bank will want to ensure that any assets it acquires yield the greatest return available.

In choosing which assets—domestic or Euro—to acquire, a bank will always consider return. However, it is with respect to Euro assets that this concern most often becomes binding. A bank can't volitionally expand domestic loans at prime, but it can normally expand with ease its Euro placement book and its participation in syndicated lending; the spreads on such business are, however, narrow.

On redeposit business, a large bank, by enjoying the natural spread of selling at the offered side of the market and buying at the bid side, will be able to pick up ⅛; often it can double that return if it takes a correct view on rates and mismatches properly. If a bank gets its timing just right at a moment that is propitious for mismatching, it may even be able to pick up 100 extra basis points on redeposit business.

On syndicated loans, spreads are more attractive than on redeposit business. Such loans have long terms, however: 6 to 10 years. With bank costs escalating yearly as a function of inflation, the profitability of booking a 10-year loan at a ⅜ spread is questionable. So long as the pace of inflation continues at 10 to 15 percent a year, a bank that funds Euro loan participations "conservatively"—insists on matching the average maturity of its assets with that of its liabilities—runs the risk of eventually putting itself out of business.

A bank that is reaching its limit with respect to leverage—that has room for only another $100 million of assets—will probably choose to put on no additional Euro assets other than foreign-currency-denominated bonds which, given the proper economic environment, offer the chance of a high return. Conversely, a bank that has room for another billion of assets on its book will feel comfortable putting on additional redeposit and syndicated loan business because a little extra income on such business is better than no extra income at all.

Return on equity (ROE). A rational observer would note that what really ought to concern a bank is not return on assets (ROA), but rather return on equity (ROE). Focusing on ROE, instead of ROA, would lead the best capitalized U.S. money market banks to immediately put on another $2, $3, even $5 billion of assets. If these assets yield—as would be expected—only a marginal return, a bank buying them would lower its ROA, *but* it would also significantly increase both its total earnings and its ROE.

This being the case, one must ask why bank managements often attach so much importance to ROA. First, bank stock analysts love a high ROA; moreover, when they find a bank that has it, they never observe that this bank's ROE could be increased significantly if the bank leveraged more and let its ROA drop. A second reason some bank managements keep ROA conservatively high and leverage conservatively low is they believe that some intangible, nonquantifiable but nonetheless real benefit accrues from a reputation for being a better capitalized bank. This benefit, to the extent that it exists, presumably causes the price of the bank's stock to be higher than it otherwise would be, and permits the bank to buy money at marginally more favorable terms than other banks can. If no such benefits exist, a bank that forgoes putting on an extra $X billion of assets to keep its return on assets and its capital ratio high is forgoing income for nothing. If high ROA produces no intangible benefits, no argument can be made for viewing it as a key variable in evaluating a bank's performance. Quite the contrary, in that case, the focus should be on ROE and total earnings.

Choosing the location of assets

A major bank that has branches in a number of foreign countries and that wants to maximize aftertax profits must view its overall Eurocurrency position not as so many separate branch books, but as a single *worldwide* book. Doing so will lead a bank to adopt the strategy of housing its assets in the branch where the *aftertax* benefit to the bank is greatest, assuming that the location is one where the asset can be funded properly.

Tax considerations. Brazil, Argentina, and Canada all impose withholding taxes on interest paid by domestic borrowers on foreign loans. The taxes withheld on such loans can be used by U.S. banks as a direct credit against U.S. federal taxes. However, the U.S. marginal tax rate at the federal level is only 46 percent whereas, in the United Kingdom, which also gives a tax credit for taxes withheld on foreign interest income, the marginal tax rate is 52 percent. To the extent that a bank can generate the same tax credit against income which is subject to a 52 percent tax rate as it can against income subject to a 46 percent tax rate, it is better off doing the former than the latter. This consideration leads U.S. banks to book loans to Brazil, Argentina, and Canada in high-tax areas such as the United Kingdom.

Maximizing aftertax return requires that a bank pay attention to and be responsive to a lot of tax-law details. Example: Canada, which imposes a 15 percent withholding tax on interest paid to foreigners, has a tax treaty with Belgium under which Belgium will grant a bank a 15 percent tax credit on certain types of loans to Canada on which Canada, in fact, withholds only 5 percent in taxes. When U.S. banks make loans to Canada falling in this category, they house them in

Brussels, since putting them there yields the bank a 10 percent tax-credit bonus.

The tax cushion problem and shell branches. A bank that adopts the strategy of viewing the sum of the Eurocurrency positions of its foreign branches as a single global book on which it seeks to maximize its aftertax return must manage its affairs carefully so that it doesn't end up with more tax credits than it can use against its federal tax bill. Because of foreign tax credits, major U.S. banks normally have no trouble working their federal tax liability down to zero. In fact, such banks do so much international business in London and other high-tax centers that they often end up with excess tax credits. In that case, the bank faces what is known as *the tax cushion problem.*

To illustrate, consider for simplicity a bank that has just two offices, a head office and a London branch. If the bank gets into a position where it has booked so much profitable business in London office that the tax credit it gets from paying a 52 percent tax on profits in the United Kingdom exceeds 46 percent of its total taxable income, it will have excess tax credits against its U.S. federal taxes. In this case, the ratio of foreign taxes paid to its total taxable income will exceed 46 percent, that is,

$$\frac{\text{Foreign taxes paid}}{\text{Total taxable income}} \times 100 > 46\%$$

and the bank has a tax cushion problem. To solve this problem, the bank needs to earn more foreign profits without increasing foreign taxes paid. A simple way to do this is for the bank to open a branch in a tax haven such as Nassau or Grand Cayman, which imposes no tax on profits. Such branches are referred to as *shell branches* because no decision making occurs at the branch and no senior bank personnel need be stationed there. Instead, the branch is run directly from head office which books loans and accepts deposits on the shell's behalf. A U.S. bank that has a shell branch in Nassau or some other tax haven will generate a lot of paperwork at the branch; this work is done by some local bank, and the resulting rise in local employment is the benefit the country sponsoring the tax haven gets out of doing so. U.S. banks run a lot of shell branches in the Caribbean because this area is in a time zone that makes it easy for major U.S. banks to deal on the shell's behalf during normal working hours.

A placement book.   Some banks are so small that the only way they can participate in the Euromarket is through their "upstream" correspondent. Small regional banks, in contrast, are large enough to run a Euro placement book but probably too small to really get into the international lending business; to do that, a bank must open a London branch, and this is a considerable expense.

An alternative for banks too small to support a London branch is a shell branch in a tax haven. There are two good reasons for doing so. One is to reap profits and tax benefits on a placement book. The other, noted below, is to gain the flexibility a placement book affords it in implementing tactics and strategies designed to alter its interest rate exposure.

Sovereign risk. While some investors feel thoroughly comfortable in placing deposits at the Caribbean branch of a U.S. bank, many others do not. This is because most investors don't understand sovereign risk. However, the educational process is ongoing, and the more that people become acquainted with the subject of sovereign risk and realize how small it is with respect to the Caribbean, the more they are encouraged to invest in that market. Doing so is easier than investing in London because of time zone considerations.

Sovereign risk has to do with the danger posed to depositors at a foreign branch by possible expropriation of the branch's assets. Many investors fear that, if Nassau or some other tax haven country suddenly turned communist and expropriated the assets of bank branches there, deposits in these branches would not be repayable.

By law, a U.S. bank is responsible for all deposits in its foreign branches unless (1) there is a change in government in a country where it has a branch, and (2) the new government is inimical to the United States. Even if a new government is unfriendly, a U.S. bank is relieved of its liability to repay depositors at the expropriated branch only to the extent that the new government succeeds in seizing the branch's assets. If 95 percent of the loans a bank booked in a branch were to major U.S. and multinational companies, these companies would—in the event of expropriation of the branch—pay off their loan obligations not to the branch, but to the bank's head office. This would protect 95 percent of the branch's assets, and thereby 95 percent of its deposits, from expropriation. If the other 5 percent of the branch's total loans were to Communist countries which recognized the new government's claim on the branch's assets and repaid their loans to the expropriated branch, the maximum loss depositors at the branch could sustain would be 5 percent. As a matter of practice, the loss would probably be zero since a major U.S. bank would be loath to have depositors lose any money placed with it.

A bank that books assets in a tax haven where the political tide might turn is careful to place only safe loans there—loans to corporations and other entities that would pay off to head office any loans outstanding at an expropriated branch. Because of this, the sovereign risk attaching to deposits in Caribbean tax havens is minimal to zero. Citibank officers who have booked over $20 billion of assets at their

Nassau branch sleep soundly; so, too, should depositors who have placed funds there.

U.S. banks should (and most do) book the large loans they make to Communist countries at head office or in a branch in a politically stable country; London office is a natural choice.

Funding considerations. In choosing where to book Eurocurrency assets, taxes are an important consideration. Another is funding. A bank needs to ensure that its Euro assets, wherever it parks them, can, if worst comes to worst, be funded locally. It has happened that barriers have sprung up preventing the funding of assets in a given branch with domestic dollars or dollars acquired by London office.

For example, some U.S. banks used to park dollar loans in their Tokyo offices. Since the Asian dollar market is thin, having the Tokyo branch buy dollars to fund loans in this market was expensive. So the banks had their London offices buy the dollars and resell them to their Tokyo offices. This worked fine, except that London office wanted a spread for its effort which led the Japanese tax authorities to conclude that Tokyo office was earning unrealistically low profits on dollar loans booked there. Maybe it was, since the Japanese tax rate on branch profits is 63 percent which means that, for a U.S. bank, it is better to book profits in London than in Tokyo. The British for their part insist that, whenever the London branch of a U.S. bank takes deposits and relends them to another branch of the same bank, the London office must get a $5/64$ spread. Except in tax haven countries, every nation wants to make sure that it gets its fair share of a bank's profits to tax.

Germany provides another example of the impact of funding considerations on where a bank books loans. Major U.S. banks negotiate a lot of loans in Germany, but because of the liquidity requirements that Germany, and Switzerland, too, impose on local foreign bank branches, it makes no sense for a U.S. bank to house dollar loans on the books of its German or Swiss branches. As noted in Chapter 14, the same rules create problems for German banks when they operate in the dollar market.

International banking facilities (IBF)[9]

On December 1, 1981, banks in New York and 11 other states with enabling legislation and foreign banks with branches in these states were permitted to open international banking facilities (IBFs). The hope in New York was that introduction of these facilities would re-

---

[9] The following section is excerpted from Marcia Stigum, "A Free Trade Zone for New York? IBFs to Be Allowed, but Fed Restrictions May Limit Growth," *Pensions & Investment Age*, September 28, 1981, pp. 20–21.

create New York as an international banking center; the chance of this occurring was, however, diminished by the restrictions that the Fed imposed on IBF activities.

The concept behind IBFs is to create a species of free trade zone for international money—primarily Eurodollars. An IBF offers a bank several advantages: deposits in the facility are not subject to reserve requirements and need not pay FDIC insurance premiums; also, income earned by the facility is specifically exempted from city and state taxes.

For depositors, one attraction of IBFs is that any interest they pay to foreigners is exempt from withholding taxes; another advantage is that the depositor will get U.S. as opposed to U.K., Bahamian, or some other sovereign risk.

U.S. sovereign risk won't attract Iranian depositors, but it should attract institutions that are loath to place funds in the shell branches that major U.S. banks have opened in Nassau and other tax havens because they don't like the sovereign risk that attaches to deposits there.

The origin of the IBFs goes back to the days when New York City was tottering on the brink of bankruptcy. At the time, the state and the city zeroed in on the banks as the culprits. The city's problems were the banks' fault because the banks kept selling the city's debt whereas they should have told the city it was bankrupt.

To add injury to insult, the city and the state raised their tax rates on bank income earned within New York State, and the city topped off its tax hike with a tax surcharge.

The imposition of punitive state and city taxes gave the New York banks a tremendous incentive to book international business in offshore tax havens, primarily Nassau and Grand Cayman which are located in a time zone that permits New York banks to deal on the shell's behalf during normal business hours.

Once this trend asserted itself and serious defections among New York banks became a distinct possibility, the state passed legislation to permit the creation in New York of IBFs. These were supposed to draw huge amounts of business back from London and the offshore shells to New York City.

For the IBFs to get off the ground, the Fed had to give them its blessing. This blessing was slow in coming because out of town banks opposed New York IBFs as unfair competition.

The Fed has a history of not making rules that favor a particular group of banks; to permit the New York IBFs to go ahead, it had to come up with a rationalization: this was that any state could pass the same legislation New York had.

A second concern of the Fed was with leakage: the movement of domestic deposits and loan business into the Euromarket. It is the

Fed's fear that further leakage would weaken its control over domestic credit and the domestic money supply.

This concern sounds legitimate but is, in fact, somewhat ludicrous, since the horse in question left the barn years ago. Today, treasurers at major domestic corporations actively and freely ferry their loan and deposit business between the domestic and the Euromarket on the basis of what best suits their needs.

When the Fed, in 1975, wrote a letter to the banks reiterating its instructions to them not to solicit Eurodeposits from domestic depositors, it forgot to send a copy to corporate America which currently buys half the Euro CDs issued in London.

Despite the fact that leakage has become a torrent, the Fed—to prevent its further growth—imposed severe restrictions on what IBFs may do; specifically, it ruled that they may not pay interest on overnight money, may not issue CDs, and may not take deposits from or make loans to domestic entities. These restrictions sharply limit the value of IBFs to banks.

No corporate depositor will settle for a two-day notice account, when he can earn interest on a Euro call account at a London or Caribbean branch.

Also, corporate treasurers will not make time deposits with IBFs when they can buy liquid Europaper in London.

Bereft of corporate deposits, IBFs will have to rely for most of their funding on the interbank market for Euros and on deposits from central banks that have large dollar holdings and that, because they wanted to diversify their sovereign risk, were already holding some dollar deposits at U.S. banks.

This contrasts sharply with the situation at U.S. banks' Caribbean branches where half of the funding comes from U.S. depositors. The restrictions that the Fed has imposed on IBFs are sufficiently stringent to make New York unattractive in comparison with London and other Euro centers.

Except for saving some bookkeeping expenses at their Caribbean shells, the only good reason New York banks have for opening IBFs is an unresolved tax conflict between the state and the banks.

The state claims that the income New York banks earn on their Caribbean books should be subject to New York taxes, since these books are run from New York; the banks counter that no tax is due because the business they do in the Caribbean is truly international.

Due to this tax tussle, the specific exemption of IBF income from state and city taxes is one attractive feature—in fact the only one—of IBFs to New York banks.

Currently, the state and city are phasing back their taxes on bank income to a more reasonable level, a move that will diminish the attraction IBFs have to New York banks. Consequently, until and unless the Fed changes its regulations so that New York becomes a true free trade zone in money, introduction of the IBFs is unlikely to produce any important change in Eurobanking.

Controlling worldwide exposure

With respect to tactics and strategies for controlling interest rate exposure, the key point to be made is that it is important for a bank to look at its total positions not piecemeal—as between the domestic book and the Eurobook—but as a single global bank. One reason is that a bank should avoid getting into a position where it has a natural hedge going for it that doesn't know about: New York is running a short domestic book, the foreign branches a long book. Alternatively, a bank does not want to end up at the oppositive extreme where both the domestic book and the Euro book are geared the same way, but so much so that the bank is taking an unacceptable risk against its interest rate outlook. To avoid either eventuality, a bank must aggregate its positions worldwide and then devise and implement strategies with respect to this global position.

A bank can avoid making too big a bet in one direction simply by setting limits on the size of the position each branch may take or on the degree to which it may mismatch its book. Doing this, however, still does not solve the first problem, which is that differences in the interest rate views taken by head office and the branches may lead to a situation where the bank has a natural hedge it doesn't want. To address that problem, a bank's head office—the central point for strategy—must regularly and frequently communicate its view on rates and its decisions with respect to strategy to its foreign branches and then track their books to make sure that these books conform to head office's rate view and choice of strategy.

A little history. Before we elaborate on developing and implementing a global strategy, a bit of history is appropriate. The head office of every U.S. bank that started operations in the Euromarket in the early 1960s initially instructed its foreign branches to accept *no* interest rate exposure in their Euro operations. A branch that acquired a 3-month, fixed-rate asset was expected to buy 3-month money against it and then sit tight and earn its spread. This situation lasted until the early 1970s. Then, gradually, U.S. banks began to allow their branches to mismatch. In those days, this almost always meant borrowing short and lending long because the yield curve was usually positively sloped.

As the 1970s progressed, head office at many banks became concerned about the risk to which the mismatch limits it imposed on the branches exposed the bank. Often these limits were couched in percentage terms. Consequently as a bank's Euro book grew, the absolute amounts represented by these percentages became large. The mismatch risk in a bank's Euro book, which initially had been minimal, became significant.

At this point, the major banks began to track their branches' mismatch regularly from head office, and they began to set tighter mismatch limits based on absolute dollar amounts. By 1975, it was not unusual for a bank to impose a whole set of limits on each foreign branch with respect to various mismatches it could have: overnight against 1-month, 1s against 3s, and so on. Coupled with this, many banks instituted a system whereby all the branches would report to head office weekly on their positions. Head office would then aggregate these reports so that it could determine at a glance the interest rate exposure on its worldwide Euro book. It would also compare that exposure with the exposure it was taking in its domestic book. For a time, banks permitted their foreign branches to operate more or less autonomously within the confines of the risk parameters set by head office.

Running a global book.   Then, in the late 1970s and early 1980s, as interest rates became higher and more volatile, a number of banks concluded that there was good reason to tighten up still further on the freedom given to the branches, to require that the branches act in conformity with rate views formulated at head office and communicated regularly to them. The path by which banks arrived at this decision was long and less than direct. Nonetheless, the decision itself was extremely important. For the first time, banks were controlling their global book from a central point.

By doing so, a bank got not only the obvious benefit of being better able to control its total exposure; it also got additional flexibility in adjusting that exposure. For example, a bank that has a lot of floating-rate loans on its domestic book is always vulnerable to a decline in interest rates. If the bank is running a global book, it can offset this vulnerability by running a short Euro book. For a major bank that fears a fall in rates and wants to run a neutral position, running a short Euro book is the way to achieve such a position.

At top banks that operate a global book, the absolute limit on running a short day-to-day position in the Euro book is liberal—several or more billion dollars. If a bank ran just a Euro book and nothing else, this limit would be so large as to permit the bank to take a tremendous risk. However, when the bank's domestic and Euro books are viewed as a whole, the offset to a huge, short Euro position is all the bank's floating-rate loans on which rates can change at the drop of a hat. Given these loans, a short Euro book can be consistent with a bank's desire to be neutral overall. As this example illustrates, a bank should never look at its domestic book on Tuesday, its Euro book on Friday. In a volatile rate environment, a bank must have a global view.

This is a conclusion that Citibank did not used to accept. In this respect, it is interesting to note that it was Citi's London office that incurred in the fourth quarter of 1980 a staggering loss that offset much of the profit earned by the rest of the bank.

Placement books.   As mentioned, a bank that is too small to open a London branch may nonetheless find it both feasible and profitable to open a shell branch in a tax haven from which it operates a Eurocurrency placement book. A bank that operates such a book can and should operate its global—domestic and Euro positions—as major banks have learned to do, as a single book. This will enable a bank running a placement book to take advantage of the same flexibility that a Euro book affords major banks in terms of structuring the interest rate exposure to which their overall position exposes them. This flexibility is particularly important to a smaller bank lacking the flexibility that access to the national CD market affords major banks.

People problems.   A bank running a global book encounters people problems at two levels. First, such a bank needs to have head-office people who know both the domestic and Euromarkets well. This expertise must be resident in the *same* persons. The worst mistake a bank can make is to have its global book run by a group of specialists in the domestic market and a group of specialists in the Euromarket. It will never happen that the two groups agree on an overall strategy that makes sense for the whole bank.

In a bank running a global book, the strategic decisions that head office makes must be carried out, in part, by individual treasurers in the foreign branches. These officers have to be made to feel that they are operating with some autonomy at the same time that they are being asked to act in conformity with the rate outlook conceived of and promulgated by head office. Achieving this requires subtlety.

The individual treasurer of a foreign branch has got to understand that, since he always knows the attitude of head office on the outlook for interest rates, he must either have his position conform to that outlook or have a good reason if it doesn't. Also, he must be prepared to accept the fact that, if head office suddenly becomes concerned that interest rates are going up, the word may go out, "Close up your exposed positions. We don't care what it costs. Just close them up." A branch treasurer may not like this, but he will do it if head office has communicated to him the necessity of, at times, having all the branches pull in the same direction.

To give branch treasurers a feeling of autonomy, it is necessary to ensure that they have some leeway for making decisions. This is possible even in a bank that permits branch treasurers to make only minor deviations from the rate view laid down by head office. Example: a branch treasurer may have to fund a large loan rollover on which the borrower opts to go six months. The treasurer thinks that interest rates will remain high for a time but not for 6 months, so he takes 3-month money against that position. This would give him a gap 3 months out, a position that would be consistent with the view at head office that interest rates will remain high in the short-run but drop 300 basis points three months hence. Against such a view, the treasurer has room to make extra money by manipulating the maturities of his assets and liabilities—by doing 6 months against 3s, or 1s against 3s.

Giving a branch treasurer some autonomy in funding will help maintain his morale in the face of tight controls from head office. But it will not solve another problem. If a bank operates a branch that is doing a lot of loan business, most of which is booked elsewhere because of tax considerations, then no matter how well the officers of this branch do their job and how much business they bring in, their branch's bottom line will show meager profits. Offsetting the potential morale problem caused by much work leading to little profit requires bankwide education. It is also important for a bank to set up an internal system that allocates bank profit in the branches on the basis of where business is originated as opposed to where it is booked. The bank should use this system to ensure that people are compensated in line with their actual, as opposed to accounting, contribution to profits.

Proper profit center analysis

To successfully run a global book, a bank must correctly organize its profit center accounting. Most banks analyze their sources of profits at a fine level of detail. Doing so is part of a bank's overall planning and budgeting process. In seeking to maximize earnings, a bank tries to determine how profitable each activity is. If the bank then runs up against a balance sheet constraint that forces it to curtail activity in some area, it can do so rationally.

The way most major banks have grown up is that their international business has been tacked on to their domestic banking activity almost as an adjunct. What these banks went through since 1960, the regional banks are going through now.

When a bank that already has a profit center analysis enters the international business, it is natural for it to treat this new business as a separate profit center. Doing so is, however, a big mistake because it impedes the free flow of funds between head office and the branches. Narrow profit center definitions will, for example, prevent a bank from taking advantage of opportunities for arbitrage that require the use of domestic funds in the Euromarket or vice versa. If the domestic and international treasuries are separate profit centers, such arbitrages can be carried out only if a transfer price can be agreed upon that will make both sides happy. This will rarely occur because as indicated by later examples, spreads are too thin.

In a bank that does international business, profit center accounting should be based on two broad profit centers: the worldwide lending and worldwide treasury divisions. Note that lending and funding are basically all a bank does.

To separate lending profits from funding profits, a bank must treat loans funded by the treasury as income-producing assets to that division and liabilities incurred to fund loans as a cost to the lending division. Under this approach, the lending division's earnings will equal the spread between the rate at which it puts on loans and the bank's cost of funds at the margin. The treasury's profit will be any savings it can realize on funding, for example, by mismatching. Dealing and trading in securities and foreign exchange is also part of the treasury function and a source of treasury profits. So, too, is the acquisition and funding of the bank's portfolio.

To illustrate what is involved in profit center accounting on a loan, suppose that London office books a new loan on which the borrower agrees to pay 50 basis points over LIBOR and opts to fix the rate for 90 days. Ninety-day money is trading at 18.5 percent. The borrower pays 19 percent, and the lending division is credited with the 50 basis point spread as income. In the bank's profit center accounting, the lending and treasury divisions of the bank are treated as if the lending division were borrowing money from the treasury at 18.5 percent. This creates a notional liability for the lending division and a notional asset for the treasury. If, in the example at hand, the treasury opts to fund the new loan by buying 90-day money at LIBOR, which is 18.5 percent, it will break even. If, alternatively, it can fund the loan at a rate below 18.5 percent (for example, by funding short), the treasury will earn a profit.

After long experience, major banks learned that to maximize overall profits, it was crucial that they treat international business not as a separate profit center, but as part of their overall lending and treasury functions. This lesson is one that regional banks would do well to learn. In entering the international business, regional banks probably already have a profit center apparatus. Thus, adding international business as a separate profit center would be an easy, almost natural mistake for them to make.

A decade ago, when the major banks treated the domestic treasury division as one profit center and their international treasury—which was part of their international banking division—as a separate profit center, they created an incentive for head office and London office to each maximize its own profits. There was no provision for having the domestic treasury work hand in glove with London office to maximize the bank's total profits by, for example, using domestic funds to support assets which London office would acquire. Creating a profit center apparatus that fosters such cooperation enables the head office and London office to earn a combined profit that exceeds the total the two could earn acting independently.

To illustrate, suppose that 3-month Euros are trading at 15⅞ while domestic CD money can be bought at 14¾. After 3 percent reserves, a bank issuing 3-month CDs has an all-in cost of about 15.20; consequently, by buying money in the domestic CD market and relending it in the Euro market, the bank can pick up over 65 basis points. There is no question that a bank should do such profitable arbitrages if the bank has a foreign branch that needs 3-month money and would, if it did not receive that money from head office, have to bid for it in the Euro market. The situation is different if none of the bank's foreign branches need 3-month money. In that case, the bank, to take advantage of the arbitrage, will have to have one of its foreign branches redeposit the money it has bought in the domestic market with some other bank operating in the Euro market. That tack, while profitable, has the disadvantage that it will balloon the bank's balance sheet and deteriorate its capital ratio.

Today, arbitrages of the sort just described must be looked for carefully. This was not so as late as the end of the 1970s. At that time, the domestic and international treasuries in most large banks were still operating as independent profit centers: therefore, they were not set up to take advantage of the arbitrage, and for that reason, U.S. and Euro rates sometimes widened to the point where such arbitrages offered a 300- or even 400-basis-point profit.

Making the global treasury function a profit center still leaves a problem with respect to interbranch transfers of funds. If the treasurer of Paris office says to London office, "How do you lend me the 3s?" he is not going to get a break from London office, which will want to make something on the trade. Head office, in contrast, would be willing to give Paris office a break in the form of money at cost to improve not its profits, but the total bank's aftertax return. With respect to maximizing the latter, the terms on which interbranch transactions occur are not crucial. The whole concept of a global treasury function is that it does not matter—except for tax purposes—whether profits are booked in London or Paris.

What does matter is not having the domestic side maximizing its profits against the international side. If this occurs, each branch is forced to do its own funding, which is undesirable because the London treasurer cannot borrow money from other banks in the domestic market as he can in the Euromarket. If domestic money is cheaper than

Euro money, the *only* way a money market bank can take advantage of this in a global sense is by having head office borrow domestic money and give it to the offshore branches.

Bank stock analysts again

We have stressed that a bank should seek to maximize its profits on a worldwide basis. In this respect, there is a lingering problem with bank stock analysts. Prior to the early 1960s, the international earnings of U.S. banks were a small part of their total earnings. Before that time, the Euromarket was tiny, and U.S. banks did almost strictly local currency business abroad.

In the mid 1960s, when the Euromarket took off, banks were able to do much more foreign business in this market than they could have had they stuck just to local currency operations, and bank profits derived from foreign operations began to be a factor in the determination by bank stock analysts of how banks were doing. Very large banks such as Citi, Chase, and Morgan during and especially toward the end of the 1970s, were deriving half or more of their earnings from international business.

Originally, bank stock analysts tended to treat a bank's international earnings as a nonrecurring event. This attitude has changed, but one still finds analysts making remarks about the "dangerous" level of international earnings that are included in the bottom lines of top U.S. banks. How legitimate analysts' concern about this is depends on where a bank's concentration of effort is, and more especially, on whether one really believes there might be limited war in Europe.

We live today in an international economy, and the earnings of top U.S. banks reflect this. Destruction of this international economy, however it might occur, would have more disastrous consequences for the economy and even for bank stockholders than a mere decline in the earnings and stock prices of money market banks.

NEW PRODUCTS AND VENTURES

No matter how attractive any new venture appears at first blush, a bank must analyze with care what effect the contemplated new venture or business will have on critical aspects of its book: liquidity, interest rate exposure, return on assets, and return on equity.

Impact on liquidity

In considering any new venture, the *first* thing a bank must look at is *liquidity*. No bank thinking of taking on new assets should do so before it has an *assured* source of funds to support those assets. The relationships between (1) the yields of the new assets and the funds needed to support them and (2) their maturity characteristics are important considerations, but the crucial first question is whether incremental funds are available.

Cash-flow characteristics of new assets and liabilities

Once a bank has determined that additional funds are available at a cost such that the spread on its new venture will be positive, it must ask how similar are the characteristics of the cash flows, into the new assets and out of the new liabilities, that the contemplated new venture will produce. For example, funding new 30-day assets with overnight funds at a positive spread will look *less* attractive when a bank recognizes that it must pay out interest on the new funds it is buying daily, while it will receive interest on the 30-day paper it is acquiring only once—30 days hence. To figure the *true* cost of the funds bought overnight for 30 days, a bank must take into account compounding, which at high interest rates can be surprisingly large on liabilities and assets that must be rolled frequently.[10]

Maturity characteristics of new assets and liabilities

Two other crucial characteristics for a bank or S&L in taking on a new venture are (1) what sort of gap between asset and liability maturities the new venture would create and (2) whether the institution wants to assume that gap. Examples of the sort of gap that a new venture could get many banks into are easy to find. Here is one: suppose that the auto market turns up and that a bank has an opportunity to make a lot of additional auto loans (such loans are typically four-year, fixed-rate paper); suppose also that our bank believes it can issue a lot more 6-month money market certificates, which are currently popular with consumers; suppose finally that funding 4-year, auto paper with 6-month certificates currently offers the bank an attractive spread, so attractive that the bank is tempted to put on a lot more such paper. However confident the bank is that interest rates will stay flat or head

---

[10] The formula for determining the *true* yield on different assets and the *true* cost of funds that must be bought when compounding is taken into account is derived in Marcia Stigum's *Money Market Calculations: Yields, Break-evens and Arbitrage* (Homewood, Ill.: Dow Jones-Irwin, 1981). This book describes many instances in which money and bond market participants should make compounding calculations, but in fact do not make them or make them incorrectly. Every bank and S&L is involved daily in many such transactions or in similar ones. The level of mathematics in this book never exceeds, except in one short appendix, that of simple algebra.

down over the 4-year period of the loan, rates might go up, and the bank might find itself earning on its new assets a zero or even a negative spread. Because of the interest rate exposure to which undertaking any new venture on which ARBL is negative exposes a bank, a bank must identify the gap associated with any new venture before it undertakes that venture and ask whether it is willing to accept the associated risk.

If a bank decides that it is willing to open up a gap, it must next ask how quickly it could close that gap if its view on interest rates were to change. This is one thing about which no bank should kid itself. For example, no bank that acquires auto paper should say to itself, "Well if interest rates rise, we will fund our auto paper with 3½-year certificates," because, by the time the bank decides that interest rates are going to rise, everyone else will think the same thing. If the general expectation is that interest rates are going to rise, the hitherto unsophisticated depositor will not want to put his money out for 3½ years; he will want to make a 6-month deposit because he too will expect interest rates to rise. This is another case where a bank's customers will fix its book if the bank has not had the foresight to act early. It is a big danger for a bank that undertakes a new venture that produces a gap to believe that it will be able to close that gap before the spread on the yields between new assets and liabilities produced by the new venture turns negative.

View of bank examiners

Another question a bank considering a new venture must examine is how taking on a new set of assets and liabilities will affect the way bank examiners look at the bank's book. Particularly with respect to liquidity and interest rate exposure, bank examiners have a different—more lenient—set of rules for money market banks than for small banks. Consider, for example, a small bank that starts from a position where it has a big interest rate exposure because it has a large mortgage loan portfolio and a big tax-exempt portfolio, and it is supporting both of these big blocks of assets with relatively short-term funds; such a bank may have little room to do more of the same even if such new business appears very lucrative at the margin. Doing so might cause the examiners to come right down on the bank, to tell them, "You cannot take any more risk than is already inherent in your balance sheet."

Return on assets

From the point of view of maximizing the bank's profits, a bank ought to concentrate on return on equity (ROE), rather than return on assets (ROA). However, as we have noted, bank analysts pay a lot of attention to ROA. If a bank that is concentrating on ROE rather than ROA has no balance sheet constraint, it might say it is going to do any new business so long as that business earns it ¼ percent. Unfortunately, that may be the wrong thing to do, particularly for a small bank. For a small bank, taking on a new business may well mean that a loan they returned down last week now looks attractive because the bank has a positive spread on it. On such a loan, the bank may be getting only a fractional extra spread that may well be offset by the imputed, but unquantifiable, cost of accepting a greater credit risk than the bank normally would.

Many banks do not think about this; they say, "Well my capital situation is good. I have more room to leverage, so I might as well do some new business." And in scratching around for some new business, they have to lend to less-and-less-good credits to build up their loan book. If a bank, in an effort to build up its ROA, lends to poorer credits, it can get a higher spread because it will be able to charge poorer credits a higher rate. Offsetting this higher rate, however, may be a higher loan loss ratio. Consequently the impact on ROA of lending to lesser credits is unpredictable. A bank thinking of taking this route must try to evaluate carefully the extra risks associated with such new business and ask itself if the extra spread is worth the associated extra risks.

A bank that wants to build up its ROA may face a balance-sheet constraint because the authorities have told the bank that it cannot leverage anymore. If so, the bank should examine spreads offered by the various asset categories available to it and seek to shift into those assets that afford it the widest spreads.

A final thought: if a bank wants to get into a new venture, chances are that all banks in its class will want to get into this venture as well, and that these banks are also all going to be looking at the same source of funds. This means, all else equal, that the spread on the new business will be much narrower than it looked initially. If so, then the bank must think hard about the degree to which it wants to commit itself to the new business at a narrower spread than currently exists.

Return on equity

Within the constraints set by its capital ratio, bank examiners, and bank analysts, a bank's goal should be to maximize ROE within whatever prudent boundaries it wants to choose. First Pennsy and First of Chicago tried to improve their ROEs by taking unacceptable risks. They are object lessons in what not to do. They did not constrain the size of the risk they were willing to take.

A bank should try to maximize its ROE with self-imposed constraints. The qualifier, "self-imposed," is important because, in the short-run, any constraint on a bank has to be self-imposed. It is not until well after the fact that authorities will impose constraints upon a bank. This is especially true when a bank is getting into a new kind of business because the authorities will not have had time to evaluate the risk associated with this business.

Deregulation

The things we have said so far would apply whether there was deregulation or not. Deregulation is creating a new situation in which more and more banks will have to buy funds at the margin to support their growth. Ultimately every bank will not have enough capital, free demand deposits, and passbook savings accounts to fund itself just with them. Eventually to grow, all banks will have to get into the business of attempting to manage their liabilities one way or another.

In the past many banks had a lot of liabilities—particularly passbook savings—that they felt they had no need to manage because they were just there. Particularly with deregulation and with the increased sophistication of small savers who had funds to invest, the trend of passbook savings to go into other bank liabilities, to invest in 6-month certificates or to leave the bank and go into money market funds, will accelerate. Depending on the pace of deregulation, banks may be facing the situation where they will, because of competition from non-bank institutions, be competing among each other for an amount of funds that is a dwindling proportion of the total money potentially available to the banking system.

Say there are X billion of funds available to the bank and to money funds in the form of consumer-type savings. Since the money funds can pay more than banks at this moment, the bulk of this money is going to money funds. If deregulation occurs and banks become more competitive in terms of bidding against money funds, the banking system may be able to recapture the bulk of that available money, but at a price.

The point is that the amount of money available to banks depends on the pace of deregulation—how fast the banks are allowed to compete against money funds—and it will depend on the ability of banks to pay competitive rates to get this money. In either event there is no going back. Eventually all of the passbook money banks now hold will disappear. Only NOW accounts, which are transaction related, will remain. A lot of banks used to think in terms of 30 or 40 percent of their liabilities being represented by passbook savings accounts, which they assumed had a perpetual maturity and a relatively fixed interest cost because of Regulation Q. Now these deposits may have a maturity of tomorrow to the extent that money funds offer a rate three times as attractive as does a passbook savings account. Banks can no longer count on such funds as a stable source of cheap money. They will have to pay a competitive rate. This creates a situation in which any bank that has passbook savings on its balance sheet is—whether it knows it or not—in the business of liability management. If the bank does not realize this, the sooner it does, the better off it will be.

A crucial point is that deregulation is going to narrow the natural spread that smaller banks typically enjoy. Small banks that have huge, natural spreads are going to see them diminish; and as that occurs, they are going to be under varying degrees of pressure to try to retain their spreads and their ROE. The only way they would be able to retain their ROE when their spreads are being compressed by outside forces is to take more risk than they used to. This brings up a point stressed throughout this book. It is not bad to take risk, but if a bank is going to do it, it should try to do it within prudent limits by consciously assessing the probability of what the payoff of any bet it makes might be. The precepts of this book are designed to provide a banker with a framework that allows him to deal with uncertainty with precision.

There is no guarantee that a bank that has been prudent will not sustain losses, but a banker who has been prudent should—when a proposition goes bad—say, "I wasn't wrong, my assumptions were." This is not any attempt to be flippant. Such an attitude means that a banker's decision was based on his best analysis of the situation and his allocation of proper probabilities to various possible outcomes. That the proposition turned out badly does not negate the correctness of the decision; all it does is show that the improbable may occur.

In formulating strategies, a bank should assess probabilities and then make a decision. If subsequently that decision turns out badly, the banker who made it can regret that he lost money because what he did turned out badly, but he cannot regret having made the decision because he made it on the best evaluation he could of possible outcomes.

For a banker, decision making is inevitable, just as for any other businessman. Rather than taking a casino approach, the banker should make decisions on the basis of the best information available to him. Then if his decision turns out badly, he should not regret having taken it. If a banker makes only prudent bets, the majority of his bets should return him a profit.[11]

---

[11] See Postscript for stories of banks that have, as this book was going to press, gotten into trouble for violating the precepts laid down in this and other chapters.

12

Futures strategies

The high level and increased volatility that have characterized interest rates in recent years have wrought a fundamental change in banking: *Today, the big risk for banks is not credit risk, but rate risk.*

To be profitable—in fact to survive—in today's markets, a bank needs more than ever the ability to restructure its assets and liabilities rapidly and on a meaningful scale. That need, moreover, becomes increasingly acute the larger the bank. Many small and medium-sized banks enjoy natural advantages in the form of (1) large free or cheap deposits and (2) protection from competition created by regulatory restrictions on intrastate and interstate banking. Such banks can operate profitably without making a great effort to implement the strategies we have described for creating and controlling interest rate exposure. In contrast, the nation's largest banks, which do business in a highly competitive environment and enjoy no natural advantages, must operate on the *hungry* principle: act as if every dollar they earn will be their last unless they work at managing their interest rate exposure. The spreads small banks earn are sufficient to live on. The spreads major banks earn on much of their business are, in contrast, so thin that the income they produce can be counted on to do little more than cover the electric bill and fixed costs. To create the level of earnings bank stockholders and analysts like to see, a big bank must live by its wits: carefully track its interest rate exposure and structure that exposure so that more often than not the bank will be making a bet on rates that pays off with increased earnings.

The markets for financial futures—bills, bonds, notes, and CDs—offer big banks and alert smaller banks opportunities for responding with increased flexibility and speed to a change in their rate outlook that dictates restructuring their balance sheets to alter their interest rate exposure. It also offers them an opportunity to get back into the business of making fixed-rate term loans.

Today, however, banks—with the exception of the dealer departments of money market banks—and thrift institutions make little use of financial futures as a tool for managing their liabilities or, more generally, for manipulating their interest rate exposure. As one dealer noted, "The talk-to-ticket ratio is high."

Banks have been slow to use financial futures for several reasons. The initial reaction of bank regulators to financial futures was that buying and selling futures contracts was a dangerous form of gambling that banks either should not get into or should use only sparingly as part of a clearly defined hedge.

A second problem is the slow pace at which banks have acquired knowledge about and expertise in using financial futures. Many bankers know little about commodities and—with the exception of a few traders down on the dealing floor—view financial futures as mysterious and potentially dangerous instruments to trade. Compounding this problem is the fact that, for a bank to become an active user of financial futures, top management must give its blessing. Unfortunately, learning about financial futures is just one of many important issues competing for the time of a bank's senior officers.

A final problem that has discouraged banks from using financial futures to hedge loans is the unfavorable way banks were, at the outset, required to treat profits and losses resulting from hedging.

Readers who are unfamiliar with financial futures and their use in hedging should begin by reading the appendix at the end of this chapter. It gives a general introduction to financial futures and describes their uses: speculation, spreading, arbitrage, and hedging. The reader should pay special attention to the workings of perfect hedges, imperfect hedges, and cross hedges: to the nature of basis risk; and to the role of basis risk as a potential source of profit.

A point made in the appendix that bears emphasis—a hedge is *not* a form of insurance. A futures market participant who hedges normally *shifts* his risk from speculation on a rate or price level to *speculation on a spread* (basis, in commodities jargon). He does *not* eliminate risk;

instead he *shifts* the nature of the risk he assumes. Normally, he also reduces the amount of risk he assumes because *he shifts the focus of his speculation from a highly variable rate or price level to a less variable rate spread.*[1]

Having made these general points, let us now turn to the subject of banks' involvement in financial futures and the opportunities this involvement offers.

ENHANCED ABILITY TO RESTRUCTURE ASSET/LIABILITY POSITIONS

No bank, large or small, can avoid assuming some natural interest rate exposure. Also, all large banks consciously seek—when the moment seems propitious—to create or otherwise manipulate their interest rate exposure to profit from it. Financial futures offer banks, large and small, a means of both shortening their response time and increasing their flexibility in reacting to market changes that call for a restructuring of their asset/liability positions.

Increasing flexibility and speeding response time

For example, a bank that gets the idea—a split second before the rest of the market does—that rates are about to move, can adjust its position more quickly in futures than in the cash market. Here's a case in point described by a money market banker:

> A few weeks ago we feared interest rates might rise in the short run. Finally, at 11 o'clock on a Tuesday, we decided we should do a half billion of 90-day CDs. You can't write much in the way of new CDs after 1 o'clock, so we figured we could do no more than $200 million of cash CDs that day, which is what we, in fact, managed. To go long $500 million of 90-day money, we sold—starting the moment we decided to move—$300 million of 90-day bill futures. When the market opened on Wednesday, rates in both the cash CD market and the bill futures market were up 40 basis points. We wrote the other $300 million of CDs we wanted at the new, higher rate and made up the extra cost by covering our short position in bill futures at a profit. Effectively doing the hedge was the same thing as having written $500 million of CDs on Tuesday at Tuesday's rate.

On a hedge transaction like this, there exists some spread or basis risk for two reasons. As short rates rise or fall, the spread between the

[1] See Appendix to Chapter 12, pp. 347–48.

rate on 90-day CDs and that on 90-day bill futures may widen or narrow. Also, even if the spread does not change, the price play in the two instruments will differ somewhat because the CD rate is an add-on rate, the bill rate a discount rate.[2]

A small banker reading through our example might think, "Big deal. Even if I were convinced that I should go out and borrow $10, $20, or $50 million of 90-day money at today's rates, there is no way I can because I lack access to the national CD market." He is right and wrong. Right that he can't volitionally sell millions of dollars of CDs in the national market. Wrong if he thinks futures are of no use to him. An attractive feature of futures is that it permits a smaller bank that has only limited alternatives for altering its asset/liability position by operating in the cash markets to adjust its interest rate exposure by taking positions in futures. A small bank that fears interest rates will rise and believes that this will eventually be reflected in a rise in its funding cost, can sell futures as a hedge. For a bank that can't sell CDs at will, shorting futures is the *only* way it can act on a view that the cost of funding its basic book is going to rise.

Escaping the balance sheet constraint

A major bank that wants to protect itself against either (1) a rise in interest rates by buying long-dated funds, or (2) a fall in rates by adding bonds to its portfolio, may feel that, to achieve the change in interest rate exposure it wants, it needs to make a $1, $2, or $3 billion move. Making such a move in the cash market may be feasible for a top bank that has preserved its good name, since such a bank has a wide variety of options open to it. If, for example, it fears a rise in interest rates, it can hedge by selling domestic CDs and Euro CDs and by buying longer-dated Euros in the interbank market.

There's a problem with this, however: that familiar friend, the balance sheet constraint. Most banks and certainly all large banks are concerned about their capital ratios. A bank that needs to make a $3 billion move to alter its interest rate exposure could do this over the long run without violating its capital constraint by letting certain of the assets and liabilities on its balance sheet run off. If, however, the bank needs to act in the short run to hedge against an imminent change in rates, there is no way it can alter its interest rate exposure without ballooning its balance sheet if it confines its activities to the cash market. For a bank concerned about its capital ratio, such ballooning, even if it is only over the short run, may be unacceptable. Again, futures come to the rescue. By assuming a large position, short or long, in futures, a bank can significantly alter its interest rate exposure with-

---

[2] See Chapter 4.

out ballooning its balance sheet. *Futures positions have the virtue of being an off-balance-sheet item.*

The reader who interprets what we have just said as amounting to saying that a bank should add speculation in futures to its kit of tools for profiting from an appropriately structured interest rate exposure, is correct. There is nothing particularly shocking about this. The sum total of a bank's or a thrift's asset and liability structure represents a bet—de facto or consciously contrived—on rates. No one would argue with the proposition that, if a given asset/liability position looks unattractive, the institution holding it should seek to alter that position by operating in the cash market. Similarly, no one should argue with the proposition that, if the institution is prevented from operating in the cash market by a balance sheet constraint, it should use futures to adjust its interest rate exposure. Using futures to alter interest rate exposure in the short run, while avoiding ballooning the balance sheet, is a useful strategy for any institution facing a balance sheet constraint, be it a small bank, a regional bank, a money center bank, or a thrift.

We stressed earlier that, for an institution using the cash market to adjust its interest rate exposure to conform to its rate view, a key rule is: don't bet the bank. The same goes for futures. A few S&Ls have gotten into deep trouble by dealing in *forward* commitments for Government National Mortgage Association (GNMA) passthroughs on the basis of an incorrect view of rates and on a scale that was out of proportion to their net worth and basic asset structure. An institution does not need futures to get into trouble making an out-sized bet based on an incorrect rate view. First Pennsy and other banks have managed this trick operating in the cash market.

Our point is that, for a bank that *carefully* tracks its interest rate exposure, formulates its rate view, evaluates its confidence in that view, and then implements reasoned bets based on its rate view, operating in the futures market is *no more risky* than operating in the cash market. Many people, including regulators, view futures positions as risky because an institution can assume a huge position in futures by putting down a margin deposit of only 5 percent or so. Rationally, it is hard to argue that this is riskier than a money market bank buying long governments which it finances almost 100 percent in the RP market. Leverage is leverage.

Much of the concern that surrounds the use by banks and other financial institutions of futures arises from the fact that human nature is such that people tend to regard old and established practices as prudent and responsible, new practices as dangerous and imprudent. If the long bond had been invented in 1978, *no one* would consider holding a 30-year government as prudent and responsible. It is only the memory of how things were in past decades that permits people to buy long governments today and believe that they are acting as prudent investors instead of high-stakes gamblers. Some decades hence, using financial futures to hedge and otherwise alter interest rate exposure will be viewed as prudent, risk-averse behavior.

Money market certificates

In recent years, the institutions that—to their great profit—could have most readily used financial futures to hedge, were thrifts and retail banks selling 6-month, money market certificates (MMCs). The maximum rate banks selling these certificates may pay equals 25 basis points over the higher of (1) the rate of discount at which 6-month T bills were most recently auctioned or (2) the average rate at the four most recent auctions.

Consider a bank that has a lot of MMCs on its book. It knows that it will have to roll them because it needs the money to fund its basic asset structure. Also, it fears that interest rates will rise. A simple and straightforward way for such a bank to hedge against the feared rise in its cost of funding is to sell 3-month bill futures. Because the rate on the MMC is tied to the 6-month bill rate, basis risk arises in this sort of hedge primarily because the spread between yields on 3- and 6-month bills may change.

To illustrate an MMC hedge, consider a bank fearing that in June of 1980, when it came time to roll the MMCs it was then selling, rates would be significantly higher. A simple ploy would have been for the bank to sell bill contracts maturing in December of that year; a proper hedge would have been to sell roughly twice the amount of bills futures as the MMC money being hedged, because the bank is hedging a 6-month instrument by shorting 3-month bills.[3] Without laboring through the relevant calculations, it is clear because of the rise in interest rates, this hedge would have saved a bank doing it roughly 600 6-month basis points, that is, $30,000 per million of MMC money hedged.

Shedding risk by hedging always has a cost. In the case at hand, if rates had continued to decline after June 1980, the bank that shorted bill futures to hedge against a possible rise in rates could have found that, by hedging, it had locked in a higher MMC cost than it would have had to pay had it not hedged. Actually, when looked at in this light, the hedge is not a bad deal for a bank, especially for a thrift. Every thrift is loaded up with low-yield, fixed-rate mortgages. For a thrift, the pain of accepting a big rise in its cost of funds in an environment of rising rates would be far greater than paying something extra

---

[3] The proper hedge ratio depends in part on what the hedger thinks a change in rates will do to the yield curve.

for MMC money when its other funds costs are falling. There is an asymmetry: The hedge will save money for the institution that puts it on when that institution can least afford a rise in funding costs. Conversely, the hedge will cost the institution money when that institution will be least pained by some extra cost.

MAINTAINING A COMPETITIVE STANCE AS A LENDER

Because of rate volatility, banks are currently unwilling to make fixed-rate loans in the 2- to 4-year area. Being able to do so would open up to banks a whole new area of lending, one that is not currently available and would be highly attractive to bank customers. The longest period for which a corporation can issue commercial paper is 270 days. Beyond that, it gets into issuing medium-term notes with all the associated problems and costs: getting a credit rating, registering the issue, paying underwriting fees, and so on. If corporations could borrow from banks at a fixed rate on an intermediate-term basis rather than going to the public market, they would. A whole market is out there waiting for banks to tap.

The one and only way banks can tap this market without taking on undue risk is by hedging. Selling 2-year note futures to hedge a 2-year loan looks possible on paper but in practice can't be done because the futures market in notes is moribund. A bank that wants to hedge a medium-term, fixed-rate loan by selling futures contracts in a market where it can do size and be assured of liquidity should sell a *strip* of CD futures—a series of contracts maturing three, six, nine, and so on months later. Actually, selling a strip of CD futures to hedge a term loan is more attractive than it sounds, because the bank will be doing its funding relatively short anyway, typically by selling 90-day CDs. Also, as rates move up and down, the bank has a lot of flexibility. Depending on its current rate view and on how strongly it holds that view, it can always lift part or all of the hedge, choose to take some longer-term money when rates are down, and later reestablish its hedge. The flexibility afforded by futures is tremendous. It is certainly sufficient to protect the lending bank, even if the hedge is imperfect.

Being able to offer fixed-rate loans gives a bank several advantages. One is the opportunity to acquire a new kind of asset that banks need. Another is that, from a credit point of view, it is better for a bank to have its customers borrowing at a fixed rate, whatever that rate is, than borrowing at a floating rate. Before a bank makes a loan, it determines that the borrower can service the debt at prevailing rate levels. If a bank lends to a customer on a floating-rate basis when prime is 16 percent, it may later turn out that the borrower just can't take six months of paying a 20 percent prime. Borrowing at a floating-rate prime can create a cash-flow problem for a corporation. If banks can offer borrowers fixed-rate term loans, they will favor both themselves and the borrower. Presumably, this will bring more business into the banking system.

The fact that banks were able to offer borrowers fixed-rate loans used to be a major attraction of bank loans to corporate borrowers. Then, as rates became volatile, banks neither would nor could accept the rate risk inherent in making fixed-rate loans. They went to variable-rate loans and shifted the rate risk they would not accept onto the borrower, which was disadvantageous to both. Now, futures offer banks the opportunity to shift the rate risk to speculators who, by their own choice, seek to accept rate risk. This is probably the most appealing, if as yet least used, opportunity that futures offer banks.

PROTECTING DEALER POSITIONS

Dealers in money market instruments and bonds were the first group to actively use financial futures to hedge, and they remain by far the most active users of these markets. At times in recent years, the only reason there was any bid in the dealer market for long bonds was that dealers were able to lay off the risk they assumed in buying bonds by selling bond futures. The same is true—if to a lesser degree—of the markets for bills, CDs, and other money market instruments.

More and more banks are becoming dealers. Regardless of whether they are recognized by the Fed, they still deal and hold dealing positions. The ability to hedge dealing positions in the futures market gives a bank more resiliency in acting as a market maker and specifically in servicing its customers.

A perennial problem a bank faces in structuring its assets and liabilities is the need to beat its customers to the draw.[4] The same problem arises in its dealer operations. When the general anticipation is that rates will rise, the customers of a dealing bank will want to sell it securities. Even if all its customers are sellers, a bank has to come up with a bid; otherwise, it will be out of business. Conversely, if the expectation is that interest rates will fall, a bank must have something to offer.

Either way, a dealing bank has to assume positions, and some of the time those positions—long or short—will entail high risk. One way a bank can protect against the risk deriving from a dealing position is to assume an offsetting position in a similar security: Offset the purchase of $100 million of one long government issue from a customer by

---

[4] See Chapter 8.

shorting $100 million of a similar issue. Often, a quicker and more efficient way to accomplish the same end is to do an offsetting trade in an appropriate futures contract.

Nonbank dealers are highly leveraged and, because of this, are acutely conscious of the risk to which position taking in volatile markets exposes them. Bank dealers have more capital behind them, but that is no reason for them to throw caution to the wind. Thinly and highly capitalized dealers all face the same risk of loss and gain on identical positions. Moreover, if a loss occurs, it is just as real to a highly capitalized bank dealer as to a highly leveraged nonbank dealer.

Many banks would earn a higher return on their dealing activities if they behaved as if they were as thinly capitalized as nonbank dealers, and in particular, if the fear of loss led them to hedge more actively. It is a story we have told before: A bank that acts as if every dollar it earns will be its last will do better than a bank that permits easy earnings from one source or another to dull its wits.

PROTECTING PORTFOLIO POSITIONS

A distinction should be made between a bank hedging its dealer position and a bank hedging its portfolio position. A bank will frequently assume positions in its dealing account that it does not want because making a bid—whatever the condition of the market—is a vital part of being a market maker. To the extent that a dealer shirks this responsibility in bear markets, it will have few customers in bull markets.

When a bank adds bonds to its portfolio, it presumably does so because its long-term outlook, in which it places a high degree of confidence, is that rates are headed down for some prolonged period and that buying long-term, fixed-rate assets is therefore a good play. The bank may be right in its forecast, but rates have a way of wiggling around their long-term trend and of casting doubt on what their true long-term trend is. This being the case, a bank that buys bonds with its own funds may find that, from time to time, it wants to hedge its position either because it thinks rates have fallen too low due to a temporary overreaction, or because it fears that the trend in rates may be changing.

Most successful hedgers are not purists who hedge a position to maturity and then retreat—their work being done—to the golf course. Quite to the contrary, the astute hedger will put on and take off hedges in response to changes in the level and tone of the market. Viewed in this context, futures offer a bank a useful and flexible tool for making week-to-week, month-to-month, or whatever-is-called-for adjustments in its interest rate exposure.

Large banks that finance their portfolios in the RP market really need to hedge not the portfolio itself, but rather *the cost of funding it.* For this reason, it is quite appropriate for a large bank to use bill futures to hedge a bond portfolio, since a bank that takes the view that, over the long term, rates are headed down, wants to hedge against short-lived hikes in short rates. A large bank seeking to hedge the cost of funding its portfolio should be prepared to put on and take off hedges as market conditions change. The best time for a bank to buy bonds that it intends to finance in the RP market is when rates are peaking, the yield curve is inverted, and carry on the position is negative. A bank that hedges its borrowing costs in that position and never lifts the hedge runs the risk of locking in a zero or negative carry.

MANAGING LIABILITIES

There are several creative ways a bank may use futures in managing its liabilities. One is to anticipate rate trends and use futures to lock in what it hopes will later be an attractive borrowing rate. We began this chapter with an example of such a play: a bank selling futures in anticipation of a rise in short rates. In our example, the futures position was unwound the following day. It could as well have been unwound a week, a month, or three months later.

A second way a bank can use futures in liability management is to reverse a previously assumed position when its interest rate outlook changes. The best example of this is in a bank's Euro book. All of a bank's Euro assets and liabilities have fixed maturities. Therefore, there is *no* way a bank can rapidly change the interest rate exposure in its Euro book other than by *adding to* its assets and liabilities. For a bank to balloon its Euro book, it must balloon its overall balance sheet and perhaps hurt its capital ratio. Even if it is willing to do this, it may be unable to. On the liability side, a bank may find that it has already used all or most of the lines that other banks have extended to it, so it can't borrow any more. On the asset side, a bank may encounter similar difficulties: e.g., find that in terms of all sorts of limits—its legal lending limit to a single credit, its self-imposed limits in terms of country risk and credit risk—it can't acquire a couple of billion of new assets. For a bank in this position, being able to do something that is off the balance sheet can be a lifesaver. A big, wrong-way position in a bank's Euro book can, as Citi's experience in the final quarter of 1980 demonstrated, really hurt a bank's earnings.

Proposing that a bank do hedges in the domestic markets using financial futures to offset interest rate exposure in its Euro book raises an issue we have discussed before, the importance of properly structuring profit centers within a bank. There is no way a bank with overly segmented profit centers will be able to use a hedge put on in the domestic market to offset a position held in its Euro book. In December 1981, 3-month Eurodollar futures began to be traded on the International Monetary Market (IMM) in Chicago. Trading in these contracts picked up only slowly for several reasons. U.S. banks could adjust the interest rate exposure in their overall book by hedging with currently trading contracts for domestic CDs and T bills. Also, the London offices of U.S. and of non U.S. banks have little expertise in dealing in financial futures and must go through the long process of training traders to use this market. The one instance in which Eurodollar futures will have a real attraction for banks is when these contracts begin to be traded on the London International Financial Futures Exchange (*LIFFE*) scheduled to open in London. The LIFFE contract will give banks and bank branches running in London a dealer position in Euro DCs the opportunity to hedge their CD position in a futures market that is open during the same hours the cash instrument trades there.

A final feature that makes futures attractive for a bank seeking to manage liabilities is that any bank can take positions in futures, whereas only a few banks have the capability of quickly altering, and in size, the structure of their liabilities by operating in the cash market. The existence of futures markets makes it possible for a small bank to place a bet that, relative to its size, is comparable to the sort of bet that Citi and other banks having access to the national CD market can make operating in the cash market.

EXPERTISE

Various factors have slowed the use by banks and thrifts of financial futures to hedge and, more generally, to alter their interest rate exposure. One is lack of expertise. Figuring out the best way to put on a cross hedge, in what ratio to establish it, when to lift it, and so on can only be done by a trader who is in constant contact with the market, has a feel for spreads—when they are wide, when they are narrow, and how they will change if rate levels change. Every money market bank has in its dealing department exactly that sort of person, and it is thus not surprising that the first big use made by banks of financial futures was by money market banks hedging their dealer positions. It is also not surprising that these same banks were the first to use futures as an adjunct to cash market operations in altering their interest rate exposure. Expertise in futures is fungible; a bank that has developed it to serve one need can use it to serve others.

Small banks do not and are never going to have the equivalent of a Chase or Morgan bill trader to do their hedging. Fortunately, the most obvious use to which they should put financial futures does not require that level of expertise. A bank does not need a hot-shot bill trader to hedge its MMC costs. It can simply make it a rule to short bill futures whenever it fears that rates will rise and it knows that the MMCs it is currently issuing or has outstanding will have to be rolled at maturity. Also, by shopping around, such a bank can find astute people in the dealer community who will give it guidance.

Impact of margin calls[5]

Expertise in the form of taking on and putting off hedges in response to changes in an institution's view as to where interest rates are headed is extremely important for a bank or S&L that hedges. Any position in futures exposes the holder to the danger of large margin calls; these will occur either (1) if rates move *rapidly* in a direction opposite from what the institution hedging fears they might or (2) if the hedging institution maintains its position in futures in the face of continuing unfavorable (for its position in futures) rate changes for a long period or, worse still, until its futures contracts mature.

A bank or S&L considering using futures should be aware that, all too often, the potentially productive strategy of hedging is illustrated in exchange literature and by people selling futures (called *futures commission merchants* or *FCMs*) with simplistic examples that ignore the pitfalls which may change the outcomes of hedges put on by the unwary. One such pitfall is that futures prices often are more volatile than cash prices.

A second, often ignored pitfall of hedging is the possibility of margin calls. When a hedger buys or sells futures, the opposite side of the transaction is taken by some other trader in futures. Each trader's contractual obligation is, however, not with his counterpart in the trade, but with the exchange. An exchange, in making itself the opposite party to both sides of every trade, assumes risk.

To control that risk, the exchange requires every trader to put up some minimum margin when he buys or sells futures. The trader will incur gains or losses as the price of the futures contracts he has bought or sold fluctuates. The amount of each day's gain (loss) is added to (subtracted from) the trader's margin account at the end of the day. Consequently, a trader starts each day having realized, through additions to or deductions from his margin account, his net gain or loss on his position since he put it on. The margin system converts, on a daily basis, what would otherwise be paper gains and losses into realized gains and losses.

---

[5] The following section is excerpted from Marcia Stigum, "Margin Call Possibility Is Pitfall Often Ignored With Futures," *The Money Manager*, September 22, 1980, pp. 12–13.

If the balance in a trader's margin account falls below the maintenance margin required by the exchange, he must immediately deposit additional *cash* in this account. Should he fail to do so, his broker is required to close out his position. If a trader has profited and his margin account has risen above the initial required amount, he may withdraw the excess money.

Risk in margin calls.   Often a hedger will establish a position in futures based on an idea of where he thinks interest rates are headed. For example, he might fear a rise in rates and sell futures to lock in a price at which he could later sell cash securities he owns. Or, he might fear a fall in rates and buy futures to lock in a favorable lending rate at some later date.

Whenever the contingency against which the hedger seeks to protect himself occurs, his position in futures will generate profits; these profits mean that funds, which he may withdraw and invest, will be deposited in his margin account. Conversely whenever the reverse occurs, that is, whenever rates move in a direction that would have been favorable to the hedger had he not hedged, the hedger—to maintain his position in futures—must deposit additional funds in his margin account.

The need to make an initial margin deposit and the possibility of subsequent fluctuations in that balance establish a real but often ignored source of uncertainty in the outcome of a hedge. If a hedge generates cash, obviously the hedger is better off because he has additional funds to invest or otherwise use. If the hedge results in substantial margin calls, the hedger may incur a significant unanticipated cost.

That cost is often ignored on the grounds that a large institutional hedger may put up income-earning Treasury bills instead of cash to meet initial margin requirements and such an institution may well have many positions in futures with the result that losses on one position are offset by gains on another.

Cost of margin calls.   The costs and risk associated with possible margin calls should not be lightly dismissed. A futures position that turns out to be unprofitable can—even when the losses on the futures position are fully offset by gains on the cash position—lead to costs large enough to materially affect the outcome of the hedge.

Consider, for example, the following scenario where the numbers were drawn from Liorex Corp.'s data base on futures. On September 9, 1979, a bank anticipating a decline in long-term interest rates decides to buy bond futures. It does not want to take delivery, and it anticipates that a fall in interest rates will affect the price of a far-out contract more than that of the maturing contract, so it buys June futures on the Chicago Board of Trade at 88-4. The portfolio manager expects to purchase approximately $1 million of bonds, so he buys 10 futures contracts with each bond having a face value of $100,000. The investor must put up a margin of $1,500 on each contract, so his initial margin deposit totals $15,000. The minimum margin it must subsequently maintain is $750 per contract or $7,500 in total.

Initial and maintenance margins differ from contract to contract and from exchange to exchange. An exchange may also, in response to changes in market conditions, alter its margin requirements at any time.

In the weeks that follow the establishment of this anticipatory long hedge, the market deteriorates. In early October, the Fed produces its famous, or more aptly infamous, "Saturday night special"—a tightening which caused a sharp rise in market rates. As a result of these developments, the following margin calls have to be met by our hedger: $8,125 on September 27, $9,275 on October 5, $9,062.50 on October 8, and $9,500 on October 9.

On October 10, our hedger, either because the time horizon for its hedge was short or because it has become convinced that the market is headed in only one direction—South—closes out its futures position at 83-12. Net on its position in futures, our hedger, who bought futures at 88–4, has incurred a loss of 152/32 (CBOT bond futures are priced in 32ds). Each 32d, or tick as it is called, on a CBOT futures contract for $100,000 of bonds is worth $31.25. Our investor's total loss on his 10-contract futures position is

$$152 \times \$31.25 \times 10 = \$47,500$$

Our hedger also has incurred a hidden loss due to the margin calls. To figure it, we assume the institution put up initial margin using Treasury bills which it would have held in any case and that the initial margin deposit was costless to it. Note this assumption would be inappropriate for any institution which had to borrow to buy the bills because the carry on a bill position at that time would have been negative even for banks which have access to the lowest borrowing rate in town, repo rate.

To meet margin calls, our hedger who puts up cash, incurs either an outright cost because it must borrow funds or an opportunity cost because it must forego investing elsewhere the funds he used.

Assume that our institution determines the annualized cost it incurs in putting up funds to meet margin calls is 15 percent. This means the total interest cost it incurs to meet margin calls, the cost of $8,125 for 13 days, of $9,275 for 5 days, etc., totals $750 over the 30-day hedge period. Since the value of $1/32$ on bonds having a face value of $1 million is $312.50, meeting margin calls adds 2.4 32ds to the price at which our institution eventually acquires its bonds.

Since the yield value of $1/32$ is small on a bond with a current maturity of 15 years or more, one could argue that from a long-term perspective, this extra cost is of small significance. It is also true that the cost of meeting margin calls on the bond hedge put on by our institution would have been vastly greater had it maintained that position over a number of months.

It is also of interest to note that, had our hedger sought to lock in a 10.50 rate on $1 million of three-month bills by buying bills futures at 10.50, the $750 cost of meeting margin calls would have lowered the effective rate at which it purchased its bills by (assuming delivery was taken) 30 basis points to 10.20.

Financing cash securities.   Buying futures is not the only way to lock in a future lending rate. Another is to buy cash securities and finance them for some period with term repo. Buying futures offers the advantage of liquidity. Buying cash securities and financing them offers the advantage that carry may be positive at times. Our example suggests that an institution that does not need liquidity should, if it can find a borrower who will not demand that collateral be repriced during the period of the loan, consider the alternative of buying cash securities and carrying them, even if carry is zero.

ACCOUNTING PROBLEMS

A second reason banks use futures less than they might has to do with the accounting treatment currently mandated for bank positions in futures. A bank is offered the option of carrying its futures position at market or at the lower of cost or market. In a volatile rate environment, this means essentially that a bank has to mark its futures positions to market every day, just as it does its dealer position.

All profits and losses that a bank realizes by marking its futures position to market run right through its P&L statement to the bottom line. This is distressing to a bank that wants to hedge fixed-rate loans, because it is likely that, for some period before the bank actually books such a loan, fluctuations in the values of the futures contracts used to hedge the loan will run through the bank's P&L statement, thereby introducing an unwelcome element of instability in its earnings.

The Federal Savings and Loan Insurance Corporation (FSLIC) has declared that S&Ls may use accrual accounting on legitimate hedges, e.g., hedging the cost of MMC money due to be rolled X months hence. No equivalent ruling has yet been made for banks. The accounting firm, Arthur Andersen, has concluded in a written opinion that, if a bank is hedging a cash asset or liability or something that will occur in the future (e.g., a fixed-rate loan to be taken down X months hence), the bank should use accrual accounting in making up a profit and loss statement for its shareholders, but that it should use marked-to-market figures in preparing reports to the Fed. This requires that banks go to the trouble and expense of keeping two sets of books. A number of banks have taken this approach so that they can use financial futures to offer their customers fixed-rate loans, the risk on which they hedge in the futures market.

The Financial Accounting Standards Board (FASB) recognizes that futures accounting is a serious problem, and, by the end of 1982, it is expected to make a definitive rule on how banks should account for futures transactions. Ideally what banks want and what they are seeking from the FASB and from legislation is a rule that any speculative positions they take should be marked to market, but that true hedges should be accounted for on an accrual basis.

Regulatory constraints

One rather ludicrous dictate that came down from the Comptroller of the Currency was that national banks could use financial futures only to hedge. A well-run bank seeks to manage its interest rate exposure in a reasoned and thoughtful way with due regard to controlling risk. Within that context, it might want to use futures to diminish, increase, change the direction of, or otherwise alter its interest rate exposure. Is every such use of futures a hedge? Define the term broadly enough, and the answer is yes. Moreover, whatever a bank has in mind when it takes a position in futures, it can always argue ex post that it was doing a hedge in whatever narrow sense a regulator chooses to define the term.

The rules and guidelines issued by regulators with respect to how banks may use financial futures have been and continue to be subject to revision. Currently, most banks are subject to guidelines put out by the Fed and the FDIC and/or to state regulations that closely follow the federal guidelines. Key guidelines currently imposed by federal regulators include:

1. Banks that engage in futures, forward, and standby contract transactions should do so only in accordance with safe and sound banking practices.
2. Such transactions should be of a size reasonably related to the bank's business needs and to its capacity to fulfill obligations incurred.
3. The positions banks take in futures, forward, and standby contracts should be such as to reduce the bank's exposure to loss through interest rate changes.
4. Policy objectives should be formulated in light of the bank's entire mix of assets and liabilities.

5. Standby contracts calling for settlement in excess of 150 days should not be issued by banks except in special circumstances and, ordinarily, such long-term standby contracts would be viewed by the agencies as being inappropriate.

None of these guidelines is particularly helpful to an institution using futures. Guidelines 1, 2, and 4 boil down to a statement that a bank should be well managed. So should every business. Unfortunately, it is the nature of free enterprise that a bad manager will rise to the top of the pile every now and then, often with calamitous consequences for the institution he manages. That fact of life is one that no pious call for every bank to be well managed will change. If guideline 3 were taken seriously and applied to a bank's operations in the cash market as well as in the futures market, it would put most of the nation's money market banks out of business.

Thrifts

In July 1981, the Federal Home Loan Bank greatly loosened the restrictions it had imposed on the use of futures by S&Ls. Under its previous rules, the nation's nearly 4,000 federally insured S&Ls were permitted only to short GNMA futures and to hold a total short position equaling no more than 5 percent of their assets. In effect, until July 1981, regulators told S&Ls that they were free to bankrupt themselves by issuing $200 billion of high-cost MMCs, but they could not hedge the ever-escalating cost of issuing this paper by shorting bill futures.

Finally, at the eleventh hour for the industry, the FHLB permitted S&Ls to short any futures contract based on a security in which they may legally invest—treasuries, CDs, and GNMA futures—to hedge holdings of these securities. Like the good regulator it is, the FHLB solemnly described the new regulations as an opportunity for S&Ls to henceforth be better managed. That gratuitous remark was akin to a doctor giving a patient he has kept on a starvation diet for a dangerously long period a cookbook for a healthy diet, which the patient will surely find highly useful if he survives the doctor's previous ministrations.

PICKING A CONTRACT

In the examples used in this chapter, the hedging medium used is often bill futures. In 1981, several exchanges began trading 90-day domestic CD futures; later, the international money market added a 90-day Euro time deposit futures contract. For certain purposes, a bank will find CD and time deposit futures a better hedging vehicle than bill futures. There is also an active and growing market in futures for Treasury notes with 6½-to-10-year maturity and carrying an 8 percent coupon, and for Treasury bonds with 20-year maturity and carrying an 8 percent coupon.

Our concern in this chapter was to point out the productive opportunities that exist for a bank or thrift to use futures in managing its assets and liabilities. Whether it should use bill, CD or other futures contracts will depend on its needs and the conditions prevailing in the various futures markets.

The first concern of an institution using futures to hedge should be that the market for the instrument it intends to buy or sell is sufficiently broad and active so that it can deal in the size it needs and be assured of liquidity.

In July 1982, daily volume in the IMM bill futures contract averaged over 25,000 contracts, which represents a total of over $20 billion of bills. In contrast, the exchanges trading futures contracts for CDs and Euro time deposits were doing a daily volume that averaged only 1 to 3,000 contracts per day, which represented a total of $5 billion of CDs. Which of the existing and proposed CD and Euro futures will survive is open to question. An interesting precedent is that, when the New York Futures Exchange (NYFE) opened its CD contract, volume in its bond contract dropped from almost 1,000 contracts a day to a few per day; then the NYFE CD contract itself died off as other exchanges opened similar contracts.

A large bank wondering whether to use bill, domestic CD, or Euro futures to hedge should ask whether the futures market in which it is considering taking a position has the volume for it to move in size and whether its continued liquidity is assured. A small bank considering using CD futures need worry less about market volume but should be concerned with continuing liquidity. Normally, hedges are unwound not by making or taking delivery, but by making an offsetting trade. Thus, market liquidity is crucial at both ends of a hedge. A hedger who took a position in the NYFE bond contract before NYFE introduced its CD contracts eventually found himself long or short a bill, bond, or contract which ceased to trade.

Moral: If you are going to hedge, don't use a contract that is or might be moribund when you want out. The history of financial futures is that many contracts have been introduced, a few were huge successes, but most quickly died or became inactive.

Acting as FCMs

Once banks get into the business of using futures to hedge, a natural extension for them of this activity is to act as *futures commission merchants (FCMs)* for their customers who want to do their own hedging.

Morgan was the first bank holding company to get from Federal Reserve Board permission to have a subsidiary to act as an FCM (futures commission merchant) for bills, bonds, CDs, and related financial futures. Because the Fed had previously approved bank holding company applications to act as futures commission merchants in bullion and foreign exchange, it was a forgone conclusion that the Fed would grant Morgan's request. Presumably, many other bank holding companies, especially the large ones, will follow Morgan's lead and open up their own FCM subsidiaries.

Appendix

The basics of financial futures and hedging[1]

The most dramatic and successful innovation in the money market in recent years has been the introduction of trading in futures contracts for financial instruments. This innovation has enabled market participants of all types—dealers, investors, and primary borrowers—to engage in a wide range of transactions that were hitherto either impossible or often unproductive because of high transaction costs.

BILL FUTURES

In January 1976, the International Monetary Market (IMM), now part of the Chicago Mercantile Exchange (CME), opened trading in futures contracts for 3-month Treasury bills. The initial reception of bill futures by the street was marked by uncertainty and coolness. Nevertheless, the volume of contracts traded in the bill futures market rose rapidly and dramatically. In fact, the market in bill futures came to be used more widely and more rapidly than any futures market ever had been.

---

[1] This appendix is adapted in part from Chapter 11 of Marcia Stigum in collaboration with John Mann, *Money Market Calculations: Yields, Break-Evens, and Arbitrage* (Homewood, Ill.: Dow Jones-Irwin, 1981).

The contract

The basic contract traded on the IMM is for $1 million of 90-day Treasury bills. Currently, a contract matures once each quarter, in the third weeks of March, June, September, and December. There are eight contracts outstanding, so when a new contract starts to trade, the furthest delivery date stretches 24 months into the future. After initiation of trading in bill futures by the IMM, other exchanges sought, without success, to trade similar contracts.

Price quotes

Bills trade and are quoted in the *cash market* on a yield basis. Consequently, the bid price always exceeds the offering price. Also, when yield rises, price falls, and vice versa. This seems reasonable to a person accustomed to trading money market instruments, but confuses someone used to trading commodities or stocks. The IMM therefore decided not to quote bill contracts directly in terms of yield. Instead it developed an *index* system in which a bill is quoted at a "price" equal to 100.00 minus yield; a bill yield of 14.50 would thus be quoted on the IMM at 85.50. Note that in this system, when yield goes down, the index price goes up, and the trader with a long position in futures profits. This conforms to the relationship that prevails in other commodity futures markets, where long positions profit when prices rise, short positions when prices fall.

Price fluctuations on a bill futures contract are in multiples of an 01, one basis point. Because the contract is for delivery of 90-day bills, each 01 is worth $25.

OTHER CONTRACTS

Since the inception of trading in bill futures, different exchanges have launched trading in various contracts, most of which have failed. As of this writing, there were—in addition to currency futures traded on the IMM—five successful contracts against debt instruments: the IMM's 90-day bill futures, CD futures, and Euro time deposit contracts, and the Chicago Board of Trade's contracts for Treasury bonds and Government National Mortgage Association (GNMA) certificates.

To illustrate our discussion of how futures are used, we will limit our examples largely to bill futures for several reasons: a bank's trader is most likely to start using bill futures; bill futures make a good hedge for MMCs; and the contrast between the volume and liquidity in the IMM bill futures market and that in the CD futures markets means that, currently, large banks often find it more useful to hedge using bill futures than CD futures.

New futures markets are scheduled for introduction in Bermuda (the world's first automated futures exchange, INTEX) and in London (the London International Financial Futures Exchange, LIFFE) existing U.S. exchanges are also proposing new contracts; finally, the Commodities Futures Trading Commission (CFTC) has proposed permitting (1) the introduction of trading on U.S. exchanges of commodity options and of options on futures, (2) the sale to U.S. citizens of such securities traded on recognized foreign exchanges, and (3), together with the SEC, the trading of futures contracts based on equity indexes.

By early 1982, futures contracts based on the Value Line Stock Index, the S&P Index, and the NYSE Index were already trading.

The INTEX market in Bermuda is seeking to set up a highly innovative exchange, one that would break with a several-hundred-year tradition of having all exchange trading in futures done by open outcry in a pit on the exchange floor. All trading on INTEX would be done via a computer-based, *worldwide, automated* system that could easily be operated 24 hours a day. INTEX's automated system will considerably benefit not only market players who want speed of execution and confirmation, but foreign participants who prefer to sleep while Chicago trades.

Market participants

The principal participants in futures markets are speculators, hedgers, arbitrageurs, and spreaders. About speculators there is little need for explanation: these individuals buy or sell futures contracts in the hope of gain. When futures prices rise or fall sharply, to the dismay of one group or another, the blame is often placed incorrectly on speculators. Actually these much maligned individuals, who statistics show lose money more often than not, perform a function essential to any futures market; they assume risks that others—namely hedgers—seek to shed.

Hedgers, arbitrageurs, and spreaders will be dealt with later in our discussion.

HEDGING

A portfolio manager who sells bill futures to limit the risk on a long position in bills and a portfolio manager who buys bill futures to lock in a rate at which he can invest an anticipated cash inflow are both managing risk by *hedging. To hedge using financial futures is to assume a position in futures equal and opposite to an existing or anticipated position, which may be short or long, in cash or cash securities.*

Delivery

An important point to note about hedging through the purchase or sale of either commodity or financial futures contracts is that delivery need not be and usually is not made or taken in connection with a hedge. Normally, hedges and speculative positions as well are closed out by making an offsetting trade in the same contract. Some newer and proposed contracts (Euro and stock index contracts) are doing away with delivery by specifying cash settlement.

The hedger attempts to put himself in a position where any loss he incurs on his cash position in the commodity (e.g., he is long and price in the cash market drops) will be offset by an equal gain on his futures position. He can accomplish this by establishing a position in futures and later closing it out. The speculator who neither owns nor desires to own the underlying commodity can also realize whatever gain or loss he makes on his speculation simply by closing out his position in futures.

If a hedger, speculator, or other futures market participant wants to make or take delivery, he is, in almost all markets, free to do so. A trader who maintains an open position in such a market at the expiration of a futures contract must settle it by making or taking delivery.

A perfect hedge

Consider an investor who has money to invest for three months and is unwilling to assume market risk. He can (1) buy a 3-month bill and allow it to mature or (2) buy a 6-month bill and sell a bill futures contract expiring 3 months hence. If he does the latter, i.e., buys the 6-month bill and hedges his resulting future long position in a 3-month bill, he will have succeeded in eliminating *all* market risk from his position in the 6-month bill, even though he will hold it for only 3 months. A hedge established using a futures contract whose expiration date precisely fits the hedger's time horizon and on which the deliverable instrument corresponds to the instrument being hedged is a *perfect hedge*.

Imperfect hedges

In practice, *hedges are common but perfect hedges are rare.* The reason is that the standardization of futures contracts required for them to be actively traded and to have liquidity is such that the hedger is normally unable to find a futures position that will give him a perfect offset to his position in the cash market. He has to settle, if you will, for a ready-made rather than a tailor-made suit, and he willingly does so for good reasons: the ability to strike a trade, the liquidity of the position he assumes, and the protection against risk of default that the futures contract offers him.

Typically, a hedger using financial futures will find that the hedge he establishes is *imperfect* for one or both of two reasons: (1) the contract's expiration date does not precisely match the time horizon in which he anticipates dealing, e.g., he sells bill futures against a position in the deliverable bill which he intends to liquidate before the futures contract expires; or (2) he has or anticipates acquiring a position in some instrument other than the deliverable security, e.g., he sells T bill futures to hedge an intended sale of 3-month CDs or an anticipated short-term borrowing need. Hedging a cash position in one security by assuming a futures position in a different but similar security is known as a *cross hedge*.

Whenever a market participant undertakes a cross hedge to control risk in a speculative position—long or short—in cash or cash securities, the precise outcome of that hedge is uncertain. How closely his gain (loss) on his futures position will track his loss (gain) on his position in cash or the cash security will depend on how the *spread* (*basis* in commodity jargon) between the rate on the futures contract and that on the cash instrument hedged changes from the time he puts on the hedge until he takes it off.

A perfect long hedge

To illustrate hedging we will consider a few examples. First, a *perfect long hedge*.

Suppose that an investor's cash-flow projections tell him that he will have a big sum of cash to invest short term in the future; that is, he is going to be *long* in investable cash. He can simply wait to invest until he gets the cash and take the rate then prevailing, or, as soon as his projections tell him how much cash he is going to have, he can lock in a lending rate by buying bill futures.

Table A–1 illustrates this. We assume that our investor knows in June that he will have $10 million of 3-month money to invest in September, and that, when September arrives, he will invest that money in bills. In June, the September bill contract is trading at 10.50. If our investor buys 10 of these contracts, he will earn 10.50 on the money he invests in September, regardless of the rate at which the cash 3-month bill is then trading.

One way he could get the 10.50 rate would be to take delivery in September of the bills he purchased at 10.50. But, to see the nature of the hedge, we assume that when his cash comes in September, he closes out his futures position and buys cash bills.

As the September contract approaches maturity, it must trade at a yield close to and eventually equal to the rate at which the 3-month

Table A–1
A long hedge in T bill futures for bills with a $10 million face value

Step 1 (Thursday, third week of June): Purchase 10 September bill contracts at 10.50. Put up security deposit, and pay round-turn commission.

Step 2 (Wednesday, third week of September): Sell 10 futures contracts; buy cash bills.

Outcome 1: Cash 91-day bill trading at 10.20.
Sell September contracts at 10.20.

Delivery value of futures at sale	$ 9,745,000
– Delivery value of futures at purchase	9,737,500
Profit on futures transactions	$ 7,500

Buy 91-day cash bills at 10.20

Purchase price of cash bills	$ 9,742,167
– Profit on futures transactions	7,500
Effective price of 91-day bills	$ 9,734,667

Calculate effective discount at which bills are purchased:

Face value	$10,000,000
– Effective purchase price	9,734,667
Discount at purchase	$ 265,333

Calculate effective discount rate, d, at which cash bills are purchased

$$d = \frac{D \times (360)}{F \times (91)} = \frac{\$265,333 \times (360)}{\$10,000,000 \times (91)}$$
$$= 0.1050$$
$$= 10.50\%$$

Outcome 2: Cash 91-day bill trading at 10.80.
Sell September contracts at 10.80.

Delivery value of futures at sale	$ 9,730,000
– Delivery value of futures at purchase	9,737,500
Loss on futures transaction	$ (7,500)

Buy 91-day cash bills at 10.80.

Purchase price of cash bills	$ 9,727,000
+ Loss on futures transaction	7,500
Effective price of 91-day bills	$ 9,734,500

Calculate effective discount at which bills are purchased:

Face value	$10,000,000
– Effective purchase price	9,734,500
Discount at purchase	$ 265,500

Calculate effective discount rate d at which cash bills are purchased.

$$d = \frac{D \times (360)}{F \times (91)} = \frac{\$265,500 \times (360)}{\$10,000,000 \times (91)}$$
$$= 0.1050$$
$$= 10.50\%$$

cash bill is trading. If a divergence existed between these two rates as trading in the contract terminated, potential for a profitable arbitrage would exist. For example, if, a few days before the September bill contract matured, it was trading at a much higher yield than the cash bill, traders would buy the contract, sell cash bills on a *when issued* basis (i.e., after the bill auction but before settlement), take delivery in Chicago to cover their short position in the cash bill, and profit on the transaction.[2]

In Outcome 1 (Table A–1), we assume that, as the September contract matures, the 91-day cash bill trades at 10.20 and the futures contract consequently also trades at 10.20. At this time, our investor sells his September contracts and buys the cash 3-month bill. He purchases his futures contracts at 10.50 and sells them at 10.20, a lower rate. Since the delivery value of the contracts is higher the lower the yield at which they trade, our investor makes (Table A–1) a $7,500 profit on his futures transaction.

When his profit on futures is deducted from the price at which he buys cash bills, he ends up paying an effective price for these bills that is $7,500 less than the actual price he pays. And this lower effective price implies that the yield he will earn on his investment is not 10.20, the rate at which he buys *cash bills,* but 10.50, the rate at which he bought bill futures.

Because the prevailing yield at which the cash 3-month bill was trading in September was lower than the rate at which our investor bought bill futures in June, he made money by engaging in a long hedge; that is, he earned a higher yield than he would have had he not hedged.

There is, however, a counterpart to this. As Outcome 2 in Table A–1 shows, if, in September, the cash 3-month bill were trading at 10.80, our investor would have lost so many dollars on his hedge that he would have earned only 10.50 on the money he invested.

Calculating in basis points. It is instructive to work out a hedge example in dollars and cents. However, it is quicker to do it in terms of basis points earned and lost. In our example, the investor buys September contracts at 10.50 and, according to Outcome 1, sells them at 10.20. On this transaction, he earns on each contract for $1 million of bills 30 90-day basis points. By buying the 3-month bill at 10.20 and maturing it, he earns 1020 90-day *basis points* per $1 million of bills

---

[2] In practice, a maturing bill futures contract will trade during the last few days of its life at a yield a few basis points higher than the deliverable cash bill. The difference reflects the extra commission and other transaction costs that an investor would incur if he bought bill futures and took delivery instead of purchasing 3-month bills in the cash market.

purchased. So *net* he earns 1050 90-day basis points per $1 million of bills purchased, a yield of 10.50 over 90 days.

Actually, the basis points earned on the cash bill are 91-day basis points and those earned on the futures contract are 90-day basis points. This difference, however, is not reflected in the numbers in Table A–1, because it affects yield earned only beyond the third decimal point.

The example we presented was a *perfect hedge*, because our investor bought a futures contract for precisely the instrument and precisely the maturity in which he planned to invest. In the case of a perfect hedge, the investor eliminates *all* risk.

Speculating on spread variation. Most investors who use the T bill futures market to hedge an anticipated long position in cash will find that the hedge they establish is *imperfect* for one or both of the following reasons:

1. Their projected investment period does not precisely match that of any futures contract or series of contracts.
2. They anticipate investing in some money market instrument other than a Treasury bill, e.g., commercial paper or bankers' acceptances.

When a hedge is imperfect, the hedger does not eliminate *all* risk. Instead, he shifts the nature of his speculation from *rate level* speculation to speculation on *spread variation*. A commodities trader would call the latter *basis risk*.

Example. Returning to our example, we now suppose that our investor's cash inflow will occur one month *before* the June contract expires. This means that, in closing out his hedge, he will sell the June contract one month before it expires and simultaneously buy the new cash bill.

At the time our investor sells his futures contract, he will be selling the right to take delivery one month hence of the then 4-month bill, while he will be buying a 3-month bill. Typically, some spread exists between the rates yielded by the 3- and 4-month bills; the futures contract, because of arbitrage, should trade nearer the 4-month than the 3-month rate.

The arbitrage that causes this rate relationship is dual. If the futures contract yielded *less than* the 4-month bill one month before it expired, a profit could be made by buying that bill, selling a futures contract, and then unwinding this arbitrage when the futures contract expired. Note that, at that time, the rate on the futures contract and the rate on the deliverable bill must be equal because they are both prices for next-day delivery of the same cash bill. This arbitrage would tend to lower the yield on the cash bill and to raise the yield on the futures contract, thereby eliminating the discrepancy between rates on these instruments. If, alternatively, the rate on the futures contract exceeded that on the 4-month bill, it would be profitable to buy the futures contract and short the cash bill—an arbitrage that would also tend to close the divergence between these two rates. The profitability of these arbitrages depends, in the first instance, on the repo rate and, in the second, on the reverse rate. Since these rates vary in relationship to bill rates, it is uncertain how close the futures contract one month from maturity will trade to the 4-month bill.

To continue our example, we next assume that, at the time our investor enters his hedge, the yield curve is upward sloping and the spread between the 3- and 4-month bills is 10 basis points. Assuming that (1) there is no change in that spread, and (2) the futures contract trades 1 month before expiration at a rate equal to the rate on the 4-month bill, the rate our investor will actually earn as a result of his hedge will be 10.40 that is, the 10.50 rate at which he bought the futures contract *minus* the 10 basis point spread between the rate at which he sold it and the rate on the new 3-month bill. Also, so long as our two spread assumptions hold, this result will occur whether the investor sells his futures contract at a low yield (Outcome 1, Table A–1) or at a high yield (Outcome 2, Table A–1).

In practice, spreads, like rate levels, are not written in stone; they change. What our investor cares about is what happens to the spread between the rate at which he sells his futures contract and the rate on the new 3-month bill. If this spread *widens* by 10 basis points from the level assumed above, i.e., from 10 to 20 basis points, the yield our investor earns will *decrease* by a like amount from 10.50 to 10.30. If, alternatively, the spread *narrows* by 10 basis points, i.e., from 10 basis points to 0, the yield he earns will rise by a like amount, from 10.50 to 10.60.

To sum up, an investor who hedges a future long position in cash must take spread relationships into account in estimating the yield he will earn as a result of his hedge. These relationships, however, are subject to variation. Therefore, the investor cannot know with certainty what return an imperfect hedge will yield, and it is in that sense that *a hedger shifts his risk from rate level speculation to speculation on spread (or basis) variation.*

Earlier we said that a second reason a long hedge is likely to be imperfect is that the investor who hedges intends to buy an instrument other than a T bill. Suppose the investor in our example intended to buy a 3-month CD and that CDs were trading, at the time he bought his futures contract, at a 30 basis point spread to bills. Then, in establishing a long hedge, our investor would be exchanging a natural speculative position on rate levels (generated by his anticipated cash inflow) for a speculation on the spread X months hence between either

(1) the rates on cash 3-month bills and cash 3-month CDs, or (2) the rates on an unexpired bill futures contract and cash 3-month CDs.

When a short futures position in one instrument (e.g., bills) is used to hedge a long position in some *other* instrument (e.g., CDs), the hedge is called a *cross hedge*.

Short hedges

The T bill futures market can also be used to hedge either a long position in money market securities or a future borrowing need. To illustrate, consider a perfect *short* hedge.

Suppose that an investor who has money to invest for three months is unwilling to accept any market risk. We assume that a 6-month bill yields more than a 3-month bill, and that the 6-month bill 3 months hence will be the 3-month bill deliverable when the nearest futures contract expires. In the absence of a futures market, our investor would have no choice but to buy the 3-month bill and allow it to mature. However, given the futures market, he should investigate the relationship among the rates on the 3-month bill, the 6-month bill, and the nearest futures contract. This relationship may be such that, without incurring market risk, he could earn more by buying the 6-month bill and selling the nearest futures contract than by buying and "maturing" the cash 3-month bill. Note that buying the 6-month bill and selling the nearest futures contract against it converts this bill into a 3-month bill, but the return on that bill will differ from that on the 3-month cash bill.

Most short hedges are *imperfect* for one or both of the same reasons that apply to long hedges: (1) a discrepancy exists between the period over which the hedge is needed and the life of any one or series of futures contracts; and (2) the instrument or borrowing need being hedged does not correspond to the instrument traded in the futures market.

Examples of imperfect hedges are easy to find:

1. Because of rate expectations, an investor wants to swap out of a long bill into a shorter bill, but for tax or other reasons he prefers not to do the swap in the cash market. He can obtain essentially the same result by selling bill futures against the long cash bill, but there is a maturity mismatch.
2. An investor or dealer uses the sale of T bill futures to hedge a long position in CDs or BAs against a rise in interest rates.
3. A corporation sells bill futures to hedge an anticipated need to borrow short term from its bank.

In each of these cases, the outcome of the hedge will depend on what happens to spread relationships. Thus, the short hedger, like the long hedger, is shifting his risk from rate level speculation to speculation on spread (basis) variation.

A cross hedge: Bill futures against prime

As an example of a cross hedge, consider a corporate treasurer who, on October 1, 1979, sold $5 million of the March bill futures contract to hedge the cost of a $5 million short-term bank loan that he expected to take out in early February 1980. At the date he puts on his hedge, the March 90-day bill contract is selling at 90.34 which corresponds to a yield of 9.66, and the prime rate is 13.25 percent. On February 5, 1980, he closes out his position in futures and borrows $5 million from his bank. At that time, the futures contract is selling at 87.86, which corresponds to a 12.14 yield, and prime is 15.25 percent.

What has the hedger accomplished? A great deal. During the time his hedge was on, the prime rate rose by 200 basis points and the rate on the March bill futures contract rose by 262 basis points. Because it was politically difficult for the banks to raise prime to a level corresponding to their marginal cost of funds, the spread between the rate on the March contract and the prime rate actually narrowed, and the $32,750 profit the hedger made unwinding his position in futures actually *exceeded* the extra cost he incurred in borrowing $5 million for 90 days because of the 200 basis point jump in the prime rate.[3]

Speculation on a spread. A futures market participant who engages in a cross hedge *shifts* his risk from a speculation on a rate or price level to a *speculation on a spread.* He does *not* eliminate risk; instead, he *shifts* the nature of the risk he assumes. Normally, he also reduces the amount of risk he assumes because *he shifts the focus of his speculation from a highly variable rate or price level to a less variable spread,* as a commodities trader would say, he assumes *basis risk.*

Many would-be hedgers do not grasp this crucial point, in part because hedging is frequently described as a form of insurance, which it is not. A person buying insurance sheds a risk by paying an insurer to accept that risk; the insurer is able to do this because it pools many independent risks, e.g., the risks of Jones, Smith, etc., each dying.

---

[3] To state the precise before and after values of the spread on which the hedger is speculating, one must convert the bill rate, which is quoted on a discount basis, to a simple interest basis and adjust the prime rate to account for the cost of holding compensating balances. Assuming a 20 percent balance requirement, the spread between the two rates was 666 basis points at the beginning of the hedge and 648 at the end. For the calculations involved, see Stigum and Mann *Money Market Calculations.* Had the borrower negotiated a smaller and currently more typical balance requirement, the rise in the spread between the two would have been even greater.

Reducing risk through pooling, the principle on which insurance works, has nothing to do with hedging. The hedger eliminates risk arising from a speculative position in cash or cash securities by taking an offsetting position in futures. Moreover, because the fit between his hedge and the position he is hedging is imperfect, by hedging he assumes a new risk; namely, he speculates on the rate spread between the cash and the futures instruments.

Imaginative hedging strategies

We have defined hedging as assuming a position in futures equal and opposite to an existing or anticipated position, which may be negative or positive, in cash or cash instruments. As our observation that hedging involves speculation on a spread suggests, this definition does *not* imply that the best way to hedge a cash position is necessarily to sell (buy) a futures contract that most nearly corresponds in maturity to the long (short) position being hedged.

Consider, again, the example of a corporate treasurer who knows he must borrow several months hence. Suppose he not only fears that the Fed might tighten, but believes circumstances are such that, if the Fed does, the yield curve will steepen. Given this, his best hedge would be to sell, not the futures contract maturing several months hence when he must borrow, but a longer contract, because the latter would lose more value than a nearby contract if the eventuality he feared, namely tightening by the Fed and a consequent steepening of the yield curve, occurred.

For a second example of imaginative hedging, consider an investor who will be long cash three months hence and wants to invest then in the 2-year maturity range. The yield curve is inverted; the investor fears that the Fed might ease shortly and believes that, if it does, the yield curve will flatten. His best hedge is not to buy a *strip* of eight consecutive futures contracts, i.e., a "synthetic 2-year note," but rather to buy eight of some long futures contract. If his fears are realized, the value of a long contract will rise more than that of shorter contracts.

Speculation on spread variation

To say that speculation on spread variation arises from "imperfect" hedges suggests that it is unfortunate that there are insufficient numbers and types of futures contracts to eliminate all risk by entering a perfect hedge. This view corresponds with the academic view of hedging, which is that the purpose of hedging is to eliminate price risk, not to create an opportunity to profit from a different sort of speculation. In textbooks, hedging is viewed as a form of insurance which has a cost that, like the electric bill, is part of normal business operating expenses.

For an investor or borrower to hedge a position—negative or positive—in cash does, in fact, insulate his business activity from price level speculation. However, it also *retains* for him the *opportunity to speculate on spread (basis) variation*. Moreover, as our examples suggest, such speculation can become a source of profit as opposed to a cost. In this respect, two comments are important. First, speculation on spread variation did not arise in the money and bond markets after and as a result of the introduction of trading in financial futures. Quite the contrary, it has long been common. A dealer or investor who, in anticipation of a fall in rates, buys a 10-year Treasury bond and simultaneously shorts—to minimize risk—an 8-year issue is doing a *bull market arbitrage* that is nothing more or less than speculating on spread variation. Many other transactions commonly done by dealers and investors are a form of speculation on a spread. What the introduction of futures trading did was to provide a vastly more efficient and less costly mechanism for taking forward positions, long and short, and a liquid market in which such forward positions could be traded.

A second important point is that the use of hedging to minimize price level speculation while simultaneously speculating on spread variation is not an innovation fathered by money market participants. Firms that produce, process, or use commodities for which futures markets exist have long understood that speculation on spread, or basis, is a potential source of profit, and they have worked to profit from it.

Once speculation on spreads is viewed as a potential profit center, it becomes clear that hedging should not be viewed as an automatic and thoughtless operation, e.g., an investor has money coming in three months hence so he buys the most nearly corresponding futures contract. Instead, hedging is an intricate activity. To succeed at it, the participant should know what spreads have been historically and what factors cause them to change. In establishing a hedge, he should also try to predict how events are most likely to affect the spreads involved in his hedge. Finally, if the unanticipated occurs, he must be prepared to alter his hedge.

The suggestion that investors, dealers, and borrowers should consider hedging as a form of potentially profitable speculation is not inconsistent with the suggestion that hedging should be used as a tool to manage risk. Any institution that holds a portfolio or anticipates borrowing is inescapably speculating on changes in rate level, since it is impossible to be long or short cash and do otherwise. To hedge and thus speculate on spread variation, is to trade one form of speculation (on a *naked* long or short position) for another, typically *less risky*, form.

ARBITRAGE

Controlling the risk associated with an actual or anticipated position in cash or cash securities by hedging is one use to which bond and money market participants put futures contracts. Another is as a tool for effecting *arbitrages*. Economists, who have a fixation for *certain* outcomes, long ago defined an arbitrage as a transaction in which the arbitrageur simultaneously buys something at one price in one market and resells it at a higher price in another market (or some more complicated variation on this theme). Such an arbitrage locks in a *certain* profit for the arbitrageur. It also works through its effect on supply and demand in different markets to bring prices in these markets into line—their being out of line is the basis for the certain profit earned by the arbitrageur on his trade.

Opportunities for highly profitable, riskless arbitrages occur only infrequently in the real world which is characterized by instantaneous communications between different markets. Yet street people constantly talk about doing arbitrages or, as they are wont to call them, *arbs*. To a street person, an arbitrage involves taking two offsetting positions, e.g., a long and a short position in cash securities or in cash securities and futures contracts, such that, if the spread between the rates at which the securities involved trade moves in an anticipated direction, the arbitrageur will be able to close out his long and short positions at a profit.

Traders put on arbitrages because they believe that spreads are out of line with what they should be now or with what they must converge to in the future. Thus, street arbitrages are a form of speculation on a spread, one in which the street has long engaged. The use of arbitrage to describe such speculation is not wholly inappropriate, however much economists may protest. Normally, such arbitrages involve a highly favorable gamble, that is, one on which the odds strongly favor the spread moving in the direction in which the arbitrageur bets it will. Moreover, because of this, the street's "risky arbitrages," like the economist's certain ones, work to pull prices into a rational pattern. The one crucial difference is that the prices being pulled into line are prices of different instruments or different maturities of the same instrument rather than prices of the same instrument traded in different markets.

The opening of markets for financial futures created a new set of instruments whose prices could be arbitraged, and street traders now frequently arbitrage between cash instruments and futures contracts and between different futures contracts. Because of the newness of the futures market, the profit opportunities it offers to arbitrageurs have been substantial, and the consequent high level of their activity has been productive in two senses: It has added liquidity to futures markets, and it has ensured that various prices, e.g., that between a futures contract and the corresponding deliverable security, bear a reasonable relationship to each other.

SPREADING

A hedger is typically shifting his risk from a speculation on rate levels to a speculation on spread variation. A speculator with no position in cash or cash securities to hedge can also speculate on spread variation. Such speculation, which is referred to as *spreading* calls for the trader to short one contract and go long in a neighboring contract on the expectation that the spread between the two contracts will either narrow or widen. Here's an example. In normal markets, the yield curve is steep at its base and then gradually flattens. Suppose, for illustration, that, in the futures market, the yield curve has the shape pictured in Figure A–1. The yield spread between the two contracts nearest

Figure A–1
Yields on bill futures contracts expiring in 3 to 15 months

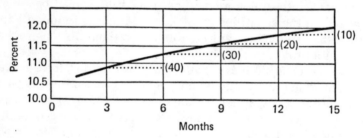

maturity is 40 basis points; there are 30 basis points between the second and third contracts, 20 between the third and fourth contracts, and 10 between the fourth and fifth contracts. The spreader assumes that, as the more distant contracts approach maturity, spreads between them will widen. Given this expectation, he might short the contract maturing in 12 months and buy the contract maturing in 9 months. If, over the next 6 months, the spread between these contracts widened from 20 to 40 basis points, he would be able to close out his position at a 20 basis point profit.

He earns a profit because, if the spread widens, the price of the futures contract in which he is long will rise in value relative to that in which he is short. Whether yields rise or fall over the holding period is immaterial to whether he profits or not. What counts is that the spread widens. His principal risk of loss is thus that the yield curve will flatten so dramatically that the spread between the contracts in which he is long and short will narrow rather than widen.

Spread traders are an important and permanent component of futures pits. A spreader who sees selling in the March contract but knows that there is a bid in the Junes will buy the Marches, sell the Junes, wait until the pressure is off the Marches, and then turn the position around. Spreaders account for over half of trading volume in the longer contracts. In carrying out operations of the above sort, spreaders perform an important market function—providing liquidity to the longer contracts.

TREASURY BOND FUTURES

T bill futures are useful for hedging short-term positions and for speculating on changes in short-term interest rates and/or the shape of the yield curve at the short end. For the manager of a portfolio of long-term bonds, there is a second interesting futures contracts, namely that for Treasury bonds.

Hedging with T bond futures

Our remarks about the usefulness of T bill futures as a hedging device all apply to T bond futures, as well. The latter can be used to hedge an anticipated cash inflow or, if the portfolio manager anticipates a rise in interest rates, to hedge a long position in bonds, governments, or corporates.

Here are a few examples. A portfolio manager who anticipates an inflow of cash and fears a fall in interest rates could buy T bond futures to lock in a future long-term yield. Alternatively, a portfolio manager who holds bonds and fears tightening by the Fed could liquidate his portfolio to prevent a capital loss, but a preferable course might be to hedge his position in bonds by selling bond futures. Doing the latter would protect his long position against a rise in interest rates while simultaneously permitting him to retain a portfolio of bonds, which he had carefully selected for properties such as credit risk and call provisions. This obviates the need for his scrambling during a subsequent market rally to purchase securities with similar properties. The bond futures market can also be useful to the portfolio manager who is seeking to minimize taxes. Consider a portfolio manager who owns long bonds in which he has a short-term capital gain that will become a *long-term* gain two months hence. The portfolio manager fears a rise in interest rates, but if he were to liquidate his position immediately, he would incur a considerable tax penalty. For him, an attractive alternative would be to hedge his position by selling T bond futures.

An investor who uses bond futures to hedge, like an investor who uses bill futures to hedge, is shifting his risk from speculation on rate levels to speculation on spread variation. For the hedger of long instruments, knowledge of what spreads are and what causes them to change is, if anything, more crucial than it is for the hedger of short-term instruments. The reason is that the hedger who uses T bond futures is likely to find that a deliverable long bond differs considerably in current maturity, credit risk, or other characteristics from the bonds he is hedging or from the bonds he intends to buy when an anticipated cash inflow occurs. For the portfolio manager, this considerable imperfection in the hedge is offset by the enhanced opportunity offered to speculate profitably on spread variation.

Factors affecting spread. To evaluate the spread between the instrument being hedged and a deliverable T bond and to determine how that spread is likely to change, a portfolio manager must consider several factors. The first is a possible change in the instrument that is *cheapest* to deliver. This consideration does not arise for the hedger who uses bill futures because the bills deliverable at the expiration of a bill contract are always homogeneous. In the T bond futures market, in contrast, several bonds that trade at different prices may be of deliverable grade at a given time. A change in the cheapest bond deliverable, such as occurred in early 1978 from the 7⅝s of 2002–07 to the 8¾s of 3003–08, will necessarily affect the spread at which T bond futures trade to other instruments.

A second important consideration is credit risk. When interest rates rise, yields on corporate bonds typically rise faster than yields on governments, and yields on low-grade corporates rise faster than yields on high-grade corporates.

A third consideration is the current maturity of the instrument being hedged. Normally, long-term instruments exhibit less yield volatility than do short-term instruments. However, because the yield value of $1/_{32}$ decreases as current maturity lengthens, long-term instruments also typically exhibit more price volatility than do short-term instruments. A bond's price volatility will also depend on whether it is selling at a discount or a premium. In a bear market, discount bonds drop more rapidly in price than high-coupon bonds; they also rise more rapidly in price than high-coupon bonds in bull markets.

Finally, the hedger should take into account possible changes in supply and demand conditions in the markets for long Treasuries and for the instrument being hedged.

The hedge ratio. A careful study of these factors is likely to suggest that the portfolio manager should hedge on a ratio basis; that is, he should sell or buy a number of contracts such that the face value of his position in futures equals some ratio of the face value of the bonds or anticipated cash flow he is hedging. To illustrate, consider a portfolio manager who is hedging a position in corporate bonds against a rise in interest rates. Because of the additional credit risk to which corporates expose the investor, he anticipates that they will drop faster than long governments in the face of rising interest rates. Therefore, to protect his position, he buys a number of futures contracts for bonds whose face value equals some ratio greater than one of the value of the bonds being hedged. To determine what ratio he should use, the hedger must consider all the factors we listed as affecting spread and, in particular, the current maturity of the instrument being hedged.

The hedger who uses bond futures, like the hedger who uses bill futures, retains, through establishing his hedge, the opportunity to speculate on spread variation and should consider such speculation as a potential source of profit. If, for example, the portfolio manager believes that any change in interest rates is likely to be upward, he should consider increasing the ratio of the contracts sold to the securities hedged so that, if interest rates do rise, this not only will not subject his portfolio to a capital loss, but will yield a gain for the portfolio. For anyone who uses the T bond futures market, other useful instruments are the actively traded GNMA futures contracts, which are for an instrument that is essentially free of credit risk and has approximately half the current maturity of the longest Treasury bonds traded for future delivery.[4]

WHO USES FINANCIAL FUTURES?

As noted, the futures contracts introduced for bills, bonds, and GNMAs have been among the most successful commodity futures contracts ever launched. An interesting question is who are the players who have entered this increasingly popular new game?

The not surprising answer is that money and bond market dealers were among the first to enter and use the market actively. They were quick to understand the market and had back offices equipped to clear and track futures trades. Also, and more importantly, they had a need to be *nimble* in the volatile markets that prevailed after the inception of trading in financial futures, and futures contracts gave them a new and extremely useful tool for moving their positions quickly and with facility.

Dealers, particularly of long bonds, quickly saw that the sale of

---

[4] In addition to the topics we have already discussed, an active trader of bill futures will want to know about *implied forward* and *implied repo rates*. Formulas for them are derived, explained, and illustrated in Chapter 11 of Stigum and Mann *Money Market Calculations*.

futures contracts was an attractive alternative to short sales as a hedging device. The use of futures to hedge has undoubtedly increased dealers' ability to bid for and position securities during difficult markets, which, in turn, has contributed to liquidity in the cash market.

Arbitrageurs, often ex-traders for major shops, who assembled capital and set up their own shops, have also been important participants in the market. The newness of financial futures has given them many opportunities to put on profitable arbitrages between cash instruments and futures contracts and between different futures contracts. Their activities are a strong force in pulling rates in the cash and futures markets into line with each other.

Another important set of participants in the markets for financial futures, as in all futures markets, has been speculators. Without the liquidity they give the market, there would be no market.

We have said a great deal about the potential usefulness of futures to end users as a means of controlling risk through hedging. Some end users have already perceived the market's usefulness in this respect and have begun to use it in the ways described above—to hedge long positions in securities and to lock in future lending rates.

The majority, however, have yet to enter the market. Some have still to understand how positions in futures may be used to control risk. Many more have understood this and are now seeking to overcome other problems that must be dealt with before they can trade futures. All sorts of potential end users of financial futures—corporations, banks, bank trust departments, and other financial institutions—have set up task forces to investigate the legal steps they must take and the accounting, clearing, and control procedures they must set up to use futures. This takes time and effort. However, the market deterioration that followed tightening by the Fed in October 1979 drove home to a wide range of potential end users the message that futures were *a valuable tool to control risk, one they needed to be able to use.* The Fed's Saturday night special that October and the subsequent shocks it has given the market have been a great advertisement for futures.

13

U.S. and foreign banks: Running a book in a non-native currency

Today, every major bank in the world is or is well on the way to becoming a multinational bank. In its country of domicile, each bank has a head office and—in the case of a few U.S. and most foreign banks—a large number of domestic branches; each also has foreign branches in London and a string of other financial centers around the globe.[1] While Americans think of major U.S. banks as being primarily domestic banks that happen to operate abroad, the English of the giant British clearing banks as domestic banks with some foreign operations, and so on, in fact, a number of the world's top banks do more business outside than inside their country of origin. Citibank of New York takes 80 percent of its deposits from foreign sources; it is multinational to the point that its foreign business is more important than its domestic business.

---

[1] Banks in Russia and other communist countries are exceptions. However, the central banks of communist countries do maintain offices in London and other centers where they transact Eurocurrency loan and deposit business, trade foreign exchange, and do other international banking.

In discussing a bank's foreign operations, one must distinguish between its operations in the highly competitive and largely unregulated Euromarket—a true international capital market—and its operations within the confines of foreign domestic capital markets. Morgan London, for example, runs a huge Euro book; in addition, it does sterling business with local depositors and borrowers. This local-currency business constitutes its local-currency book. When Morgan runs a sterling book in London, Citibank a French franc book in Paris, or Credit Lyonnais a dollar book in New York, these banks are operating books in a *non-native currency,* that is, *a currency other than that used in their country of origin.*

Running a book denominated in a non-native currency within the confines and regulations of a foreign country poses problems for a bank. In this chapter we consider these, looking first at U.S. banks and then at foreign banks. The positions of these two groups of banks differ in that at least the Euro operations of U.S. banks are primarily in their native currency, the dollar, whereas the foreign operations of foreign banks, including their Euro operations, almost always involve running books in non-native currencies.

LOCAL CURRENCY BOOKS OF U.S. BANKS

As preface to our discussion of the local-currency books of U.S. banks, two points should be made. First, for every currency, there is a distinction between the currency as a Eurocurrency and the currency as a domestic or local currency. Within every country, the accepting of deposits, the making of loans, and other banking activities carried out in the currency of that country are subject to some or all of a wide range of controls: reserve requirements, liquidity requirements, capital constraints, deposit lids, lending controls, constraints on the acceptance of deposits from foreigners, exchange controls, and so on. There is little purpose in cataloging these, since they are subject to frequent change. In the case of some currencies—the U.S. dollar and the British pound—the differences between the domestic currency and the Eurocurrency are small but nonetheless real. For example, since the United Kingdom abolished exchange controls, it is legal for banks that receive deposits of Eurosterling to lend these funds to UK firms for financing domestic activities. However, the Bank of England has requested that banks not do this, and as a general rule, banks never do what the Bank of England asks them not to do; that is the way bank regulation in the United Kingdom works. With respect to the dollar, deposits made in the United States are subject to reserve requirements, but Eurodollar deposits held by U.S. and foreign banks outside the United States (or in an IBF) are not.

Second, we recall that only a few financial centers in the world are highly attractive as Euro centers. London owes its preeminence as a Eurocenter to its political stability and to the fact that it imposes no liquidity or reserve requirements on the Eurocurrency operations of banks there, no restrictions on their taking of Eurodeposits or making of Euro loans, no restrictions on their foreign exchange trading, and no withholding tax on interest paid to foreign holders of Eurocurrency deposits. Judged by these standards, few other Euro centers are as attractive. Some, Tokyo and most continental centers in particular, are quite unattractive.

Foreign branches of U.S. banks that are located in major financial centers, as opposed to tax havens such as Nassau, do a mix of Eurocurrency and local currency business. This mix depends in part on how favorable the climate in the center is for doing Eurocurrency business and on the restrictions imposed on the activities of foreign banks in the local market.

Gathering local currencies

A first and overriding concern of a U.S. bank operating a local-currency book in a foreign country is obtaining that currency. Foreign branches of U.S. banks operating in a local market usually obtain little in the way of *current accounts* (foreign jargon for demand deposits) from corporations because these branches do little operational business, such as check processing, lock box collections, and other non-credit services that corporate customers normally pay for with compensating balances.

In foreign countries more often than not, banking is highly concentrated with the bulk of the business being done by a handful of national or regional giants. These local giants have a lock on local consumer business. In the United Kingdom, for example, people who need a checking account open it with one of the clearing banks. A similar situation exists in France, Belgium, Germany, Japan, and other countries where the size and vigor of the local economy makes the opening of branches attractive to U.S. banks.

In the United Kingdom and a number of other countries, retail and corporate current accounts all operate on an *overdraft* basis. This means that a person or corporation keeping a current account for transactions purposes may have a balance that is either positive or negative. A positive balance represents a net deposit of funds, a negative balance a borrowing.

Because the giant local banks control all the consumer business in the country, the net amount of funds they get from current accounts—positive balances minus overdrafts—totals a huge sum. This cheap money gives local banks a big advantage in terms of their cost of funds over the foreign branches of U.S. and other foreign banks. An analogous situation exists in the United States. There, American banks enjoy a big advantage by virtue of the large amounts of costless—except for the allocation of overhead—demand deposits that they receive but which foreign bank branches operating in the United States have difficulty in garnering.

The asymmetry in who gets local deposits means that U.S. bank branches operating in the United Kingdom, France, Belgium, and elsewhere can't really be competitive as intermediaries because they must buy every bit of money they lend. To justify their existence, these banks must do other things to earn profits—trade foreign exchange and run a Eurocurrency book if local regulations permit. A foreign bank branch can be competitive in running a Eurodollar book because, in the Euromarket, there are no free current account balances. In 1981, for example, when rates peaked and the yield curve was inverted, Euro call money commanded rates in the top teens—with daily compounding on 255 business days, an 18 percent call rate compounds to an effective cost of funds of 19.71 percent—a long way from free money.

In many European countries, there are controls on the flow of the domestic currency either inward, outward, or both. In this respect, the situation in Brussels is not atypical. Morgan Brussels may run a Eurocurrency as well as a local Belgian franc book. The branch, however, may use only to a very limited extent borrowed Eurodollars to create, via a swap, Belgian francs to fund its local Belgian franc book.[2] Controls also exist on the use of local currency to acquire other currencies. On the other hand, deposits of Euro French francs or Eurodollars may be used by a bank's Paris office to acquire DM-denominated bonds, a double whammy play—a bet on interest rates and on an exchange rate—that we described in Chapter 11. The way we described, in that chapter, the treasurer of Morgan Paris buying DM-denominated bonds is, in fact, not the way the deal would typically be done. Nor-

---

[2] Controls on the creation, inflow, and outflow of local currency are all designed by the local monetary authority with the intention of insulating the domestic capital market from the Euromarket so that the domestic monetary authority may pursue some semblance of an independent monetary policy with respect to controlling the local money supply, the level of local interest rates, and the exchange value of the local currency.

European authorities blow hot and cold on the issue of pegging or at least smoothing fluctuations in exchange rates. Currently, the volume of short-term funds sloshing around in the world capital market makes it near futile for Europeans to do much about the rate at which their currencies exchange against the dollar, but they do try to minimize fluctuations in the rates at which various European currencies trade against each other.

mally, the treasurer in Paris office would bid for a deposit of Euro DM; the lender of these DM would take in a Eurodollar deposit, swap the dollars into DM, and then charge the treasurer of Morgan Paris a rate on the DM deposit equal, approximately, to the rate paid on the Eurodollar deposit plus (minus) the annualized cost of swapping dollars into DM. This example illustrates and emphasizes a point made in Chapter 6: the bulk of nondollar Eurocurrency deposits does not result from natural Eurodeposit business in nondollar currencies, but is rather Eurodollars with a swap tagged on. When foreign exchange is obtained via a swap, there is no foreign exchange risk.

Antiestablishment position

Any bank trying to do business in another country—whether it is a New York bank trying to do business in Paris or a French bank trying to do business in New York—is an outsider and, as such, finds itself in an antiestablishment position. In this context, the establishment is represented by the large local banks: Credit Lyonnais in Paris, Chase Manhattan in New York.

Being in an antiestablishment position puts a lot of pressure on the foreign branches of U.S. banks operating in a local market. In France, the big banks are nationalized; in Belgium they are quasi-nationalized because they operate hand in glove with the central bank and the exchequer. An important function of the central bank in any nation is to act as a lender of last resort to local banks. In Germany, the Bundesbank lends to the foreign branches of U.S. banks operating in Germany on the same basis that it lends to German banks. As a rule, however, the foreign branches of U.S. banks operating a local-currency book do not have lender of last resort facilities with the local central bank, which lends to local banks only. Foreign banks operating in the United States used to face the same problem—lack of access to the discount window at the Fed—until passage in 1978 of the International Banking Act.

Lending techniques to garner
local business

A foreign branch of a U.S. bank operating a local-currency book is at a disadvantage to local banks because it has difficulty garnering much in the way of current account balances. Consequently, its funding costs compared to those achieved by local banks are high.[3] Despite this

---

[3] An exception is when local interest rates are low and the cost of maintaining an extensive branch network makes the cost to a native bank of current account money high.

disadvantage, the only way these branches can get a foot in the door and do local business is by cutting loan rates, which is precisely what the foreign banks did when they came to the United States.

Cut-rate lending by foreign branches of U.S. banks started in London. These branches would call up local corporations and say, "Why borrow on an overdraft basis from the big clearing banks when they are killing you? Their base lending rate is much too high. We will lend to you at 50 basis points over what it costs us to borrow sterling in the interbank market; and you can borrow for whatever period—one, three, or six months—you choose, at a fixed rate."

In doing this sort of business, London branches of U.S. banks were booking loans at spreads that barely covered their overhead. Their strategy was to offer a loss leader, get some business on the books, establish a relationship, and hope that, as time passed, they would be able to break into the regular lending business and get a portion of the normal banking business done by companies to whom they had sold loss-leader advances.

The practice of U.S. bank branches calling up local borrowers and offering them cut-rate loans priced off the cost of buying funds in the interbank market came to be known as *hotline business*. From the United Kingdom, hotline business quickly spread to France, Germany, Belgium, and elsewhere. The local banks were about as enthusiastic about this as were U.S. banks—who wanted to lend to everyone at prime in the U.S. market—when the U.S. branches of foreign banks started offering American borrowers term loans at a floating rate equal to the Fed funds rate plus ¼ percent. But foreign banks trying to gain a foothold in the U.S. market had the wherewithal to absorb the losses generated by this sort of business, and they did it. Their offering of cost-plus loans to U.S. borrowers did as much as anything to accelerate the move toward cost-plus lending by American banks in the domestic market. Similarly, the competition that the foreign branches of U.S. banks gave to local banks in foreign countries forced banks there to bite the bullet and move to various forms of cost-plus pricing, their only alternative being to permit the U.S. banks to take a big chunk of local business away from them.

When narrow margins on loans priced at a spread over the lender's cost of funds become common, this means that competition has become rampant, and that borrowers are shopping for rate, period. In conditions other than these, no bank should lend at a margin that leaves no room for profits.

Another point about narrow margins is that they make liquidity and interest rate exposure considerations paramount. A bank that has no profit margin also has no margin for error. The bank really can't get it wrong, because, if it does, it will be out of business. Thus, all we said in previous chapters about liquidity and interest rate exposure considerations applies with even greater force to the running by a foreign branch of a local-currency book.

Shoring up the availability of local currency

Usually a bank that operates a local-currency book in a foreign branch has no lender of last resort facility with the central bank. Consequently, foreign branches operating local-currency books have to come up with some ingenious means of shoring up their liquidity with respect to the local currency. Since the difficulties U.S. banks experience in getting deposits of local currency in their European branches differ little from those experienced by European banks seeking to garner dollar deposits at their U.S. branches, it is common for big multinational banks based in different countries to set up mutually beneficial reciprocal agreements. (It takes mutual benefit to get an agreement between natural competitors.) For example, Morgan Paris needs a more stable source of local French francs than their access to the French franc market provides, since circumstances might arise that would impair their access to that market. In theory, the problems faced by the New York branch of Credit Lyonnais are fewer, since it can draw dollars from the vast Eurodollar market, but still, the dollar for them is a non-native currency, and the possibility always exists that the United States might impose stricter controls on the import, if you will, of Eurodollars into the domestic market. It did, under the International Banking Act of 1978, subject the dollar operations of foreign bank branches in the United States to reserve requirements.

Given the above considerations, it is to the mutual benefit of a U.S. and a foreign bank to create a *reciprocal deposit scheme* and a *reciprocal standby agreement.* The first is a scheme that enables both banks to augment immediately and for a long period their resources of the reciprocating bank's local currency at the lowest cost possible. The second is a lender of last resort facility discussed at the end of this section.

Reciprocal deposit schemes are drawn for some fixed amount, say $50 million on the dollar side and an equivalent sum on the French franc side. Usually such agreements last for a long period: 7, 8, or even 10 years. This gives the participants an assured source of funds over a sufficiently long period to make strategic plans for business development. It is also especially useful to German banks that operate under liquidity rules that require that some minimum portion of their liabilities have a maturity of four years or more.

Normally, reciprocal deposit agreements are kept fully drawn at all times. One reason is technical: doing so prevents some banks from violating the covenants in capital note issues they have sold.

The terms of reciprocal deposit schemes are fairly standard. The dollar sums we have quoted are reasonable for major money market banks. The amounts may seem small, but these agreements are in addition to all of the other credit arrangements—lines extended for Euro placements, foreign exchange trading, and other activities—that these banks carry on with each other. A U.S. bank must be particularly concerned about the *total* credit lines it extends to another bank because it may lend only a limited amount equal to a small percentage of its capital to another bank.

In a reciprocal deposit scheme, there is no commitment fee, since the facility is of benefit to both banks, and a fee would, therefore, make no sense. Each party to such an agreement obtains funds from the other at some agreed upon spread above the cost of funds to the latter. The borrower (deposit receiver) normally has the option, within limits, of fixing the maturity of the deposit he gets—to take 1-, 2-, 3-, or 6-month money—depending on his view on rates.

In addition to entering into reciprocal deposit schemes which provide participating banks with a *long-term* source of a foreign currency, the same banks will draw up a *reciprocal standby agreement* under the terms of which they may borrow from each other local currency on demand in cases of extreme need.

Because U.S. banks are limited with respect to the size of the reciprocal deposits and standby agreements they make with a single foreign bank, they will often enter into several such agreements with different banks in a single country. By setting up agreements with a number of large French banks, Morgan, for example, can increase the total base of French francs available to it while simultaneously limiting its credit exposure to any single French bank.

Given that multinational banks from different countries are constantly competing with each other in the international and in their own domestic markets, one might expect them to be mutually antagonistic. In fact, their interests have become so mingled around the world that they have become mutually dependent—and this despite the fact that, in their day-to-day relations with customers, they compete actively with each other. One of the most, if not the most, important minglings of interests and sources of mutual dependence is the need we have just described for all banks operating foreign branches with local-currency books to look to local banks for deposit and line agreements to shore up their branches' liquidity in local markets.

With respect to competition between U.S. and foreign banks, it is interesting to note that it was U.S. banks that first invaded the home turf of foreign banks. These same U.S. banks, while they did not welcome the later incursion by foreign banks into the U.S. market, did nothing to stop it. They argued, with considerable justice, that the foreign banks were doing nothing to them in the American market that they had not earlier done to the foreign banks in their local markets.

Also, they argued that the business of banking is an expanding pie. Consequently, increased international competition should, on average, be consistent with domestic banks in all major countries continuing to grow both in their local market and in foreign markets.

To anyone who takes seriously the lesson preached by Adam Smith and later theorists that free competition will produce efficient markets and stimulate innovation, international banking produces a showcase example of how competition on a worldwide scale works to benefit all. The entry of foreign banks into closed and highly concentrated local banking markets has frequently benefited local bank customers by forcing local banks to adopt practices that better serve the customer.

In some cases, international competition among banks has put pressure on regulators to change certain rules of the local banking game so that banks operating in the local market could do so more efficiently. Regulations, especially in banking, often lack economic justification but, once on the books, are hard to change, partly because they often come to protect some group's vested interest. A case in point is American restrictions on intrastate and interstate banking.

The interbank market for local currency

The one place foreign branches of a U.S. bank can normally buy local currency at market rates is in the local interbank market for the currency. To enter this market, a bank must first go around to local banks and establish relationships. In the United Kingdom an American bank entering the local market would go to the big clearing banks and other banks supplying sterling to the interbank market and say, for example, "Gee, I don't know if you have heard of us, but we are Bankers Trust . . . ." Of course they have heard of the bank if it is a big money market bank, perhaps not, if it is a smaller regional. In any case, chances are that local banks will want to do business with the new foreign branch; certainly they will if the new branch belongs to a top bank. So the local banks will establish lines against which the new branch may buy (borrow) funds from them in the interbank market. These lines, like those in the U.S. Fed Funds market, are usually not *advised*, that is, the bank granting the line does not tell the grantee the size of the line. Over time, banks granted lines by other banks can usually accurately guess the size of these lines by observing what amount of funds topside different banks will lend them in the interbank market.

Usually business in the interbank market is done through local brokers; only rarely do banks deal directly with each other. In the UK sterling market, a U.S. branch that puts in a bid with a broker may find out from him that it is getting 20 million pounds from National Westminister, 50 million pounds from Barclays, and so on.

Over time, a bank should keep careful tabs on the size it can do with other banks and use this information to develop a sense of its size overall in the market. Other things being equal, a bank's presence in the market should grow as the market grows, and interbank markets always grow, reflecting growth in the money supply due to inflation and expansion of local economic activity.

Each year, a foreign bank branch should notice that the amount of funds it can buy in the interbank market is increasing. Over time, banks there will enlarge their lending lines to the branch to obtain an outlet for the increasing amount of funds placed with them. Also, new banks are likely to come onto the scene, and they will want to establish lines to foreign branches. It is important for a branch to monitor and to build its presence in the market as a taker of funds because of a rule of prudence we have stressed: *To control liquidity risk, a bank must always maintain a presence in the market that exceeds that needed to support its basic asset structure.*

Foreign banks participate in the U.S. interbank market for funds on much the same basis that U.S. banks participate in foreign interbank markets for local currencies. One crucial difference is that the Fed funds market is primarily an overnight market, the market for term Fed funds being limited in size. In foreign interbank markets, as in the market for Fed funds, prices rise and fall with ebbs and flows in the demand for and supply of funds.

In Chapter 11 we noted that one reason for the existence in many foreign countries of a broad interbank market for local currency deposits over a wide range of maturities is the success local banks have in obtaining time deposits. Another reason is that the demand in the foreign exchange market for forward quotes—as part of swap transactions or hedges—creates a demand for deposits of different currencies over a range of maturities: 1-week fixed; 2-week fixed; and 1, 2, 3, 6, 9 and 12 months. At times, trading in deposits over even longer maturities occurs in the interbank market. Often, such long deposits, known as *long dates,* derive from foreign exchange transactions.

If a bank customer wants to do a forward transaction nine months hence, say DM against dollars, either because he anticipates receiving DM then and wants to lock in a rate at which he can exchange DM for dollars or because he wants to do a 9-month swap of dollars into DM, a bank foreign exchange trader can quote the customer a nonarbitrary forward rate only if he can base his quote on the rates being paid on 9-month deposits of dollars and marks. It is off the difference between these two rates that the equilibrium forward rate between DM and dollars quoted in the foreign exchange market is normally derived. We say normally because the expectation of an imminent change in exchange rates can drive the forward rate at which a currency is quoted to a premium above or discount below the "normal" value implied by deposit rates.

In our example we used dollars and marks. There is only a very thin domestic market for 9-month term Fed funds. However, this creates no problem in the foreign exchange market, because there is an active market for Eurodollar time deposits in all maturity ranges, including nine month.

The need for long-dated deposits arises when the occasional customer who wants to hedge a position for two or three years asks his bank to accommodate him. A bank faced with such a request has to find institutions willing to accept and place currency deposits of this length to quote a rate without exposing itself to a liquidity, interest rate, or foreign exchange risk. For example, a customer whose native currency is the dollar, asks a British bank to quote it a rate on a 3-year swap into sterling. For the bank to quote such a rate without exposing itself to risk, it must take in a 3-year deposit of sterling and make a 3-year placement of dollars. The swap rate it quotes the customer will be a function of three things: the spot dollar/pound exchange rate, the rate it earns on the dollar deposits it places, and the rate it pays on the sterling deposit it takes.

The corporate deposit market

Negotiable CDs. Outside the United States there is only one country, the United Kingdom, where there is a large established market for negotiable CDs denominated in *local* currency. Singapore has such a market, but it is still in the fledgling stage. In the United Kingdom, sterling CDs issued by the foreign branches of U.S. banks to support their sterling books are surprisingly well accepted. Because of the high concentration in British banking, the number of local banks that issue sterling CDs is limited. To achieve diversification, a big investor in the sterling CDs is forced to buy sterling CDs issued not only by local banks, but also by the London branches of top U.S. banks.

Unfortunately for the New York branches of foreign banks, no analogous advantage exists for them. U.S. investors have so many domestic names among which to choose that they can adequately diversify without buying dollar CDs issued by foreign bank branches. These branches do sell dollar CDs in the New York market, but they cannot issue in large volume without having to pay up. Also, their paper carries the disadvantage that, because many fewer investors will buy it, it is less liquid than paper issued by top U.S. banks.

Time deposits. In major countries other than the United States and the United Kingdom—France, Germany, Belgium, Switzerland, Japan, and Hong Kong—there is no market for negotiable CDs. Instead, banks take straight time deposits from corporate customers. The foreign branches of U.S. banks cultivate relationships with local institutions to obtain such time deposits. Doing so, however, is not without its problems. If a bank has a time deposit relationship with a client whereby it takes his money for three months, six months, or whatever, that client comes to depend on the bank to pay him a reasonable rate. This is especially true in countries where investors with excess cash have few investment alternatives because the number of instruments traded in the domestic money market is limited.

France is an example of a country where this is true. When money is tight in France, all banks, including the foreign branches of U.S. banks, solicit deposits from local corporations. Then when money turns easy or when the French government in its wisdom decides to limit bank lending, a bank that has gone out and solicited deposits will find itself holding deposits which it really does not need. This poses a two-edged problem for the foreign branches of U.S. banks. While they don't need the money, they want to continue to pay a competitive rate to keep depositors with whom they have carefully cultivated a relationship. In doing so, the foreign branches of U.S. banks are at a considerable disadvantage. Local banks have big profit margins because of all the free current account money they get from small depositors. Consequently, they can afford to bid up for corporate money even when they do not need it.

To sum up, for the foreign branch of a U.S. bank soliciting time deposits from local corporations is a chancy affair. For liquidity, the branch needs to maintain continuity of these deposits. However, these deposits can, from time to time, become costly because the branch either can't use the money or can use it only at a rate so low that the branch's spread is narrowed practically to zero.

Secondary markets for bank paper

The extent to which both the foreign branches of U.S. banks and local banks, as well, can rely on the secondary market for bank paper for liquidity varies considerably from country to country. Next to New York, the most elaborate money market is that in London. London trades everything New York does except repos. However, *bill brokers* or *discount houses*, which are roughly the equivalent of U.S. money market dealers, do the equivalent of repo with the Bank of England.

In England, it used to be that bill brokers, who finance the paper they buy with the Bank of England, would buy only BAs created by British banks. This has, however, changed. Currently, the BAs of foreign banks operating in London are acceptable for trade, provided that these securities meet certain criteria. This change means that the use of BAs provides foreign bank branches in London with a viable means of creating self-liquidating paper.

The British change of heart with respect to the acceptability for trade of BAs issued by U.S. bank branches was no gesture of generosity. British banks operating branches in the U.S. have lobbied long and hard to have their paper acceptable to the Fed as collateral when the Fed, in the course of open-market operations, does repo with the dealers. In effect, the Fed and the Bank of England struck a reciprocal deal, each agreed to accept as eligible collateral BAs issued by local branches of banks headquartered in the other's country.

The conditions under which a foreign branch of a U.S. bank can liquidate some of the paper it generates in the local secondary market—to the extent that the latter exists—vary from country to country. Generally, there is some means by which a foreign branch can be assured of liquidity by issuing various forms of trade paper. However, in doing so the foreign branch is generally at a competitive disadvantage vis-à-vis local banks because foreign branch paper is usually discounted at higher rates than is local bank paper, which sells at what are known as *fine rates* in the trade.

Commercial paper and BAs form a huge part of the U.S. money market. In foreign countries assorted variations on these themes are common. In the United Kingdom, there are bills of exchange, also called commercial bills. On a BA, a bank has the choice, after it has accepted the paper, of giving it back to the drawer to sell or of discounting the draft and then either holding it or selling it in the market. Generally, a commercial bill is an accepted BA that is turned back to the drawer of the draft because the bill is not a BA in the true sense; it finances a mercantile transaction but not one specifically involving the import, export storage, or shipment of goods. Commercial bills represent one source from which firms can raise working capital by operating through an accepting bank. To this extent, they serve much the same purpose as does the sale of commercial paper in the United States.

In Japan, which has yet to develop a sophisticated domestic money market, there is a commercial paper market of sorts, but it works through the banks. Japanese banks make working capital loans to corporations. They then sell the paper generated in these transactions as commercial paper through an elaborate dealer network. This dealer network is, in turn, supported by the Bank of Japan, which informs the dealers of how much paper it will hold and what rate it will pay for this paper. This is the way the Bank of Japan controls short-term interest rates. In running open-market operations, the transactions medium for the Fed is primarily bills and repo, for the Bank of Japan, it is basically commercial paper.

In France, there is a commercial paper market that works much as the Japanese market does. The paper generated in this market may be sold directly to an arm of the Banque de France, which performs the same function as the Bank of Japan. Every day, the Banque de France makes known how much paper it is willing to buy and at what price. A bank that generates such paper and wants to sell it to the central bank, as opposed to financing it in the interbank market, offers its paper to the Banque and takes its turn.

Swaps to obtain local currency

In some countries from time to time—regulations in this respect are subject to change—it is possible for the branch of a foreign bank to create local currency via swaps. For example, the foreign branch of a U.S. bank can buy Eurodollars or borrow dollars from head office and swap them into the local currency. In most countries where this can be done, the extent to which it can be done is controlled by the local central bank. In Belgium, for example, every foreign bank branch has a tranche that sets a limit on the amount of Belgian francs it may produce via swaps. A typical tranche might amount to $50 million.

Using swaps to produce local currency involves several dangers. The first and foremost is that the authorities can arbitrarily change the rules. A foreign branch that comes to rely on swaps as a source of local currency to finance its basic asset structure runs a liquidity risk; at any time, the local monetary authority can say, "Sorry, but economic conditions have changed. You can't do that any more." If this occurs, the branch will have to scratch around for funds to replace those previously produced by swaps. As noted, expanding existing sources of local currency or producing new ones can be difficult and costly for a foreign branch.

A second danger with using swaps to produce local currency is that the cost of funds produced this way can be volatile and may, at times, get out of hand. In theory, the cost of local currency produced by a swap out of dollars should equal the interest rate paid on the borrowed dollars plus (minus) the annualized cost of (return on) the swap.

If a bank branch operating in a country where local interest rates are low, borrows dollars to swap them into the local currency at a time when dollar interest rates are high, the cost of the local funds produced should be much lower than that of the dollars borrowed. The reason is that the local currency being produced through the swap should sell at a premium in the forward foreign exchange market. Therefore, the annual cost of the swap will be negative. When that cost is subtracted from the rate paid on the borrowed dollars, the net cost of the local funds produced will be less than that of the dollars borrowed. How much less? If markets are efficient and free to reach an equilibrium price, the cost of producing local currency through a swap should closely approximate the cost of borrowing it in the local market.[4] In practice, however, the relationship between rates in the local market and rates on this currency when it is produced via a swap may get out

---

[4] See Chapter 12 in Marcia Stigum in collaboration with John Mann, *Money Market Calculations: Yields, Break-Evens, and Arbitrage* (Homewood, Ill.: Dow Jones/Irwin, 1981).

of whack because (1) government regulations prevent the arbitrage necessary to bring rates into line or (2) expectations with respect to a realignment of exchange rates overwhelm the impact of interest rate differentials on forward rates.

Japan in the early 1970s provides a case in point. At that time, foreign bank branches operating in Tokyo were allocated liberal swap lines. They could borrow dollars, convert them into yen, and use the yen proceeds to finance loans to local businesses. Yen interest rates were lower than dollar interest rates, and the forward yen, consequently, should have sold at a premium. It did, but the premium was much greater than that which the differential between yen and dollar interest rates should have caused, because the market anticipated revaluation of the yen. The upshot was that, for foreign bank branches operating in Tokyo, the cost of obtaining local currency via dollar swaps was actually *negative*. This was an anomaly that should have been arbitraged out. In the free Eurocurrency markets it was; in Japan it was not, due to government controls.

For a foreign bank branch, the cost of yen produced via swaps out of dollars during the year 1971 was in the neighborhood of minus 2.7 percent! No bank can complain about having a negative cost of funds. There is a danger, however, in such situations. The effective cost rate may suddenly change due to a change in the exchange rate, in interest rate differentials, or in expectations. This happened in the case of the yen. The big profit on swapping dollars into yen during 1971 reflected the market's conviction that the Japanese had to revalue the yen. Once revaluation occurred, that expectation disappeared, and the cost of producing yen via swaps out of dollars reverted to a level that reflected interest rate differentials. Suddenly, the cost of yen produced via swaps rose from minus 2.5 percent to plus 14 percent. For a bank financing yen assets yielding 10 percent, this resulted in a dramatic change in spread profits.

Relying on swaps to produce local currency exposes a bank not only to a liquidity risk, but to interest rate risk. This is not to say that it should not be done. However, it is a strategy that should be employed with care and caution.

Standby lines

Earlier we talked about reciprocal deposit schemes which banks of different nations negotiate with each other. These agreements are designed to provide partners to the agreement with a dependable source of a nonnative currency. Consistent with this purpose, reciprocal deposit arrangements are fully filled at all times.

Standby lines, always a *committed facility,* are a different arrangement. When a bank of one nationality negotiates a standby line with a bank of another nationality, its intent is to obtain a *lender of last resort* facility for one of its local-currency books; e.g., a U.S. bank for its French franc or DM book. By definition, a bank will never use a lender of last resort facility except in extremis—the facility being designed to provide the bank with liquidity when there is absolutely no other source it can tap to obtain a needed currency.

A U.S. bank wanting to establish a standby line for a particular currency will find a foreign correspondent for which this currency is a native currency. It will then make an agreement with the bank whereby the latter stands ready to lend the U.S. bank its currency in an emergency. In exchange, the U.S. bank commits itself to lend dollars to the foreign bank in an emergency.

When the two banks negotiating a standby facility *both* seek to satisfy a need for a lender of last resort facility for borrowing a foreign currency, *no* fee is charged by either bank for the line. Having a commitment fee in place is *always* an incentive for a facility to be used, because the fee stops accruing if the facility is used. On a standby line, for neither party would such an incentive be appropriate.

A bank obtaining a standby line wants an insurance policy on which it hopes it will never have to collect. The implicit understanding between the contracting banks on a standby facility is that this facility will never be used by either bank unless one party runs out of the other's currency. In practice, this occurs only rarely. When a bank is forced to draw on a standby line, it normally is unable to obtain a particular currency because the banking system in the currency's country of origin is, for some reason, terribly illiquid, e.g., Chase cannot get French francs because the French central bank is pursuing an extremely tight monetary policy.

Earlier we said that standby lines carry no fee. This is not to say they are free. A bank obtaining a standby commitment from another bank has altered its liquidity position *in its native currency* for the worse. Specifically, the bank has committed itself to lend on demand to a foreign bank, and that demand, if made, is more likely than not to occur at a time when the lending bank itself will have difficulty obtaining its own currency. This is a second reason that it is in the interests of both parties to a standby agreement that the line never be drawn upon.

Pricing of standby loans. The pricing of loans taken down under standby agreements is difficult. Since such lines are most likely to be drawn upon during periods of extreme illiquidity in the lender's capital market, it may be difficult to ascertain the rate at which the borrowing should be priced, because lending money is likely to be a real imposition on the lender. The rate charged on a takedown under a standby agreement is usually a workout rate. Reflecting this, such agreements often specify that the rate at which a loan will be made under the agreement should be "the best rate available" or "a rate such that both parties may agree upon it." In some cases, the agreement may specify that the rate will be determined after the fact on the basis of what the money was, in retrospect, worth in terms of convenience to the borrower and inconvenience to the lender. Standby lines are to be used in extremis, and a bank in extremis worries about getting money, not the price it pays for it.

The reason standby lines are crucial for a foreign bank branch operating a local-currency book is that such branches normally have no lender of last resort facility at the local central bank. One exception is Germany. There, standby lines are less important to foreign branches running DM books because these branches may borrow at the Lombard rate—German equivalent of the discount rate—from the Bundesbank. To do so, they must use as collateral German government securities. There is no repo market in Germany in which such securities may be financed, as are U.S. bank holdings of treasuries. This means that a U.S. bank branch operating in Germany has to use *its own* funds to hold German government securities. Consequently, by discounting these securities at the Bundesbank, it can raise real cash. For the same U.S. bank to borrow from the Fed at the discount window against treasuries would make no sense; such a bank can and does finance its holdings of governments in the repo market. Because it never uses its own funds to finance its holdings of governments, a big U.S. bank can't use them to raise real cash.

Size. The size of the standby lines a bank negotiates in a given currency should be an amount based on the proportion of its purchased liabilities in this currency that it considers to be vulnerable. This amount is subject to change and should be reviewed constantly.

When a bank negotiates a standby line, its concern is *strictly with liquidity, never with interest rate exposure.* What the bank wants is the ability to get its hands on money when money is available nowhere else. The standby lines a bank negotiates really amount to converting its ability to garner large amounts of its domestic currency into an ability to garner amounts of various foreign currencies.

A one-way need. Sometimes a bank will find itself operating in a country where local banks have no U.S. branches and are not heavily involved in the Eurodollar market. Argentina is an example; local banks there are forbidden to do dollar business. A U.S. bank with a branch in Argentina needs a standby line for obtaining Argentine pesos, but local banks have no need for a standby line to obtain dollars. This means that a U.S. bank will have to pay a fee to get a peso standby line from a local bank, unless it has something of value to offer the Argentine bank in return. In Spain, the situation is similar.

Herstatt crisis. While standby lines are rarely used, *no foreign branch can do without them.* This was demonstrated when the Herstatt Bank failed in 1974. This failure caused big Middle Eastern depositors of dollars to be concerned about the credit of even large non–dollar-based banks. These depositors observed that the Herstatt failure caused banks from many countries to lose large sums of dollars; they reasoned that banks to which the dollar was a native currency could easily withstand such losses, but wondered whether banks to which the dollar was a non-native currency could.[5]

Because of this concern, the large Middle Eastern depositors, who had been placing their money in many banks, concentrated their deposits in a handful of top U.S. banks and insisted on making huge call deposits. The four or five U.S. banks that received all this short-term money dropped their bid rate by 2 or 3 percent in an attempt to turn away the tide of money flowing to them.

For these banks, the period was one of mixed blessings. On the one hand, the spread between the bid rates at which they took in money and the offered rates at which they redeposited it with other banks was so large and the amounts of money involved were so huge that the period was the most lucrative they had ever experienced in their Euro operations. On the other hand, these high profits came at the price of balance sheet distortions and the acceptance of additional credit and liquidity risk. First, the receiving banks—because they ended up redepositing or otherwise lending the funds deposited with them to banks to which the Middle Eastern depositors were no longer willing to lend—ended up accepting a big (in terms of volume) credit risk that the Middle Eastern depositors wanted to shed. Second, the receiving banks were ballooning their balance sheets and deteriorating their capital ratios. Third, because most of the depositors would place their money not for periods such as one, three, or six months, but only at call, that money could disappear tomorrow. Consequently, the receiving banks were forced to violate two basic rules of liquidity: (1) never take a big portion of your funds from a single source, and (2) never accept too large a proportion of your deposits at call.

During this period, some of the banks with which Middle Eastern depositors would no longer place dollars had to call on standby lines with top U.S. banks which, in this way, were also forced to accept credit risks that, at that point, the ultimate depositors were unwilling to accept. The widening spreads and profits of the top five U.S. banks during the post-Herstatt period were compensation to them for the

---

[5] Failure of the Herstatt caused many banks to lose dollars because Herstatt was a big dealer in foreign exchange, and it failed owing money to many banks from which it had purchased foreign exchange; foreign exchange is always settled in dollars.

extra risks and other deleterious balance-sheet effects that they accepted by doing all of this extra business.

If another disaster like Herstatt occurred today, exactly the same scenario would ensue because no other mechanism exists to deal with it. The circumstances of a "disaster" today might, for example, be failure by a big LDC (less developed country) borrower. Such a failure would cause no big bank to fail, but it might cause a flight to quality by large depositors similar to that caused by the Herstatt failure.

An aside. There is an interesting parallel in the U.S. market. If a *very* large U.S. corporation failed tomorrow, the commercial paper market would shrink, bank loans would rise, bank footings would rise in step, and firms that used to buy commercial paper would buy bank CDs. The very largest U.S. banks would benefit most from this flight to quality, and they would face much the same extra profits and extra problems they faced in the wake of Herstatt. Perhaps they would have no liquidity problem, since U.S. depositors would probably be rational enough to buy 1-, 3-, and 6-month CDs rather than insist on leaving their money at call. However, the top U.S. banks would face a ballooning of their balance sheets, a deterioration of their capital ratios, and a credit risk, because at least some of the commercial paper issuers to whom they had extended backup lines would no longer be able to sell their paper and would, therefore, be forced to draw upon these lines for loans.

THE OPERATION OF FOREIGN BANKS IN NON-NATIVE CURRENCIES

Major foreign banks, like their U.S. counterparts, have all become to varying degrees multinational banks running big Euro books and local-currency books at branches scattered around the globe.

The bulk of what we said in Chapters 9 and 11 and in this chapter about interest rate exposure in a Euro book, the importance of running a worldwide Euro book, and the special problems associated with running local-currency books at foreign branches applies equally to major foreign banks and their U.S. counterparts. The opportunities and problems U.S. and foreign banks face in their international operations, and the means they should use to capitalize on these opportunities and to solve the associated problems bear strong similarities.

There is, however, one difference that warrants attention. The dominant currency by far in the Euromarket is the dollar, which is a *native* currency to U.S. banks. Thus, in operating in the Euromarket, U.S. banks are operating primarily in their *native* currency. In contrast, foreign banks, in operating in the Euromarket, are operating primarily in a *non-native* currency. This distinction puts foreign banks at something of a disadvantage with respect to liquidity risk.

RELATIVE RISK OF OPERATING IN DOLLARS VIS-À-VIS OTHER CONVERTIBLE CURRENCIES

The Eurodollar market is the largest market in the world, $1,170 billion on a gross basis and $577 billion on a net basis.[6] This means that there is money to go around for everyone. Moreover, that money is available to a wide range of banks. Any credit worthy bank of some size can obtain from other banks lines that will enable it to buy in the interbank market Eurodollar deposits of varying maturities: overnight, 1-month, 3-month, 6-month, and longer.

To that extent, dollars are much more available to foreign banks than are foreign currencies to U.S. banks. Moreover, few restrictions—other than reserve requirements—exist or are likely to be imposed on the "import" by foreign banks of Eurodollars to fund their U.S.–branch dollar books. Most of the time, the widespread availability of dollars should make it possible for a major foreign bank to operate, without severe liquidity risk, both a Eurodollar book and a local-currency book at its U.S. branch.

Most of the time is, however, not all the time. In operating in dollars, foreign banks do face—despite the normally widespread availability of dollars—special liquidity risks because the dollar is, for them, a non-native currency.

The flight to quality risk. One risk we have mentioned in connection with the Herstatt crisis is the potential flight to quality by depositors. At the time of the Herstatt crisis, standby lines were insufficient to bail all foreign banks out of the ensuing difficulties they experienced in obtaining dollars. The foreign banks that experienced the greatest liquidity problems post-Herstatt were the Japanese banks. At that time, their Eurodollar books were in bad shape, and all the other banks knew it. The Japanese banks had made a lot of fixed-rate loans for five, six, even seven years and were carrying these loans with day-to-day money. Pre-Herstatt that looked great because the yield curve was positively sloped and dollars were readily available to all major banks. To banks that were potential lenders of dollars to the Japanese, the same situation post-Herstatt looked terrible, because foreign banks, as a group, were experiencing a liquidity problem with respect to the dollar.

---

[6] See Table 6–5.

The post-Herstatt plight of the Japanese banks illustrates a point made in Chapter 8. If the yield curve is positively sloped, a bank can be technically illiquid—e.g., fund 6-month assets with 1-month money—for some period, make money, and not get into trouble. However, to do so on a large scale is dangerous because, inevitably, circumstances will change, and they may change in a way that will kill the bank.

Post-Herstatt, the Japanese banks had to pay up to get dollars not only because they were non–dollar-based banks, but because they were losing money hand over fist on their dollar business. The latter caused other banks to demand an extra premium for giving dollars to Japanese banks or to refuse to lend them dollars at all. The situation became so difficult for the Japanese banks that the Bank of Japan had to bail them out. Fortunately, it could easily do so. Japan had been running a balance of payments surplus, so the Bank of Japan had official dollar reserves invested in U.S. Treasury bills which it could easily convert into cash and deposit with Japanese banks experiencing a liquidity problem.

Once the Japanese banks, which are extremely strong, got back on their feet with respect to their dollar business, the Bank of Japan imposed liquidity restrictions on their operations in dollars. Specifically, it said to these banks, "If you make a loan for a year, you must fund it with a deposit of at least equal maturity, and the same goes for loans of longer maturity." The Bank of Japan imposed these liquidity requirements even on rollover loans, because its concern was not with price but with availability. The liquidity requirements imposed by the Bank of Japan on the dollar operations of Japanese banks caused these banks to become leaders in developing a new form of Eurodollar paper: *floating-rate Eurodollar CDs with multiyear maturities.*

Exchange controls.   Many countries impose or have imposed and may again impose various forms of exchange control that limit the availability of dollars to local banks or even preclude local banks from dealing in dollars.

The imposition of exchange controls to protect the exchange value of the domestic currency is not inconsistent with permitting local banks to be active in the Eurodollar market or even from preventing local financial centers from being Euro centers. Britain, which had exchange controls until they were dismantled in 1979 is a prime example. The Euromarket was born and flourished in London during the period when tight controls existed on sterling. That was possible because the Euro activities of banks, in London, British included, were separated from their activities in the domestic sterling market by a clearly defined and well-respected set of rules established by the Bank of England. The smoothness and polish with which the British were

able to pull off this two-separate-markets-side-by-side routine probably reflects the unique, informal, but effective method by which the
Bank of England regulates banks operating in London.

In any case, a foreign bank that runs a Eurodollar book either in a
domestic financial center—e.g., a French bank in Paris—or in a foreign
center such as London faces the danger that its activities may be cur-
tailed and, in particular, its dollar liquidity threatened by the imposition of exchange controls on its native currency. The United States
imposed relatively mild exchange controls only once since the end of
World War II, during the period 1964–74, which did restrict the inter-
changability for banks of domestic and Eurodollars.[7] Most other countries have imposed exchange controls to prevent either the depreciation or appreciation of their currency more frequently than has the
United States and with greater severity. Thus, for foreign banks, depending on their country of origin, the possibility of alterations in
exchange control rules and a consequent change in the liquidity of
their dollar position is a constant and real risk.

Sovereign risk revisited. A country that imposes exchange controls may often follow the pattern of the United Kingdom. UK banks
were permitted to engage in Euro operations, but—to protect the exchange value of sterling—they were forbidden to use more than a
small amount of their sterling resources to produce dollars via swaps
and then lend these dollars offshore. This is reasonable from the point
of view of protecting the exchange value of the local currency, but the
arrangement does raise a question in the minds of depositors. Effectively, such exchange controls mean that a bank's capital, which is in
local currency, is unavailable—however large it may be—to meet depositor claims for dollars in the event that the bank experiences dollar
losses.

This is a strictly theoretical issue, since depositors have, in fact,
never suffered losses due to such an eventuality. Nevertheless, if there
is no way a foreign bank can use its capital to produce dollars to pay off
dollar debtors, this should cause some trepidation on the part of depositors who are considering placing dollars with it.

Currently, having an inconvertible currency produces the biggest
problem for banks from a country such as Brazil that has very strict
exchange controls. All the resources of a Brazilian bank are denominated in cruzeiros which may *not* be taken out of the country without
permission from the exchange control authorities. This creates a problem for a Brazilian bank that wants to open a branch in, say, New York.
To lend dollars there, the branch has to get dollars which it can do only
by paying a premium for them. As a practical matter, no one believes

---

[7] See Chapter 6.

that, for example, the Banco do Brazil is in danger of going out of business. The premium reflects depositors' concern that the bank's cruzeiro resources would *technically* be unavailable to pay off any dollar obligations its New York branch might incur.

For a bank that faces this sort of difficulty and wants to open a New York branch, it would be natural to open up both reciprocal deposit schemes and standby lines with U.S. banks operating in Brazil. Doing so would help; it is, in fact, a necessity. But such a bank is still forced by exchange controls to operate at a disadvantage in dollars.

Capital and liquidity requirements. Different countries regulate domestic banks quite differently. For example, U.S. banks are subject to reserve requirements, but not to specific liquidity or capital constraints. German, Belgian, and Swiss banks, in contrast, are not required to hold reserves, but must meet stringent liquidity and capital constraints. British banks are regulated quite informally. The Bank of England "suggests" what it thinks banks should and should not do; such suggestions prove, in practice, much more difficult to evade than do detailed regulations of the sort imposed by the Fed.

Currently, the leading banks in the Euromarket are U.S., British, Canadian, French, and Belgian banks. This list is not precisely the one a person would expect based on country size and vigor of the local economy. The conspicuous absence of German and Swiss banks from the list reflects the liquidity and capital constraints to which these banks are subject. Liquidity and capital constraints do not prevent these banks from doing all the local currency business available to them, but they do become binding constraints when these banks seek to do Eurobusiness. Putting on a lot of Eurobusiness is bound to balloon a bank's balance sheet and thereby worsen its capital ratio. Also, given the way the Euromarket operates—long-term rollover loans are financed with purchases of short-dated funds—Euro operations can easily cause difficulties for a bank that must meet stringent liquidity requirements. Since margins on domestic business are usually more attractive than margins on Eurobusiness, especially for European banks, liquidity and capital constraints—to the extent that they become binding constraints on expansion—will and have caused the affected banks to forgo Eurobusiness rather than domestic business. The choice between the two sorts of business is no choice at all. A bank that can do only so much business will always opt to do the business that is most profitable to it.

German banks have attempted to make an end run around the Bundesbank's liquidity and capital requirements by booking their Eurobusiness in Luxembourg subsidiaries. However, German authorities are threatening to end this play by forcing German banks to meet liquidity and capital constraints on the basis of their consolidated balance sheets; i.e., to combine, for compliance purposes, the balance sheets of their foreign subsidiaries with that of their head office.

The acceptance of foreign-bank, dollar-denominated paper

CDs in London. There are two places foreign banks can seek to raise dollars by selling their own paper, London and New York. There is a huge (multibillion-dollar) market for Eurodollar CDs in London. With respect to this market, one must distinguish between (1) *trading paper* that is sold to investors such as corporations that truly want liquidity and may eventually sell the paper, and (2) *lockup paper* which is sold to banks that want to hold negotiable CDs to give their assets the appearance of greater liquidity but that, in fact, intend to hold any CDs they buy to maturity.

The bulk of the Eurodollar CDs issued in London and sold to investors in the United States constitute trading paper, and generally only top U.S. names are acceptable to U.S. investors. However, foreign banks can and do issue dollar-denominated CDs in London to banks seeking lockup paper. Often they are able to issue such paper at rates close to or on top of the rates that top U.S. banks pay, but to sell their paper at such favorable rates, they must carefully ration the amount they write. A foreign bank can raise dollars by selling Eurodollar CDs in London, but only a limited amount, the amount being a function of its name and size.

CDs in New York. A foreign bank that makes a reasonable attempt to cultivate relationships with domestic banks can easily gain access to money in the Federal funds market. However, since this market deals primarily in overnight funds, foreign banks wanting to obtain financing for longer periods must rely on the sale in the New York market of either their CDs or their BAs. Foreign banks, however they may be viewed in the world market, face the same problem in New York that U.S. banks face in operating local-currency books in foreign financial centers; they are in an antiestablishment position. In the U.S. CD market, the sale of foreign bank CDs is thwarted by a chicken and egg problem. Most investors are unfamiliar with foreign bank names, don't know their credit, and so shy away from buying their paper even though such paper trades at more attractive rates than do CDs issued by top U.S. names. Dealers, who are always looking for a new product to peddle, would like to sell foreign bank CDs to domestic investors but are leery of positioning much of this paper, since they know it is difficult to sell to investors. The reluctance of dealers to position foreign paper, in turn, decreases the willingness of investors to buy it, because paper that dealers won't position is, by definition, illiquid, and most investors place a high value on liquidity.

This is not to say that foreign banks can't and do not sell CDs in New York. They do, and a goodly bit of such paper passes through the hands of and is traded by dealers. However, the quantity of paper foreign banks can sell in New York is small relative to that which U.S. banks of similar size and credit worthiness sell in the same market. Over time, the acceptance of foreign bank CDs has grown among U.S. investors, but the recent switch in Fed policy toward permitting short-term rates to be more volatile has hurt the sale of such paper; volatile rates encourage dealers to seek profits on turnover rather than on positioning, a development which, in recent years, has strengthened the preference of dealers for paper that is readily salable to a wide range of investors.

BAs. The problems foreign banks face with respect to their CDs—foreign banks are neither well known to nor accepted by investors, so dealers do not want to position their paper—also apply to BAs issued by foreign banks. There is, however, an exception, Japanese BAs. Normally, these trade at a premium to U.S. acceptances, but they do trade well and are actively dealt in by New York dealers. In one way or another, the Japanese are involved in about half the acceptance business done in the United States. This forced the Fed at one point to bite the bullet and decide against their traditional rules that Japanese acceptances, if they meet the same criteria that domestic BAs must, would be acceptable as collateral when the Fed—as part of open-market operations—does RP with the dealers and banks. The Fed's stamp of approval on such Japanese paper has made it acceptable to a wide range of domestic investors who would otherwise never have touched it, this despite the foreign sound of Japanese banks—Sumitomo, Mitsubishi, Daiwa—to American ears.

Non-Japanese banks have tried several ploys to sell acceptances to U.S. investors. They have asked top U.S. banks to endorse their acceptances, creating, in effect, two-name paper, but U.S. banks have been loath to do so since foreign banks operating in the United States are their direct competitors. Also, when a U.S. bank adds its name to a foreign bank acceptance, it charges a fee for doing so which increases the foreign bank's borrowing cost.

Another ploy foreign banks have tried is to say to regional banks: "We will create acceptances and have them guaranteed by our head office back home. Will you then commit to buy some of that paper from us at an attractive rate and peddle it to investors in your local sphere of influence?" This is a way for foreign banks to circumvent the New York dealers.

Double reserves. Since passage of the International Banking Act in 1978, the U.S. branches of foreign banks are required to maintain reserves against any deposits of dollars they receive from domestic sources or buy in the Euromarket to fund their U.S. book. As noted in Chapter 11, arbitrage causes Euro rates in any maturity range to equal or nearly equal domestic CD rates grossed up for reserve costs and the cost of FDIC insurance. This means that, if the New York branch of a foreign bank relies on funds purchased in the Euromarket to fund itself, it will have a higher cost of funds than major U.S. banks do because it will, in effect, be required to pay the reserve cost twice, once because the Euro rate incorporates this cost, again because the foreign bank must deposit reserves with the Fed on any Eurodollars it uses in the United States.

The passage of legislation putting foreign banks in the position of having, de facto, to pay reserves twice seems less than fair. Certainly passage of this legislation must have been a disappointment to foreign banks, which—after having lost money for years by making cut-rate, loss-leader loans to domestic corporations in an attempt to buy their way into the U.S. market—were probably hoping to finally be able to operate profitably in the United States.

On the other hand, U.S. banks face a similar disadvantage if they use Eurodollars to fund at least some of the local-currency books they run abroad. Also if, for example, Citi New York buys Eurodollars at a rate grossed up to compensate for U.S. reserve requirements and then swaps these dollars into sterling to finance its sterling-denominated portfolio of gilts, it must hold reserves against the resulting deposits, since they are booked on the U.S. balance sheet.

GLOBAL INTEREST RATE EXPOSURE

Earlier we made the point that a U.S. bank—especially in times of volatile interest rates—should, in controlling its interest rate exposure, run a global book: integrate its domestic and Euro books in measuring its interest rate exposure and be willing to use a position in one book to offset exposure in the other. We also noted that, at times, a U.S. bank may be able to adjust its interest rate exposure more rapidly in its Euro book than in its domestic book. Therefore, if a change in the bank's interest rate forecast requires a quick change in its interest rate exposure, the better place for it to make that adjustment in the short run may be in its Euro book.

Local-currency books represent probably something on the order of 10 to 15 percent of the total books of top U.S. banks. The more closely an economy is tied to other Western economies and to the free world economy as a whole, the more likely it is that interest rates in that country will move up and down roughly in step with Eurodollar rates which, in turn, closely track U.S. domestic rates. There are, however, exceptions to the assumption that interest rates in major free world countries will move together.

An example is the United Kingdom which is a special case because of its oil production. If the price of oil (which is invoiced in dollars) rises, Britain might decide to lower its interest rates to prevent the pound from appreciating, while, simultaneously, West Germany might decide to raise its interest rates to prevent the mark from depreciating and to dampen the inflationary impact of a rise in the price of oil.

A major U.S. bank running a global book should seek, to the extent possible, to integrate its local-currency books into its global position. Doing so, however, will require careful judgments as to whether anticipated movements in dollar interest rates will be tracked and, if so, to what degree, by rate movements in the various countries where the bank runs a sizable local-currency books.

The issue of whether rates in a given country will or will not move in step with dollar rates is even more crucial for foreign banks running big dollar positions. Ideally, such banks should run global books for the same reasons U.S. banks should; doing so is by far the best way to track a bank's overall interest rate exposure and to adjust that exposure so that the bank may profit from any insight it has into how interest rates are likely to move in the short run.

To the extent that a foreign bank feels confident that rates in its home country will move in step with rates in the Euromarket, it is, if anything, probably better placed than a U.S. bank to adjust its global interest rate exposure by altering its Euro book. Typically, European banks earn higher profit margins on domestic business than major U.S. banks do. This means that—from the point of view of maintaining an acceptable return on assets—a foreign bank is better able to add low-margin Eurobusiness to its balance sheet to alter its global interest rate exposure than is a major U.S. bank.

How feasible it is for a foreign bank to better control its interest rate exposure by running a global book will depend directly on the correlation between dollar interest rates and interest rates in its country of origin. If that correlation is high, running a global book will offer a foreign bank a significant opportunity for better managing its overall interest rate exposure. If, alternatively, the correlation is low, a bank—to manage its overall interest rate exposure—will have to make separate interest rate forecasts for domestic and dollar rates and to run its domestic and Euro books with a degree of independence greater than that which would be appropriate for a U.S. bank running both a domestic and a big Eurocurrency book.

14

A postscript:
Banking debacles occurring as this book went to press

As this book went to press, an unprecedented spate of difficulties at, and sometimes failures of, major financial institutions, domestic and foreign, was rocking both the domestic U.S. and the Euromarkets. Brief descriptions of each of these and of its implications for sound bank management are given below.

DRYSDALE SECURITIES

The market in repos and reverses is not only one of the largest, but one of the most complex sectors of the domestic money market.[1] Dealers do repo transactions to finance their own inventories of securities and reverses to borrow securities when they must make delivery on issues they have shorted; on such transactions, dealers, bank and nonbank, act as principals in the transaction.

Investors sometimes also do repo to leverage their position. More

---
[1] See Chapter 12, "Repos and Reverses," in *The Money Market: Myth, Reality, and Practice* (Homewood, Ill.: Dow Jones-Irwin, 1978) by Marcia Stigum.

commonly, they reverse out securities, i.e., borrow cash against them, as part of a profitable arbitrage: typically, an arb pointed out to them by a dealer in or by a broker of repo. Finally, the Fed does repos and reverses as part of its open-market operations.

Any institution participating in a repo or reverse repurchase transaction is, regardless of the side it takes, exposed to some credit risk unless its counterpart in the trade is the Fed. The same is true of any institution that brokers repo or acts as an agent in repo or reverse repo transactions. One important source of credit risk in RP transactions is that the institution taking one side of the transaction may be making a bet on rates: running a short book in anticipation of a fall in rates or a long book in anticipation of a rise in rates; should rates move in a direction opposite to that in which the institution is betting they will move, the resulting losses incurred by that institution may be so large as to preclude it from honoring the obligations imposed on it by the RP transactions into which it has entered.

Because credit risk is inherent to all participants in repo and reverse transactions, a maxim of the street has always been: *know thy customer*. Street participants were dealt a rude reminder of this maxim when Financial Corporation of Kansas City went bankrupt in 1975. Financial Corp., which, when it went under, was holding $1.8 billion of governments, was the creation of Eldin Miller, a man who has been described as a nonsmoker, nondrinker, who looked like a church deacon and inspired confidence in all he met.

Eldin's initial strategy was to purchase governments and to finance these with loans of much shorter maturity in the RP market: to run a short book in the expectation that rates would fall. In fact, rates rose; this eventually led Miller to try to reverse his strategy and at the same time to raise cash, but he acted too late to avoid disaster.

When Financial Corp. went under, people assumed that street firms had been so chastened by its failure and by the Winters debacle in Ginnie Mae forwards that they would either institute new credit controls or enforce strictly those they already had in place: that prudent firms would again take to heart the maxim know thy customer.

When in early 1982 Drysdale—a small, new dealer on the street got involved in a big way with Chase, it was following a strategy opposite to Financial Corp.'s initial plan; namely, it supposed that interest rates would rise. To take advantage of the anticipated rise in rates, Drysdale shorted governments; to make delivery, it borrowed securities primarily from Chase under its securities lending program and also from other banks in smaller amounts. Chase's program involved lending 1) securities held by its customers on a prearranged fee basis and 2) securities reversed in from other institutions through repo brokers.

During the period Drysdale was actively shorting the government market and covering by reversing in securities, its transaction generated, because of the different ways in which governments are priced for purchases and for use as repo collateral, a goodly bit of cash flow for Drysdale; specifically, Drysdale had to pay only principal on the securities it reversed in from Chase, but it sold these same securities for principal *plus* accrued interest whenever it made a short sale.

Had interest rates gone up, as Drysdale believed they would, the firm would have made a big profit on its short sales. Instead, rates fell. Presumably Drysdale did not bank the cash flow generated from the short sale of securities which it had reversed in. In mid-May Drysdale was unable to come up with $160 million it owed Chase to cover coupon payments due on securities it had borrowed from Chase, coupon payments that Chase was obligated to pass on to the investors on whose behalf it had lent these securities.

On the transactions in question, Chase was acting as an agent; this is indicated by the fact that the tickets for these transactions were written not with Chase Bank *as principal* but for the XYZ *stock loan* account at Chase.

It is a *street convention* that, when an investor lends securities through a bank that is acting as an agent, as Chase was, then whenever the term of the loan encompasses a coupon date, the borrower of the securities will collect the coupon and turn the proceeds over to the agent who will, in turn, pass them on to the lender of the securities.

Large, savvy investors who lend securities through a bank that is acting as an agent for an anonymous dealer or investor ask the agent for a letter that says that, while the bank is acting on behalf of a customer in lending out the customer's securities, it is for all intents and purposes, and in particular with respect to the payment of accrued interest on coupon dates, acting as principal. This is another *street convention*; since not everyone is familiar with this convention, not everyone asks for such a letter.

In acting as an agent in securities-lending transactions, a bank is probably getting ½ percent, which on Drysdale's estimated $4 billion position would have amounted to $2 million per year in fee income. The presumption is that fees of this magnitude represent payment not just for writing tickets, but for providing anonymity to one or both sides of the transaction and for assuming any credit risk inherent in the transaction.

When Drysdale failed, Chase found itself being asked by the institutions whose securities it had lent to ante up $160 million of coupon interest that was due them but which Drysdale lacked funds to pay. At first, Chase refused to pay saying that, in its capacity as agent, it was not legally bound to do so. This position caused Chase to be put under a lot of pressure from a wide range of market participants to pay up. Perhaps because of this pressure, Chase realized that, if it failed to pay the interest due, its action might trigger the failure of other firms, which in turn might cause the whole dealer market in governments to collapse. In any case, Chase finally agreed to pay the $160 million of accrued interest due while reserving the right to pursue claims against third parties.

In the context of this book, two points should be made. First, Chase got into trouble only because it lacked or failed to implement proper credit controls. The drawing up and enforcement of strict credit controls is fundamental to the operation of any financial institution.

A second point relates to what we said in Chapter 12 about a bank making a strategic decision to enter a new line or to expand an existing line of business. Deciding to run a big securities lending operation—a strategic decision made by Chase—is, as we note, a decision that should be made by a bank only on the basis of a careful evaluation of the risks, as well as the possible rewards, associated with the new venture.

Partly as a result of pressure from bank analysts, all banks today are looking for ways to raise their return on assets (ROA); whereas banks used to want to be the biggest in terms of footings, today they seek to have the best ROA. This means banks are all scrambling for service business that will bring them fee income without ballooning their balance sheets. Running a securities lending operation, because it has no impact on the balance sheet of the institution running it, is a natural for banks wanting to raise ROA. The catch is that, if all big banks and dealers are scrambling for the same business, they can all do increased amounts of it (build bigger books) only by dealing with less-and-less-creditworthy customers. Or to put it another way, competition will tend to erode the initially attractive fee offered on this service because entry of many institutions into the provision of this service will raise the notional, but nonetheless real, credit risk associated with it, which in turn will lower the true spread earned on it.

FAILURE OF THE PENN SQUARE BANK

In the summer of 1982, the Penn Square Bank failed with substantial losses to uninsured depositors—the first time this had happened in FDIC history. With respect to the precepts laid down in this book, the main point that should be made concerning Penn Square's failure is the same one we made above. When a bank decides to enter a new line of business that appears to offer attractive spreads—in this case, energy lending—a lot of other banks are going to make the same decision. As a result, as banks do more and more of this sort of business, they are likely to find themselves lending to poorer and poorer credits.

A bank should recognize this, but banks, like investors in anything from tulips to common stock, are subject to crowd psychology. When a particular investment becomes a new, hot fad, they feel compelled to get into it. Thus, when REITs were the fad, most banks—to their later regret—got into REIT lending. Because energy loans were a fad until oil prices peaked out, Penn Square not only made a lot of questionable energy-related loans, but was also able to peddle participations in these loans to big banks who should have known better: $1 billion to the Continental Bank, $200 to $300 million to Chase, $400 million to Seafirst Corp., $200 million to Michigan National Corp., and $125 million to Northern Trust Corp.

DOME OIL AND THE CANADIAN BANKS

While U.S. banks were making or otherwise participating in energy-related loans to their later regret, the same was occurring north of the border on an even grander scale. In Canada, energy-related lending became a fad not only because energy prices were rising, but because Trudeau convinced Canadians—economic theory to the contrary notwithstanding—that a massive capital outflow resulting from the buyout by Canadian companies of American properties in Canada would be in the long-run economic interest of Canada. This created an atmosphere in which Dome Petroleum, the giant of the Canadian energy industry, could, with the aid of bank loans, attain a leverage ratio of $30 of debt to $1 of capital. To put things in proportion, note that Dome is a nonfinancial business corporation not a bank which is supposed to make money by being highly leveraged: if Citibank or any other major U.S. bank were to attain a 30-to-1 capital ratio, the regulators would be knocking on its door asking bank management just what they thought they were doing and what their plans were for reducing their debt or bolstering their capital.

Currently, Dome, which is in dire financial straits, has outstanding from the major Canadian banks loans equal to roughly 40 percent of the total equity and reserves of these banks. Clearly, the Canadian government, since it cannot permit widescale collapse of its domestic banking system, must eventually decide to bail out either Dome or the Canadian banks.

CONTINENTAL ILLINOIS

During the spring and summer of 1982, Continental Illinois saw its image as one of the nation's top banks tarnished by a number of events. It was a big taker of participations in the energy-related loans Penn Square was making; on these, Continental had to take a second-quarter, pretax write off of $220 million. Later in the summer, Nucorp

Energy—for which Continental, as leader of a group of nine banks, had put together a \$300+ million revolving credit agreement—filed for protection under Chapter 11. Energy-related loans were not Continental's only problem. It had also made big loans to Braniff, International Harvester, Massey-Ferguson, American-Invesco, Dome Petroleum, Wicks, and other firms that either had gone bankrupt or were experiencing severe financial problems.

The upshot of Continental's numerous sour and souring loans was that it faced a liquidity problem. One of the precepts of this book is that the first and foremost concern of a bank must be to maintain its liquidity: its ability to ensure the availability of funds to meet its commitments at a reasonable price at all times. For a bank, liquidity is crucial because liquidity is what keeps the bank's door open in the short run and what permits the bank to be profitable over the long run.

To maintain liquidity, a bank, even if it is in the top 10, must make every effort to keep its name pure in the market place because, from everyone's point of view, there is *no* penalty for not lending to a bank that has let a shadow be cast over its good name.

Because of the large losses—real and potential—deriving from Continental's loan portfolio, investors by the summer of 1982 did not want to and felt no need to hold Continental's paper. As a result, Continental, the nation's seventh largest bank, was forced to ask CD dealers to remove its name from the list of top banks whose CDs traded—because they were viewed as all being issued by top credits—on a no-name basis. Continental was also forced to ask the IMM to delete its name from the list of banks whose paper was deliverable on a maturing futures contract for 90-day CDs; prior to doing so, Continental was the bank whose CDs were most frequently delivered at the expiration of a CD futures contract.

For a top bank, going through a period when it cannot sell its CDs in volume in the national market is not fatal: First of Chicago did it. Doing so, however, is costly to a bank because the inability to tap the national money market in volume inevitably raises the bank's cost of funds, which in turn has a negative impact on its profitability so long as the condition persists.

Fortunately for the Continental, it continued to be able to buy Fed funds without being forced to pay up: other banks did not expect the Continental to go bankrupt overnight. Continental did, however, have to pay up 20 to 50 basis points for Euros. For a bank that relies heavily on bought money, having its cost of funds on other than overnight money raised 20 to 50 basis points must have a marked impact on its ROA.

To regain the confidence of investors and thereby liquidity—the ability to obtain money when it needs it at a *reasonable price*—Continental will have to do what First of Chicago did: take its lumps in the form of loan losses, slim down its loan portfolio to creditworthy names, and regain a respectable and consistent record of profitability. Once it does this, investors will again be willing to lend to the Continental on the same terms on which they lend to other top banks.

THE BANCO AMBROSIANO

In June 1982, the Italian central bank requested that the chairman, Mr. Robert Calvi, of the Banco Ambrosiano, then Italy's 11th largest bank and largest private bank, provide it with details concerning the $1.4 billion of loans that the Banco Ambrosiano Holdings S.A., a Luxembourg financial holding company, had extended through its Latin American subsidiaries to a number of Panamanian companies. Shortly thereafter, Mr. Calvi was found hanging from a London bridge in a position that suggests that, unless he was an extraordinary athlete, his death was a result of foul play.

From there on, the Ambrosiano story unfolded like a good yarn spun by Paul Erdman. Unfortunately for Euro bankers, however, the story was fact not fiction.

On July 12, the Midland Bank—agent for a syndicate of banks that had lent $40 million to Banco Ambrosiano Holdings (BAH)—declared BAH in default because of long-overdue payments of interest and principal. Other banks in other syndicates followed suit; and on July 14, BAH's assets were frozen by a Luxembourg court.

Subsequent investigations uncovered the fact that the $1.4 billion of loans extended in early 1980 by the Latin American subsidiaries of BAH and financed by BAH and other Ambrosiano subsidiaries were to paper corporations that were nominally owned by the Vatican Bank. The operations of this bank, known officially as the Instituto per le Opere de Religione (IOR), have, until recently, been shrouded in total secrecy; IOR owns at least 1.58 percent of the Banco Ambrosiano and is suspected of owning much more. Apparently in many matters—the full story has yet to be told and may never be—the Vatican Bank acted as a de facto partner in various ventures with the Banco Ambrosiano. Certainly Calvi was known in Italian circles as "God's banker."

A most peculiar aspect of the loans financed by BAH in Latin America is that Archbishop Paul Marcinkus, the American-born president of the Vatican bank, signed "letters of patronage" for the Panamanian ghost companies that received loans from BAH. Marcinkus's letters stated that the companies were controlled by the Vatican bank and were apparently written to serve as references or guarantees for the lender. However, after the letters were written, Calvi secretly rendered them legally worthless by absolving the Vatican Bank from any responsibility in these loan transactions. As of August 1982, no one knew what had happened to the $1.4 billion of money lent by Ambrosiano subsidiaries to paper companies in Panama.

The declaration by the Midland Bank that BAH was in default and the subsequent disclosure of the irregular, to say the least, activities in which the Banco Ambrosiano had engaged (often in confusing partnership with the IOR) caused the Banco Ambrosiano to face a *liquidity* crisis. When it became apparent that this bank could no longer meet its obligations, the Bank of Italy, working with a consortium of major Italian banks, put together an aid package designed to permit the Banco Ambrosiano to make timely payments on its obligations. This arrangement continued until early August when the Bank of Italy stated that the remnants of the Banco Ambrosiano's assets would be reconstituted into a new bank that would be controlled by the bank consortium formed in July to bail out Ambrosiano. By ordering a liquidation of the assets of the Banco Ambrosiano, rather than declaring the institution bankrupt, the central bank permitted Ambrosiano to continue its normal banking activities without interruption.

In announcing the establishment of the new bank, called the Nuovo Banco Ambrosiano, the Italian treasury minister stressed that this new bank would in no way assume the liabilities of BAH or of its Latin American subsidiaries. The support given by the Bank of Italy to the Banco Ambrosiano is in line with what one would expect. Since the failure of the Herstatt, no major free-world country has permitted one of its top banks to fail with losses to depositors.[2]

While the fate of the Banco Ambrosiano has been settled, the question of what institution, if any, would assume responsibility for paying off BAH's liabilities remained an open issue in August 1982. As Italian authorities sought to pierce the veil of secrecy and diplomatic immunity surrounding the operations of the Vatican Bank and threatened to bring fraud charges against three of its directors, the IOR, for its part, refused to accept any liability for the debts of BAH, which as a practical matter the IOR could not pay off in full since these debts exceeded its net worth.

The Bank of Italy argued that it was under no legal or moral obligation to pay off the debts of BAH because the company was a holding company located in Luxembourg. Luxembourg, for its part, washed its hands of responsibility for BAH's debts on the grounds that BAH was not a bank but a holding company.

All this was troubling to Euro bankers for several reasons. First,

---

[2] Penn Square is no exception. Unfortunately for Penn Square depositors, this bank was small enough on the American scene so that regulators felt they would permit it to fail with losses to depositors without bringing down the whole house of cards—the domestic banking system—with it. That would not have been the case if Citibank or one of the nation's other top banks had gotten into difficulties of equivalent severity, as evidenced by the expensive and time-consuming federal bailout of the Franklin National.

they stood to lose $526 million on loans to and notes issued by BAH and perhaps a good bit more on deposits with its Latin American subsidiaries.[3] Second, Euro bankers feared that default by BAH might ring the death knell of the Basle convention. In this convention, signed in 1975 following the failure of the Herstatt Bank, central bankers agreed to assume responsibility for the solvency of foreign-based bank subsidiaries set up by their country's commercial banks. While BAH falls technically outside the convention because it is a foreign subsidiary of a holding company, Eurobankers feel that default of BAH would violate the spirit of the Basel agreement and thereby weaken one of the foundations on which confidence in the vast interinstitutional market in Euros is based. Whether that will prove so, and if it does, the extent to which the Euromarket will be affected over the long run, remain to be seen.

Apart from its Euromarket impact, most of the rest of the Ambrosiano story, including the involvement of the Vatican Bank, points to a simple and obvious moral: permitting a bank to operate with great secrecy—total secrecy in the case of the Vatican bank—invites bankers, who, like other businessmen, have human failings, to engage in questionable if not fraudulent activities. It is not without good reason that publicly owned banks in the United States and other major countries are subject to outside audit and are required to publish periodically income statements and balance sheets.

EAST EUROPEAN LENDING

A final cloud over the banking scene in the summer of 1982 was the huge loans U.S. and foreign banks had outstanding to East European countries. Certainly in the case of Poland, there was no realistic hope that it could or would repay its loans in the foreseeable future. Yet bankers clung to the hope of rescheduling Poland's debts to obviate the necessity of huge loan writeoffs.

In this respect, it is interesting to note that the German banks, which are among the most heavily regulated of Western banks, had made, relative to their size, the biggest loans to East European countries and that they had done so partly at the behest of German authorities who were anxious to further the cause of detente.

Strict bank regulation and sound banking do not necessarily go hand in hand for two reasons. First, as in the case of Germany, strict

---

[3] The miasma of intergroup transactions that linked the Banco Ambrosiano, the numerous subsidiaries of its holding company, the Vatican bank, and other Eurodollar market participants are portrayed schematically in the *Financial Times*, August 5, 1982. A lot of the dollar flows in the chart that lead to the Vatican bank are marked with question marks.

regulation in no way prevents a government from encouraging domestic banks to take imprudent actions if the government feels it is in the national interest that domestic banks do so. Second, U.S. bank regulators, the Comptroller's Office in particular, are noted for not blowing the whistle when they find that a bank is slipping into deep trouble and actually violating one or more of the many rules the bank is required by statute to respect; fearing that adverse publicity might create a run on a bank in trouble or, worse still, a run on all banks. The policy of the Comptroller's Office is to elicit a promise from a wayward bank to do better in the future. All too often when the examiners return, they find to their dismay that the bank that promised to do better is in worse shape than ever. That was certainly the case with Penn Square, which had been under the eye of the Comptroller's Office since 1980.

GLOSSARY

Common banking, money market, and bond market terms

Accretion (of a discount): In portfolio accounting, a straight-line accumulation of capital gains on discount bonds in anticipation of receipt of par at maturity.

Accrued interest: Interest due from issue or from the last coupon date to the present on an interest-bearing security. The buyer of the security pays the quoted dollar price plus accrued interest.

Active: A market in which there is much trading.

Add-on rate: A specific rate of interest to be paid. Stands in contrast to the rate on a discount security, such as a Treasury bill, that pays *no* interest.

Aftertax real rate of return: Money aftertax rate of return minus the inflation rate.

Agencies: Federal agency securities.

Agency bank: A form of organization commonly used by foreign banks to enter the U.S. market. An agency bank cannot accept deposits or extend loans in its own name; it acts as an agent for the parent bank.

Agent: A firm that executes orders for or otherwise acts on behalf of another (the principal) and is subject to its control and authority. The agent may receive a fee or commission.

All-in cost: Total costs, explicit and other. Example: The all-in cost to a bank of CD money is the explicit rate of interest it pays on that deposit *plus* the FDIC premium it must pay on the deposit *plus* the hidden cost it incurs because it must hold some portion of that deposit in a non–interest-bearing reserve account at the Fed.

All or none (AON): Requirement that none of an order be executed unless all of it can be executed at the specified price.

Amortize: In portfolio accounting, periodic charges made against interest income on premium bonds in anticipation of receipt of the call price at call or of par value at maturity.

Arbitrage: Strictly defined, buying something where it is cheap and selling it where it is dear; e.g., a bank buys 3-month CD money in the U.S. market and sells 3-month money at a higher rate in the Eurodollar market. In the money market, often refers: (1) to a situation in which a trader buys one security and sells a similar security in the expectation that the spread in yields between the two instruments will narrow or widen to his profit, (2) to a swap between two similar issues based on an anticipated change in yield spreads, and (3) to situations where a higher return (or lower cost) can be achieved in the money market for one currency by utilizing another currency and swapping it on a fully hedged basis through the foreign exchange market.

ARBL (assets repriced before liabilities): This number, which may be calculated for various time periods, is a measure of the mismatch in a bank's book and thus of its interest rate exposure. Since ARBL is the difference between two numbers, it may be positive or negative.

Asked: The price at which securities are offered.

Away: A trade, quote, or market that does not originate with the dealer in question, e.g., "the bid is 98–10 away (from me)."

Back up: (1) When yields rise and prices fall, the market is said to back up. (2) When an investor swaps out of one security into another of shorter current maturity (e.g., out of a 2-year note into an 18-month note), he is said to back up.

Bank discount rate: Yield basis on which short-term, non–interest-bearing money market securities are quoted. A rate quoted on a discount basis understates bond equivalent yield. That must be calculated when comparing return against coupon securities.

Bank line: Line of credit granted by a bank to a customer.

Bank wire: A computer message system linking major banks. It is used not for effecting payments, but as a mechanism to advise the receiving bank of some action that has occurred, e.g., the payment by a customer of funds into that bank's account.

Bankers' acceptance (BA): A draft or bill of exchange accepted by a bank or trust company. The accepting institution guarantees payment of the bill.

BANs: Bond anticipation notes are issued by states and municipalities to obtain interim financing for projects that will eventually be funded long term through the sale of a bond issue.

Basis: (1) Number of days in the coupon period. (2) In *commodities* jargon, basis is the spread between a futures price and some other price. A money market participant would talk about *spread* rather than basis.

Basis point: One one hundreth of 1 percent.

Basis price: Price expressed in terms of yield to maturity or annual rate of return.

Bear market: A declining market or a period of pessimism when declines in the market are anticipated. (A way to remember: "Bear down.")

Bearer security: A security the owner of which is not registered on the books of the issuer. A bearer security is payable to the holder.

Best-efforts basis: Securities dealers do not underwrite a new issue, but sell it on the basis of what can be sold. In the money market, this usually refers to a firm order to buy or sell a given amount of securities or currency at the best price that can be found over a given period of time; it can also refer to a flexible amount (up to a limit) at a given rate.

Bid: The price offered for securities.

Block: A large amount of securities, normally much more than what constitutes a round lot in the market in question.

Book: A banker, especially a Eurobanker, will refer to his bank's assets and liabilities as its "book." If the average maturity of the liabilities is less than that of the assets, the bank is running a **short** or **open** book.

Book-entry securities: The Treasury and federal agencies are moving to a book-entry system in which securities are not represented by engraved pieces of paper but are maintained in computerized records at the Fed in the names of member banks, which, in turn, keep records of the securities they own as well as those they are holding for customers. In the case of other securities for which there is a book-entry system, engraved securities do exist somewhere in quite a few cases. These securities do not move from holder to holder but are usually kept in a central clearinghouse or by another agent.

Book value: The value at which a debt security is shown on the holder's balance sheet. Book value is often acquisition cost ± amortization/ accretion, which may differ markedly from market value. It can be further defined as "tax book," "accreted book," or "amortized book" value.

Bridge financing: Interim financing of one sort or another.

British clearers: The large clearing banks that dominate deposit taking and short-term lending in the domestic sterling market in Great Britain.

Broker: A broker brings buyers and sellers together for a commission paid by the initiator of the transaction or by both sides; he does not position. In the money market, brokers are active in markets in which banks buy and sell money and in interdealer markets.

Bull market: A period of optimism when increases in market prices are anticipated. (A way to remember: "Bull ahead.")

Bullet loan: A bank term loan that calls for no amortization. The term is commonly used in the Euromarket.

Buy-back: Another term for a repurchase agreement.

Calendar: List of new bond issues scheduled to come to market soon.

Call money: Interest-bearing bank deposits that can be withdrawn on 24-hours notice. Many Eurodeposits take the form of call money.

Callable bond: A bond that the issuer has the right to redeem prior to maturity by paying some specified call price.

Canadian agencies: Agency banks established by Canadian banks in the United States.

Carry: The interest cost of financing securities held. (See also **Negative** and **Positive carry.**)

Cash management bill: Very short-maturity bills that the Treasury occasionally sells because it is low on cash and needs money for a few days.

Cash market: Traditionally, this term has been used to denote the market in which commodities were traded, for immediate delivery, against cash. Since the inception of futures markets for T bills and other debt securities, a distinction has been made between the cash markets in which these securities trade for immediate delivery and the futures markets in which they trade for future delivery.

Cash settlement: In the money market, a transaction is said to be made for cash settlement if the securities purchased are delivered against payment in Fed funds on the same day the trade is made.

Certificate of deposit (CD): A time deposit with a specific maturity evidenced by a certificate. Large-denomination CDs are typically negotiable.

CHIPS: The New York Clearing House's computerized Clearing House Interbank Payments System. Most Euro transactions are cleared and settled through CHIPS rather than over the Fed wire.

Circle: Underwriters, actual or potential as the case may be, often seek out and "circle" retail interest in a new issue before final pricing. The customer circled has basically made a commitment to purchase the note or bond *or* to purchase it if it comes at an agreed-upon price. In the latter case, if the price is other than that stipulated, the customer supposedly has first offer at the actual price.

Classified loan: A classified loan is one cited by bank examiners as being at risk to some degree. A classified loan may or may not be nonperforming.

Clear: A trade carried out by the seller delivering securities and the buyer delivering funds in proper form. A trade that does not clear is said to fail.

Clearinghouse funds: Payments made through the New York Clearing House's computerized Clearing House Interbank Payments System. Clearinghouse debits and credits used to be settled in Fed funds on the first business day after clearing. Since October, 1981 these debits and credits have been settled on the same day in Fed funds.

Commercial paper: An unsecured promissory note with a fixed maturity of no more than 270 days. Commercial paper is normally sold at a discount from face value.

Committed facility (line of credit):   A legal commitment undertaken by a bank to lend to a customer.

Competitive bid: (1) Bid tendered in a Treasury action for a specific amount of securities at a specific yield or price. (2) Issuers, municipal and public utilities, often sell new issues by asking for competitive bids from one or more syndicates.

Confirmation: A memorandum to the other side of a trade describing all relevant data.

Consortium banks: A merchant banking subsidiary set up by several banks that may or may not be of the same nationality. Consortium banks are common in the Euromarket and are active in loan syndication.

Convertible bond: A bond containing a provision that permits conversion to the issuer's common stock at some fixed exchange ratio.

Corporate bond equivalent: See **Equivalent bond yield.**

Corporate taxable equivalent: Rate of return required on a par bond to produce the same aftertax yield to maturity that the premium or discount bond quoted would.

Country risk: See **Sovereign risk.**

Coupon: (1) The annual rate of interest on the bond's face value that a bond's issuer promises to pay the bondholder. (2) A certificate attached to a bond evidencing interest due on a payment date.

Cover: Eliminating a short position by buying the securities shorted.

Covered interest arbitrage: Investing dollars in an instrument denominated in a foreign currency and hedging the resulting foreign exchange risk by selling the proceeds of the investment forward for dollars.

Credit risk: The risk that an issuer of debt securities or a borrower may default on his obligations, or that payment may not be made on sale of a negotiable instrument. (See **Overnight delivery risk.**)

Cross hedge: Hedging a risk in a cash market security by buying or selling a futures contract for a different, but similar instrument.

CRTs: Abbreviation for the cathode-ray tubes used to display market quotes.

Current account: Foreign jargon for demand deposits.

Current coupon: A bond selling at or close to par, that is, a bond with a coupon close to the yield currently offered on new bonds of similar maturity and credit risk.

Current issue: In Treasury bills and notes, the most recently auctioned issue. Trading is more active in current issues than in off-the-run issues.

Current maturity: Current time to maturity on an outstanding note, bond, or other money market instrument; for example, a 5-year note 1 year after issue has a current maturity of 4 years.

Current yield: Coupon payments on a security as a percentage of the security's market price. In many instances the price should be *gross* of accrued interest, particularly on instruments where no coupon is left to be paid until maturity.

Cushion bonds: High-coupon bonds that sell at only a moderate premium because they are callable at a price below that at which a comparable noncallable bond would sell. Cushion bonds offer considerable downside protection in a falling market.

Day trading: Intraday trading in securities for profit as opposed to investing for profit.

Dealer: A dealer, as opposed to a broker, acts as a principal in all transactions, buying and selling for his own account.

Dealer loan: Overnight, collateralized loan made to a dealer financing his position by borrowing from a money market bank.

Debenture: A bond secured only by the general credit of the issuer.

Debt leverage: The amplification in the return earned on equity funds when an investment is financed partly with borrowed money.

Debt securities: IOUs created through loan-type transactions—commercial paper, bank CDs, bills, bonds, and other instruments.

Default: Failure to make timely payment of interest or principal on a debt security or to otherwise comply with the provisions of a bond indenture.

Demand line of credit: A bank line of credit that enables a customer to borrow on a daily or an on-demand basis.

Direct paper: Commercial paper sold directly by the issuer to investors.

Direct placement: Selling a new issue not by offering it for sale publicly, but by placing it with one or several institutional investors.

Discount basis: See **Bank discount rate.**

Discount bond: A bond selling below par.

Discount house: British institution that uses call and overnight money obtained from banks to invest in and trade money market instruments.

Discount paper: See **Discount securities.**

Discount rate: The rate of interest charged by the Fed to member banks that borrow at the discount window. The discount rate is an add-on rate.

Discount securities: Non–interest-bearing money market instruments that are issued at a discount and redeemed at maturity for full face value, e.g., U.S. Treasury bills.

Discount window: Facility provided by the Fed enabling member banks to borrow reserves against collateral in the form of governments or other acceptable paper.

Disintermediation: The investing of funds that would normally have been placed with a bank or other financial intermediary directly into debt securities issued by ultimate borrowers, e.g., into bills or bonds.

Distributed: After a Treasury auction, there will be many new issues in dealers' hands. As those securities are sold to retail, the issue is said to be distributed.

Diversification: Dividing investment funds among a variety of securities offering independent returns.

DM: Deutsche (German) marks.

Documented discount notes: Commercial paper backed by normal bank lines plus a letter of credit from a bank stating that it will pay off the paper at maturity if the borrower does not. Such paper is also referred to as **LOC** (letter of credit) **paper.**

Dollar bonds: Municipal revenue bonds for which quotes are given in dollar prices. Not to be confused with "U.S. Dollar" bonds, a common term of reference in the Euro bond market.

Dollar price of a bond: Percentage of face value at which a bond is quoted.

Don't know (DK, DKed): "Don't know the trade"—a street expression used whenever one party lacks knowledge of a trade or receives conflicting instructions from the other party (for example, with respect to payment).

Due bill: An instrument evidencing the obligation of a seller to deliver securities sold to the buyer. Occasionally used in the bill market.

Dutch auction: Auction in which the lowest price necessary to sell the entire offering becomes the price at which all securities offered are sold. This technique has been used in Treasury auctions.

Edge Act corporation: A subsidiary of a U.S. bank set up to carry out international banking business. Most such "subs" are located within the United States.

Either/or facility: An agreement permitting a bank customer to borrow either domestic dollars from the bank's head office or Eurodollars from one of its foreign branches.

Either-way market: In the interbank Eurodollar deposit market, an either-way market is one in which the bid and asked rates are identical.

Eligible bankers' acceptances: In the BA market an acceptance may be referred to as eligible because it is acceptable by the Fed as collateral at the discount window and/or because the accepting bank can sell it without incurring a reserve requirement.

Equivalent bond yield: Annual yield on a short-term, non–interest-bearing security calculated so as to be comparable to yields quoted on coupon securities.

Equivalent taxable yield: The yield on a taxable security that would leave the investor with the same aftertax return he would earn by holding a tax-exempt municipal; for example, for an investor taxed at a 50 percent marginal rate, equivalent taxable yield on a muni note issued at 3 percent would be 6 percent.

Euro bonds: Bonds issued in Europe outside the confines of any national capital market. A Euro bond may or may not be denominated in the currency of the issuer.

Euro CDs: CDs issued by a U.S. bank branch or foreign bank located outside the United States. Almost all Euro CDs are issued in London.

Euro lines: Lines of credit granted by banks (foreign or foreign branches of U.S. banks) for Eurocurrencies.

Eurocurrency deposits: Deposits made in a bank or bank branch that is not located in the country in whose currency the deposit is denominated. Dollars deposited in a London bank are Eurodollars; German marks deposited there are Euromarks.

Eurodollars: U.S. dollars deposited in a U.S. bank branch or a foreign bank located outside the United States.

Excess reserves: Balances held by a bank at the Fed in excess of those required.

Exchange rate: The price at which one currency trades for another.

Exempt securities: Instruments exempt from the registration requirements of the Securities Act of 1933 or the margin requirements of the Securities and Exchange Act of 1934. Such securities include governments, agencies, municipal securities, commercial paper, and private placements.

Extension swap: Extending maturity through a swap, e.g., selling a 2-year note and buying one with a slightly longer current maturity.

Fail: A trade is said to fail if on settlement date either the seller fails to deliver securities in proper form or the buyer fails to deliver funds in proper form.

Fed funds: See **Federal funds.**

Fed wire: A computer system linking member banks to the Fed, used for making interbank payments of Fed funds and for making deliveries of and payments for Treasury and agency securities.

Federal credit agencies: Agencies of the federal government set up to supply credit to various classes of institutions and individuals, e.g., S&Ls, small business firms, students, farmers, farm cooperatives, and exporters.

Federal Deposit Insurance Corporation (FDIC): A federal institution that insures bank deposits, currently up to $100,000 per deposit.

Federal Financing Bank: A federal institution that lends to a wide array of federal credit agencies funds it obtains by borrowing from the U.S. Treasury.

Federal funds: (1) Non–interest-bearing deposits held by member banks at the Federal Reserve. (2) Used to denote "immediately available" funds in the clearing sense.

Federal funds rate: The rate of interest at which Fed funds are traded. This rate is currently pegged by the Federal Reserve through open-market operations.

Federal Home Loan Banks (FHLB):   The institutions that regulate and lend to savings and loan associations. The Federal Home Loan Banks play a role analogous to that played by the Federal Reserve Banks vis-à-vis member commercial banks.

Figuring the tail: Calculating the yield at which a future money market instrument (one available some period hence) is purchased when that future security is created by buying an existing instrument and financing the initial portion of life with a term RP.

Firm: Refers to an order to buy or sell that can be executed without confirmation for some fixed period.

Fixed dates: In the Euromarket the standard periods for which Euros are traded (one month out to a year) are referred to as the fixed dates.

Fixed-dollar security: A nonnegotiable debt security that can be redeemed at some fixed price or according to some schedule of fixed values (e.g., bank deposits and government savings bonds).

Fixed-rate loan: A loan on which the rate paid by the borrower is fixed for the life of the loan.

Flat trades: (1) A bond in default trades flat; that is, the price quoted covers both principal and unpaid, accrued interest. (2) Any security that trades without accrued interest or at a price that includes accrued interest is said to trade flat.

Float: The difference between the credits given by the Fed to banks' reserve accounts on checks being cleared through the Fed and the debits made to banks' reserve accounts on the same checks. Float is always positive, because in the clearing of a check, the credit sometimes precedes the debit. Float adds to the money supply.

Floating-rate note: A note that pays an interest rate tied to current money market rates. The holder may have the right to demand redemption at par on specified dates.

Floating supply: The amount of securities believed to be available for immediate purchase, that is, in the hands of dealers and investors wanting to sell.

Flower bonds: Government bonds that are acceptable at par in payment of federal estate taxes when owned by the decedent at the time of death.

Footings: A British expression for the bottom line of an institution's balance sheet; total assets equal total liabilities plus net worth.

Foreign bond: A bond issued by a nondomestic borrower in the domestic capital market.

Foreign exchange rate: The price at which one currency trades for another.

Foreign exchange risk: The risk that a long or short position in a foreign currency might, due to an adverse movement in the relevant exchange rate, have to be closed out at a loss. The long or short position may arise out of a financial or commercial transaction.

Forward Fed funds: Fed funds traded for future delivery.

Forward forward contract: In Eurocurrencies, a contract under which a deposit of fixed maturity is agreed to at a fixed price for future delivery.

Forward market: A market in which participants agree to trade some commodity, security, or foreign exchange at a fixed price at some future date.

Forward rate: The rate at which forward transactions in some specific maturity are being made, e.g., the dollar price at which DM can be bought for delivery three months hence.

Free reserves: Excess reserves minus member bank borrowings at the Fed.

Full-coupon bond: A bond with a coupon equal to the going market rate and consequently selling at or near par.

Futures market: A market in which contracts for future delivery of a commodity or a security are bought and sold.

Gap: Mismatch between the maturities of a bank's assets and liabilities.

Gapping: Mismatching the maturities of a bank's assets and liabilities, usually by borrowing short and lending long.

General obligation bonds: Municipal securities secured by the issuer's pledge of its full faith, credit, and taxing power.

Give up: The loss in yield that occurs when a block of bonds is swapped for another block of lower-coupon bonds. Can also be referred to as "aftertax give up" when the implications of the profit (loss) on taxes are considered.

Glass-Steagall Act: A 1933 act in which Congress forbade commercial banks to own, underwrite, or deal in corporate stock and corporate bonds.

Go-around: When the Fed offers to buy securities, to sell securities, to do repo, or to do reverses, it solicits competitive bids or offers, as the case may be, from all primary dealers. This procedure is known as a go-around.

Good delivery: A delivery in which everything—endorsement, any necessary attached legal papers, etc.—is in order.

Governments: Negotiable U.S. Treasury securities.

Gross spread: The difference between the price that the issuer receives for its securities and the price that investors pay for them. This spread equals the selling concession plus the management and underwriting fees.

Haircut: Margin in an RP transaction, that is, the difference between the actual market value measured at the bid side of the market and the value used in an RP agreement.

Handle: The whole-dollar price of a bid or offer is referred to as the *handle*. For example, if a security is quoted 101-10 bid and 101-11 offered, 101 is the handle. Traders are assumed to know the handle, so a trader would quote that market to another by saying he was at 10-11. (The 10 and 11 refer to 32nds.)

Hedge: To reduce risk, (1) by taking a position in futures equal and opposite to an existing or anticipated cash position, or (2) by shorting a security similar to one in which a long position has been established.

Histogram: A bar chart displaying a probability distribution in which the assigned probabilities add up to 100 percent.

Hit: A dealer who agrees to sell at the bid price quoted by another dealer is said to *hit* that bid.

IBFs (International Banking Facilities):   Shell branches that U.S. banks in a number of states may form at head office to do limited types of Eurobusiness.

In the box: This means that a dealer has a wire receipt for securities indicating that effective delivery on them has been made. This jargon is a holdover from the time when Treasuries took the form of physical securities and were stored in a rack.

Indenture of a bond: A legal statement spelling out the obligations of the bond issuer and the rights of the bondholder.

Interest rate exposure: Risk of gain or loss to which an institution is exposed due to possible changes in interest rate levels.

Investment banker: A firm that engages in the origination, underwriting, and distribution of new issues.

Joint account: An agreement between two or more firms to share risk and financing responsibility in purchasing or underwriting securities.

Junk bonds: High-risk bonds that have low credit ratings or are in default.

Leverage: See **Debt leverage.**

Leveraged lease: The lessor provides only a minor portion of the cost of the leased equipment, borrowing the rest from another lender.

LIBOR: The London Interbank Offered Rate on Eurodollar deposits traded between banks. There is a different LIBOR rate for each deposit maturity. Different banks may quote slightly different LIBOR rates because they use different reference banks.

Lifting a leg: Closing out one side of a long-short arbitrage before the other is closed.

Line of credit: An arrangement by which a bank agrees to lend to the line holder during some specified period any amount up to the full amount of the line.

Liquidity: A liquid asset is one that can be converted easily and rapidly into cash without a substantial loss of value. In the money market, a security is said to be liquid if the spread between bid and asked prices is narrow and reasonable size can be done at those quotes.

Liquidity diversification: Investing in a variety of maturities to reduce the price risk to which holding long bonds exposes the investor.

Liquidity risk: In banking, risk that monies needed to fund assets may not be available in sufficient quantities at some future date. Implies an imbalance in committed maturities of assets and liabilities.

Locked market: A market is said to be locked if the bid price equals the asked price. This can occur, for example, if the market is brokered and brokerage is paid by one side only, the initiator of the transaction.

Lockup CDs: CDs that are issued with the tacit understanding that the buyer will not trade the certificate. Quite often, the issuing bank will insist that it keep the certificate to ensure that the understanding is honored by the buyer.

Long: (1) Owning a debt security, stock, or other asset. (2) Owning more than one has contracted to deliver.

Long bonds: Bonds with a long current maturity.

Long coupons: (1) Bonds or notes with a long current maturity. (2) A bond on which one of the coupon periods, usually the first, is longer than the others or than standard.

Long hedge: *Purchase* of a *futures* contract to lock in the yield at which an anticipated cash inflow can be invested.

Make a market: A dealer is said to make a market when he quotes bid and offered prices at which he stands ready to buy and sell.

Margin: In an RP or a reverse repurchase transaction, the amount by which the market value of the securities collateralizing the transaction exceeds the amount lent.

Marginal tax rate: The tax rate that would have to be paid on any additional dollars of taxable income earned.

Market value: The price at which a security is trading and could presumably be purchased or sold.

Marketability: A negotiable security is said to have good marketability if there is an active secondary market in which it can easily be resold.

Match fund: A bank is said to match fund a loan or other asset when it does so by buying (taking) a deposit of the same maturity. The term is commonly used in the Euromarket.

Matched book: If the distribution of the maturities of a bank's liabilities equals that of its assets, it is said to be running a *matched book*. The term is commonly used in the Euromarket.

Merchant bank: A British term for a bank that specializes not in lending out its own funds, but in providing various financial services such as accepting bills arising out of trade, underwriting new issues, and providing advice on acquisitions, mergers, foreign exchange, portfolio management, etc.

Mismatch: A mismatch between the interest rate maturities of a bank's assets and liabilities. See also **gap** and **Unmatched book.**

Money market: The market in which short-term debt instruments (bills, commercial paper, bankers' acceptances, etc.) are issued and traded.

Money market (center) bank: A bank that is one of the nation's largest and consequently plays an active and important role in every sector of the money market.

Money Market Certificates (MMCs): Six-month certificates of deposit with a minimum denomination of $10,000 on which banks and thrifts may pay a maximum rate tied to the rate at which the U.S. Treasury has most recently auctioned six-month bills.

Money market fund: Mutual fund that invests solely in money market instruments.

Money rate of return: Annual money return as a percentage of asset value.

Money supply definitions currently used by the Fed:
    M-1:   Currency plus demand deposits and other checkable deposits.
    M-2:   M-1 plus overnight RPs and money market funds and savings and small (less than $100,000) time deposits.
    M-3:   M-2 plus large time deposits and term RPs.
    L: M-3 plus other liquid assets.

Mortgage bond: Bond secured by a lien on property, equipment, or other real assets.

Multicurrency clause: Such a clause on a Euro loan permits the borrower to switch from one currency to another on a rollover date.

Municipal (muni) notes: Short-term notes issued by municipalities in anticipation of tax receipts, proceeds from a bond issue, or other revenues.

Municipals: Securities issued by state and local governments and their agencies.

Naked position: A long or short position that is not hedged.

National banks: National banks are federally chartered banks that are subject to supervision by the Comptroller of the Currency. State banks in contrast are state chartered and state regulated.

Negative carry: The net cost incurred when the cost of carry exceeds the yield on the securities being financed.

Negotiable certificate of deposit: A large-denomination (generally $1 million) CD that can be sold but cannot be cashed in before maturity.

Negotiated sale: Situation in which the terms of an offering are determined by negotiation between the issuer and the underwriter rather than through competitive bidding by underwriting groups.

New-issues market: The market in which a new issue of securities is first sold to investors.

New money: In a Treasury refunding, the amount by which the par value of the securities offered exceeds that of those maturing.

Noncompetitive bid: In a Treasury auction, bidding for a specific amount of securities at the price, whatever it may turn out to be, equal to the average price of the accepted competitive bids.

Non-native currency: A currency used by an institution other than the currency used in its country of origin; e.g., French francs to the Chase bank.

Nonperforming loan: A loan on which interest is not paid as it accrues. Since banks are examined only periodically, a nonperforming loan may or may not be classified.

Note: Coupon issues with a relatively short original maturity are often called *notes*. Muni notes, however, have maturities ranging from a month to a year and pay interest only at maturity. Treasury notes are coupon securities that have an original maturity of up to 10 years.

NOW (Negotiable order of withdrawal) accounts: These amount to checking accounts on which depository institutions (banks and thrifts) may pay a rate of interest subject to federal rate lids.

Odd lot: Less than a round lot.

Off-the-run issue: In Treasuries and agencies, an issue that is not included in dealer or broker runs. With bills and notes, normally only current issues are quoted.

Offer: Price asked by a seller of securities.

One-man picture: The price quoted is said to be a one-man picture if both the bid and ask come from the same source.

One-sided (one-way) market: A market in which only one side, the bid or the asked, is quoted or firm.

Open book: See **Unmatched book.**

Open repo: A repo with no definite term. The agreement is made on a day-to-day basis and either the borrower or the lender may choose to terminate. The rate paid is higher than on overnight repo and is subject to adjustment if rates move.

Opportunity cost: The cost of pursuing one course of action measured in terms of the foregone return offered by the most attractive alternative.

Option: (1) **Call option:** A contract sold for a price that gives the holder the right to buy from the writer of the option, over a specified period, a specified amount of securities at a specified price. (2) **Put option:** A contract sold for a price that gives the holder the right to sell to the writer of the contract, over a specified period, a specified amount of securities at a specified price.

Original maturity: Maturity at issue. For example, a 5-year note has an original maturity at issue of 5 years; 1 year later, it has a current maturity of 4 years.

Over-the-counter (OTC) market: Market created by dealer trading as opposed to the auction market prevailing on organized exchanges.

Overnight delivery risk: A risk brought about because differences in time zones between settlement centers require that payment or delivery on one side of a transaction be made without knowing until the next day whether funds have been received in account on the other side. Particularly apparent where delivery takes place in Europe for payment in dollars in New York.

Paper: Money market instruments, commercial paper and other.

Paper gain (loss): Unrealized capital gain (loss) on securities held in portfolio, based on a comparison of current market price and original cost.

Par: (1) Price of 100 percent. (2) The principal amount at which the issuer of a debt security contracts to redeem that security at maturity, *face value.*

Par bond: A bond selling at par.

Pass-through: A mortgage-backed security on which payment of interest and principal on the underlying mortgages are passed through to the security holder by an agent.

Paydown: In a Treasury refunding, the amount by which the par value of the securities maturing exceeds that of those sold.

Pay-up: (1) The loss of cash resulting from a swap into higher-price bonds. (2) The need (or willingness) of a bank or other borrower to pay a higher rate to get funds.

Pickup: The gain in yield that occurs when a block of bonds is swapped for another block of higher-coupon bonds.

Picture: The bid and asked prices quoted by a broker for a given security.

Placement: A bank depositing Eurodollars with (selling Eurodollars to) another bank is often said to be making a placement.

Plus: Dealers in governments normally quote bids and offers in 32nds. To quote a bid or offer in 64ths, they use pluses; for example, a dealer who bids 4+ is bidding the handle plus $4/32 + 1/64$, which equals the handle plus $9/64$.

PNs: Project notes are issued by municipalities to finance federally sponsored programs in urban renewal and housing. They are guaranteed by the U.S. Department of Housing and Urban Development.

Point: (1) 100 basis points = 1 percent. (2) One percent of the face value of a note or bond. (3) In the foreign exchange market, the lowest level at which the currency is priced. Example: "One point" is the difference between sterling prices of $1.8080 and $1.8081.

Portfolio: Collection of securities held by an investor.

Position: (1) To go long or short in a security. (2) The amount of securities owned (long position) or owed (short position).

Positive carry: The net gain earned when the cost of carry is less than the yield on the securities being financed.

Premium: (1) The amount by which the price at which an issue is trading exceeds the issue's par value. (2) The amount that must be paid in excess of par to call or refund an issue before maturity. (3) In money market parlance, the fact that a particular bank's CDs trade at a rate higher than others of its class, or that a bank has to pay up to acquire funds.

Premium bond: Bond selling above par.

Prepayment: A payment made ahead of the scheduled payment date.

Presold issue: An issue that is sold out before the coupon announcement.

Price risk: The risk that a debt security's price may change due to a rise or fall in the going level of interest rates.

Prime rate: The rate at which banks lend to their best (prime) customers. The all-in cost of a bank loan to a prime credit equals the prime rate plus the cost of holding compensating balances.

Principal: (1) The face amount or par value of a debt security. (2) One who acts as a dealer buying and selling for his own account.

Private placement: An issue that is offered to a single or a few investors as opposed to being publicly offered. Private placements do not have to be registered with the SEC.

Prospectus: A detailed statement prepared by an issuer and filed with the SEC prior to the sale of a new issue. The prospectus gives detailed information on the issue and on the issuer's condition and prospects.

Put: See **Option.**

RANs (Revenue anticipation notes): These are issued by states and municipalities to finance current expenditures in anticipation of the future receipt of nontax revenues.

Rate risk: In banking, the risk that profits may decline or losses occur because a rise in interest rates forces up the cost of funding fixed-rate loans or other fixed-rate assets.

Ratings: An evaluation given by Moody's, Standard & Poor's, Fitch, or other rating services of a security's credit worthiness.

Real market: The bid and offer prices at which a dealer could do size. Quotes in the brokers market may reflect not the real market, but pictures painted by dealers playing trading games.

Red herring: A preliminary prospectus containing all the information required by the Securities and Exchange Commission except the offering price and coupon of a new issue.

Refunding: Redemption of securities by funds raised through the sale of a new issue.

Registered bond: A bond whose owner is registered with the issuer.

Regular way settlement: In the money and bond markets, the regular basis on which some security trades are settled is that delivery of the securities purchased is made against payment in Fed funds on the day following the transaction.

Regulation D: Fed regulation that required member banks to hold reserves against their net borrowings from foreign offices of other banks over a 7-day averaging period. Reg D has been merged with Reg M. Reg D has also required member banks to hold reserves against Eurodollars lent by their foreign branches to domestic corporations for domestic purposes.

Regulation Q: Fed regulation imposing lids on the rates that banks may pay on savings and time deposits. Currently, time deposits with a denomination of $100,000 or more are exempt from Reg Q.

Reinvestment rate: (1) The rate at which an investor assumes interest payments made on a debt security can be reinvested over the life of that security. (2) Also, the rate at which funds from a maturity or sale of a security can be reinvested. Often used in comparison to *give up* yield.

Relative value: The attractiveness—measured in terms of risk, liquidity, and return—of one instrument relative to another, or for a given instrument, of one maturity relative to another.

Reopen an issue: The Treasury, when it wants to sell additional securities, will occasionally sell more of an existing issue (reopen it) rather than offer a new issue.

Repo: See Repurchase agreement.

Repurchase agreement (RP or repo): A holder of securities sells these securities to an investor with an agreement to repurchase them at a fixed price on a fixed date. The security "buyer" in effect lends the "seller" money for the period of the agreement, and the terms of the agreement are structured to compensate him for this. Dealers use RP extensively to finance their positions. Exception: When the Fed is said to be doing RP, it is lending money, that is, increasing bank reserves.

Reserve requirements: The percentages of different types of deposits that member banks are required to hold on deposit at the Fed.

Retail: Individual and institutional customers as opposed to dealers and brokers.

Revenue bond: A municipal bond secured by revenue from tolls, user charges, or rents derived from the facility financed.

Reverse: See Reverse repurchase agreement.

Reverse repurchase agreement: Most typically, a repurchase agreement initiated by the lender of funds. Reverses are used by dealers to borrow securities they have shorted. Exception: When the Fed is said to be doing reverses, it is borrowing money, that is, absorbing reserves.

Revolver: See Revolving line of credit.

Revolving line of credit: A bank line of credit on which the customer pays a commitment fee and can take down and repay funds according to his needs. Normally the line involves a firm commitment from the bank for a period of several years.

Risk: Degree of uncertainty of return on an asset.

Roll over: Reinvest funds received from a maturing security in a new issue of the same or a similar security.

Rollover: Most term loans in the Euromarket are made on a rollover basis, which means that the loan is periodically repriced at an agreed spread over the appropriate, currently prevailing LIBOR rate.

Round lot: In the money market, round lot refers to the minimum amount for which dealers' quotes are good. This may range from $100,000 to $5 million, depending on the size and liquidity of the issue traded.

RP: See **Repurchase agreement.**

Run: A run consists of a series of bid and asked quotes for different securities or maturities. Dealers give to and ask for runs from each other.

S&L: See **Savings and loan association.**

Safekeep: For a fee, banks will safekeep (i.e., hold in their vault, clip coupons on, and present for payment at maturity) bonds and money market instruments.

Sale repurchase agreement: See **Repurchase agreement.**

Savings and loan association: Federal- or state-chartered institution that accepts savings deposits and invests the bulk of the funds thus received in mortgages.

Savings deposit: Interest-bearing deposit at a savings institution that has no specific maturity.

Scale: A bank that offers to pay different rates of interest on CDs of varying maturities is said to "post a scale." Commercial paper issuers also post scales.

Seasoned issue: An issue that has been well distributed and trades well in the secondary market.

Secondary market: The market in which previously issued securities are traded.

Sector: Refers to a group of securities that are similar with respect to maturity, type, rating, and/or coupon.

Securities and Exchange Commission (SEC): Agency created by Congress to protect investors in securities transactions by administering securities legislation.

Serial bonds: A bond issue in which maturities are staggered over a number of years.

Settle: See **Clear.**

Settlement date: The date on which a trade is cleared by delivery of securities against funds. The settlement data may be the trade date or a later date.

Shell branch: A foreign branch—usually in a tax haven—which engages in Eurocurrency business but is run out of a head office.

Shop: In street jargon, a money market or bond dealership.

Shopping: Seeking to obtain the best bid or offer available by calling a number of dealers and/or brokers.

Short: A market participant assumes a short position by selling a security he does not own. The seller makes delivery by borrowing the security sold or reversing it in.

Short bonds: Bonds with a short current maturity.

Short book: See **Unmatched book.**

Short coupons: Bonds or notes with a short current maturity.

Short hedge: *Sale* of a *futures* contract to hedge, for example, a position in cash securities or an anticipated borrowing need.

Short sale: The sale of securities not owned by the seller in the expectation that the price of these securities will fall or as part of an arbitrage. A short sale must eventually be covered by a purchase of the securities sold.

Sinking fund: Indentures on corporate issues often require that the issuer make annual payments to a sinking fund, the proceeds of which are used to retire randomly selected bonds in the issue.

Size: Large in size, as in "size offering" or "in there for size." What constitutes size varies with the sector of the market.

Skip-day settlement: The trade is settled one business day beyond what is normal.

Sovereign risk: The special risks, if any, that attach to a security (or deposit or loan) because the borrower's country of residence differs from that of the investor's. Also referred to as **Country risk.**

Specific issues market: The market in which dealers reverse in securities they want to short.

Spectail: A dealer that does business with retail but concentrates more on acquiring and financing its own speculative position.

Spot market: Market for immediate as opposed to future delivery. In the spot market for foreign exchange, settlement is two business days ahead.

Spot rate: The price prevailing in the spot market.

Spread: (1) Difference between bid and asked prices on a security. (2) Difference between yields on or prices of two securities of differing sorts or differing maturities. (3) In underwriting, difference between price realized by the issuer and price paid by the investor. (4) Difference between two prices or two rates. What a commodities trader would refer to as the *basis.*

Spreading: In the futures market, buying one futures contract and selling a nearby one to profit from an anticipated narrowing or widening of the spread over time.

Stop-out price: The lowest price (highest yield) accepted by the Treasury in an auction of a new issue.

Street: Brokers, dealers, and other knowledgeable members of the financial community; from Wall Street financial community.

Subject: Refers to a bid or offer that cannot be executed without confirmation from the customer.

Subordinated debenture: The claims of holders of this issue rank after those of holders of various other unsecured debts incurred by the issuer.

Swap: (1) In securities, selling one issue and buying another. (2) In foreign exchange, buying a currency spot and simultaneously selling it forward.

Swap rate: In the foreign exchange market, the difference between the spot and forward rates at which a currency is traded.

Swing line: See **Demand line of credit.**

Swissy: Market jargon for Swiss francs.

Switch: British English for a swap, that is, buying a currency spot and selling it forward.

TABs (tax anticipation bills): Special bills that the Treasury occasionally issues. They mature on corporate quarterly income tax dates and can be used at face value by corporations to pay their tax liabilities.

Tail: (1) The difference between the average price in Treasury auctions and the stop-out price. (2) A *future* money market instrument (one available some period hence) created by buying an existing instrument and financing the initial portion of its life with term RP.

Take: (1) A dealer or customer who agrees to buy at another dealer's offered price is said to take that offer. (2) Eurobankers speak of taking deposits rather than buying money.

Take-out: (1) A cash surplus generated by the sale of one block of securities and the purchase of another, e.g., selling a block of bonds at 99 and buying another block at 95. (2) A bid made to a seller of a security that is designed (and generally agreed) to take him out of the market.

Taking a view: A London expression for forming an opinion as to where interest rates are going and acting on it.

TANs: Tax anticipation notes issued by states or municipalities to finance current operations in anticipation of future tax receipts.

Technical condition of a market: Demand and supply factors affecting price, in particular the net position—long or short—of dealers.

Tenor: Maturity.

Term bonds: A bond issue in which all bonds mature at the same time.

Term Fed funds: Fed funds sold for a period of time longer than overnight.

Term loan: Loan extended by a bank for more than the normal 90-day period. A term loan might run five years or more.

Term RP (repo): RP borrowings for a period longer than overnight, may be 30, 60, or even 90 days.

Thin market: A market in which trading volume is low and in which consequently bid and asked quotes are wide and the liquidity of the instrument traded is low.

Tight market: A tight market, as opposed to a thin market, is one in which volume is large, trading is active and highly competitive, and spreads between bid and ask prices are narrow.

Time deposit: Interest-bearing deposit at a savings institution that has a specific maturity.

Tom next: In the interbank market in Eurodollar deposits and the foreign exchange market, the value (delivery) date on a Tom next transaction is the next business day. (Refers to "tomorrow next.")

Trade date: The date on which a transaction is initiated. The settlement date may be the trade date or a later date.

Trade on top of: Trade at a narrow or no spread in basis points to some other instrument.

Trading paper: CDs purchased by accounts that are likely to resell them. The term is commonly used in the Euromarket.

Treasurer's check: A check issued by a bank to make a payment. Treasurer's checks outstanding are counted as part of a bank's reservable deposits and as part of the money supply.

Treasury bill: A non–interest-bearing discount security issued by the U.S. Treasury to finance the national debt. Most bills are issued to mature in three months, six months, or one year.

TT&L account: Treasury tax and loan account at a bank.

Turnaround: Securities bought and sold for settlement on the same day.

Turnaround time: The time available or needed to effect a turnaround.

Two-sided market: A market in which both bid and asked prices, good for the standard unit of trading, are quoted.

Two-way market: Market in which both a bid and an asked price are quoted.

Underwriter: A dealer who purchases new issues from the issuer and distributes them to investors. Underwriting is one function of an investment banker.

Unmatched book: If the average maturity of a bank's liabilities is less than that of its assets, it is said to be running an unmatched book. The term is commonly used in the Euromarket. Equivalent expressions are **open book** and **short book.**

Value date: In the market for Eurodollar deposits and foreign exchange, value date refers to the delivery date of funds traded. Normally it is on spot transactions two days after a transaction is agreed upon and the future date in the case of a forward foreign exchange trade.

Variable-price security: A security, such as stocks or bonds, that sells at a fluctuating, market-determined price.

Variable-rate CDs: Short-term CDs that pay interest periodically on *roll* dates; on each roll date the coupon on the CD is adjusted to reflect current market rates.

Variable-rate loan: Loan made at an interest rate that fluctuates with the prime.

Visible supply: New muni bond issues scheduled to come to market within the next 30 days.

When-issued trades: Typically there is a lag between the time a new bond is announced and sold and the time it is actually issued. During this interval, the security trades, **wi,** "when, as, and if issued."

Wi: When, as, and if issued. See **When-issued trades.**

Wi wi: T bills trade on a wi basis between the day they are auctioned and the day settlement is made. Bills traded before they are auctioned are said to be traded wi wi.

Without: If 70 were bid in the market and there was no offer, the quote would be "70 bid without." The expression *without* indicates a one-way market.

Yankee bond: A foreign bond issued in the U.S. market, payable in dollars, and registered with the SEC.

Yankee CD: A CD issued in the domestic market (typically in New York) by a branch of a foreign bank.

Yield curve: A graph showing, for securities that all expose the investor to the same credit risk, the relationship at a given point in time between yield and current maturity. Yield curves are typically drawn using yields on governments of various maturities.

Yield to maturity: The rate of return yielded by a debt security held to maturity when both interest payments and the investor's capital gain or loss on the security are taken into account.

Index

Regulation Q—*Cont.*
  deregulation of interest rate lids, 9–10,
    23, 27–28, 90–94, 290–91
  on large-denomination CDs, 38–39,
    93–94
  as a stimulus to the Euromarket, 121
Repos; *see* Repurchase agreements
Repurchase agreements (RP), 43–45, 95–
    97, 386–87
  bank use in funding, 71, 74, 75, 76, 84,
    95–97, 111–12, 239, 255
  credit risk, 95–96, 387–89
  dealer use in financing, 44
  Drysdale case, 386–89
  by the Fed, 44
  Fed open market operations, as part
    of, 45, 97
  Fed proposal to impose reserves on,
    296–97
  investors in, 95–96
  RP rate, 44
  term RP, 44, 96
Reserve requirements, 23, 26–27, 82,
    90–92, 96, 149, 172
  bank holding company paper, 104
  on Fed funds purchased, 95
  on foreign banks, 9, 160–61
  Regulation D, 99, 137
  as a stimulus to the Euromarket, 121
  by type of deposit, 90–91
  use to control money creation, 23–26
Return on assets (ROA), 302–3, 318–19,
    389, 391
Return on equity (ROE), 303–4, 319–20
Reverse repurchase agreements, 43–45,
    386–89
  to cover shorts, 45, 386–89
  credit risk, 96, 386–89
  Fed open market operations, as part
    of, 45, 97
  investors in, 96–97
  term transactions, 97
Riding the yield curve, 85
RPs; *see* Repurchase agreements

S

Savings and loan associations, 189, 237,
    326, 338
  assets of, 19
  borrowing at the discount window, 28
  capital ratios, 186–87
  FHLB aid and regulation, 35–36, 92,
    211, 299, 338
  hedging borrowing rates, 327–28, 336–
    37, 338
  MMCs, 94, 108, 111, 211
    hedging rate on, 327–28, 332–33,
      336–37

Savings and loan associations—*Cont.*
  NOW accounts, 10, 27–29, 30
  rate lids, 92–94
  reserve requirements, 23 n, 27–28, 91
Securities and Exchange Commission
    (SEC), 41, 342
Security Pacific National Bank, 72
Shorting, 45
  dealer positions, 45
  use of reverses to cover, 45
Sinkley, Joseph F., 190 n
Sovereign risk, 127, 129, 153–57, 306–7,
    331, 380–81
Spero, Joan E., 190 n
Spreading (bill futures), 354–55
Standard & Poor's, 42
Stock index futures, 342
Swaps
  Eurocurrency swaps, 149–152
  extension swaps, 86–87
  into local currency, 368–69, 372–73

T

T-accounts, 20
Term Fed funds; *see* Federal funds mar-
    ket
Term RP; *see* Repurchase agreements
Thrifts; *see* Savings and loan associations
Treasury bills; *see* U.S. Treasury secur-
    ities
Treasury-Fed accord, 78–79, 168
Treasury securities; *see* U.S. Treasury
    securities
Treasury Tax and Loan (TT&L)
    accounts, 217 n

U

U.S. balance of payments deficit, 122
U.S. Treasury securities, 33–35, 56
  auction procedures, 33–34
  bank holdings of; *see* Commercial
    banks, government portfolio
  bills, 33
    auctions of, 33
    futures contract, 35, 324–25, 327–28,
      332, 339–41, 344–47
    yield at auction, 52
    yield calculations, 47–53
  bonds, 33–34
    auctions of, 34
    call provisions, 56–57
    futures contract, 35, 341
    rate lid on, 34–35
  book-entry form, 56 n
  dealers in, 34, 76, 386–89
    hedging by, 329–30